nuanua

TALANOA

CONTEMPORARY PACIFIC LITERATURE

Vilsoni Hereniko, General Editor

Alan Duff *Once Were Warriors*
Albert Wendt *Leaves of the Banyan Tree*
Hone Tuwhare *Deep River Talk: Collected Poems*
Epeli Hau'ofa *Tales of the Tikongs*
Patricia Grace *Potiki*

nuanua

pacific writing
in english

since 1980

selected with an introduction by

albert wendt

TALANOA

CONTEMPORARY
PACIFIC
LITERATURE

UNIVERSITY OF HAWAI'I PRESS

HONOLULU

In memory of

TALOSAGA TOLOVAE
FRANCIS TEKONNANG

Amuia le masina e alu ma toe sau . . .

Introduction and selection © Albert Wendt 1995
Copyright in original stories and poems remains with the authors
All rights reserved

Published in North America by
UNIVERSITY OF HAWAI'I PRESS
2840 Kolowalu Street
Honolulu, Hawai'i 96822

Published in New Zealand by
AUCKLAND UNIVERSITY PRESS
Private Bag 92019
Auckland

Publication is assisted by Te Waka Toi Council for Maori and South Pacific Arts and
the Literature Programme of the Arts Council of New Zealand Toi Aotearoa.

Part-title illustrations by Sina Wendt, reproduced with kind permission of
Longman Paul.

Printed in Singapore by South Wind

Second Printing 2007

Library of Congress Cataloging-in-Publication Data
Nuanua : Pacific writing in English since 1980 / edited by Albert
Wendt.
    p. cm. — (Talanoa)
    ISBN 0-8248-1731-1 (acid-free paper)
    1. Pacific Island literature (English) 2. Islands of the Pacific—
Literary collections. I. Wendt, Albert, 1939- . II. Series.
PR9645.8.N83   1995   94-45613
820.8'0996—dc20   CIP

CONTENTS

v

CONTENTS

CONTENTS

ACKNOWLEDGEMENTS

The editor and publisher are grateful to The South Pacific Creative Arts Society, PO Box 5083, Raiwaqa, Suva, Fiji and to the Institute of Pacific Studies, University of the South Pacific, PO Box 1168, Suva, Fiji for permission to reproduce stories and poems first published in *Mana* magazine and other publications. All the material reprinted from these publications is copyright to the publishers and to the authors, whose permission we gratefully acknowledge: Apelu Aiavao, 'The Married Couple'; Prem Banfal, 'I Remember'; Lemu Darcy, 'Cars You Have My Wantoks' and 'Women and Housework'; Pasitale Faleilemilo, 'Funeral in Savai'i'; Konai Helu Thaman, 'No More Guava', 'Langakali' and 'Sunday Sadness' in *Langakali* (SPCAS, 1974); Vilsoni Hereniko, 'The Unfinished Fence'; Jon Jonassen, 'Saved'; Kauraka Kauraka, 'Sixteen Bags' and 'Taunga of the Great Moko' in *Dreams of a Rainbow* (Mana Publications, USP, 1987); Celo Kulagoe, 'Where Leaves Had Fallen', 'The Toothpick', 'Culture Shock' and 'My Gods' in *Where Leaves had Fallen* (SPCAS, 1980); Jully Makini (previously Sipolo), 'Civilized Girl' and 'A Man's World' in *Civilized Girl* (SPCAS, 1981); Tasi Malifa, 'Christmas in Samoa, 1978'; Pio Manoa, 'Invitation', 'Laucala Bay'; Nemani Mati, 'Reflections on a Night Out in Town'; Grace Molisa, 'Custom', 'Neo-Colonialism' and 'Status Costs' in *Black Stone I* (Mana Publications, 1983) and 'Ni-Vanuatu Women in Development' in *Colonised People* (1987); Sampson Ngwele, 'Peripheral Politicians' and 'Island Chant' in *Bamboo Leaves* (SPCAS, 1990); Rexford T. Orotaloa, 'Raraifilu' in *Suremada* (Mana Publications, Suva, 1989); Som Prakash 'An Act of Love'; John Saunana, from *The Alternative* (Mana Publications, 1989); Vianney Kianteata Teabo, 'Abatekan'; Francis Tekonnang, 'Beia and Ioane'; Makiuti Tongia, 'To God', 'Storyteller', 'Return the Noonday Star' in *Korero* (Mana Publications, USP, 1977); Joseph C. Veramo, 'Onisimo' in *Black Messiah* (SPCAS, 1989). Momoe Malietoa Von Reiche, 'Solaua, a Secret Embryo', 'My House Idea' and 'My Guest' in *Solaua, A Secret Embryo* (Mana Publications, 1979); Steven Edmund Winduo, 'The Dancer', 'The Mother and Child', 'Nuigo Market', 'Different Histories' in *The Dancer* (SPCAS, Fiji, 1991).

Acknowledgement is also made to the publishers and copyright holders listed below, for permission to reproduce copyright material. *Ondobondo* (Book House, Literature Department, University of Papua New Guinea, PO Box 320, Port Moresby, PNG): Nora Vagi Brash, 'Mass Media, Mass Mania'; Loujaya Kouza, 'The Expatriate'; Joyce Kumbeli, 'Caught Up'; Jack Lahui, 'We Are Tukes'; Russell Soaba, 'Kuburabasu'; Kumalau Tawali, 'The Song of the Rower'; Thomas Tuman 'Kum Koimb'; Vincent Warakai, 'Dancing Yet to the Dim Dim's Beat'; Peter Watlakas, 'Speak Up'. First appeared in *Ta'unga* (published by The Creative Writers' Society, Cook Islands): Vaine Rasmussen 'A Book and a Pen' (1984); Florence Syme-Buchanan, 'Boat Girl' (1984); Mona Matepi Webb, 'Grandmother and the Mat' (1984). Published by *Samoa Observer*: Sano Malifa, 'Rain' and 'Night' are from *Song and Return* (1992); Ruperake Petaia,

'Poems in the Rain', 'Freedom Day' and 'Papeete by Night' are from *Patches of the Rain* (1992); Noumea Simi, 'Peace', 'In Life' and 'What Are We' are from *Sails of Dawn* (1992);Tate Simi, 'Birdcall I', 'Poem to My Father' and 'Taumeasina' are from *A Deeper Song* (1992). Published by the Institute of Pacific Studies, University of the South Pacific:Tom Davis, *Vaka* (1992); Kauraka Kauraka, 'Darkness within the Light' from *Return to Havaiki* (1985); Makerita Va'ai, 'Song of Discovery', 'I Thought of You' and 'At Claire's Place' from *Pinnacles* (1993); Julian Maka'a, 'An Unexpected Gift' from *The Confession* (1985). Alistair Te Ariki Campbell, *The Frigate Bird* (Reed, Auckland, 1989); 'The Dark Lord of Savaiki' and 'Soul Traps' are from *Stone Rain:The Polynesian Strain* (Hazard, Christchurch, 1992); Litia Alaelua, 'Ghosting' and Johnny Frisbie Hebenstreit, 'The Bed' first appeared in *Metro*; Apisai Enos, 'Moon'; Sudesh Mishra, 'In Nadi', 'Confessions of a Would-be Brahmin' and 'Beachcombers' from *Rahu* (Vision International, Fiji, 1987); 'Elegy' and 'Detainee II' from *Tandava* (Meanjin Press, Melbourne, 1992); Satendra Nandan, *The Wounded Sea* (Simon & Schuster, Australia, 1991); 'Siddarth' and 'Ballet for a Sea-Bird' from *Faces in A Village* (1976); Seri, 'Pigeon Park', 'Sione, God . . .', 'From Tiata and Liz' in *Frustrated Actors*; Subramani, 'Tell Me Where . . .' in *The Fantasy Eaters* (Three Continents Press, Washington, 1988); John Pule, *The Shark that Ate the Sun* (Penguin, Auckland, 1992); John Kasaipwalova, *Sail the Midnight Sun* (Credit Melanesia, Trobriands, 1980); Ignatius Kilage, *My Mother Calls Me Yaltep* (OUP, Melbourne, 1980); Steven Thomas Lyadale, 'The Frost', *The PNG Writer*, vol.1, no.1, Sept. 1985; Russell Soaba, *Maiba* (Three Continents Press, Washington, 1985); *Naked Thoughts* (Papua Pocket Poets, Institute of Papua Studies, 1978); 'Looking Thru Those Eyeholes', PNG Poster Series; Epi Enari Fuaau, 'The Olomatua' from *Sister Stew* (Bamboo Ridge Press, Hawaii, 1991); Emma Kruse Va'ai, 'Ta Tatau' from *Short Stories from New Zealand* (ed. Alistair Paterson, Highgate/Price Milburn, Wellington, 1988); Albert Wendt, 'I Will Be Our Saviour . . .' from *Birth and Death of a Miracle Man* (Penguin, Auckland, 1986); Clara Reid, 'Island' and 'Violent Storm' from *7 Tutuila Writers* ('O si'uleo o Samoa, Samoa, 1987); Eti Sa'aga, 'Birthday Present' and 'Of Butterflies and Bubbles'; Caroline Sinavaiana, 'Ianeta's Dance' and 'War News';Talosaga Tolovae, 'Polynesian Old Man' and 'Crucifixion on Sunday' from *The Shadows Within* (Rimu Publishing, 1984); Momoe Malieto a Von Reiche, 'Nostalgia' and 'Who is Lili Tunu?' from *Tai, Heart of a Tree* (New Women's Press, 1988); Albert Wendt, 'Parents & Children', 'Knife', 'Shaman' from *Shaman of Visions* (AUP, 1984); 'The Wall' first appeared in *Nightlife*, in *Sport* vol.3, Spring 1989 and 'In Your Enigma' in *Landfall* vol.187, Autumn 1994; Sam L. Alaisa, 'The Parrot' from *Hostage* (USP, Solomons, 1988); Jully Makini (nee Sipolo), 'Roviana Girl' from *Praying Parents* (Aruligo Book Centre, 1986); Pesi Fonua, 'Point of No Return' from *Sun and Rain and Other Stories in English* (Vavau Press,Tonga, 1983); Epeli Hau'ofa, *Kisses in the Nederends* (Penguin, Auckland, 1987) and 'To the Last Viking of the Sunrise'.

The editor and the publishers were unfortunately unable to trace the copyright holder for Sano Malifa, *Midnight Sonnets*. If contacted, we shall be pleased to include acknowledgement in any future reprints and/or new editions.

GENERAL EDITOR'S NOTE

Teachers of Pacific literature and interested members of the general public will welcome this anthology of prose and poetry. Between the covers of this volume will be found a representative selection of creative work written since 1980, when *Lali*, the first collection of Pacific writing, was published. Edited also by Samoan novelist and poet Albert Wendt, *Lali* was a huge success, in part because of Wendt's careful and thoughtful selection of material. The same concerns are evident in this anthology, appropriately titled *Nuanua*.

As in a rainbow, each poem, story, or extract in this collection is a unique shade and hue, though some of their themes, such as colonialism, love, nature, or identity, inevitably overlap. Written mostly from a personal perspective, each poem or story is colored by the author's experience, gender, political beliefs, cultural background, and choice of language, to name a few of the many factors that influence any artistic creation. Thus each cultural product has its own internal logic that gives it shape and meaning; each embodies a mood, a sensibility, and a truth about life in the contemporary Pacific.

Like the various colors of a rainbow, the selections in this volume complement and enhance each other, reflecting back to the reader an aspect that is sad, serious, happy, confused, and forever changing in its shape and focus. The Pacific portrayed in this collection is complex and complicated. It is a rainbow of many colors that will delight, entertain, and instruct its readers about matters of concern to Micronesians, Melanesians, and Polynesians.

Thank you, Albert Wendt, for this rainbow of poetry and prose.

VILSONI HERENIKO

INTRODUCTION

In many of our Pacific languages nuanua means rainbow, an appropriate description of the diversity of cultures and languages, of fauna and flora found in Polynesia, Melanesia and Micronesia. It also aptly describes the richness and variety of our literatures, both oral and written.

People have been living in some parts of our region for at least 45,000 years. During that enormous span of time we explored the whole Pacific and settled most of it. Our Pacific ancestors were able to sail for hundreds of miles in set directions, to return home and then to repeat those journeys. Through these acts of discovering, exploring and settling the vast Pacific our forebears created and shared a larger inhabited world.

As soon as written languages were introduced into the Pacific in the nineteenth century, literacy spread rapidly, first through Polynesia, then through the rest of our region. Literacy was used primarily by the missionaries to convert the people to Christianity. The first converts were in turn used as missionaries to convert other Pacific countries. Contrary to popular belief, most of the missionaries who won the Pacific for the Christian God were our own people.

Literacy in the indigenous languages also allowed our people to correspond with one another and thereby start a written literature, conduct business and even set up printing presses. As with other introduced technology and influences, we indigenised writing, using it for our own purposes.

Up till the 1960s, most of the written literature about Polynesia, Melanesia and Micronesia was by outsiders. Only a few literary works by Pacific Islands writers had been published. For example, Florence 'Johnny' Frisbie, of the Cook Islands, published *Miss Ulysses of Puka Puka* (New York: Macmillan, 1948), an autobiographical story of a young girl and her life with her papa'a father on the island of Pukapuka. She has continued writing since and *Nuanua* contains 'The Bed', one of her recent stories. It seems that our literature has come full circle.

Perhaps the first novel by a Pacific Islands writer to be published was *Makutu*, by Tom and Lydia Davis (1960). This is the tale of a young English doctor and a 'narrow-minded New England spinster' who come to work on the imaginary island of Fenua Lei. She is makutu-ed, as it were, for breaking the tapu of the island's most sacred shrine. It is interesting that after a series of careers as a doctor, scientist and politician, Tom Davis has again published a novel, *Vaka* (IPS, 1992). An extract from *Vaka* appears in this book.

1

But apart from those examples and the work of Alistair Te Ariki Campbell in Aotearoa/New Zealand in the 1950s, poetry, fiction and drama written in English by indigenous writers did not start to emerge until the 1960s and 1970s, with the establishment of high schools and tertiary institutions such as the University of Papua New Guinea and the University of the South Pacific. This literature was part of the process of decolonisation and the cultural revival that was taking place in our region, inspired by and learning from the anti-colonial struggles in Ireland, Africa, the Caribbean, and India, the civil rights movement in the United States, the international student protest movement and the opposition to the Vietnam War.

Though our region remains a mix of the colonial and the post-colonial, what can be called post-colonial literature in English is now well established and growing all the time. For the purposes of this anthology I define Pacific literature as that written or composed by Pacific Islands peoples, especially the indigenous peoples.

Colonial literature (fiction, non-fiction, poetry and drama) was part and parcel of the arrogant process of colonialism in which we were viewed as part of the fauna and flora, to be studied, erased, 'saved', domesticated, 'civilised' or 'developed'. We were viewed almost wholly from a Eurocentric perspective. That literature was by Europeans who had supposedly 'discovered' us and the islands we had discovered and settled over hundreds of years; they were traders, missionaries, colonial adminstrators, development experts, journalists, novelists, poets, anthropologists, literary critics and papalagi settlers and their descendants. Colonial literature assumed, whether consciously or unconsciously, that the coloniser's language was superior to ours and part of saving and civilising us was therefore to convert us to that language. The results of this were devastating. In Australia, for instance, many Aboriginal languages (and their speakers) were destroyed. In Aotearoa, te reo Maori nearly suffered the same fate, and it is still under threat. In Hawai'i the same thing happened.

If we appeared at all in colonial poetry and fiction we were seen as exotic, as peripheral, as 'extras' in the epic, as stereotypes or as noble and heroic forms of escape. In non-fiction we were specimens to be studied and analysed. The histories written about us were really about the colonisers and their activities among us. Much colonial literature justified the very process of colonialism and our conversion to progress and development!

Colonial literature created a whole mythology about us. This is still being perpetuated in some of the supposedly post-colonial anthologies and in writing by the descendants of the Papalagi/Pakeha settlers. Today some writing considered by Pakeha/Papalagi writers to be post-colonial, we consider colonial.

Even in Australia, Aotearoa and Hawai'i, which from the viewpoint of their indigenous populations are still colonies, our post-colonial literature declares itself to be different from and opposed to colonial literature. We need only read the work of the Aboriginal playwright Jack Davis and the novelist Mudrooroo, the Maori writers Patricia Grace, Witi Ihimaera and Keri Hulme and the Hawaiian poets Joseph Balaz and Haunani Kay Trask to see that.

How does our literature show itself to be post-colonial? By what it says and how it says it. We have indigenised and enriched the language of the colonisers and used it to declare our independence and uniqueness; to analyse colonialism itself and its effects upon us; to free ourselves of the mythologies created about us in colonial literature.

Colonialism has changed us radically but I don't support the outmoded and racist theories, such as the fatal impact theory, which underpin most colonial literature about us. According to these theories and views, we, the indigenous, have been hapless victims and losers in the process of cultural contact and interaction; our cultures have been 'diluted' and 'corrupted'; we have even 'lost' them. All cultures are becoming, changing in order to survive, absorbing foreign influences, continuing, growing. But that doesn't mean they become any less Samoan or any less Tongan. We and our cultures have survived and adapted when we were expected to die, vanish, under the influence of supposedly stronger superior cultures and their technologies. Our story of the Pacific is that of marvellous endurance, survival and dynamic adaptation, despite enormous suffering under colonialism in some of our countries. We have survived through our own efforts and ingenuity. We have indigenised much that was colonial or foreign to suit ourselves, creating new blends and forms. We have even indigenised Western art forms, including the novel.

For me the *post* in post-colonial does not just mean *after*; it also means *around*, *through*, *out of*, *alongside*, and *against*. In the new literatures in English it means all these. Our literature has, since the 1960s, been inventing and defining itself, clearing a space for itself in relation to colonial (and other) literature. It is not surprising that our literature began and gained euphoric power and mana within and alongside the movements for political independence in our region; movements which worked to decolonise our countries and to forge national identities rooted firmly in our own ways of life and in our own pasts. Post-colonial literature was part of the drive for roots, cultural revival and rebirth. (Its most recent political phase is the attack on our corrupt elites and the injustices perpetuated by neo-colonialism.) And as our anti-colonial political movements were inspired by other anti-colonial movements, our literature was inspired by and learned from the post-colonial literatures that emerged out of those movements.

Our literature puts us at centre stage, with our accents, dress, good and evil, dreams and visions. As in other former colonies, much of our early literature is nationalistic, angry, protesting, lamenting a huge loss. That loss is defined differently from country to country. The literature attempts to reconstruct what has been lost or changed. Consequently much of it is a fabulous storehouse of anthropology, sociology, art, religion, history, dance and music. Novels like *The Crocodile, Maiba, Potiki, the bone people, Leaves of the Banyan Tree* and *Dr Wooreddy's Prescription for Enduring the Ending of the World* show this well.

Much of our early literature saw the colonial and the indigenous as in irreconcilable opposition, the colonial as the evil destroyer; no benefits at all were seen in colonialism or the emergence of blends and mixtures and fusions of the indigenous and the foreign, even though our literature itself is living proof of that. It is often modernist and uses the realist mode — here again is the influence of Western/colonial art, literature and education on our writers. Much of our fiction is of political and social commitment, with a heavily tragic, pessimistic vision of our times; it shows the other features of modernism too: deliberate ambiguity and complexity, irony, unified structures and characterisation, the search for originality and uniqueness, and the concealment of artifice in the hope of transcending time and place. You can read Eliot, Yeats, Pound, Forster, Auden, Woolf, Faulkner, Hemingway, Wright, Ellison, Lessing and others in that literature.

Many of these influences came to the Pacific through our writers' university education and reading and through literature courses which also included post-colonial writers like V. S. Naipaul, George Lamming, Derek Walcott, Chinua Achebe, Wole Soyinka, Bessie Head, Ngugi wa Thiongo, and Kwei Armah. The so-called magic realism of Jorge Luis Borges and Gabriel García Márquez has also entered our literature. So now we have a complex and expansive blend of realism and magic realism in our writing. But at the heart of all this are the indigenous ingredients: the techniques of oral storytelling and other oral traditions; art, dance and music; and indigenous philosophies and visions.

Features of the postmodern can also be seen. Like the post-colonial, postmodernist literature is still defining itself, clearing a space for itself, declaring itself against some of the tenets of modernism. The postmodern is deliberately pastiche and parody; it is playful and does not bother to hide the process that writing is; it is self-referential and consciously literary; it is often anti-elitist and goes for the 'discontinuous narrative' and inconsistent character development; it sees art as a commodity, the reader and buyer as crucial participants in the making of art; it sees reality as relative and changing; it is often a mix of realism, fantasy, autobiography, parody, and so on; it tends to condemn the moralistic and didactic features of realist fiction. Postmodernist writers like Calvino and Eco have been influential in our region. However, postmodernism is not new to Pacific indigenous cultures, where storytelling is always seen as a process which changes according to the mood of the teller and the reactions of her audience, and where art is a commodity produced for the community.

Lali

Lali: A Pacific Anthology, published in 1980 and reprinted several times, was my first attempt to anthologise a representative selection of prose and poetry in English from the Cook Islands, Fiji, Kiribati, Niue, Papua New Guinea, Vanuatu, Solomon Islands, Tonga and Samoa. Initially when I planned *Lali*, I wanted to include in it work by Tangata Maori, Tangata Aborigine and Tangata Hawai'i. But in the end I decided to confine the selection to English and to the countries I've mentioned for the following reasons. There are over 1200 different languages in our region; it is impossible to anthologise in one volume all the literatures in those languages. The writing by Tangata Maori, Tangata Aborigine and Tangata Aborigine was already being anthologised in their countries. Being more conversant with the writing in English, I restricted the anthology to that language which, after two hundred years in our region, is now our major language for regional communication, education, business and trade. Through my work at the University of the South Pacific from 1975 to 1987 I helped encourage, foster and publish that writing, particularly in the countries of that university's region. So I drew mainly on the literatures of those countries.

The same constraints and considerations have made me restrict the selection in *Nuanua* to prose (mainly fiction) and poetry in English and to the same countries. I have chosen only from work published since 1980.

After *Nuanua* the urgent need is to publish national anthologies in our indigenous languages. Whatever money is available should be devoted to that. If our indigenous languages are to remain strong and inventive their literatures should be taught and read widely.

A word of caution: *Lali* and *Nuanua* may create the impression that the strongest and most extensive literature in our region is represented by fiction and poetry. That is not so. Like writers everywhere, more Pacific writers write non-fiction than fiction or poetry or drama. Led and inspired by the publishing programme of the University of the South Pacific's Institute of Pacific Studies, under the dedicated editorship of Ron Crocombe, our writers have produced works of history, autobiography, economics, politics, geography, sociology, science and much more.

The literatures in our indigenous languages continue to flourish and grow. Our oral literatures, which stretch back hundreds of years, are astounding collections of mythologies, genealogies, poetry, stories, songs, chants and incantations. These are still our richest literatures even though most of them have not been recorded or passed on to our young people through our education systems. Many of our writers continue to draw their strength and inspiration from our oral traditions; some reuse or reinvent our ancient mythologies to map the present, some use the techniques of oral storytelling and recitation and oratory. There are many examples of this in *Nuanua*. John Kasaipwalova's *Sail the Midnight Sun* and Rexford Orotaloa's stories in *Suremada* take the use of those techniques to greater heights.

Since *Lali*

Much has changed in our region since the publication of *Lali*. At that time there was no country called Vanuatu: now the New Hebrides has become independent Vanuatu. Most of our countries are now either independent or self-governing. However Indonesia, the US and France continue to hold on to most of their Pacific territories, using them as nuclear testing sites and military bases. After the US was forced out of Vietnam it turned many of its Pacific territories, especially in Micronesia, into heavily armed and sophisticated military complexes; and thus denies the indigenous people their political independence. Though American Samoa is still an American territory, I have grouped it in this book with Western Samoa because our fa'a-Samoa and aiga ties are still firm. In New Caledonia, French Polynesia, East Timor and West Irian the indigenous movements for independence have gained strength although many of their leaders and supporters have been killed or imprisoned by the colonial settlers and authorities. A literature in French by the indigenous peoples is developing but not as fast as ours in English.

The indigenous peoples of Aotearoa, Australia and Hawai'i, now minority groups in their countries, continue their valiant struggle for sovereignty and self-determination. That struggle has led to a remarkable renaissance in indigenous ways of life and in all the arts. The Tangata Maori renaissance with its exciting developments in the arts is a truly innovative movement of wordwide significance. Our artists and writers in other Pacific countries are learning from it.

Decolonisation still inspires much of our writing. Colonialism, racism, modernisation and their effects on us remain major preoccupations in our literature. A sense of profound loss still pervades that writing. At the same time in those countries struggling for their independence the writing is full of anger and of hope.

Since the Second World War, and particularly since independence, there has been a rapid growth in the populations of our countries. Urbanisation is intensifying and is causing political and social dislocation, overcrowding, major health problems, rising crime rates, widespread unemployment and poverty. Most of our governments do not have the resources to create jobs, feed, educate, and house our populations adequately. Consequently foreign aid, in all its forms, has become the biggest industry in our region. Most of our national economies are heavily dependent on it: without it they would collapse. Some of our economies have been described as 'remittance' economies, dependent for their survival on money sent by our migrants living abroad. So much for the enchanting myth of South Sea paradises free from foreign influence and control!

Since the 1960s, especially, many of our people have migrated to get work and better education for their children. Countries such as Aotearoa, Hawai'i and the US now have large Pacific Islands populations, including third-generation Pacific Islands people. In 1991 there were almost 168,000 Pacific Islanders (or 5 per cent of the total population) in Aotearoa. They are influencing and changing sports, dance, theatre, art and literature. Some of our writers now live outside their countries of birth. Alistair Te Ariki Campbell, who went to Aotearoa as a young orphan from the Cooks, is now one of that country's major poets and novelists. The Samoan poet Talosaga Tolovae lived and taught high school in Tokoroa; he died there in August 1994. John Pule went from Niue to Aotearoa when he was five.

Apart from losing many of our most energetic and adventurous people, our countries suffer the other political, social and economic problems and ills which plague most developing countries. Much of our writing focuses on these problems and their effects on individuals, families and communities. Our writing is also examining and attacking the growing corruption and abuse of power in our elites. Disillusionment, irony, anger and cynicism are the most obvious features of that writing.

But our writing also celebrates what all literatures celebrate: love, sorrow, joy, death, pain, happiness, and through it, language and the gift of speaking, saying. Styles range from the lyrical realism of Russell Soaba and Konai Helu Thaman, through the wild and savagely delightful satire of Epeli Hau'ofa and the complex storytelling style of Rexford Orotaloa, to the surrealistic poetry–prose mix of John Pule.

Expanding tertiary education, radio, television and video, newspapers and other media, and the growth in the production, distribution and study of writing within our region have brought our writers closer together, made them aware of what is happening and being written throughout the region. Now the work of our leading writers is influencing the writing of our younger ones. It is also shaping how we see ourselves and our cultures and how we are seen by others, and destroying some of the stereotypes and myths created about us by outsiders.

Selection

As in *Lali* I have selected stories, extracts from novels, and poems which give a representative picture of what is being written and which, in a combination of ways, have appealed to me as things well discovered, well said, well sung; as things new, striking, energetic; poetry and prose which continue exploring the possibilities of language and what we are and the forces shaping us and our ways of life, giving face and body and voice to us and our magnificent ocean.

We have very few full-time writers — you can't earn a living from it! Some, like Momoe Malietoa Von Reiche and John Pule, are also artists. Others are bank managers, politicians and advisors to politicians, senior civil servants, actors, dancers and musicians, and teachers in the universities or other educational institutions. Many of the writers who were in *Lali* are not in *Nuanua*, either because they have stopped writing altogether or because they have not published new work. One of the main features of our writing is the large number of writers who publish a few pieces and then disappear, perhaps quite appropriately, into the civil service, politics, the professions and business. Some of them, like Vincent Eri (who died in early 1994), Maori Kiki and Paulias Matane, have become businessmen or ambassadors or heads of government departments.

Some of the writers in *Lali* are here again. Since 1980 many of them have published substantial books of poetry or prose or both. Exciting new writers have also published work over the last fourteen years. They are showing other ways of using English and enriching that language further.

Pacific literature is now taught in many countries within and outside our region. Teachers and researchers are now adding very sensitively to the critical commentary and analysis of our literature. They are also enthusiastic supporters and promoters of it. And more publishers are willing to publish it too.

Anyway, wantoks, here at last is *Nuanua*.
Malo le onosa'i! Ia manuia pea le tapuaiga!

Over the years taken to compile *Nuanua* many people have helped and advised me. I am particularly grateful to John Barnett for his detailed and expert editorial assistance, to Elizabeth Caffin and Gillian Kootstra of Auckland University Press, and to Reina Whaitiri, Loata Vuetibau and Helen McArdle of the University of Auckland.

ALBERT TUAOPEPE WENDT
Auckland, Aotearoa, 1994

COOK ISLANDS

ALISTAIR TE ARIKI CAMPBELL

from *The Frigate Bird*

It was the first time I'd met the Purple Lady. I passed her as I walked up the outside stairs to my motel unit. It was dark, but there was a little light from a window above my head — enough to see that her face was as smooth as an egg and that she was wearing a purple coat. I can't explain why I felt uneasy, because she was ordinary enough and polite as well. In response to my greeting, she flashed her teeth at me — and big shiny teeth they were.

I'd had an exhausting day on the Northerner express and arrived late in Auckland. I took a taxi to my motel and after a few drinks in the house bar I went to bed, trying not to be aware of the disgusting bed-cover, which was grimy and reeked of stale sweat and cheap perfume. This was supposed to be a high-class motel, and I couldn't understand why my room was so obviously substandard. I had always got on well with the management, so why did they give me this room? I was puzzled and irritable.

It seemed I'd no sooner closed my eyes than I woke up to the sound of gentle knocking on my door. I cursed and put on the light and was thoroughly confused. I thought I was still at home and kept opening a door and finding myself in the wardrobe, tangled up with clothes-hangers and my jacket and overcoat. And where there should have been a door leading to the living-room there was a blank wall. I finally sorted out where I was and opened the front door, only to find that the secret knocker had gone.

I was now in a state of panic — the rats were in the house. I had the heebie-jeebies. I was going nuts again. I was certainly not in the right frame of mind to fly to Rarotonga and from there take a boat to Penrhyn, my mother's homeland. Only yesterday my sister had asked me why I was going. Good question, I thought, but aloud I told her I had promised my editor a story about our childhood in the Islands.

I took a taxi to the airport and felt my spirits sinking all the way. Not even the dry sense of humour of the gruff taxi-driver could raise them. But I did manage a ghost of a smile when he told me about one particular passenger he'd picked up.

'Even an old fellow like me,' he said, 'is got at by women who want to have sex in the cab. One night a handsome well-spoken woman in her early forties — a night nurse at some hospital — tried it on. She waved a ten-dollar note in my face and said, "I don't suppose you can change this. Hop over to the back and we'll call it quits."

'I looked at her through the rear-vision mirror and said, "No thanks — I have plenty of change."

The flight to Rarotonga was a nightmare, and when we arrived in the early hours in the humid heat, I felt a wreck. Fortunately, I got through customs without the usual hold-up. I checked in at my motel, took a sleeping tablet and went to bed utterly wretched. Why did I think of that building society manager with whom I had discussed my loan application? I told him I was short of money, but things would get better.

He looked at me and said mournfully, 'Things never get better, mate.'

Several times I get up in the night and go to the toilet, and in my delirium I argue with that sad defeated man. 'Should I send a loan application to God? I shall ask him for a sound mind. Surely that's not asking for too much.'

There's a deep sigh from my familiar in the corner. I shall get to know him well before journey's end.

A young girl brings in my breakfast. I tell her I'm from Wellington.

'Oh,' she says, 'that's no good.'

'Have you been there?'

'No — but my friends have, and they say it's no good.'

I tell her that her friends are mistaken, but she wanders off with a pretty shrug of her shoulders. She is about eighteen, plump and breasty. But now she comes back and leans against the door and asks me, 'Do you know that lady in the purple coat? She got here last night when you did — on the bus.'

Panic flares in my stomach. How can that be? I saw no such person either on the plane or in the bus that brought me and a few sleepy guests to this motel.

'No — I don't know her.'

Later in the morning I visit the local doctor, a heavy owl-eyed Scot, and tell him I'm depressed. He asks me to describe my symptoms, and I mention a feeling of panic, insomnia and heavy legs. He looks searchingly at me and writes out a prescription for a hundred and twenty anti-depressant tablets. 'Take four each night before bed. You should start feeling better again in about a fortnight or three weeks.' Why does he look at me with such bitterness? Three weeks! How can I possibly last that long?

Feeling better now that I am stocked up with enough tablets to see me through the voyage, I buy some food to take back to my unit: a filled roll, a bag of oranges and a large pawpaw. I try to eat the roll, but my mouth is too dry. Eating is going to be a problem on board, and that worries me. I'll have to stick to fruit. I am exhausted. That encounter with the doctor has drained me of energy. I sprawl on my bed and watch a tiny white lizard. He is swift and agile. He darts forward, flicks out his tongue, withdraws, darts forward again, withdraws — then vanishes. How can I bear this agony?

I manage to call a taxi — that takes some doing — and I share it with a young Singaporean Chinese who is here to attend a seminar on making concrete bricks from coral sand. He is under the impression that I am paying the fare for both of us and is inordinately grateful. His face drops when I pay only for myself. I feel too apprehensive to worry about his feelings. For there she is — the same dirty old ship that took my sister and me to Penrhyn some years ago. I remember her squalor and stench and I have to steel myself before I can face going aboard.

I haven't mentioned that I saw the Purple Lady yesterday — how could I forget? I had to steady myself against a tree. The Premier's limousine passed me, pennants fluttering, and there she was looking out at me, big teeth exposed in a grimace. The Premier must then have said something funny, because both were laughing, and he was holding a finger to his sunglasses to stop them falling off. It was so bizarre that my skin crawled. The car stopped — and I fled to lose myself in the crowd.

The odd thing is that the breasty young Island girl keeps popping up everywhere I go. It may sound paranoid, but I suspect that she and the Purple Lady are in this thing together — though don't ask me what thing. And once I caught her laughing. Sometimes I become so tense that I move like a puppet — jerky and uncoordinated. When crossing the road, I take a step forward and snap my head to the left. There's no fluency in my movements — it is stomp, stomp, stomp, on my wooden legs. Is it any wonder that the Island girl laughed? But I hate her for it.

I had to fight for my bunk. I had moved my gear into the cabin and was resting up in my bunk when a young man — actually, little more than a pretty boy — came in, black eyes flashing, and said severely, 'What are you doing in that bunk?'

I was flabbergasted. 'Doing? What do you think I'm doing? The cabin boy brought me here — and I'm staying put. Yours is the lower bunk.'

'It's not my bunk — it's my mother's,' he said, sulkily.

The mother turned out to be a reasonable woman. 'I'm sorry about that,' I told her.

'That's all right,' she said.

This little spat drained me of all my energy, and I was relieved when they went out and left me alone. I was so tired, I actually fell asleep, which I seldom do during the day, and when I woke up we were at sea. I was again disoriented and at first had no idea where I was and how I'd got there. Worse still, my mouth tasted vile, and I was in a blue funk. The ship was rolling heavily. One moment my feet were higher than my head, and the next the reverse was true. I had the awful feeling that when my feet were uppermost fluid was seeping from my stomach into my mouth. I sat up in despair. If that was the case, I was done for. It was 1.30 a.m. Should I get the skipper out of bed and explain to him my predicament? Would he be prepared to turn the ship round and return to Rarotonga? He'd think I was mad if I told him that the drug wouldn't work as long as it seeped into my mouth. Should I put it to him — for he seemed a reasonable bloke — that if I had a bunk that ran parallel to the ship the problem would be solved?

Then, in a flash, the solution came. What if I kept my head at all times higher than my body? There'd be no leakage then. An inspiration — brilliant! I arranged my pillows against the bulkhead and sat bolt upright. And at once I had doubts. I would have to sit that way throughout the entire voyage. I'd look ridiculous — and the little kids would come and point their fingers at me and laugh. Then came another flash. If I was suffering from seepage, than surely the others would be too, but you don't see them sitting up in their bunks and whining about it. Why? Because we are all engineered so that these things don't happen — stupid! I felt much as Rutherford must have done when he split the atom.

I tried to have my first meal with the others, but the food, curried chicken, turned to ashes in my mouth. My whole body was on fire, and *whoosh* — I had an attack of prickly heat, spreading downwards from my head, until my whole body was on fire.

'Not eating?' asked the cook.

'Not hungry,' I replied, pushing my plate away and beating a hasty retreat.

The woman who has the bunk below me tells me she's going to Penrhyn to buy pearls. She is married to a Penrhyn man and knows the people well. She's like a doll — never a hair out of place, clear blue porcelain eyes and a flawless complexion. Naturally, I call her Living Doll. She tells me we won't reach Penrhyn until the weekend after next. I count on my fingers and work out that the tablets should be biting by then.

We are standing off Aitutaki and there's a lot of movement on deck. Somebody throws a sack of oranges into the cabin, and I sit up and see one of my cabin mates peeling a green orange with a flick-knife. He is a powerfully built man, about my age. He is a Penrhyn man, with that little dash of pride that Penrhyn people seem to have.

He hands me the peeled orange, and I thank him. I tell him what Living Doll has told me about marrying a Penrhyn Islander, and he snorts angrily.

'He married to an Australian man, not a Penrhyn man.'

I've noticed that Islanders sometimes say 'he' when they mean 'she'. Why did Living Doll lie? Is she part of the conspiracy? She looks squeaky clean, but you can never be sure.

I feel safe in my bunk. It's my castle, and if it comes to the Final Test, it will be fought here.

Last night I had a strange and terrifying experience. I could sense the

Giant Toad — have I mentioned him to you? No? Well, I could sense him stirring in my solar plexus, but before he could harm me I lobbed a hand grenade — a tablet — at him and set him back. But he stirred again and grew so huge — to an increasing roll of drums — that I had to fling five more grenades at him and knock him for a six. Then suddenly all sorts of things happened — like in a Marx Brothers movie. Rockets went off in the sky, my ears whistled, my nose steamed, and nerves all over my body popped and sizzled. All of which I found so interesting I stood aside — so to speak — and observed. But I didn't forget my deep breathing. I was conscious that I might be under surveillance, so I kept my mouth under the sheet.

As far as I know, Living Doll is the only person on board who knows of my condition. I told her yesterday I was having a nervous breakdown, and she was kind enough to fetch me a glass of water so I could take my pills. But I can't get over her lying to me.

Another quite extraordinary thing happened to me — when was it? I get so confused, it's frightening. Anyway, I felt this nerve twitch in my solar plexus. It inched its way like a worm up my body and round my heart, then headed for my neck. A door slammed and the nerve went out like a light. This happened several times until the nerve took a new course, went straight up my body and my neck, made contact with my brain and blew a fuse. The flash made me gasp and sit up. This happened many times, and I felt I had to defend myself by concentrating hard and thwarting the Enemy. I heard Living Doll asking me if I was all right, but I wasn't letting on. You can't be too cautious in enemy country. Was it appropriate that I thought of Jacob wrestling with the Angel?

I am certain now that the crew is aware of my condition — and the passengers too. I heard two boys go past, and one said to the other, 'That fellow there is going crazy.' I was so indignant I almost called out. And the other night, when the deck passengers were holding their evening service, I was convinced they were praying for my soul. They believed I was possessed by demons and they were exorcising them with gusto.

I have been worrying about Living Doll. Is she one of them? I saw her teeth when she snapped at the cabin boy, and they looked awfully big and white and sharp. I need no reminding of when I saw them before.

There's a fat pig of a man who drifts about the passenger quarters. He has the loudest voice I have ever heard — and doesn't he use it. He's in the next cabin at this very moment, bellowing like a bull. Big Mouth, I call him. The other day I got so angry with his shouting that I went next door and asked him to keep his voice down. He was so astonished, he stood there and gawped at me. It had occurred to me that he was one of *them*, but no, he can't be — he's too stupid.

We're plodding along somewhere in the wide Pacific. My muscular friend tells me we should reach Manihiki at midnight. I don't know if I can trust him altogether. That knife looks awfully sharp — and he's a bad-tempered man, easily aroused to fury. He hacks the top off a drinking coconut as if decapitating an enemy — a good man to have on your side in a brawl. He hands me the coconut he has topped, and I drink gratefully. He's a wild man is Muscles, but he's all right.

I realise now that I have been barmy. It takes a lot to admit such a thing — you'll agree, I'm sure. Well, I should have been able to read the signs, but somebody keeps changing the rules. Last night I went to the toilet, and was trying to piss, when I heard the Devil roaring in fury. I opened the door and looked out and saw nobody. I tried to piss again, but my knees were knocking together, and nothing came. The roaring started up again, and I was so scared I almost took to my heels. Then I made a big discovery: that was no Devil roaring but the sea in the outlet pipe. At least I think it was. I popped another pill to be on the safe side.

What does the Devil look like? His face is that of a huge insect, brown and armour-plated, with hundreds of eyes. That's all I'm allowed to say. And the Praying Mantis is his courtier at table. Courteous to your face, but look away and — wow! — he's crunching your head like a stick of celery.

One night I had this experience. It was decidedly odd. I thought I was lying in my bunk, which kept moving its position to different parts of the ship. It was a dream of dissolution, I suppose. Then, as I was dropping off, I thought I was lying alongside some kind of stockyard that was divided into small pens containing no animals. One moment Big Mouth was bawling beside me, and the next he was half a mile away, shouting his stupid mouth off. You wouldn't have him for a friend, would you? Anyway, he must have been trying to tell me something — but God knows what.

Rua the cook is an odd bird, I must say. He looks no more than a grubby kid, but he's all of twenty-five. He's small and stocky, with lank black hair through which he peers uncomprehendingly at the world. His face is shiny with sweat. He speaks slowly and incoherently. I can't understand what he's trying to say most of the time. It makes me mad. Is he drunk or popping pills? Muscles comes in and urges me to eat, 'Go on — have your breakfast. Eat. Kaikai good today.'

'What did you have for breakfast?'

He clams up and looks uneasy, as if he's given too much away. I rephrase the question, but it's no good — I've lost him.

We are standing off Manihiki, and though it's still early in the morning, it seems that the whole population is swarming all over the ship. Outside my cabin, the winch is chugging away. Groan, groan, groan go the steel hawsers unloading the cargo and, later in the day, loading copra. It's strange that although the engines are making a hell of a din you can talk quite softly and be heard. There are many strong smells about, from smoking oil to the stench of the bilge, but no matter how overpowering these may be you can still smell a fart.

Big Mouth is back. He went ashore to terrorise the natives and is now next door thundering in his usual style, but I take no notice of him. It would be clear to a blind man that he's trying to rile me, but I have other things to worry me and I ignore him. I'm not getting any better. There was rain about, but I think it bypassed us. I stare through the porthole, feeling absolutely rotten. We are passing a string of pretty islets, some quite tiny and supporting a few palm trees, others quite big and densely covered.

The men are trawling for barracuda, big game fish that fight to the end. There is much laughter and horseplay. They hack at the struggling fish and slice off chunks to hand around. It becomes a feeding frenzy — the knives flash and raw gobbets are consumed. Even I get caught up in the excitement, grab a piece and scuttle off to my hidey-hole. But, alas! I gag on it and almost choke. This is a hell of a life. I lie down.

I must have slept, for it's quite dark now and we are lying off some island, engine stilled. Rakahanga — no, by God! Manihiki. Living Doll tells me we've come back to pick up passengers. I am confused. I thought the plan was to pick them up on the way back from Penrhyn. 'It's all changed,' she says.

'Are we sailing direct to Rarotonga after leaving Penrhyn?'

'Nobody knows.'

'Nobody knows!' Think of it. It's a farcical situation. I'm terrified of the irrational. It seems pretty barmy to trawl for fish in a cargo ship, wasting hours of time (not to mention oil), when we could have sailed to Rakahanga. I now learn we have returned to Manihiki to pick up a Catholic priest to take him to Rakahanga. Even a priest at the heart of this confusion does little to ease my mind. And what was it that Living Doll said to me when she returned to the ship after going ashore? 'Oh, by the way — a lady sends her regards . . .' That was below the belt.

'A la-lady?' I stammered.

'Yes — she sends her regards.' Living Doll laughed. 'And her nose is purple, too. She must have been drinking.'

How could she laugh when my mind was at risk? Suddenly I was frying inside my skin. I felt weak and very threatened. I had to lie down.

I'm in the eleventh day of my Great Ordeal, and I don't feel the slightest bit better. In fact, I feel worse — much worse. I'm in terror of the Giant Toad.

The Fat Boy who occupies the fourth bunk in the cabin came in just then — he must have scented blood — looked around and went out again. He's a glutton. He sometimes lies in his bunk and eats steadily for an hour or more

16

— biscuits, oranges, bananas, sweets, coconut flesh — all are stuffed into the gaping hole in his face. Fatty is from Penrhyn, I'm told. Heaven preserve me — we might be related! Which reminds me — I expected Rua to bring me my dinner. Stuff you, mate! I'll survive in spite of you.

Will they ever be able to transplant minds? One day they may have the technology and the know-how. But the church would be against it — bound to be. They'd find some moral obstacle. And I'm not sure how I'd feel if my mind were transplanted into a body that had bad breath or dandruff, or was deficient in some respect . . .

I'm under siege! The pipes are clanging, and a stone strikes the steel deck above my head, veering off with a clatter. Somebody old is approaching and stops outside my door. He sniffs and shuffles closer. And closer.

'Is that you, Grandfather?'

Someone is mumbling gibberish — Christ, it's me! A dog barks quite clearly. They say that the spirits can imitate any sound. Shuffle, shuffle, closer and closer. The pipes go haywire and thump like mad. I hum to keep my spirits up, and somebody joins in. It's insane. Very distantly the same dog howls and immediately yelps as if somebody has kicked it. And now a fly buzzes in my ear, and another, and another, until the whole cabin vibrates with their buzzing.

He's here — the Lord of the Flies — and every hair on my body is standing up!

The torment went on all night. Once a powerful voice roared out in a sudden rage. Wrapped tightly in a sheet, with only my mouth exposed, I tried to pray, but a giant fish struck the underside of my bunk and my prayer dried up. God help me! There was a roaring in my ears, and I gabbled the Lord's Prayer over and over, made mistakes and panicked.

Then I thought that the spooks were Polynesian and couldn't understand English, so I babbled the Cook Island benediction, 'Te Atua te aroha'. There was an explosion of light. I jack-knifed and sat bolt upright in my bunk, my eyes wide with terror, only to see that the cabin light was on. My muscular friend was staring at me and growling, 'Did you take my knife?' That brought me back to sanity.

'Knife? I haven't seen your knife.' I wanted to ask him if he'd seen the Purple Lady, but I didn't like the way he was looking at me.

'You all right?' he asked.

'Yes — I'm all right. I often go to sleep trussed up like this.'

'I thought I heard someone shouting.'

'You couldn't have. I've been here all along, and I heard no shouting.'

That was a close shave. I watch him clambering onto his bunk. He has two large suitcases standing end to end, taking up half the width of his bunk and leaving him a narrow ledge to lie on. It's a wonder he doesn't fall. And what are in those suitcases that he guards so jealously? A cut-up body?

Muscles is looking at me. 'Skipper he say we get to Penrhyn in two days.' Panic stations! How can I possibly get better in that time?

I have this conviction that my tormentor is Fat Boy. He's often hanging about in the corridor when I go out. This morning I heard a tentative whistle. It fingered my brain like an aerial root. I got up and looked out the door. Nobody. Oh, he was there, all right. There was just a hint of sulphur as if he'd suddenly, well, vaporised. Tormentors are born psychologists, quick to sniff out weaknesses and play on them.

Fat Boy could have thrown the stone that ricocheted about the deck. It's the sort of mindless thing that would give a stupid adolescent a lot of twisted pleasure.

Sometimes he comes into the cabin sucking an orange or a stick of sugarcane and steals a furtive look at me. I pretend I'm not troubled by his little tricks — and off he goes to think up something more diabolical.

It's the twelfth day, and still no sign of my liberation. As the man says, 'Things never get better.' Fat Boy is not a demon — of that I am certain. I give him one out of ten for intelligence. He's a low-grade agent. He's certainly not bright enough to orchestrate all the sounds that have been driving me crazy. Orchestrate? Absurd. This ancient tub is a whispering gallery, and he threatens me no more than the pillow I rest my head on. But why did he enter the cabin just then wearing a purple shirt?

Living Doll tells me we reach Penrhyn tomorrow. She looks at me slyly from the corners of her eyes while her pink tongue explores her upper lip. She exposes her large white teeth, but whether in a smile or a snarl I'm not certain. Then suddenly I have this incredible experience — it is joy I feel, pure joy! But now that it has passed, the old doubts return. Is she the Purple Lady? I don't know and I don't much care. Does that mean I'm getting better?

The Dark Lord of Savaiki

I am the one in your dreams,
master of passion,
favourite child
of Tumu and Papauri.
Te Ara o Tumu

I Under the Tamanu Tree

Who, who and who?
Who is the dark Lord of Savaiki?
  Crab castings
        convulsions under the house
where the landcrabs
  tell their grievances
to the roots of the tamanu tree.
Agitation of the leaves,
  the palm trees clash
              their fronds,
and the wind hurries past
  clutching in its fingers
the leaf-wrapped souls
      of children torn
          from the eyelids
of despairing mothers.
                    Hung
on spiderwebs for safekeeping,
      they will dangle there,
until the spirits come
              and eat them.

II The Witch of Hanoa

When Kavatai died,
    his son Paroa, as chief mourner,
wrapped his corpse in mats
and hung it from the ceiling
    to decay in decent isolation,

neighbour to the stars
    and the grieving wind
that rode the rooftree
      for three months
and terrified Te Tautua people
  with its groans
    and high-pitched whistling.
All this time,
      his widow Puatama,
feared throughout the kingdom
  for her sorcery,
fed his spirit at her breast
    until it grew so vast
it burst apart the ribcage
  of the house,
      a monstrous storm
that tore up trees
  and levelled villages,
    rampaging
to the west as far as Manihiki.
Her grief assuaged,
  she called his spirit home,
as she would a dangerous child,
and, chastened,
  he returned
      upon a mango's back
and beached at Hanoa,
where he lies in peace
  with Puatama
      in an unmarked grave.

III Teu

Mother, you were there
  at the passage
    when our ship arrived.
The sea, heavy as oil,
  heaved unbroken
    on the reef,

the stars
     lay in clusters
             on the water,
and you wept
     when you laid
             the Southern Cross
upon our eyes

IV At Nahe

At Nahe, attended by a sandshark,
     I waded in the shallows
that seemed as white and pure
             as happiness,
or the shark itself.
I was happy being a child again,
     and, careless as a child
             in a treasure house,
I ripped up chunks of coral
     to take home.
             Horrid amputation!
The living creatures seemed
             to shriek,
and bled a kind of ichor.

V The Doves of Pauma

The surf breaks on the mouth
     of the passage at Pauma,
where the black doves used to play
     when crickets and grasshoppers
drowned out the murmur of the sea,
     and the wind was drugged
by the scent of tipani
             and tiare maori
that flowered abundantly
     along the roadways
now overgrown and sunk in ruin.

21

VI Tapu

The sea gnaws at Paroa's bones
    where he lies at Nahe,
but Paetou,
    beloved of Maringikura,
sleeps secure at Hanoa
under an untidy heap of stones.

VII Brother Shark

The black mango
        is a priest
in his marae
    of blazing coral
where Ataranga's sunken house
    tilts
        towards Savaiki
and the setting sun.

VIII Omoka

It will be like this one day
    when I sail home to die —
the boat crunching up onto the sand,
then wading through warm water
        to the beach,
the friendly voices
    round me in the darkness,
the sky dying out
    behind the trees of Omoka,
        and reaching out of hands.

IX Trade Winds

You were just a girl,
    one of two wild sisters,
when he came to Tongareva,

a gloomy trader,
his soul eaten away
by five years
in the trenches.
You followed him
from island to island,
bore his children
only to see your dreams
break up
on the hidden reef
of Savaiki.
Mother,
your footsteps falter
outside my window,
where you have waited
fifty years
for your children
to return.
The moon comes out,
lovely
as a mother's face
over a sleeping child.
The trade winds
are your fingers
on my eyelids.

X Bosini's Tomb

Ancestral shapes
on the beach,
lying beside their drawn-up boats,
chatting and laughing softly
as they await the dawn —
so many names to remember,
so many names to honour!
Grandfather Bosini,
why do you beckon
from the deeper shadows
beyond your tomb?
The children of Marata
join hands

with the children of Tumu
and have peaceful dreams.
                    They smile to see
Father and Mother
        walking hand in hand
across the swirling waters
                    of Taruia Passage,
where the leaping dolphins
            celebrate the dawn.

from *Soul Traps*

I A Stranger from Rakahanga

A stranger has arrived from Rakahanga.
        Nobody knows how he came:
                no strange canoe has been reported —
none could survive in such a sea.
        Our villages are awash, and our dead groan
                as they sit up to the chin in water.
Such a stranger, you would think, would be
        so singular, so arresting,
                once seen, nobody could forget him.
Nobody remembers a single thing —
        the look on his face (if he has a face),
                his size, or if he is young or old.
He arrived, some say, a few hours ago,
        others claim it is more than a week,
                since he was first seen at Omoka.
On one thing, though, all are agreed:
        he is a traveller from Rakahanga —
                but why Rakahanga, they can't say.
They stand around in silent groups, expecting
        the worst — but not a thing happens.
                No deaths or accidents are reported.
They will turn soon to urgent tasks, repair
        the storm damage, but strangely empty
                as if nursing a disappointment.

II Sina

You were a tender girl, Sina,
    fragrant as the komuko
        of the young coconut tree.
Throughout our adolescence
    our entire universe
        was the floor of a canoe
where we lay together
    drifting among the motu.
        Every night I would pluck
for your breasts and hair
    the flowers of the sky.
        And then one night
we drifted far from shore
    through the scented darkness,
        oblivious of the reef
until too late — aue!
        Now you are a woman
            lovelier even than the girl
I lay with long ago,
    and another suitor
        drinks from your calabash . . .
Ru the fisherman
    knows all the secret places
        in the ocean floor.
His spear is probing
    for an answer.
        I watch and wait.

III Akaotu

Surging over the reef,
    surging over the reef,
        the sea has breached
the canoe of Akaotu
    and now she lies becalmed
        in the shallows of Sanganui.
Her splendid lovers have fled,
    leaving her to the mercy
        of her jealous consort,

25

red-haired Atea,
　　Lord of Light, who grumbles
　　　　in his sleep, causing
the sky to flicker.
　　But the Lady Akaotu
　　　　turns with the tide.
She smiles as she dreams
　　of atolls in their green birth
　　　　　pricking the white horizon.

XIII Mahuta

The gourd is overripe,
　　but it is the yam you steal
　　　　from our ocean gardens,
Mahuta, lover of night.
　　late of Rakahanga.
　　　　The beautiful young girl
sighs as she holds
　　each heavy breast
　　　　within a heavy hand.
Stunned, stunned —
　　the dragonfly bows its head
　　　　to the blows of the rain.
Lightning scribbles its name
　　above Katea Village
　　　　where a young man lies
dying, who only yesterday
　　was anointed ariki
　　　　Mahuta, night-walker,
what are the fishermen saying
　　as they wade hip-high in the sea?
　　　　It is easier to net the tide
than to trust in Mahuta,
　　gatherer of souls.

TOM DAVIS

from *Vaka*

When the canoe came into his hands, Te Arutanga Nuku renamed her *Te Pori o Kare* after his wife. Before he could sail her to places where he could show her off, he and his grand uncle, Apainga, the tutor and navigator priest he had chosen, and the fifty crew, had a great deal to learn about sailing the big canoe. Far fewer than fifty were needed to man her, but the extra number not only made handling easier, it also provided a warrior force for protection against attack and challenges from freebooters roaming the ocean. Apainga had been in charge of *Te Tia* and Atonga had been reluctant to release him to take charge of *Te Pori*, but Te Arutanga Nuku's argument that there was nobody else with Apainga's experience to manage such a large canoe finally convinced Atonga. The quirks and peculiarities in sailing her were going to be more than those of *Te Tia*, which was half the length and much less in actual size. 'Besides,' he added, 'Apainga has done a fine job in training his nephew, Te Matangi Parapu, to take over from him and he is fully qualified to take over.'

Te Pori lay in her canoe house where Atonga's 'birds' had left her as *Te Manu Ka Rere*. Her mast, spars, rigging, sail and other gear were stowed neatly beside her. The canoe house, which looked enormous before, seemed to have shrunk. In it now also lay spares of all kinds. There were spare sails and numerous coils of rope of different sizes, sitting in orderly piles on the floor. The sculling oars and long steering paddles were all there. The people of Upolu now understood why Atonga had ordered such a large orau, but there was still enough space left for other temporary uses.

The arched rafters of the orau made them strong and, since they were fastened firmly into the ground, it made them resistant to hurricanes. Sometimes they were the only shelters available either during or after a cyclone. But, even more frequently, they were used to house people of a malaga, known in Eastern Polynesia as a tere. As ancient as Polynesia itself, this was a popular pastime which involved groups of people visiting their relatives and friends in other districts or islands. These touring groups might range from twenty to as many as a hundred or more. Smaller malaga were housed in the special guest house which every Samoan high chief kept for that purpose, but larger groups were bunked in public meeting houses, or when a particularly large group turned up, the orau was pressed into service.

Malaga were popular because they were fun affairs where relatives were visited, new places seen, new people met, new relationships made and lavish entertainments enjoyed. They broke the monotony of life and, for each malaga, new songs, dances, chants and poems were created.

Among the young, many of the relationships resulting from a malaga became permanent. This helped maintain good inter-tribal relationships. Whether intended or not, it was also a way of mixing the genetic pool. Tradition demanded that the visitors receive every kindness and courtesy. Often the exchange of gifts was extensive. By the time a malaga departed, usually in a torrent of tears on both sides, the visitors would have eaten the hosts out of house and home. Malaga were expensive, but the Polynesians loved them and they served an important social purpose in the extended family sense. It was a foregone conclusion that *Tè Pori* would become involved in them. It was, thought Te Arutanga Nuku, one way of showing her off when the time came.

The canoe house was a convenient place for men to gather, talk over current events and tell the stories of history over and over. Tales of the hero warriors were favourites. Current events and scandals were even more popular. Many of the ancient voyages of discovery were credited to the five Maui brothers who fished the islands of Polynesia out of the sea. One of them, Maui Marumamao, went to the continent at the far eastern end of Te Moana Nui a Kiva and brought back some plants, including the kumara, and new customs. These were the sagas of history which the tumukorero historians loved to allegorise, involving the gods, deifying the participants and adding the fanciful to confuse the future seekers of historical truth. More often than not, everybody just gossiped and the chiefs drank kava. In the heat of the day, the orau was a nice place to be.

Tè Pori's size made her a daunting problem for launching and hauling. Some asked Atonga to work his magic and have his birds do the work. Atonga answered them with a huge, but silent, grin. Some took his unwillingness seriously. In legend, the Manu Aitu clan, which had apparently moved the canoe effortlessly, were classified as mana'une (menehune, manahune). In almost every way they were the equivalents of elves, leprechauns and goblins of other societies. They were small in size, had magical powers and were given to performing feats beyond the capability of ordinary mortals. There were even entities similar to fairies, separately known as patupaiere.

The size of the canoe posed problems of maintenance and handling under sail. There were big canoes of the same generic type as the kalia of Tonga Nui, Vava'u and Lakemba and the drua of the Fiji Islands, but none of them, they believed, were as big as *Tè Pori*.

Although Apainga, now fully transferred from *Te Tia* to *Te Pori*, had solved the matter of hoisting the sail, everyone wondered about the difficulties of tacking. These, along with a number of difficulties associated with size, were some of the reasons why many of the large canoes 'perished ashore'. However, in *Te Pori*'s case, her fine qualities and the love Te Arutanga Nuku had for her made these difficulties insignificant. His solution was to hand the canoe over full time to Apainga and his crew. Apainga always took his responsibilities seriously, and this assured tender loving care for the future of *Te Pori*, at least for the period of Apainga's remaining lifetime.

Apainga's experience made him immune to the new difficulties posed by the size of *Te Pori*. It was, he thought, only a matter of putting more power into the system. This could only mean more manpower and a system of distributing that power so that nobody got in each other's way. His rigging of *Te Pori* with four halyards was a case in point.

The matter of moving canoes between the sea and their places ashore was an important one. It determined the length of their lifetime. Too long in the water, they became sodden, barnacle encrusted and riddled with the teredo worm. Too long ashore, they dried up, planks cracked and seams opened. Therefore, a balance between use in the water and rest ashore in a canoe house, had much to do with the longevity of a canoe.

Apainga called upon the crew and experienced men he had used for the same purpose in moving the smaller *Te Tia*. He explained the difficulties and his plan for overcoming them. Normally the bigger canoes were moved by sliding poles under them and using the poles to lift and carry them.

'I think,' he told them, 'the poles will need to be longer and stronger, and there will need to be more of them, to allow about one hundred and fifty people on the main hull and about half that number on the smaller hull. Two hundred and thirty to two hundred and fifty men should be enough to do the job,' he concluded.

'Can we get large and long enough poles from the toa trees to allow enough people on them without too much bending?' asked a captain of the watch.

'I think we can,' replied Apainga. '*Te Pori* is two roa at the widest, but comes in as you go down to the keel and towards the ends. A four-roa pole along which men can be distributed can only get better to handle as we move to the ends. Distributing the men along a pole will result in less bending.

'I don't think it's a problem,' interjected an old, experienced sailor. 'There are enough toa trees with long straight trunks and branches to meet our needs. We just need to go and get them.'

All seemed to agree and it was settled. After all, they had done this often on smaller canoes. Apainga was right, it just needed more of the same for this giant canoe. More poles to go under the canoe and more people on them to lift and carry it.

Rollers or skid surfaces were rarely used. Fijians, who used living humans as rollers, did so only on the first launching as a sacrificial christening procedure. After that, they also carried their canoes between canoe house and water. Normally Polynesians moved their weighty burdens by carrying them. One Polynesian could move his own weight more by lifting it than by pushing or pulling it. The limiting factor was the awkwardness of obtaining a proper grip and leverage. In most, if not all cases, this was solved by attaching poles on which the lifter or lifters could get a hold.

So it was with moving *Te Pori o Kare* to the water of the lagoon. With canoes of seven to ten roa, men just got a grip on gunwales, iato, outrigger and anywhere else they could and carried the canoe bodily. To Polynesians, canoes were valuable. They took time and skill to make, and caring for them was important. Only under extreme circumstances were they dragged with or without rollers, which did not work well on sandy beaches anyway. Getting enough people to carry a canoe of whatever size was only a matter of spreading the word.

In the case of canoes of the size of *Te Pori*, it was only a little more complicated because it took more organisation and time to get everything together to do the job. A day and a morning were devoted to the project. Men spent all of one day scouting for the right size saplings, cutting and trimming them to size. It was brutal work, and the help they got from the youth of nearby villages was much appreciated. They were careful about the work on the poles, for after use they would be stored in the orau and used over and over again. Next morning, the poles were put in position.

Much earlier in the same morning, others prepared and cooked food in several umu for workers and hangers-on at the launch. Later in the morning, others harvested green drinking coconuts. Women sat on the ground in groups and deftly plaited half-roa-long baskets from coconut fronds, cut and brought to them by young men and boys. These were to hold the food and carry it to where it was needed.

Preparing food for important occasions always had a strong social aspect of its own. Although the work started soon after midnight, people doing it socialised and had fun. One would think those who would be responsible for the work during the major event next day would take time off to rest. That is not the Polynesian way. The organisers, those who would carry the canoe and many others who would play a major role in the day's launch operations, joined those butchering the pigs and dogs and those preparing the chickens and fish as well as those preparing the umu for firing. They did this, not so much to help with the work, but to socialise and gossip. It seemed no one wanted to miss anything whenever and wherever it might occur. Food and fun were the major returns for the services rendered that day.

The day of the launch broke with a bright sun. Out to seaward, some clouds hung low on the horizon and several tumurangi rose high into the sky, sitting firmly on their dark rain-spilling bottoms, but the deep blue of the sky overhead was interrupted only by a scattering of fair-weather clouds making their way in the general direction Savai'i to the west.

For all, except perhaps the carriers and organisers, it was a picnic. The launching and hauling of a big canoe was not such a frequent event that it did not attract attention. In the case of this very big canoe, it was a very special event. A large proportion of the matakeinanga had taken a part, small as it might have been, in the building of *Te Pori o Kare*.

Someone had to cut the pandanus, prepare it and make it available for the deft hands of women who made the sails. Coconuts had to be husked and the fibres prepared for old men to twist into strands on their thighs to make the sennit for rope makers to turn into cordage of all sizes needed for *Te Pori*. Young men, armed with stone axes and wedges, went into the bush to cut timber from which the planks and spars were prepared. Boys bled sap from breadfruit trees and ran it to those stitching the planks to use as caulking. Very young children, using left-over or inferior material, practised the many operations in building a canoe. Hardly anybody was left out of participation in the building of their canoe.

The crowd was gathering fast. The promise of a fine sunny day, perhaps even a scorcher, continued. Many plaited themselves hats out of coconut fronds. Others twisted ei katu out of ferns which served almost the same purpose, but were more chic. Married ladies and matrons wore the more common simple bonnet with a small brim to which flowers and leaves in every possible design were attached to produce the required shade from the sun. Many were decked out in their best white tapa clothing and viewed the event as an opportunity to add to contemporary fashion. That stylish clothes might be discarded in a moment of carefree exhilaration to join a dance or go for a swim did not concern them. Some from a village came dressed in identical uniforms to emphasise that they formed a close-knit club.

The younger women came more briefly dressed, outdoing each other in the use of flowers to adorn themselves. Their aim on this occasion was to catch the eye of a suitable young buck as a companion for later. In contrast the men wore only maro, but were not averse to bedecking themselves with a flower over the ear, an ei katu on the head and a lei around the neck. With a glaze of light sweat, their brown skin, variously blued with tattoos over rippling muscles, shone in the sun.

From early morning, the beach and lagoon were full of yelling and screaming children cavorting and chasing one another on the beach, in the water and under the shade of groves of coconut, pandanus and fau trees.

A drum band and its dancers had, on their own initiative, made an appearance to add to the festive air of the occasion. The band was playing a quiet tantalising rhythm while the dancers sat in the shade, not yet into their act. The rhythm was not wasted. Little girls and boys were taking full advantage of it and doing a creditable job of dancing, encouraged by their elders.

Each household had brought food and drink of their own. No one was going to go hungry or thirsty. As usual, a shortage of food at a picnic or any occasion was something feared with horror by Polynesians.

While preparations for the launch proceeded, the drums beat out their rhythms and the dance team of a hundred couples moved in graceful military unison. They were ably supported in the rear by very young children, for this is how they learnt.

By mid-morning the finicky finishing touches to the preparations had been completed. Nobody was in a hurry. In operations requiring the coordinated effort of a large number of people there is a pace which, if exceeded, would disrupt the natural rhythm of people adjusting their minds for the undertaking and coordination of effort required.

Polynesians understand this very well. No one tries to hurry things just for the sake of getting the job done quickly. Yet it is usually done with speed and efficiency. Neither is there unnecessary talk and instructions about how the job is to be done. These fall in place naturally with time and circumstance, but there is always the murmur of talk Polynesians find necessary when adjusting with one another in a combined physical effort of this nature. Only the loud voices of those in charge, standing apart, can penetrate it and bring the silence of order when they judge that everybody has adjusted.

A busybody, who believes that others are more stupid than he, can do more harm than just being a nuisance. If such are around, everybody ignores them. Sometimes they work themselves into positions of charge. When that happens the project is doomed. Everybody goes home or does not turn up at all. On that day, however, there did not seem to be any serious nuisances around. A good omen.

All the omens for the canoe had been good. Even the deaths of Orokeu and Oroinano were interpreted as good omens. Since they were of high rank, their deaths served as a desirable sacrifice to launch this canoe on a distinguished career. Polynesians, especially those of Samoa, did not indulge in human sacrifice as did the Fijian Melanesians on such occasions. However, if it occurred on its own account, it was rationalised as a good omen.

The steps of the operation moved forward smoothly towards the moment when everything would be completed and ready. There had been no problem in obtaining volunteers for the lifting and carrying. Everyone wanted a part of the action, as had always been the case on such occasions.

Finally the moment came. As usual the crowd sensed it and became quiet. The lifters took their positions. Women of all ages quickly formed on either side of the canoe, leaving room for the lifters. Men formed behind them. These were the chanters and were composed mainly of men and women who came to facilitate the spectacle as well as contribute to it. Several elders took up strategic positions around the canoe. They were to ensure that the chant would be performed in unison. With a walking stick, Talamasua took up a position where he could be seen by the others. The job of ensuring unison in this part of the launching operations had fallen to him. It was not pre-arranged. He saw the need and stepped in to meet it. Now that everybody was in position, the quiet deepened to silence. Only the steady beat of the rollers on the distant reef interrupted it. The high priest called the karakia for such occasions, asking the gods to be with those who sailed on *Te Pori o Kare*. Te Arutanga Nuku's chief orator spoke to thank all those who came to help at the launching and needlessly pointed out there was plenty of food and drink for all.

The lifters bent to their poles. Talamasua slowly raised his walking stick and, after a pause, brought it down in a cutting motion. The males, all except the lifters, started the chant that was now known to all:

Men:	Orokeu e Oroinano
Women:	Orokeu e Oroinano
Men:	Orokeu e Oroinano
Women:	Orokeu e Oroinano
All:	Tu Popongi te tini o Kuporu
	Matakitaki i te rakau e.

The chant was repeated over and over in strict cadence. During the first chorus, the lifters took hold of the poles. At the second, they took the strain. On the third, they lifted the canoe. With the fourth, they moved forward in strict time with the cadence of the chant.

The mesmerising repetitious chant had its effect on the carriers, chanters and spectators alike. It was stimulating and, because the great canoe moved, the chant took on a purposeful quality and meaning and drove the beat of its message into all. Now it was a great roar in perfect cadence. The women danced alongside the carriers, exhorting them by hand movements in time with the chant. All knew that strict cadence was important to the carriers. The spectators, further behind the chanters, were now in full cry, emulating them.

The canoe moved forward like some great millipede, determined and inexorable. When it reached the water's edge, carriers, chanters, spectators and the ladies in their fashionable finery took no heed. They chanted and danced into the sea until the great canoe was afloat. Reluctantly, as it were, the chant ended, and all shouted at each other in sheer joy at the success of the operation. One of her anchors was lowered and *Te Pori o Kare* floated serenely while swimmers cavorted around her like playful dolphins. Screaming and yelling children swarmed aboard, using her as a diving platform.

Te Pori was coaxed to shore with one end resting on the beach and one of her anchors holding her there. With a biped structure of poles, the tall mast was stepped and its running stays roved through the leads at each end of the hull. Shrouds and stays were positioned and made fast. The sail and its spars were laid on the lee side of the mast. The four halyards, already roved through the great horn, were fixed to the boom at one end and to the great cleat at the other.

By the evening, all the big and little things to fit a ship for sea were completed. Te Arutanga Nuku and Apainga could not contain their impatience for the sea trials planned to take place next day.

Te Pori lay anchored on the still waters of the lagoon, patiently awaiting the future that would take her to many places and involve her in many adventures. She was anchored on one of her six anchors, three for each end. Each anchor was made of basaltic rock through which a hole had been bored for fastening the anchor rope. *Te Pori* was high on her waterline, dry wooded and empty hulled.

Toward sunset, almost every day, the east wind diminished and the on-shore breeze lulled to nothing. Later the offshore breeze intermittently rattled a coconut front and whispered its way onto the lagoon. In this peaceful time of the day, Te Arutanga Nuku and Apainga noted there were others on the beach, just sitting. Like them, they could not take their eyes off the graceful canoe reflected in the still waters turning pink and yellow in the setting sun. Soon it was dark and they went home.

For Te Arutanga Nuku, it was anything but a restful night. He tossed and turned. The launching had been successful and tomorrow was the great day of putting the canoe through her paces, and his impatience for the day to dawn played its part in denying him sleep.

The canoe and its launch had stimulated him. The last sight of her sitting on the lagoon like a beautiful woman would not leave him. What she meant to him, combined with rapid passing thoughts of what he would do with her, excited him. He realised that the canoe had the same effect on him as a woman. She would not let go of his thoughts.

He got up and went out into the warm night. There was not a breath of moving air. The waning moon was in its half-moon phase of korekore akaoti, the end of the third quarter. Apropos of nothing, except perhaps to think of something else than the canoe, he pondered that this phase of the moon was not particularly good for fishing or planting, but it was to be followed by the three nights named for the god Tangaroa, which were good for fishing.

He looked towards Te Pori's sleeping quarters and suddenly felt the need for her company. He went the few steps to reach her. In the light of the moon coming through a rolled-up matting shutter, he could see her sleeping peacefully. In the warm night, she lay on her back, spread-eagled with the light tapa blanket rucked up around her hips and waist. Her softly rounded thighs and legs lay comfortably apart in the repose of sleep. Just a wisp of the black curls of her pubis peeped out from under the covering. One arm lay outstretched and the other lay across her body below her firm breasts that had not yet suckled a babe. She was a picture of tranquil and youthful beauty. He thought, 'You are as beautiful as the canoe. Perhaps only you can take my thoughts off her.'

He gently moved her outstretched arm and lay beside her. Her response was a small whimper and a sleepy snuggling in to him. He held her close. She came slowly awake and nuzzled him with her lips and nose. She could feel the hardness of him rising against her. She pressed her body against it and he could feel the wetness of her responding.

Earlier in the evening she had sensed his preoccupation with the canoe which she was beginning to see as a rival. She could see his obsession with the canoe was not too different from that of a man for a lover. This realisation brought a pang of jealousy and she mulled it over before falling asleep. But now he was hers and he had come to her for solace for whatever bothered him. She pushed harder against him. There was no need for words. Sensing her compliant response, he thought, 'You can give me what the canoe cannot,' and, moving over her, entered her with strong urgent thrusts which soon ended in a gasping pulsating climax. She was not able to follow his demanding passion, but was happy to satisfy it, for she sensed the canoe had aroused him, but only she could take care of it.

She could not sleep. She was still on a sexual high that Te Arutanga Nuku's love-making had not assuaged. His deep breathing announced he was asleep. She watched the moon through the space of the rolled-up matting. She noted its phase. By where it lay in the sky, she knew it was early in the time period after midnight, turuaipo-mamaiata. She thought about the launching and the ease with which it had taken place. She thought about the fun everybody had and the vast quantities of food they ate. She smiled when she remembered how some of her friends had walked, chanting heedlessly, into the sea with all their fashionable finery.

The moon moved beyond the space of the open shutter. 'Ka moe, must sleep,' she said to herself, but suddenly there was the image of Atonga watching the launching proceedings from afar. The remembrance of him standing there brought the episode of her part in obtaining the canoe vividly before her. She remembered the build-up of the sexual feeling between them as she pounded the poi and how, at the height of it, Atonga had come to her, removed her clothing and made love to her. She remembered her passionate response.

Now she was roused and she needed Te Arutanga Nuku to do for her what Atonga had. She looked over at her husband and thought, 'My dear husband, I will show you how I got the canoe for you.' With that she came close to him and reaching down fondled him as tenderly and skilfully as she knew how.

He came awake and grew hard in her hand. Climbing on her, he entered her. The urgency was now all hers. Realising he had been premature that first time, he resolved to give her all the pleasure he could. Then she thought of Atonga. The climax coming to her was reaching to every part of her. She cried out with the excruciating, gripping force of it. Te Arutanga Nuku joined her with an orgasm that drove deep into him, excelling the one before. As he rolled off, she said to herself, 'That is how I got the canoe for you, my husband, and I will not let her come between us.'

Until sunrise, they slept the sleep of complete mental and physical relaxation.

The fore–aft profile of the hull of *Te Pori* was symmetrical. Therefore, its centre of resistance to leeward drift was always amidships. When the canoe tacked, the whole ensemble of sail, spars, mast, sheet and steering oar went symmetrically to the other end. For she came about by the stern becoming the bow and the bow becoming the stern. Therefore, on either tack, the centre of pressure of wind on the sail was always forward of the centre of resistance of the hull to leeward drift. This relationship between pressure of the wind on the sail and resistance of the hull to leeward drift is true for all sailing craft. If it is not correct, steering will not balance. The balance needed on *Te Pori* was one by which, when the steering oar was let go, she would come up into the wind slowly, but not come about. Coming about was not desirable in a vessel designed to sail always with the same hull to windward.

Apainga was apprehensive about this relationship. It could be tuned by moving the yard and its socket more to the ends or more amidships. It could also be done by leaning the mast to a greater or lesser degree to take the sail forwards or sternwards on the tack under consideration. Invariably the setting on one tack worked on the other. With some fine trimming, on certain points of sailing, she should sail herself. By inspection, Apainga had not been able to ascertain that the relationship was correct. In his experience, builders tended to err on the side of not enough separation between the two centres. This made it hard work on the steering paddle to prevent the vessel from coming up into the wind. Tomorrow would tell the story. Otherwise, he found no reason for complaint. The canoe was properly conceived, executed and finished.

As is customary among Polynesians, everybody was up with first light in the period of mamaiata. After a breakfast of taro, left-over fish or meat and a draught of coconut juice, they would be about the business of the day. Some would be off to feed their pigs at the limits of the village. Others would be preparing for fishing in one or other of the forms in which it was practised. Still others would be heading inland with their digging sticks to plant, and at the end of the day would bring back a harvest of breadfruit, yams, coconuts and bananas slung at both ends of a pole carried over one shoulder. Some, who would have been fishing during the night, slept on.

Today it was different. There was the intrusion of the great canoe sitting on the lagoon in her pristine freshness. *Te Pori* shone and glittered in the first yellow-pink rays of the rising sun. It was the time when the offshore breeze dissipated and the onshore breeze was yet to ruffle the lagoon and chuckle its way through the trees. It was also the time of day for the chore of waking up, whispering softly to one another till the spell was broken by the brightness of the morning and a fast increasing east wind noisily rattling the foliage and moaning urgently through the thin spindle-leaved casuarina trees.

The time for starting the sea trials had been set for the end of the period called popongi and the start of the period called popongi-avatea. At this time the sun hangs midway in its journey from the horizon to its zenith, avatea. It was also the time when the wind from the east starts to freshen and create white caps and a good sailing breeze each day. It would allow *Te Pori* to sail north on a broad reach for the reef passage and out on to Te Moana Nui a Kiva.

To Te Arutanga Nuku, Apainga and the crew, the sun had slowed. It was as though the legendary Maui had once again cast his net to slow its passage. It was taunting their impatience to sail this canoe and discover its personality, qualities and faults. Te Pori, the woman, had requested to come along. She stood next to her husband on the control deck wrapped in a dog-skin cloak against the chill of the morning. She exuded an air of unconcerned interest.

On the time planned for departure, there was no sign of the expected breeze. Apainga notice the tightening of Te Arutanga Nuku's grip on the rail. He felt sorry for the young man who had yet to learn the virtue of patience. But they did not have long to wait. It came with increasing strength. It flopped the sail from one side to the other as it was being raised. The anchor rope was brought up short. Then the sail was up. When *Te Pori* swung with her smaller hull to windward, the anchor was weighted, the sheet hauled in and, with a creaking mast step, a squeaking stretch of shrouds, and the squealing and grunting of the iato cross-beams in their bindings, the lightly loaded and dry timbered *Te Pori* shot forward with unbelievable acceleration. Before they knew it, they had run out of lagoon and were shooting through the passage with foaming billows crashing on the coral reefs on either side. *Te Pori* flew into the open sea at eighteen knots by a later form of reckoning.

Apainga stationed himself on the main deck next to the helmsman. Nearby were two standby helmsmen. He had arranged this in case *Te Pori* showed signs of hard steering. In the past he had had occasion to abort sea trials because the vessel could not be prevented from running up into the wind. However, he was pleased, *Te Pori* steered well. His nagging of the builders and riggers had paid off.

Maintaining this northerly course, he ordered the sheet men to pull the sheet in a little more. *Te Pori* responded instantly with what was to become the familiar mast step grunt, the stretching screech of bindings, the rigging squeal of pleasure and the visible increase in speed.

Apainga and the helmsman used the smaller windward hull and the amount it was exposed above the water as a gauge to how much the vessel could be driven before things became critical. Later, when they became used to her, they would not need anything other than the feel of her to tell them of her sailing status. The wind was now at full trade-wind strength. Still on a reach, *Te Pori* hissed her way over the swells, cutting cleanly through the seas and short chop raised by the wind. She was enjoying herself and so was everybody aboard.

In direct contrast to a ballasted monohull, a multihull has its greatest stability when it is upright. As it heels, stability decreases in proportion to the degree of heel. Te Arutanga Nuku and Apainga decided that this was not the time to test *Te Pori* to the limit. She was as light as she would be and it was not fair to test her in this state. In such large canoes the windward hull was never flown purposely out of the water. It served no purpose and was asking for trouble, because a mere shift in body weight would have no effect. Only in serious circumstances such as a race, a chase or an escape would a large multihull be pressed to such extremes. Her long water-line gave her an advantage over smaller vessels to make such immoderate measures usually unnecessary.

Upolu was falling far astern. It was time to tack. Apainga joined Te Arutanga Nuku, Te Pori and Talamasua on the control deck. Talamasua had been included in the trials with some of his carpenters so that structural alterations could be made on the spot. They all needed a good view of the tacking procedure. The ship's company had never had such huge spars and expanse of sail to handle in tacking. Te Arutanga Nuku and Apainga glanced upwards to the great spars and sail and, looking at each other, shook their heads in disbelief at what had to be done.

It was now a full sailing breeze. All were alert and waiting for the order to tack. It came with the small word, 'Pa'e!'.

Tè Pori was brought slowly to windward, but not into the wind. The sheet was let go and the sail flapped with thunderclaps, rattling the mast and spars. The canoe shook from end to end. With the help of the wind and the men hauling and easing on the running stays, three men grabbed the yard, lifted it out of its socket and started the walk to the other end. They passed along the narrow end deck, along the main deck, to the lee of the mast and its lee shroud, over the decking of the other end and thunked it into the socket there. With this manoeuvre the sail and its spars were moved from one end of the canoe to the other. The mast which was slanting in one direction before, was now slanting in the other. The vessel now lay abeam. The steering oar was in its new place, as was the sheet. The sheet was hauled in, the sail filled and *Tè Pori* accelerated with speed in the opposite direction and on the other tack.

This first try was awkwardly done. The difficulty was in the work of the three men controlling and walking the tack assembly, which was shaking and gyrating with the flapping of the sail. Since there was no room for more than three, the watch captains worked out that if there were three lines on the end of the yard, three men on each, holding them in different directions, could assist in controlling the assembly at the tack. Next time around, this arrangement was found to be of help and became part of the tacking procedure. For the rest of the day, they practised and practised, tacking and sailing the canoe on all angles with the wind.

They put her through her paces for apparent wind sailing. This was important because any other way of sailing her downwind produced no speed at all. Straight downwind sailing produces similar results with most sailing ships. With the rig used on the alia, it produced even worse results. In most sailing vessels only the addition of spinnakers of twice the area of a mainsail and special large downwind sails can offset the lethargic nature of this point of sailing.

In an alia, the arrangement of its single sail and yard is such that, when sailing directly before the wind, the sail will not stand flat to the wind. In small sailing canoes of this rig, the sail can be made to stand better by propping the boom out with an additional spar. This is not easy on a large canoe such as *Tè Pori*. Therefore, apparent wind sailing and tacking downwind is almost a necessity, the high speed obtained by this technique being a bonus. It also avoids the necessity of spinnakers and other downwind sails to overcome this slowest point of sailing. Windsurfers and iceboats of today sail by no other means, but only sailing vessels which achieve high speeds can be sailed in this mode. Most monohulls lack the speed capability for apparent wind sailing, wherefore the necessity for spinnakers, stunsails and other downwind sails.

On all points of sailing, *Te Pori*'s performance could not be faulted. Te Arutanga Nuku and Apainga were pleased. The crew were pleased too, but they had worked hard.

In the late afternoon, those ashore watched *Te Pori* returning in a powerful, surging reach towards the passage. She was a sight to behold. Her small bow wave belied her speed, but she was moving fast, for the canoe's company were letting her have her head. With unabated speed, she shot through the passage, made short work of the distance to her anchorage, rounded up and dropped her sail. When way was lost, she was exactly over her anchorage. She let go of her anchors and lay back on them, seemingly with a grateful sigh of a job well done. It was a manoeuvre everybody appreciated. Yes, those ashore thought, Te Arutanga Nuku, Apainga and her crew were proving worthy of such a canoe.

Boats are made of wood and other dead material. Despite this the craftsmen who design and build them, without consciously knowing it, build in characteristics which make a vessel unique in behaviour. These are the men who build part of the soul that goes into a vessel and makes her a living being. It is the men who command and sail her who complete the process. If these men are good at their jobs and are in empathy with her, a boat comes to life and evokes a soul and personality of her own. *Te Pori* was no exception. Out of these early sea trials, she was already developing a recognisable character. Even those watching from shore could feel it beginning to emanate from her timbers, spars, sail and from those who sailed her.

On going ashore, Talamasua sent riggers and carpenters aboard to tighten the lashings of the iato booms which joined the two hulls. These were the places of greatest strain. After its first stretch, the quality of sennit and its freedom from changing length when wet and dry precluded the need for re-tightening lashings for some time to come.

Next day, they were out again. They practised more tacks. With each one their proficiency improved. Te Arutanga Nuku and Apainga now felt confident that, when they took the canoe to other places, they could handle the close quarters of small harbours under sail.

They practised shortening sail under adverse conditions. Although it was unlikely they would meet with severely adverse conditions, they still could practise the procedures. The first was to shorten sail for an increase in wind strength. They practised using the spiller line which is attached to the boom and roved over the great horn of the mast; hauling on it raises the boom. This effectively reduces the frontal area of sail facing the wind, but it ruins its aerodynamics for close windward work. The degrees of sail reduction by this means are infinite. They practised taking off sail and bending on a smaller sail. This reduces sail area, but maintains windward capability. With a large crew and the long boards of ocean sailing, this is not the problem it seems.

In imagined squalls, they practised dropping the sail until the squall passed. In a fake full storm, they rehearsed bare pole sailing downwind or lowering one or more anchors to act as a drogue and hold the bow into the wind and the seas for a slow downwind drift. By going through the motions they became familiar with what each procedure could do.

When shortening sail by hauling the spiller line which ran over the great horn with the halyards, it would not budge. A climb up the mast showed that it was jammed under the halyards. Apainga was vexed because the riggers should have known that, with multiple halyards, the likelihood of this happening was about ninety-nine to one. Apainga told the crew to leave it alone. Instead he ordered Talamasua to have his tufuga carpenters, who came with materials for just such an emergency, to fashion a cleat with two holes to be installed on the mast just below the horn. Through the holes two new spiller lines were passed. This took a little time and effort, but it was done and the training could go on. Later, in port, the job was done properly.

In the following days, they practised taking the sail off and bending others on. In pretended squalls, they dropped sail and set it again and again until they could do it blindfolded and quickly. They also did some more training in tacking. Although the strongest trade wind could not match the conditions of a full storm, they let the anchors down forty fathoms several times and confirmed that the procedure did a fine job of keeping the canoe headed into wind and seas. This procedure was greatly aided by leaning the bare mast downwind to act as a weathervane to keep the canoe into the wind.

With sail stowed and keeping time by chanting, they practised sculling in unison. The height of the canoe above water precluded the use of standard paddles on this class of vessel, and sculling was resorted to for propulsion. This was achieved by long oars which passed through hourglass apertures in the main deck. There were eighteen of them. The method could not make much headway against thirty knots of wind or even fifteen, but that was not their purpose. It was to move the vessel in calms, away from reefs, in and out of sheltered harbours, and just to propel them on their course when there was no wind at all.

Te Arutanga Nuku and Apainga decided that the crew needed a good rest. They were getting stale from the days of hard training. But their spirits were high because they had, they believed, tamed *Te Pori* to their will. Apainga divided the crew into three, one to be aboard to take care of the canoe while the other two were off duty. By rotating the three, everybody got a good rest. As was usual, this procedure was adopted for watches under sailing conditions. A few days later they were at it again, but with an easier pace.

Atonga, now in his forty-fifth year, envied them, but he talked himself into being satisfied that the canoe was in good hands. He was also satisfied that Te Arutanga Nuku could take care of the ali'idom on his own. He was feeling restless and wanting a change. Te Pori, his daughter-in-law, still disturbed him sexually and his want of her was often an aching throb. It would be best if he left Upolu and went to his other haunts to discover how his other families were getting along. He also pined to see his grandfather, Toi, who had settled in Tahiti and with whom he had been very close in earlier days. He thought about taking *Te Tia*, but that would disturb the nice way things were. So when a big kalia from Vava'u turned up on its way to Tahiti, preparing for the long tacks into the prevailing southeast wind, northeast to Tongareva, then south to Tumutevarovaro and northeast again to Tahiti, finally reaching the Iva islands (the Marquesas), no one was surprised when he joined her. Later they heard he stopped off in Tahiti and was living with his grandfather, Toi.

JOHNNY FRISBIE HEBENSTREIT

The Bed

Make no mistake, the bed belongs to Rere who has gone to New Zealand to become a nurse. We all know this, but she is far away and her sister, Vaerua, sleeps in it now. She proudly refers to it as 'Toku roki akaperepere'. She loves this treasured bed so dearly she actually sleeps in it.

On our island some beds are treated with reverence, as one would a delicate tiare blossom. They are largely ornamental, often unused for their normal function, the owner sleeping on a cool pandanus mat on the floor beside it.

Rere's bed, in this intimate village, is typical. Its heavy, cast-iron frame is bent and rusted. But it is lovingly covered with a tivaevae, a colourful hand-embroidered version of the ubiquitous patchwork quilt. The pillows are encased in hand-sewn, multicoloured cases, and propped neatly against the headboard for everyone to admire. Laid side by side in formal display on the bed are stiffly starched clothes, coconut-fibre hats, and an assortment of seashell leis. Other objects of less value are stored away in boxes under the bed: used razor blades and pocket knives, blunt needles and discoloured threads, rusty fishhooks from Japan and layers upon layers of chipped enamelled plates from China.

Every morning while the family sleeps, Vaerua routinely emerges from the jumbled mass of the kapok mattress, wraps a pareu around her thick waist and makes up the bed by patting and moulding the scattered cotton wool back into the centre. The mound that is formed is then evenly distributed by smacking it forcefully with a pliable coconut broom. Vaerua then covers the mattress with the beautiful hand-embroidered red, white and royal blue tivaevae, her large breasts touching the bedspread, and gently and lovingly she supports them with one plump arm.

Having arranged the tivaevae to her satisfaction, sometimes she becomes disenchanted with the position of the bed in the small square room and must ask the aid of two or more strong men of the village to shift it. As they help, the men usually take advantage of the opportunity to tease her with half playful but nevertheless hopeful remarks.

'E Vaerua, e. When will you share this fine bed with me again? I recall this to be a very receptive mattress, don't you agree?'

As she is good-natured, Vaerua will laugh, covering her dark freckled face with graceful fingers. Then, tightly securing the knot of her pareu as if to say 'Keep your hands off', she will reply. 'Te witoki i te tama nei. The only thing a cheeky fellow like you could woo is the next door witch's old hen!'

The men join in the merriment, and soon the bed is shifted to Vaerua's satisfaction.

Vaerua is not the libertine these remarks might suggest. In fact, she is really quite sober and hard-working. Not only that, she has had only one lover. Everybody in the village admits that Vaerua is a lovely girl of the most obvious femininity, and that the men cannot be blamed for their wishful teasing.

She is at work by seven o'clock every morning Monday through to Friday. She is proud to be the housemaid for two important neighbours from New Zealand, washing chinaware daily, and hanging out to dry imported garments that are not seen elsewhere on the island.

'One day I will have clothes just like the ones I washed today. I will sit in a private living-room by the seashore, counting the waves breaking over the reef, greeting the early morning sun with a song. I will own an icebox, full of everything they have, including ice. It will be a fine change from the usual village fare of tea, cabin bread and tinned beef.'

She devotes Saturdays to cleaning her room, the most important ritual being to strip the bed and carry the mattress outside to air and dry. She then cleans under the bed, and spends considerable time wondering what to do with the many treasures belong to her sister: those treasures recall many seasons past, and Vaerua must not discard them even to make way for her own things.

One Saturday afternoon, while the village men are away at sea fishing, women gather around the burning umu in the weekly ritual of preparing the Sunday banquet. A chattering of many voices emerges from the smoke, sounding like the evening cacophony of the mynah birds in the mighty purau tree.

'That bed is not well cared for these days,' says one in a malicious tone. 'You ought to see it. There are days when it is left unmade.'

'Yes, you are right. Rere saved long and hard to buy her bed,' crows another smoke-filtered voice. 'Sometimes, I see dirty clothes on it, for no reasons at all except that Vaerua is insensitive. I'll have to write Rere, and tell her how the bed is being mistreated.'

A pause, and then another whispering voice, sly and confiding. 'She embraces the young man from the upper village in that bed, I swear. I hear giggles that are not the result of dreams. Lucky wench!'

'Yes, I too, admit that I am envious,' retorted another.

As such gossips are common around the umu, little importance is given to them.

Soon after this therapeutic exercise, the radio warns of an enormous hurricane approaching. The European community scurry to secure the roofs of their square houses with heavy ropes, and to fill numerous containers with water against the rains that would fill all plumbing with discoloured water mingled with gravel, remnants of roots, and earthworms. The villagers, however, leave their thatched-roof houses unprotected, for they would be easy enough to rebuild. Instead, they climb the swaying coconut trees, trimming off superfluous fronds so the trees might offer less resistance to the wind and survive. This done, they strip the village cookhouses of any boards suitable for surfing and watch eagerly the darkening sky over the rising, fervent sea.

When the barometer drops, tempers have a way of flaring up. In particular, the temperamental matriarch of the household next door is suspicious of the activities of one of her many boarders, a girl of twenty, who is Vaerua's third cousin. These suspicions involve her own husband, and the matriarch, prompted by the brewing hurricane, decides that her health is suffering from sleeplessness caused by the constant vigil necessary to keep a nightly watch. She would solve the problem by ejecting the girl!

There is a sudden eruption of thundering verbal abuse, and the animated villagers quickly gather in the village square to be entertained.

The angry matriarch is storming, bellowing to be heard in the gusty competing winds.

'You are a tramp. You can't keep your dirty hands off other women's men. Leave my husband alone or I'll pluck out your hair. A naked hen you'll end up to be.'

The inspired third cousin spits in rebuttal, ejecting the saliva towards the trembling red-faced matriarch, then turns and strides slowly and confidently across the open square, dragging behind a bundle of bedclothes.

'Puaka matu, like Iro's fat pig!' she shouts for all to hear, simultaneously thrusting out her right hip. 'You say I slept with your equally fat husband, but you have never caught us together, not yet.' She thrusts outward her favourite hip again, while pulling up her skirt, exposing a bare brown bottom. Then, feeling that she had put enough distance between herself and her antagonist, she throws the bundle of bedclothes dramatically to the ground and makes as if to sleep there; waiting, as well, for someone to offer her lodging and protection from the impending hurricane.

Vaerua, who has seen it all, takes pity on her relation for she herself had once been thrown out of the matriarch's house, but by the husband, who felt he had not been shown the proper attention. Although she does not have a house of her own, she could offer to share her bed, and this suggestion the cunning cousin quickly accepts.

As often seems to happen after a warning, the hurricane does not come after all. But Vaerua's third cousin stays on, and soon the tone of the women's voices around the umu takes on a new bitterness.

'That wretched night owl — sleeping on Rere's bed! That vampire. E tamaine ori aere ua. She has enough fire between her legs to scorch every man on earth.'

'She ought to sleep on the floor. I should throw her there myself. I shall certainly write Rere.'

So, when the monthly *Taveuni* weighs anchor for Auckland, in addition to its cargo of canned orange juice, green bananas and copra, it carries the fat woman's letter describing in detail the village drama of the past week.

The reply comes the following month, addressed not to the fat woman, but to Vaerua.

'Dear Sister,' Rere writes, 'news has come from a notable gossip (the name I shall withhold since you know who she is, anyway) that you have committed an unforgivable sin by allowing a certain siren to sleep in my bed. (Our mother would certainly turn in her grave.) I am so angry at you I can't seem to find the right words to continue with this sad letter. Therefore, dear younger sister, bend to me now so we may kiss in conclusion.'

'I have been wrong in allowing you to sleep in her bed,' Vaerua confesses in the midst of continuous sobbing. 'I will ask my lady boss to find you a bed of your own. You must agree to sleep on the floor from now on. I have wronged my sister.'

It is not long before the third cousin is informed that she will soon possess a bed of her own. She immediately begins describing the bed she envisages: a luxurious four-poster, a double bed, decorated at the top with frilly white lace. In short, one like Rere's. She is relieved to know that she will no longer have to sit out in the dark, or turn her back, when Vaerua welcomes her lover from the nearby village.

Alas, there is absolutely no room left in the house for another mammoth bed, nor is there enough money in the collection for such a bed. The third cousin does not seem worried by this lack of money and proudly hands over the remaining balance the very next day. The total is now enough to purchase a plain but sturdy army bunk which the third cousin immediately places next to the window facing the house of the matriarch. There is some speculation as to where the money comes from, and indeed, the matriarch creates another vitriol when she discovers her monthly bread money is gone. However, as everyone happily agrees, the third cousin now has a bed of her own and Vaerua will no longer be criticised by the village gossips.

And while the third cousin is experiencing new joy, Vaerua consoles her troubled heart in silence, for her lover has been frightened off by the unusual attention recently paid to the bed, and some nights have passed during which he failed to appear. Her fears have grown that she has lost her chance to marry. She even takes to sleeping on the floor as an act of punishment, while the bed stands alone, unruffled, in its royal grandeur.

Naturally, this distressing digression cannot exist for long. Vaerua's lover returns some nights later, on a specially selected evening, when the moon lends little light. First, he must enter the sleeping house without noise, and to accomplish this feat he must further prove his prowess by leaping stealthily like a goat over the pebble path to the doorway. He succeeds, landing with a light and gentle thud on the concrete floor. Several of the discerning insomniacs are relieved that the lovers have united and they lie in anticipatory silence for their rewards, which come immediately. There are whispering exchanges of an affectionate nature, followed by the lusty sounds of smacking lips, in Rere's bed.

These nightly trysts have continued, and everyone knows about them now. But, as these particularly unique villagers are seldom anxious to disrupt the excitement created by a successful secret love affair, and since it is a foregone conclusion that the lovers are going to marry as soon as the unborn baby makes itself known, no one wishes to inform Rere. Even the matriarch is silent, for her favourite hen now nests on the bed by day, and this gives Vaerua some power over her, until the day the chicks are hatched.

Jon Jonassen

Saved

God save the Queen
At last the British have come
To claim a dot on the map
Months after the Jack
Was flown by Ariki Nui Makea
High chief of a district
Through urgings from a British
In fear of the French

Praise them Kiwi men
For taking from the British
Full responsibility
For all of Rarotonga
And all her little satellites
To lump them all together
And call them Cook Islands

Sorry for the locals
Who never had a say
In all this hanky panky
They probably never knew
That they were really merely
A card on the table
Useful when needed
And ready for the deal

KAURAKA KAURAKA

Sixteen Bags

Sixteen bags
of passion flowers you collected for me
The aroma sweet purple
colour fresh and alive
Each blossom unique on my tongue
Perfect for my cup of tea

Hot water from the earth
releases your healing steams
of catnip music and chamomile lullaby
of peppermint spears and lavender shields
I am nurtured by your hands of rosemary fern

Great green taunga of Manoa
I taste your dew-kissed lips
keeping leaves moist in the rising sun
You cool my boiling mind
Your taste needs no artificial sweetening

When the sun is high you open your arms
to demand the passionate vines be green
When the sun is low your legs you spread
to receive the shadows of the day
into sixteen valleys of the night

Taunga of the Great Moko

Oh Taunga of the Great Moko
Immense calabash of mana
Your sacred ground guarded
by long-tusked boars
from profane fingers of man
Oh Daughter of the Sun who directs light

into the cave where black spiders live
Oh lover of the rainbow who obeys
the commands of water and fire
Oh proud rider upon the back
of the great white shark
The blind chanter to entertain
Tangaroa at his deep-sea banquet in Kauai
The four winds carry news
of your korero like lightning

Today our canoe landed
and your great white herons
led us from the beach
through the spider-webbed cave to your marae
at the foot of Anahola hills
but we dare not step upon
your sacred ground without invitation
lest we disturb the wild moko
Oh Taunga of great powers from Havaiki Nui
according to foreign nostrils
you stink of decaying corpses
but from where we stand
the smell of your sweet maire and ava
increases with time spent
waiting upon you

Darkness within the Light

Show off with your New Zealand degree!
Think you're smart?
Let's compete climbing for coconuts!
Can you husk my number of nuts?
Can you dive and fill the sack with pearl-shells?
Think you're smart?
Count, see who's got the most?
You really think I'm dumb?
You're not aware of the darkness within your light.

How I pity you!
Foreign knowledge has blinded your heart.
When I welcomed you with a greeting kiss

you offered your cheek to someone else.
When I slapped your thigh to say Hello
you thought I was seducing you.
I spoke to you in Maori but you replied in English.
You wouldn't lend a hand unless I paid cash
I despair, my friend, you leave me desolate!

VAINE RASMUSSEN

A Book and a Pen

When I was young
They gave me a book and a pen,
A set-rule and a calculator to play with,
Test tubes and bunsen burners
To experiment with,
And then a piece of paper
That said
'Academically qualified to matriculate at any University'.

When I was at University
They gave me another book and pen,
Marx's theories and Solzhenitsyn's literature
To debate, discuss and agree over,
Political thought and administrative procedures
To digest,
Then another piece of paper
Called a BA.

When I came back
They gave me a job.
I used books and pens,
Letterheads and folders
To fill up with trash.
A paypacket to cash
At Tamure or Tumunu.

When I grew old
They gave me a pe'e
A legend, a song
And a language to master.
A dying culture I had lost
In my search.
And I grew up at last
Realising I had missed a lot.

FLORENCE SYME-BUCHANAN

Boat Girl

She impatiently looks forward to the monthly visits by the regular ship. She will walk down to the wharf and watch men and machines busily strain underneath the Pacific sun unloading goodies for her island.

But the watching is not for long, she has a different purpose. The sailors, bored with weeks of oceans, gaze at her with unveiled interest from the decks of their ship and blatantly express their desire. They are not gentlemen, but hard men deprived of female companionship for too long. This does not worry her, for she has no pretensions at being anything other than a boat girl who is there to sate the sailors with longed-for sex. Boats mean business for this island girl and her clientele's harsh crudeness is accepted without complaint.

In her gay floral dress she will sneak past bored Port Authorities in their drycleaned uniforms and try to beat her girlfriends on board.

A few moments on board are spent choosing a customer (or vice versa) and settling the cost of pleasuring him. She will be lucky if her client can offer a drink. One drink can lead to many and a drunken sailor is easier to manipulate, or cheat.

Rima turned seventeen on board a ship last week. She cannot remember whether it was the *Fetu Moana* or the *Tiare Moana*, only that two days were spent in drinking and sweaty sex in the mephitic atmosphere of the cramped cabins. Everybody had wanted a try of the birthday girl, who eventually stumbled off the vessel two hundred and fifty dollars richer.

On this particular morning Rima opened her sleepy eyes and recognised the familiar surroundings of her shabby room. There is no ship in today.

Tired eyes focus on the digital watch strapped to her thin wrist. The watch, a present from a now obscure lover and an object of envy amongst the other girls, told her it was 2.47 p.m.

She unsuccessfully tried to recall the previous night's events before kicking off a thigh her partner had carelessly flung over her after a night of heated sex. She rolled off the lumpy, sweat-dampened mattress and wrapped a faded pareu around herself.

Not bothering to glance at sleeping Ioane, Rima crept out of the old house and ran to the rickety shower-house made of corrugated iron. Her mother, Vera, had attempted to conceal the rusted roofing by planting kopi around the outside. Despite Rima's hangover she noticed the kopi flowers smelt particularly lovely this morning.

The cold shower washed away her hangover, fatigue and traces of the night's primitive crudities. Rima reminded herself to buy another bottle of shampoo on Monday and for the time being resorted to using Lux instead. Gathering her pareu around her lean wet body, she remembered her nosy neighbours and dashed into her clothes-strewn bedroom.

She flicked her wet hair over Ioane's sleep-creased face.

'Oi, get up'.

The sleeping figure mumbled an unintelligible oath and came to life. 'You'd better get up and put your clothes on — and you might as well go home.'

Rima made it sound more a command than advice.

Ioane reluctantly raised himself, unable to conceal the typical morning self-consciousness at his naked body.

After the youth left, Rima tidied the room, which she usually shared with two younger sisters, and counted her last boat takings after folding away the last of her clothes. A hundred and ninety-five dollars left; the Banana Court had been the recipient of sixty-five dollars last night and God knows who else she had bought drinks for apart from Ioane and herself. And Vera would be asking for money to buy food for the family, and her sisters needed new uniforms. She'd be lucky if thirty dollars would be left over after her family had their handouts.

Lighting her first cigarette of the day, Rima quietly comforts herself that another boat is arriving tomorrow.

It is during the few solitary moments like this, Rima often wonders about love and remembers how she became a boat girl.

Her first visit to one of the ships was to accompany a friend, a hardened, older boat girl, to meet a prospective customer. The boat seemed enormous and exciting, and fascinated the naive fifteen-year-old virgin. Rima did not know exactly what prostitution was, or what the word meant. She only had a vague idea why her friend Tutai was on board the ship. Tutai introduced her to some sailors who welcomed the young girl so profusely she found it overwhelming. Nobody had ever made her feel so wanted.

In the stale, stuffy cabin, Tutai explained to the younger girl about being a boat girl.

'Plenty money,' Tutai told her confidently. 'You can make over a hundred dollars in one night and all you have to do is open sesame'. To Rima this sounded simple enough. The money temptation was hard for the young girl to resist, and her family's poverty was quite well known in Tupapa.

Anyway, her virginity would be lost sooner or later, and in the process of losing her virginity she might as well earn some money, Tutai reasoned.

Rima's first customer was one of the officers whose seniority gave him privileges which were not confined by ship rules. He was a big, hairy, rough man who crushed the young girl to the narrow bunk, making it difficult for her to breathe, and when she was able to gasp for air, it sickened her stomach to inhale the papa'a stale breath.

Three hours later, Rima left the ship, no longer a virgin, a hundred dollars clutched in a nervous small hand and unsteady on her feet after her first taste of rum and Coke.

From that day ships became a means of quick finance and an easy exit from the boredom of school. Her parents eventually gave up trying to stop Rima, and only acknowledged her presence when money was needed in the family or chores had to be done when her sisters were not home. Rima didn't mind, it left her bereft of parental nagging and she could do what she pleased.

Except fall in love and be loved.

It would be nice to fall in love, whatever love may be, Rima constantly assured herself. Often the young girl would ask herself whether love was the safety of marriage and children or the seemingly never-ending nights of fulfilling desire . . . merely as a vessel accommodating sailors with sex. Rima yearned to exchange the short soulless business ventures for permanent love. But the money she earned from 'business' she could not afford to sacrifice.

But local men don't fall in love with boat girls, she sadly reminded herself. Her occupation was common knowledge, and marked her like an ugly tattoo as far as the local males were concerned. She provided for only the few who were hard-up for loose sex, and then there were never any dates or rendezvous afterwards.

Rima always assured herself that one of these days a handsome local fellow (preferably one who had come back from New Zealand) would fall in love with her (or her love-making) and marry her. She would be such a good wife.

But the other boat girls, especially the older lot, laughed at Rima's thoughts.

'No guy will want to marry you, you're just a taramea,' they would say.

Rima gave up sharing this dream with her friends, but kept on hoping.

Epilogue

It is six years later and Rima is twenty-three; most people think she is older; the haggardness of her face tells of struggle, disappointment and approaching alcoholism. The constant bouts of VD have also left their wrinkles on the once smooth, attractive face. Her figure is still slim, but her belly protrudes even though Rima is not pregnant. She doesn't make as much money from the boats; the regular sailors are tired of her and seek the younger girls.

You will see Rima at the Banana Court hanging onto a post because she can't stand upright. As usual she has had too much to drink after spending her last boat takings.

A good boat night means thirty dollars these days, all of which is spent on drink, and Rima still prefers rum and Coke.

Most of the BC males know Rima by sight and try to avoid her. Unwary tourists passing her by will be shoved an empty glass with the plea that it be refilled, and if they stay long enough, will hear Rima speak with sadness in her large unfocusing eyes about her one hope, to fall in love with the right man.

'I'll make such a good wife,' she'll tell.

MAKIUTI TONGIA

Return the Noonday Star

Fifty thousand years ago
I ran those mountains for kaikai
plucked feathers to decorate my dance
I tilled the yam gardens
with brother cousins
and felt the karem leg
search love.
I lived dreamtime worlds
with bush fires talking to the spirits
and voyaged distant mountains
touching the sky.
Fifty thousand years ago
I was here.

But I was not happy long
Youth dictated I search the world
In my canoe I sailed my journey
to islands of legends
I was crazy drunk with
the novelty of travel
But youth is youth
My penis was then strong
In the legend lands
I danced the karem leg
planted my seed in kumara plots.
Women and Melanesian hair
and Micronesian eyes babied my child
later I hungered for
Searching home
I called her name
But elders reminded my
time was past to catch
home islands in the dew.

(They float at dawn to
new grounds fostering
their roots)
But I return still
in the noonday star
and search

Fifty thousand years today
I touch the karem leg
My head is crazy
My youth dead.
Strange cousin brothers
stare in my face
They no laikim mi
in my prodigal skin
I touch their skin
sweat in the betel spit
paint lime to my lips
in red teeth
But all afraid me
They no laikim mi.

Fifty thousand years ago I was here.
Your fathers were my brothers
your mothers my sisters
Time furthered the path
we travelled
And a big ugly star
mark my face as a
foreigner to your eyes
But I no care stories
you tell to immigration officers
I no care the legends
you'll twist and turn
me truly to a beast of
the sea.
I only care to return
the noonday star to Eberia.

To God

The tamanu timbers fell victim
to the fire's fury, as the temple
    burned like a scout's bonfire.
While the Christian fire burned down
the last temple of the pagan gods
he shouted:
    'From ash to ash,
    God, deliver this evil
    away from your land!'
Then he cast his mana over
my ancestors and they knelt and
worshipped him.

Storyteller

Hungry faces sit in a half moon,
listening to the storyteller
journeying the evening,
mixing laughter with fear.
Then the half moon gets smaller
and smaller,
until all the bodies touch, nesting
a pool of fear in childhood minds.
The storyteller exhausted
sleeps alone with a smile.

Mona Matepi Webb

Grandmother and the Mat

She sat cross-legged on the bare concrete floor, her slight frame bent over the pandanus mat she had been weaving for the past hour. Her aged fingers moved with practised ease along the fresh row of criss-crossing pandanus strips, the right thumb pressing the pandanus down as the index finger of the left hand swept up a handful of pandanus strips with lightning speed.

The room was sparsely furnished: a little table stood in one corner. On top of it was a well-worn Bible. The binding had come off at one stage; it was now held in place with row upon row of sellotape. Beside the table was a single bed. The kapok mattress that had once been on it was now replaced by a new spring mattress. A mat similar to the one the old woman was making covered the floor on that side of the room.

In the still of the afternoon, only the rhythmic clip-clipping of the pandanus strips could be heard in the old house. While her fingers weaved intricate designs on the border of the mat, the woman's mind wandered as she reminisced of her youth gone past.

The only daughter of a family of six, she was the favourite of both parents. She was also the envy of the girls in the tapere for she never had to tramp inland to weed in the taro patches. Not once did she have to wade knee-deep in mud to get mamio for the family meal. She was one of the lucky ones. The loving yet strict upbringing by her parents prevented her from partaking in the village gatherings of the mapu. Her beauty attracted many suitors, but all were to no avail. Only the best would be considered for the hand of Tetonga's daughter in marriage.

Pre-marriage courting was frowned upon in those days. If a man desired a woman, it was the correct procedure to approach the parents concerned for permission to marry. The old woman smiled whimsically, as she recalled the first day her late husband had approached her parents' house. He brought with him an a'ai, which, he explained to her parents, was a gift for their daughter, Makitae.

During the days that followed, he paid regular visits to her parents' house, always with some kind of offering in the form of food such as pork or chicken cooked and still hot from the umu, a kit of mamio and an a'ai, for he was a reputed fisherman. The old woman shifted slightly to ease the cramp in her legs. She sighed and muttered, 'Yes, he was a great fisherman', and with that her thoughts lapsed again into the past.

It was about a month after he had first brought the fish for her that her mother had allowed her to speak with her benefactor. But only for a short while. Out of all the mapu in the village, he was the only one that had awakened her interest, and the following day her mother told her of the forthcoming marriage to him. There would be a lot of work involved and much feasting. She remembered her mother's words before the wedding.

'E ine, we have watched over and protected you for twenty-five years. You have been a good daughter, but now it is time for you to leave us. Tomorrow you will have a new parent. He is a good man, he is strong, he is clever. A lot of the village girls would give their right hand to be in your position, for you are a lucky girl. You must not disgrace us, you must be a good wife for him: cook his meals and keep him clean, for that is the duty of the wife.'

Then the obedient answer — 'Ae, e Ma.'

She remembered being carried on the pa'ata from the church to her new home, her husband's home. A fleeting smile stole across her lips as she recalled the speech her father gave at the wedding feast that followed. He had addressed her husband — 'E unounga, akonoia tau tamaine, are i topa-purumu!' The old woman chuckled at the memory. Her wizened eyes cast a saddened look around the room. Within these walls were imprisoned the memories of her youth and a happy marriage.

'Now I am on my own, Nga is gone.' She did not realise that she had spoken out loud.

'E Ma! E Ma!' The voice of her youngest grandchild floated into the room. He was calling to her from outside. The old woman chuckled again.

'Tera tamaiti, e Pa, do you remember our son at that age? Aue, teia mai!'

The grandson toddler leapt into her arms, tangling himself in the strips of pandanus on the unfinished mat.

'Why do you sit in here making those stupid mats, Grandmother?' he demanded in his childish voice. 'My mummy bought a new mat today, it's made of plastic and it's easy to clean! Come and see it, Grandma!' He tugged at the old woman's arm. But she shook her grey head at him, smiling in her gentle way.

'No, my child, I have seen the new plastic mat; but this,' she held up a roll of the dried and flattened pandanus leaves, 'toou arikiriki teia, the pandanus is your mat, the plastic one is imported. Now, you look at this mat,' she patted the one she'd just been weaving. 'Your grandfather was born on a mat like this one, and his father before him. Even your father was born on a mat like this. It is one thing you can hold and say it is truly yours. But the plastic? No, that is the papa'a mat. Not yours, not the Maoris'.' She fingered the stripped pandanus leaves lovingly. 'This has been here since the beginning of time and here it will remain and be known.' Then she looked into the puzzled eyes of her mokopuna and dropped a light kiss on his forehead. 'Run outside and play, child. Someday I will tell you the meaning of the mat.'

As the grandson ran off, the woman returned to her reminiscings, her old gnarled fingers once again busy, weaving.

FIJI

PREM BANFAL

I Remember, I Remember

The memory of my mother was sacred. I gathered it to my heart each night as I lay down to sleep beside my sister on the old mattress placed on the floor and covered with a worn-out sheet. I though of her as I lay on the mattress and stared at the pale-blue walls.

My earliest recollection of my mother was when, one day when I was a child, she had taken me into the shower with her. I distinctly recall the shock of the water as she held me under the shower; I remember how I struggled and gasped for breath, frantic with fear — then the feel of her warm, soft body and the fear was gone. I clung to her.

My thoughts dwelt on her often — as I washed the never-ending line of plates and pyaalaa and pots black with soot which had to be scrubbed clean with coconut fibre, soap and ash from the fire outside; as I walked home from school with my sister and as I struggled with my homework at the end of a long and tiring day. In the morning there wasn't much time to think about anything — I just rushed through everything in order to get my sister and myself ready and to get to school on time.

One afternoon as I was folding the clothes I had taken off the line, I worked out the circumstances which might have led her into taking me into the bathroom with her. My paternal grandparents who lived with us must have gone to work on the piece of land behind our house. My father must have been at work. There was no one at home she could have left me with so she must have closed all the windows and doors and taken me into the bathroom with her.

I finished folding the clothes and after I had sorted them out I sat on the box and looked at the sky. As the clouds scudded past I imagined her sitting on a cloud and sailing through the sky. As the breeze blew through the trees I imagined the leaves sighing with sadness as they whispered her name.

There were also other memories which in later years dominated my thoughts, but they were no longer sacred.

After the death of my mother my father married again. I had been very close to my father as a child, but after my father married again my stepmother made sure that he devoted all his time to my half-sisters and half-brothers. My half-sisters and half-brothers did not have any feelings of resentment towards my sister and me, but my stepmother made a point of fostering feelings of jealousy and resentment.

In the afternoons after school my sister minded my half-sisters and half-brothers while my stepmother did the cooking and I helped her. Sometimes they would cry for no reason. My stepmother would be charging over, flourishing a plate or rolling pin or whatever came to hand shouting, 'What is she doing to you? She's pinching you. She's hitting you. If you can't look after my children leave them alone.' I can distinctly recall the expression on my sister's face. She was only seven years old, and the idea of being cruel to a small child would never have occurred to her because she was by nature kind and gentle.

I finished my primary schooling at the age of twelve, and I was admitted into the third form at Dudley High School. I recall my first day at my new school. I wore socks and shoes instead of sandals which everybody else wore. The shoes were black lace-ups. They were a bit small for me and pinched my toes, but I kept wearing them because I felt that they enhanced my status at my new school.

Somewhere along the line I had acquired the habit of chewing my tongue as I concentrated on something. I must have been chewing my tongue because the principal, who was teaching us during the period, thought I was chewing gum and she told me to leave the room. There was a bench on the verandah outside the classroom. I sat on the bench for a while, then I stood on the bench and peeped inside. The principal saw me and she was very angry. It was a bad start to my first day at my new school.

I remember my first day at school when I started primary school. My grandmother had taken me to school with her that day. I wore my new school uniform and new sandals and I carried the school bag my father had bought for me. I was teased by everyone in my class because my school bag was the sort that boys used. I went home and told my parents about it, but they insisted that there was nothing wrong with it and that I should continue taking it to school with me. My parents finally gave in when I refused to go to school unless they bought me a more suitable bag.

That first day I clung to my grandmother's skirt and refused to let go. After the formalities in the head-teacher's office my grandmother took me to the classroom. Whenever Grandma tried to say goodbye to me I clung to her laahgaa and wouldn't let go.

My teacher asked my grandmother to stay with me for a while. When I saw the other children, some of whom were crying, I felt much better. I started making friends, and I did not notice when my grandmother slipped away.

My sister and I loved to be with my grandmother. It was more fun to be with her than with my mother who was so strict about everything. If you coughed without putting your hand over your mouth or if you ate with your mouth open Grandma did not say anything, whereas Mother was very quick to correct you.

I shall never forget how she punished me one day for being greedy. She usually gave my sister and me a bowl of Ovaltine every night before we went to bed. One night I wanted my sister's bowl of Ovaltine because it seemed to me there was more in her bowl than in mine. She gave it to me, and after I had finished drinking that she put the other bowl in front of me and said, 'Now drink this.' I could not drink all of it, but she insisted that I finish it. I did my best but ended up being sick.

My grandmother and grandfather grew rice for home consumption. The rice was broadcast in the dry field at the back of our house, then transplanted to the wet field further down the road.

I remember my grandmother milling the rice in the home-made mill and winnowing it. After the paddy had been brought in from the field, it was put out in the sun to dry on a big paal which was made up of jute bags called basthaa, opened up at the seams and joined together. For winnowing, a plaited bamboo soop was used. Grandma would check the direction of the wind and after filling the soop with the rice which was in the process of being milled, she would lift up the soop to slightly above shoulder level and shake it gently, letting the rice fall on to the paal. As she did this the chaff blew away in the wind.

For milling, a home-made mill was used. The mill was made up of a long piece of thick, heavy log painted black. At one end a much smaller piece of wood was nailed on at right angles to the main log. This contraption was called a dhekii. It was fixed into the ground in such a way that when pressure was applied at the free end, the other end moved. The end with the piece of wood attached rested in a shallow hole in the ground. This hole had gentle slopes and was plastered over with mixture of cow-dung and earth. The paddy for milling was placed in this shallow hole.

The other end of the dhekii rested in a hole in the ground deeper than the other one. On either side of this hole there were two uprights for the operator to hold onto. The operator applied pressure at this end of the dhekii, and the other end, with the piece of wood at right angles, went up into the air. As it fell back into place the end with the piece of wood at right angles came down onto the heap of paddy, placed in the shallow hole in front of it.

Grandma usually sat near the hole with the paddy in it and shifted the paddy gently from side to side with her hand so that the rice was milled evenly. Grandma had perfect timing, for every time the dhekii came down she would take her hand away.

My sister and I would sit beside her while she was milling the paddy. Sometimes we would try to imitate her, but she was very quick and would put out her hand and stop us before we could lay our hands on the paddy.

When my father married again, together with a new mother we acquired a new grandmother and many aunts and uncles. Two of these aunts were almost the same age as my sister and I. We used to have a lot of fun together.

I remember the school holidays when we built the little hut we used to play in. School was over for that year and there was a lot of time to play and have fun.

One day as I was sitting on the steps not very far away from the 'tunnel' I had a great idea. I ran up the steps to look for Muni, one of my newly acquired aunts, and my sister, Geeta. I found them raking up the leaves under the mango tree. I told them about my idea. They started raking up the leaves as fast as they could so that they could finish the work quickly.

I went inside the house to get the key for the 'under the house'. This was an area which was enclosed by the four walls of the house and which had outcrops of soapstone and soil all over it. The outcrops were uneven; in some places they touched the floor of the house, in others they didn't. The area was used for storing things, like uncles' and aunts' wedding presents, gardening tools and the like.

Soon Muni and Geeta joined me, and we walked over towards the jungle which was on the other side of the gully. It hadn't rained for a while and the water in the gully was low. We stepped from stone to stone, occasionally slipping on the slippery ones, and very soon we reached the jungle.

We chose four strong branches from the bau trees growing there. We made sure each branch had a fork at one end, and we set to work to cut down those branches. We had only one knife, so we took turns in hacking at the branches. Every time we felt we had cut deep enough into a branch we would run away from it in case it fell on us. When the branches did not fall we ran back laughing, and hacked at the branch once again. Finally, we managed to cut down the four branches we needed. We also stripped lengths of bark from the bau trees. We dragged everything to the empty space near the 'tunnel' and sat down to rest.

What we needed now was a spade to dig holes for the four posts of our house. Nobody wanted to go to the 'under the house' to get the spade. I decided either Muni or Geeta should go. I picked up a leaf from a nearby tree and put it in my right hand. I put both my hands behind my back and asked them to guess which hand the leaf was in. Muni guessed right, but I pretended that she was wrong and let her go and get the spade.

Muni brought the spade over and we dug up four holes in the ground. We used a piece of string to make sure that the holes were at equal distance from each other. We planted the four forked branches into the holes. Now we had the four posts of our hut.

What we needed now were some branches for the roof and dry coconut leaves for the thatching. We made another trip into the jungle to get the branches and the dry coconut leaves.

When we got back from the jungle we placed four branches on the forked ends of each of the four posts and made them secure with strips of bark from the bau tree. We also placed branches at intervals on top of these branches. We cut up the dry coconut leaves into suitable lengths to place over the top as thatching. Our hut was now ready. We put some jute bags on the ground, and we used a sheet of corrugated iron to give shade on the side where the sun was coming in. We sat down to enjoy the coolness of the hut.

Soon one of the aunts called out from the house that it was time for lunch. We had rice and dhal and mango achaar for lunch. We ate our lunch in our hut and played Ludo and Snakes and Ladders for the rest of the afternoon.

Every Christmas holidays we helped Grandma to make a steamed Christmas pudding. We would buy stale bread from the shop, and after breakfast we would rub the bread into crumbs. We would spend the morning doing that while Grandma would go to town to buy other things like mixed peel, sultanas and raisins, etc. to put into the pudding.

We also made a fire outside to heat a kerosene drum full of water. Grandma would come back from town about lunch time. She would change into her home clothes and she would sit on the floor in the middle of the kitchen and give orders: 'Pass me that big aluminium basin' and 'Now add the butter and rub it in.' We would run up and down while we obeyed her orders.

Finally, the pudding would be mixed, put into a cloth, tied up firmly and placed into the kerosene drum full of boiling water on the fire. We would then sit down to lick the basin in which the pudding had been mixed.

The pudding would have to be boiled for eight hours because of the eight cups of flour which had gone into it. We would find packing cases and sit on them and sing Christmas carols while we kept the fire going.

I finished fifth form at Dudley High School and went to Suva Grammar School to study for the New Zealand University Entrance Examination. Most secondary schools in Fiji did not have sixth forms at that time and so Suva Grammar School started a multi-racial sixth form. Only the sixth form was multi-racial, the rest of the school was for Europeans or children who had some European blood in them.

A new phase of my life started at Suva Grammar School. Dudley High School was a school for Indian girls run by the Methodist Mission, whereas Suva Grammar School was co-educational. I had never had much contact with boys, and I had no idea how to talk with them or how to conduct myself in front of them. I used to wonder about things like whether it would embarrass a boy if a girl talked to him about shaving his beard just as a girl would feel embarrassed if a boy talked to her about shaving her armpits. That year was spent learning about boys, and as a result I failed University Entrance and had to repeat the following year. I stayed on for another year at the school in order to apply for a scholarship to study at a university in New Zealand.

After the scholarship results came out, one of the Education Officers from the Education Department came to brief us on university life in New Zealand. I remember asking him how we should dress up at university. He had shouted at me, 'Dress up! You are not going there to dress up.' I was very embarrassed by his reaction. After spending a few months in New Zealand I learnt the difference between 'to dress up' and 'to dress'. During most of my school career the emphasis in the learning of English had been placed on reading and writing and I had had very little practice in using the language orally and in conversation. I can remember another instance when I had made a similar mistake. We were having lunch and a European girl was sitting beside me. She had bought a tomato with her and she squeezed it to get at the juice. The juice squirted onto me and I said to her, 'Did you pinch your tomato?' She said hotly, 'I didn't pinch it. My mother bought it from the market.'

My three years at Suva Grammar School led me to a new awareness of myself, a further estrangement from my father and a growing alienation from my own community. I remember how I tried to show my growing feelings of independence and the desire to assert myself as an individual in my own right. I got a dress made with slits on both sides and I shaved all the hair on my legs. The day after I left school I wore the dress and painted my lips with bright red lipstick.

Soon after, I started to make preparations to go to New Zealand. I went through all the red tape and got everything ready.

I distinctly recall the feeling of panic and anguish inside me as I walked up to the aeroplane which was bound for New Zealand. All of us Fijian students travelled on the same plane, and we consoled each other as we left the soil of our homeland for the first time in our lives. As I left Fiji, I also left my childhood behind to start a new phase of my life in a strange country, among strange people.

VILSONI HERENIKO

The Unfinished Fence

Work for Jimi began at eight o'clock and ended at five, Mondays to Fridays. His alarm clock wakes him up at seven-fifteen, he has a quick shower, a quick cup of coffee and toast, and he leaves the house at seven-forty-five, just in time to get to Mrs Davidson's house at eight.

Usually Jimi walked to Mrs Davidson's house. He only had to pass the telephone booth and the post office before he was in sight of the old lady's house. Jimi preferred walking as he did not feel comfortable on the crowded bus among strange and indifferent people. And, anyway, it wasn't a long walk. Also, since the post office was on his way, he could post letters to his wife and family as he passed it.

The old lady was kind to Jimi. Sometimes she called Jimi inside the house and they had afternoon tea. She found a sympathetic ear in Jimi and they often talked for hours — about her husband who died in the Navy, about her children who preferred to live miles away, and about her flowers. She always paid Jimi for these missed hours of work. Money she had lots of, as her son owned a business and her daughter was a nurse; both keep her happy and satisfied by sending her money every two weeks.

The first two weeks Jimi spent weeding under the apple trees, planting flowers and trimming the hedge. He often mused that the job was too light for a man. In Fiji, it was a woman's job. I bet my wife would call me a lewa if she saw me, he often thought. He counted himself really lucky to have got this job. And for two dollars an hour. Incredible! His friends Jone and Mua had been less fortunate and had to be satisfied with a factory job.

Occasionally, Jimi's thoughts wandered back to Fiji, to his wife and to his two children. Did they miss him as much as he missed them? There were so many people and yet he felt lonely. What if he died while walking on the street! Would someone pick him up? The people all seemed so impersonal to him — like the doll he sent over to his daughter for Christmas; and why were they always hurrying? Couldn't they walk slowly? He consoled himself that in two months' time his three-month tourist visa would expire and he would return.

Jimi's wife, Mere, wrote fairly often — letters which Jimi could remember offhand, as he had read them over and over again. He replied to every letter she wrote, always mentioning how much he missed her and how much he longed to return. His wife's letters were his only consolation in an unfriendly country.

The only thing Jimi had in common with Mrs Davidson was their loneliness and their love of letters. It seemed that the written word had so much power over both of them. Part of Jimi's job was to collect the old lady's mail every day on his way back from lunch. Jimi enjoyed doing this because he loved to watch the expression on Mrs Davidson's face, and he loved to think that he was partly responsible for the happiness of this old lady who lived alone in her huge and lonely mansion.

Jimi finished trimming the hedge and began to work on the wooden fence which surrounded the house. One whole week was spent scraping off the old paint. He couldn't understand why so much time and money had to be spent on such a structure which did not seem to serve any useful purpose at all, except of course to isolate the old lady further.

Painting the fence was boring. It was a tedious kind of job. Sometimes he thought it better to work in a factory. At least there would be people to talk to. He thought of the people in the village who always worked in groups. Work was fun. They would joke about the women, talk about their farms, their biggest catch and, before they realised it, the work had been completed. Now he had to work alone and time seemed to drag.

A month passed. Soon he would be back. He counted the days and looked forward to the day when he would return.

Mrs Davidson seemed happier each day and generously praised Jimi for his hard work. Jimi worked hard and she paid him well. It seemed an ideal relationship.

But one day something happened that upset their normal routine. It was on a Monday. Jimi, having assured the old lady that he would not forget to collect her letters on his way back from lunch, left the house in high spirits. At the foot of the driveway leading to the house was the mailbox. Jimi peered into the hole and saw a few letters and a parcel. He smiled, knowing that Mrs Davidson would be pleased. He made it a point that he'd pick them up when he returned.

Turning right, he followed the main road until he reached the corner. He turned left and passed the post office. He looked at his watch and quickened his steps. Then passed the telephone booth.

The street was empty. Odd. How come? No one else was walking besides him, Jimi realised. Then a strange feeling came over him. He felt the urge to run. He began to sweat.

A screech of brakes! Jimi froze. He tried to control himself. Two men in a blue car, one fat and the other thin, both wearing caps on their heads. Leaning his left arm on the window, the fatter man announced,

'We are the po–lice. You un–der–stand?'

Silence. Jimi swallowed and blinked his eyes. Again the man said,
'We are the po–lice. Where are you go–ing?'

Relax, relax, Jimi told himself. Nothing's wrong.

'To the shop.'

'Where did you come from?'

Pause.

'Over there.' The thin man felt in his shirt pocket and took out a notebook
and a pen.

'And what is your name?'

'Jimi.'

'Is that your surname?'

'No.'

'What is your surname?'

'Viliame.'

The thin man wrote furiously.

'And where is your home, Viliame?'

'Arcadia Road.'

'No, I mean your real home. Tonga?'

'Fiji.'

Must be brave . . . be brave . . .

'And you said that you were going to the shop? And this is your lunch-
hour, isn't it, Viliame? Where do you work?'

'I'm not working.'

'What is that on your hands?'

Jimi faltered.

'Paint.'

'What were you painting, Viliame?'

'Our house.'

Silence.

'Okay Viliame. That is all.'

The fumes of the car clouded Jimi's eyes and he stumbled. He ran, turned
left, and barely missed a rubbish bin. He slowed down a bit, turned left again
into Arcadia Road.

Jimi stumbled up his steps. He got the key from his pocket, pushed the
door and slammed it hard. He leaned on the door, panting. His knees shook;
he slumped on a chair. He felt a strong urge to relieve himself.

Jimi took his time in the bathroom. His mind, his senses seemed to have come
alive. The silence was unbearable. Then . . . a familiar sound. Jimi jumped. The
blue car pulled up and stopped. Three men. The fat man got out first . . .

Mrs Davidson looked at her watch. Three o'clock and Jimi had not returned.
She dropped the *Woman's Weekly* she was reading and went to get the letters
herself.

Pio Manoa

Invitation

Sometimes
as a frog feels
the coming rain
so my awkward fingers
sense the end
of laughter.

Therefore,
friend,
before the wind shakes
and the sky gathers
let us sit a moment
by the hum's edge
and the fringe of light,
the quiet water under
the bullfrog's assertion
where the finger of water
points into silence.

There our words
will find the delicate filaments
that anchor brain to belly or heart,
words to tease other words
and words
that bear unseen
the source
which we must touch
to see.

Laucala Bay

(for Al)

There is no wind
to lift the darkness
crouching upon this strip
of browning water,
only the masks of disparate
voices floating in unison
of foam and bubbles,
from the hills again
sloughing off
towards two islands.

The reef is loud
with the rages of the undersea.
Above, the cornered stars
withdraw.
Other corners of sky gather
beyond the voices
(engine room of a berthing ship)
knowing. The fisherman
beyond the reef
by his lamplight waits.

It is the night for the unquiet
sleepers' walk,
in which one may see
the many dead returning —
before the gown of the white woman
startled your afternoon sleep,
rustling through your passage
and into sunlight,
before the pet beast
savaged her child in its sleep,
before the conflagration,
the raging flames
for bewildered men,
before the powder flash
and the limp club and spear
and the might of war canoes

of Bau and Rewa
trembling on the water
sealed the fitful destinies,
the strange meeting
of musket and Word —
the alphabet of the mercenary
word,
the savagery of submission,
the crossed flag and the arrogant cross,
the saving flag, the redeeming cross.
The water tasted of the dead
or you walk with the tang of ashes.

Beyond the night of the strangers' ship
going down, and the voices of men and women
mingled in the wind
rounded the promontory
into these delta waters.

Before the roar of amphibians,
the engines of a modern war
and the thud of fliers' heels,
there is Kau the strong
an ancestor of phallic fame
sailing his courting poems
for the maiden of Suva,
the lady of Nukulau,
sending his sons far out
wooing wives
for his old insatiable mats
and the houses of Vugalei.
There goes Rokola
with the huge oar
poling his canoe
to a friend to clothe his sons.

Tomorrow I shall hear
the stadium battles roar,
and tell my Pacific brothers
of the spirits that we plundered
and their imminent second coming.

Nemani Mati

Reflections on a Night Out in Town

last saturday morning
in a desperate effort
to organise and direct
my life somewhat more orderly
i confessed
to my best friend
deep down inside me
i was a cold-blooded liar

the night before
i had watched
my twenty-five years of life
floating in a carton of beer
spent the night out
in town boogying
in the grooviest joint
dead stoned drunk with
two friends of mine and
ghost-like faces of people
who never seemed to care

well the night ended
like all nights with
half-flown moons
and circling half planets
deep in the concentric circles
of my tormented conscience

the bouncer
he growled at me and
said i shouldn't sleep
in public places then
he threw me out
and i flew down
an eagle without wings
the stairway was mine
for a second i was
the king

my glasses broke
shattered the five-dollar bill
sank in the gutters
of man's inhumanity
and my pelvis ached
hammered with pain
pieces of concrete
swarmed in my veins

i fought
screamed
swore
cried
and said i am a human being
you can't do this to me
my rights are guaranteed
in the constitution
(heaven knows what that is)
anger took me
shaking with fear
of violence unknown
to our people

it is now sunday morning
as i drown my sorrows
in a cup of milo
the *fiji times* lies crumpled
in the wastepaper basket
and there is an uneasy
feeling of uncertainty
depression and failure . . .
of being rejected and misunderstood
like being caught with your pants down
somewhere on the streets
lamenting the death of traditions

what went wrong i asked
did i run after the wrong gods
my head hurts
from too much
introspection
a thousand needles dance
before my eyes

exploding in the sky
i pick up the pieces
there are holes everywhere
and the books are dusty
from non-use
i am confused
by the many choices
i cannot find my way
(in a day-to-day reality)
i cry and swear
and curse the nature of things
but whose fault i asked
is it mine
is it yours
or is it ours

tonight i must
drag myself once more
to the edge of the sea
where once among the
ghost conscious roots
of my forefathers
i sat and dreamed
of the things i
would like to do
while the waves rose and fell
undisturbed by my presence
well such is the nature of
things existing on their own
but all obeying
a timeless rhythm
while the mind dwells
on the infinite disorientation
of life's order
a problem
inside another
look and behold as
the crack widens
on the cosmic cosmic wall
but alas there is no light
only darkness
and no hope
but dreams of salvation

SUDESH MISHRA

In Nadi

On wet days the stench of squashed toads,
skins glued to the asphalt,
assails the spaces in your memory;
you stroll the bylanes
gathering the maggots of your past
from lumps of dog-shit;
foraging the common refuse
for a canefield and a wooden house
gay with white ants,
you stumble upon the banks of a river
with a cow for its name:
once after the puja you launched
a ship of coconut and flowers
and watched it sail into the village
where native boys with fins and gills
float all day with ease.
The vessels you launch today
founder with a hiss,
sinking to the embrace of algae
and ageless riverweed; turning away
you clear the clog of camphor
from your nasal passages
breathing gently from memory to memory.

*

On dry days hunting for words
packed with frost
you meet dawdlers lazing
around a tanoa.
Gulping a bowlsum
you enter the gossip with a fat tongue.
Forgetting the disparity
between people and poetry,
between truth and reality,
you cheat at cards
and watch cigarette smoke

strangle the Knave of Spades.
Accessory to a thematic murder
you crush peanuts between teeth
and wonder if the tanoa
harbours a miniature Loch Ness
and wonder if anything
ever coheres and whether the tanoa
houses a Monster Muse.
The sun sews patterns
above the pavement
as you figure out a way
to restore the Dark Knight,
regain the confidence
and the equilibrium of the outset.
But torpor sets in
and kava filters into the brain,
you transmute into a 'lazy-eyed'.

If only you could walk away
from the drug and heat.

Confessions of a Would-be Brahmin

O Shiva   O Parvati   O Durga
I have sinned.
I have used my right hand to explore cracks
Other than those of sculptures.
I have picked my nose with Cow-Eaters
Breaking Manu's Ram knows which law.
I have smoked ganja with Angrez mlecchas
Envying them, all the while, their pigment.
(You see, I even dispute
Your affidavit that they are albinos.)
On the side, I have bedded a washerwoman;
Pissed in the Ganges when no one was looking;
And for the edification of the Hindu Society of Australia
Recited the *Ramayan* with (they later said)
Beer on my breath.

O Shiva O Parvati O Durga
Though I have crossed the kala pani
And lost caste
Forgive me my trespass.

O Shiva O Parvati O Durga
You'd be pleased to know
Some things never change
The left hand still cleans my arse.

Beachcombers

Safe luxury liners won't satisfy; two-a-penny whaling barques
with nothing but a bubblegum between them
and the Spanish galleons through which the hammerhead smiles
they fossick for, from jetty to pier to quay.
Deckhand, cook's boy, stowaway; all try a hundred trades
to secure a wreck (with a Man Friday Foot branding the stern).
Melville managed it with Dr Long Ghost off the topaz
of Tahiti, except no tell-tale flotsam accompanied them.
Four weeks for mutiny in the charnel-house
they breathed the virginal oil from a Gauguin canvas
and trafficked fantasies of semening the splayed pages
of banana leaves under a thatch of uneasy stars.
Two fortnights before, from the *Lucy Ann* they saw the yarning polyps
bricking barricades for voluptuous thighs, twig-brown
and arrow heading into a patch of tar-deep night.
Neither polyps, nor the cabined captain could dissuade them:
Papeete glowed a pastoral furrow eager for foreign seed.
'To Tamai then', they sang from the Calabooza Beretanee
and watched their libidos swim through a sea of Lory-Lorying bodies;
and while the thwanging waves concaved upon the shore,
two sticky worms ghosted the entourage of Bougainville, Wallis, Cook,
and bored through sandal-pasted shrubs, entering the heavenly warren
that wets the dream of every pox-afflicted beachcomber.

Elegy: Dr Timoci Bavadra

No fox can foul the lair the badger swept.

W. B. Yeats

I

Rafters of rain fell in Samabula;
Rumours congealed like fat on the radio.
A prankster, it seems, had cut the lights off;
The act ended before it was over.
The watchers in the stadium cannot see,
Yet cling steadfastly to the single belief
In the municipal generator —
Our *deus ex machina*. A people's faith
In the theatre is perhaps more tragic
Than a hero's parting distich. But when
A man, more than the sum of his masks, walks
The stage, the artifice fails: the playhouse
Vanishes, only the vision remains.

II

You were too ordinary
For this carnival
Of the extraordinary;
But surely the marvel
Was your humility
Amid all the vainglory
Common as tea
Between this and that Tory.

III

Uluivuda, you have taught us something.
Act and intention must wed in everything,
Thought and deed are bound to a moral need:
This minus that: a priest without a creed.

IV

A man is more than a penny slogan,
More than the digits of demography.
Such menhirs of truth several ignored,

Others abhorred. A modest wagon
Of firm believers gather by the sea,
Hoping to catch pectorals of a word,
Which, like an ancient runic message,
Would guide us through this difficult passage.
Some choose to vanish in dormitory
Cities, where suburbs are silent enclaves,
And your neighbour just an anomaly.
All, all were in there for the lottery,
The priest and soldier, the trader and knave.
Not one had faith in ideals of parity.
O how toads trumpet the tyrant's sonnet,
And many starve that the few may banquet.

V

I watch from the balcony
The ocean's marauding cavalry;
The interminable chorale
Of the surf rises metaphysically
Above the general drawl
Of hucksters, quibblers and sophists.
The interim beasts of recent history
Roam the wondrous forests,
Abode of our children's children,
Leaving an augury of pug-marks
Which neither man nor Heaven
May succeed in undreaming.
You were Noah to our Ark.
Once everything had much meaning.

Once everything had much meaning.

VI

A soft rain falls on a grave
In Vuda, raising a cairn
In praise of a man who gave
Without claiming a stake,
Without wooing the fake.
On his grave falls a soft rain.

Detainee II

(for Som Prakash)

That night my vague jailers left a mattress
Sweating faeces, I slept on philosophy.
Twelve days and I share my inquisitor's
Myopia, his U-smile and rhetoric.
A 40-watt gourd perspires inside my den,
Modestly pendulous, inviolable,
Almost the moon. My mind's tungsten is burnt.
At breakfast I yearn for the snap and jerk
Of the cold Sten. This is the fatal catch,
This is the Black Roulette. One surreal night
Whispers gnawed outside my grilled crate. I cried:
'Is this the witching hour, tell me — Shiva,
Great God, I'll waltz widdershins round thy church.'
Conspiratorial sniggers assembled
With the new light. Lieutenant Pio Chara,
Studiously urbane, arrived with portmanteau
Queries and uriny tea. 'Mr Prakash,
You are a Security Risk, a threat
To the Republic. Publicly recant
All you have said of our Saviour, our State.'
Ogres, in urban legends, overtax the hero
At the level crossing. *That*, my friend, is the fatal catch.

SATENDRA NANDAN

from *The Wounded Sea*

At the airport, just before I was allowed to leave the terminal and board an Air Pacific flight for Sydney, a young female reporter from Radio New Zealand asked me:

'What were your thoughts as you were being driven to the military barracks by the gunmen?'

'I was glad my father was dead,' I replied.

She looked puzzled.

I tried to explain: he wouldn't have survived this betrayal; this fatal stroke.

'Oh, I see.' She looked enigmatically at me, without seeing anything.

'You see, I survived: not one but *two* coups,' I told her, without being asked.

As I boarded the rainbow-coloured aircraft, and before I went in, I stopped on top of the gangway and looked back towards my village. It was scattered amongst the sugarcane fields. Like the bruise in my beard, it was now hidden. I had received that bruise from the butt of a gun.

I fastened my seat-belt. The No Smoking sign hadn't been switched on yet. The Fijian air hostess smiled with her teeth, red lipstick darkening her hibiscus face.

The headline in the newspaper lying on the next seat said: 'They died instantly.' The chief's neck was broken, his wife's face bashed. Two prominent Fijians from the West were dead. 'Carnage on the roads is becoming commonplace,' the report stated. It did not matter to me. I didn't know them.

Besides, they were Fijians. I remembered how Litia Moses, one morning in the staff lounge of the University, told a Fijian colleague that a family of four had drowned near Suva Point.

'Isa lei,' sighed my colleague. How sad.

'But, they were Indians,' Litia assured, in Bauan dialect.

My Fijian colleague looked embarrassed. I pretended I hadn't heard. We continued to measure our concerns with cups of coffee.

There's nothing like instant death; we all know that. Or almost all of us. That we are dying every instant is another matter. That edge of awareness comes often a little too late.

Air Pacific announced the departure — finally. We taxied and took off over canefields and little houses and coconut palms; and then as we turned towards the foam-filled sea, my heart leapt. Not exactly like a rainbow in the sky . . . but a great, deadly weight had lifted.

The island receded. Nadi town looked like an overturned box of jewels as my flight made its ascent through the darkness, and the red light on the right wing of the plane glowed — glowed like a burning pyre seen from the distance of a wounded sea.

I felt as if I had clambered from a life-raft onto a cruise liner.

I was leaving my country, at Christmas, with death on my mind.

I asked the Fijian air hostess for a bottle of champagne.

My father's death was a harrowing affair. My mother had grown old and gaunt caring for him. And my brother, a doctor, had aged in the four years he had kept him alive. The pain of death is for the living. The dead are lucky. That's why I said there's nothing like instant death. Life can be so very long.

Years ago when my father was ruining his health with kava — the bane of my village — I wrote a poem at school entitled 'My Father's Son'.

Ratu Reddy, our principal, read it. Then he expressed his 'deepest condolences and sinceremost sorrows' to me.

I protested. 'Sir, my father is still alive.'

'Oie! I'm very, very sorry, boy,' Ratu Reddy had muttered, folding his palms. 'I thought the poem was really about the death of your father.'

It was. Four years later when I stood near the funeral pyre on the Wailoaloa Beach cremation ground. I recalled the poem and marvelled at the accuracy of my observations, at the details — the minutiae of details.

By then I'd become a student of literature; and thought, Art really makes Life.

The sadness in my heart began to slowly evaporate in the brilliant sunshine that spread itself on the airport houses like the sea crawling over barren rocks. My grizzled brother lit the pyre while the local pundit, Birbal, shouted several 'Oums' in the wind and hurled incomprehensible shlokas into the ocean. And as the sugar-and-ghee smoke blew towards the Fijian huts on the other side of the village I was glad the old man was dead, now being burnt, and his ashes were to be thrown tomorrow into the sea. The Pacific Ocean, part of the Indian Ocean, part of the holy Ganga . . . it was comforting.

The sea is one, I thought. Only we in our ignorance call it by different names — depending from which shore we are gazing while the seagulls shriek, dive and die.

Then I saw Pratap — the 'mad boy' of our village. He was running towards the cremation ground in his ragged, filthy clothes. Shorn hair full of dust, feet bleeding and calloused, a face of grief. I remembered a bare tree on a bare hill, and a cow mooing under it.

'Ram, Ram, Bhai.' Pratap kept mumbling his greetings in the name of Lord Rama as he passed a number of people. They'd just paid their last respects to the dead man and were now making their way towards the Fijian fish vendors about a mile away from the funeral grounds. Feasting after a funeral is — or was — a Fijian way of life: as these people returned to their offices in Nadi town they would be carrying a bundle or two of fish or crabs.

'Ram, Ram, Bhai.' Pratap rushed, faltered, fell towards the flames. The tiri-tiri logs crackled; a smell of camphor and ghee rose with the smoke. Birbal the pundit distanced himself as Pratap stood near the flaming pyre, close and dumb. I looked at him: his face was covered in brown dust, tears were rolling down his scarred cheeks. No one stood near him; no one consoled him. He was alone.

My father was being consumed by fire, the flesh of my father was being charred.

My father was born in Fiji. His father had come from India — from a little, obscure village called Sultanpur near the Taj Mahal — under the indenture system. Slavery was abolished — at least on paper — in 1833; a new system had begun in 1834. My grandfather, who never mentioned the Taj Mahal, had signed his girmit — he couldn't pronounce 'agreement' — for ten years with the coolumber, the Australian overseer who called his number every morning as he reported for work.

After serving and surviving ten years of his girmit, he married a girmitya woman. Father was their second son. I did not know much about my grandmother except that she had four other sons and then had eloped with a slightly fairer girmitya — named Ramsuroop — a jehajibhai, a mate, a traveller on the same ship from India.

'Baba' as I called my old grandfather — it never ever occurred to me that once upon a time he must have been young — never remarried. Whenever Father talked about Grandma, Baba would either curse his brown spindly-legged mare, or curse Kallu, the mongrel dog who would always be dozing nearby, and threaten him with starvation.

Baba looked after his 'Pandavas' as he called them and lived with Father. He would visit the homes of his other sons, but he would always sleep in the special bure built for him by my father. No matter how late in the night these visits finished, Baba would always ride his mare back home. And as he arrived he'd shout:

'Arre, chodou, everybody sleeping?'

'Arre, buddou, go to sleep. Food's in the kitchen. Don't wake up the children!' Father would yell back, waking everyone.

Baba would then go through his ceremonies, rather noisily: he'd feed his mare; wash himself at the well; sing a few couplets from the *Ramayana*; change into his dhoti, white and clean; caress Kallu; and then come into my bure.

Then he and I would eat bread with herrings in tomato sauce.

Happiness depends on such little things. The dead live on in their acts — insignificant in life, immeasurable in death.

But one night Baba didn't return.

Next day Father announced he had been taken to Nadi hospital.

'He's been appendixed,' Father revealed. 'A minor operation is needed.'

Dr Ponia assured Father that Baba would be in specialist care. He would personally take charge of the operation. 'Satyam,' he said touching the big ash mark on his forehead.

To me, Dr Ponia looked more like Kalpu — our pujari, the village witchdoctor. But Father was reassured, because Dr Ponia had got his medical degree in India in a college called Gurukul.

A doctor trained in India; a man of faith, too.

Of course, we didn't know that Dr Ponia could defeat divinity.

It was past midnight. I was studying hard for the Senior Cambridge — that curse of the children of the British Empire, an examination that followed the Bible and the English language everywhere. Ratu Reddy, as usual, had given me several maths problems to solve. I always suspected he couldn't do them himself. Midway through the class, he would suddenly look at me and say: 'Continue the work, I've got to go to the office. I'm expecting a direct call from Mr Bray, the Chief Education Officer, from Suva . . . ' And he would stride out of the classroom purposefully, leaving me to solve the problems on the blackboard, pockmarked like his face. Of course I knew he'd gone to gossip with Doris, an English teacher from New Zealand . . .

I head Father's tractor come to a screeching halt. Then a deadly silence. A few seconds later I heard a terrible wail — like the hooting of an owl and the baying of a dog together. I came out of my bure. The moon lay its beams on the marigolds. I saw my father crying. I had never seen him cry before. He was a huge, strong man — like a tree. His voice could shake the whole village.

Baba had died in the operating theatre.

According to Dr Ponia the operation had been successful, but complications had developed due to an overdose of anaesthetic by his Chinese assistant. Father didn't understand, nor did he care to know the details.

He wept like an orphan. His father from India was dead.

Pratap came to spend the night with us. 'Mausa,' he said. 'Don't cry, you'll wake up the whole village.'

Father whimpered. Pratap held his hand for a while then sang: gita bhajans he called them.

> Thou grievest where no grief should be!
> For the wise in the heart

Mourn not for those that live,
      nor those that die.
No I, nor thou, nor any one of these,
Ever was not, nor ever will not be,
Forever and forever afterwards.
All that doth live, lives always . . .

That which is
Can never cease to be
The Life is, spreading life through all . . .
And like the ocean, day by day receiving
Floods from all lands, which never overflows;
Its boundary line not leaping, and not leaving,
Fed by the rivers, but unsucceeded by those . . .

So he sang, bits from many songs. It was all a mumble to me.

Then Pratap asked me to pound some kava and we made the grog. The first bowl I poured was for the taukei, the Fijian spirit on whose land we dwelt. Father would never touch kava unless the taukei was served first.

As I was about to give a bowl to Father Pratap whispered, 'One for Baba.'

I poured out some in the corner of the bure. A frog leaped in the darkness.

My father was a big man. I think a brave man, too. His face had power, the solidity of a boulder on a farm. As a schoolboy I once witnessed his bravery.

Two factions in our village were threatening to burn and rape for a month. One afternoon they tried to kill. Bisnath's gang attacked Baburam's. Baburam's gang chased Bisnath's down the hill — ten grown men pursued by five men with cane knives and iron bars. And Bisnath shouting, 'Mausa, bachao, sala killing us!'

Father emerged from the bure, rushed down the hill and, lifting both his hands above his head, yelled so loudly that I wet my shorts:

'What's this Mahabharat? Stop! Look! Listen!'

He must have picked that up from the sign at the railway crossing.

Baburam's murderous men stopped at the foot of the hill, confronting Father's shadow in the evening sun. I stood between Father's legs.

'Mausa,' Baburam pleaded. 'Get out of the way. We have to kill Bisnath before the sun goes down.'

Father moved. Baburam clutched his cane knife. His four bloodied companions looked ferocious.

Father pleaded. One of Baburam's men said something rude to Father. Suddenly Father snatched Baburam's cane knife. I was knocked to the ground. When I raised my dusty head, the offender lay prostrate before Father, Baburam begging that he be let up.

Father relented, very reluctantly. He turned back towards me and winked.

Revolution, I read later, began with a wink.

Bisnath's men by this time had disappeared into the canefields. Baburam's men turned and went home, their knives hanging like horse penises in the evening paddock.

Father had saved a man's life that day. We returned home and Father sat on the kerosene drum without a shirt, looking larger than life under the stringy, gnarled tamarind tree. A beautiful man with plenty of hair on his bare chest.

The second time Father cried was the day I left Nadi Airport for Delhi. I was going away for four years to study, on a scholarship. As my other relatives left the airport, Father sat on the corrugated iron bench and wept.

Why did he weep? Was it because his own father, at almost my age, had made an earlier journey from India to Fiji — and never returned? Something, as a father, he was now beginning to understand.

Or was it because he himself could never make the journey to his father's village? The CSR company owed Baba a passage back to India, and as the girmitya didn't go, it was his son's. But who would Father have seen in Sultanpur? Baba, being illiterate, had never written to his family. Maybe Baba was escaping from the subcontinent? Just as I was escaping from an island?

The thought haunts me now. Was this my father's first death?

Every Tuesday at 4 p.m. an Air India flight would arrive from Sydney. It was a special flight to Nadi. I remember how they advertised it: Nadi, Shiva's bull with a garland of hibiscus round its neck, a tikka on its forehead and an Air India hostess performing arti. I didn't see the bull with any particular interest, but the air hostess! Her silk sari, moon face, big eyes, her shawl draped delicately on her Kama Sutra bosom, the shape of her silken buttocks . . . she *still* haunts me long after the flights ceased to operate. She was my first awakening to sexual beauty — an air hostess's picture next to a holy bull.

To Father, Air India was the idea of India itself. India, for Father, was a grain of sand in an oyster: it troubled him, then crystallised into a pearl in his imagination . . .

Every Tuesday Pratap accompanied Father to the airport on our ageing Ferguson tractor. And as the flight landed — always at 4 p.m. — they would watch every passenger alight, then the air hostesses and the pilots. I was never there. They would wait till the aeroplane door closed. Then they would drive back home, sit outside the bure, drink grog and stare at the stars.

*

A few bat-eaten mangoes were scattered on the bare ground and the summer flies were buzzing around them. The mulkaam tree had always been fruitful. An old man lay under the shade of the tree, his eyes wide open, staring into the sun. His eyes a fragment of it, perhaps: *I am the inseparable in the separate; skull and bones — a sugar sack full of stones.* A few well-fed flies were crawling over his unshaven face as do ants on a khatai that Mother put in dhal to make it delicious.

The sun found the old man's granitic face and lent it a revenant radiance. His bald, stony skull reflected the character of a coastal landform battered by sea and high winds and, like it, had acquired an illusory and elusive dignity. You do not see that kind of face in my generation. The old man had learned to live between the sea and the land on our little island — that indefinable border of existence we call life. The wise, they say, see life as maya: the human illusion, a mere heartbeat away from the other illusion — death.

Kallu dozed next to the old man. They were fond of each other. Kallu would never touch his food until Baba had arrived home and caressed his excited muzzle as if blessing him. The decrepit dog would then yawn, stretch and smile.

Baba also had his dun-coloured mare, Rani. He rode on her daily, selling sukhi, baigans ('Baigani! Eggyplants!' he yelled when he saw any Fijians) and 'toomatoos'. The faithful mare knew the route Baba would take early in the morning and return by late in the evening. Kallu and I were always excited at their return. Baba would take the saddle gently off Rani's perspiring back and pull the bridle from her foaming mouth. I would then lead her to the well for buckets of cool water. First I would splash a few buckets all over her and Rani would shiver and neigh in sheer delight. Then I would tie her to the tamarind tree and lay her meal before her with a biscuit tin full of water from the well.

Baba would follow with his lathi in one hand and the hurricane lamp in the other. He would sneeze loudly as he passed the bure of my parents and then, at the well, wash his hands, feet and face. No one worried much about him — he had developed his own rhythm of life, like a transplanted tree among the native shrubs. His moods, it seemed, were controlled by distant memories as the tides are by the moon.

After washing himself and sprinkling water in the four directions, he would stand facing the moon or, when the moon was not visible, the brightest star, and when it was a moonless and starless night, he would look at the flame burning steadily inside the hurricane lamp and chant a few mantras. What he echoed I didn't understand: to me he was an illiterate old man. Slowly he would plod his way to the bure with the broken door. Kallu would make way for him at the entrance; I would be inside waiting expectantly on his bamboo plaas.

'This door will never get fixed until I die!' he lamented ritually and cursed the mother of his son. 'Accha, come, come, chodou,' he would call me fondly, 'see what's in the brown bag.'

He would then hand me the brown paper packet from Trikambhai's shop. Inside I would behold a tin of herrings in tomato sauce, a loaf of stale bread from Lum Hop's cafe, a single apple and a tin of IXL blackcurrant jam from Australia. I would take out each of these gifts with great care and heap them on the Fijian mat in front of Baba, who by now had changed into his white dhoti, his face beaming with coconut oil. He seldom wore a shirt in the evening. His nipples looked like dried prunes and his Gandhi-like chest was covered with strands of white hair suppressed and knotted as if some stubborn patch of grass had been under the wheel many a time.

'Accha, chodou, where's the tin-cutter?' he would enquire.

I would search frantically under the mat, in the four corners of the bure, in the biscuit tins full of tobacco leaves. Usually my search would be in vain except for an onion or a leaping, pissing frog. 'At least you've found something useful, chodou,' he would compliment me, taking the tin-cutter from under his half-lifted left buttock. And he would let out a contented fart.

Then we would all sit together, with Kallu blocking the doorway, salivating at the smell of the herrings. Baba would open the tin carefully while I would slice the loaf of half-burnt bread with a cane knife. Onions would be chopped and mixed with the herrings and green chillies. Baba would then lift, reverently, a morsel of fish and bread to his forehead, and then — and only then — put the first morsel into my mouth. Kallu was given two herrings and two slices of bread, which he'd gulp down greedily, waiting for more. The rest Baba and I would eat slowly, taking an occasional sip of maatha — skimmed milk — which I detested.

Baba would ruminate: 'Two things about food, betu: chew it well, and never waste even a single grain. Every grain is a gift from the gods and every grain has the eater's name written on it,' he would tell me, philosophically baring a perfect set of teeth. 'Look at Lali, how she chews all the time.'

Lali was our cow — holy, sacred and milk-giving. Once Baba caught me riding on Lali's back up a hillslope. He was outraged and gave me a mighty slap. I didn't eat for two days. He was distraught. On the second evening that I didn't eat, he came to my bure where I was lying looking feverish, and he explained to me: 'Riding a holy cow is paap, betu, never do that. Otherwise when your Baba dies, Lali's children won't give their tails to your Baba to help him swim across the Baitarini — the river dividing narak from swarg.'

He would then tell me why cows were given as holy gifts to priests. I listened to him fascinated, frightened. Lali became my most loved animal.

One evening Lali didn't wind her way home. We searched for her all over the village. Two mornings later we heard Kallu barking in the middle of the canefield. Baba made his way through hornets' nests to where Kallu was barking furiously. Lali was lying there, eyes wide open, unable to move. Flies were exploring her plaintive nostrils.

Soon half the village was there muttering and cursing. Who could have done such a terrible deed? Lali had been speared in the belly. I was reminded of frogs I had seen impaled and struggling on the sharp iron and bamboo spears that some Fijian youths carried while fishing.

Baba uttered a single word: 'Rakshasas!'

Lali was transported home on a ghasita to recuperate under the tamarind tree by the well. Baba minded her as he would have minded me had I been hurt. He looked weary and haggard — and every time Lali mooed, he would jump out of his plaas and sit by her. Lali's wound, plastered with cow dung, was washed daily with warm water. When after a month she was healed, Baba took her into the middle of the Nadi River and gave her a good bath, washing every part of her body. Then with his right hand on Lali's left horn, he stood staring at the sun for quite a while.

I never saw Baba read, but he had a reservoir of gripping tales from the *Ramayana*. His favourite story was of Ram's exile with Sita, his princess wife. Baba didn't think much of Ram's younger brother, Laxman, possibly because he had mutilated the nose of a woman — Supnekha, Ravan's sister. And Baba even tried to make us understand why Ravan had abducted Sita and taken her to Lanka. Wouldn't you do that, chodou, if your sister's nose was chopped off?'

I didn't understand the moral or metaphysical implications of the cowardly deed of Laxman or Ravan. But Baba's own fury was reserved for Kekeyi, who had forced Ram into exile.

'Why was Ram sent into exile, Baba?'

'Because Kekeyi wanted her own son to be king of Ayodhya.' Baba paused before reflecting: 'Exile, betu, is common. Valmiki wrote about Ram's exile, so that we could bear ours. That's how I have lived here, chodou!' His voice faltered.

I began to see things in perspective. On the eve of his coronation, Ram was exiled for fourteen years by his selfish stepmother. In Ram's story I saw our Fijian Indian lives mirrored. And I began to understand the myths on which our civilisation was founded. Both their potency and impotence.

After Lali's brutal spearing I noticed Baba's life change suddenly. He started telling me stories from the *Mahabharat* — that most terrible and wisest of books; the first recorded holocaust of humanity. His eyes would burn with a fire of the sort I had seen my mother stir to cook Father's special rotis. Years later I was to see it in a lovo at the feet of Ratu Sukuna's statue in front of the Queen's Parliament.

Baba became interested in local politics. 'What's Boothalingam Reddy doing now, chodou?'

'He wanting to stand for election, Baba,' I would read from the newspaper.

'Naam baria, karam garia,' he would comment to himself — big name, bullshit work.

I would tell him that Chimmach C. Ali was also standing for the Legislative Council.

'Arre, chodou, all these are crooks,' he'd say cynically, pulling my ears with some passion.

Once Father heard him singing out a vile couplet denouncing local members of parliament and came rushing into our bure: 'What rubbish are you teaching the boy?' he demanded.

Baba replied, calmly: 'Arre, chodou, what do you know? They've chopped Mother India's arms, her breasts. She fed all of us. We came in the same ship — jehajibhais — now they want separate seats in this tin-drum island. And they killed Gandhi, too,' he concluded vehemently.

Father shouted, 'Gandhi was killed by a mad Hindu. Didn't you hear on the radio? It was in the *Fiji Tem*, also. Wasn't it?' seeking confirmation from me.

'Arre, son of an ass, how long will you believe radio and noospaper? This is kaliyug — the age of evil. And the truth will never be known.' Baba's anger had subsided.

Almost thirty years later I began to understand Baba's battles with his son. Baba's prejudices were part of his being, like air and water are integral to nature. It intrigued me to find that a man who could tell such marvellous tales about Ram and Sita could also be full of petty prejudices against a community. But that was Baba — he had carried in his holdall from his obscure village in India his heritage and multicoloured obscenities. This island was the last place to change his subterranean thinking: an archipelago, surrounded by more than a cannibal ocean.

Once as we sat late and the evening sun was diving into the sea in all its naked glory, I asked Baba: 'Why are there no elephants here?'

'Arre, chodou,' he pulled me closer to him. 'Elephants are huge.'

'How big, Baba?' I asked with wonder.

'Like those mountains.' He pointed to the gaunt peaks in the Sabeto Range which hemmed our village and gave it dignity and definition. Some nights we would see fire on the mountains where Turam Khan had his goat farm. Baba would simply observe, 'The rakshasas are cooking stolen cows tonight.'

Elephants, he said, couldn't live on our island. The land was soft and they would sink into the ground. I believed him and dreamed of elephants often. Huge and mighty creatures. My island country had only wild boars and mongoose. Not even jackals until the day of the jackals — or the colonel — did arrive, but by then Baba was gone and I had grown up and seen elephants.

From fragments of fragmented lives, this is the dream that the old man, my Baba, gave me: to see elephants where there were none.

As I looked out of the window of my hot timber–tin house, Baba would be lying under the mulkaam tree like a shard of discarded boulder. Then along would come Rahul, my brother's son, chewing a stick of sugarcane. I would feel a shiver of joy. The mango tree was sullen in the heat and shimmering silence lay on the cane tops. I would hear his old voice: 'Arre, chodou, give me a piece of your sugarcane!' And the splendid, bubbling laughter of a child who knew the old man would never catch him; who knew none of the sorrows of the lonely sun burning, burning.

A child and a shadowless man, pursuing life on a pullulating island.

★

That Father was too fond of yaqona was known to everyone in the village except, apparently, himself. His skin had shrivelled up like the bark of the raintree which stood old and ageless behind one of our bures, and Mother continually grumbled that if his old veins were ripped, yaqona would drip from them instead of blood. Nothing, however, would deter Father from his grog (as the muddy stuff was popularly and warmly known). His irrefutable excuse: 'The Queen drink grog, don't she?' (And it was true: whenever the Queen or any member of the Royal Family came to Fiji, the Yaqona Ceremony was one of the highlights of the visit.)

Besides, Father was holder of a unique honour: he was employed at the Nadi International Airport, out near our village of Votualevu. He was the first descendant of an indentured labourer to have been given a job there. It was 'statusfying' for the whole village, and Father, sometimes in an extravagant mood, would claim this as a 'first' in the entire world. The villagers started calling him Boss. Only Mother remained unimpressed.

Our home, which consisted of three bures, was about a mile from the airport, on top of a red hill. Every evening as a Qantas jet landed, Father would mount his bicycle and rush to the airport. He would return after about two hours with a few Qantas spoons, cheese for the chickens, a couple of toilet rolls in which to wrap eggs for Lum Hop's cafe, and usually some pictures of air hostesses which were subsequently stuck to the bamboo walls of Father's bure between some brilliantly coloured portraits of Hindu gods and goddesses. (Several years later, when my brother inherited the honour, we discovered that Father was the sole and chief person-in-charge of the international airport's rubbish tip.)

On his way back from the airport, Father would buy a bundle of kava roots from Lum Hop's. His arrival home was always announced by Kallu, and the village would ring with the pounding of kava till long after midnight. Birbal, the pundit from India, often joined in. The conversation would range from the *Ramayana* to the shining silver birds (the aeroplanes), and Birbal would quote from the holy book to show that the *idea* of the aircraft was first mooted by the great Hindu sages. At this, Father would serve (only himself) another bowl of cool kava, after stirring it passionately.

No one knew when the grog session gave over. At eleven the next morning Father would wake and arise, and by twelve he would have his breakfast. Rarely could he be persuaded to go down to the river for a bath — his legs looked like dalo uprooted days ago. When Mother got furious, he would say:

'Look, the coolumber. He bright and white. He never bathing — he tol' me hisself, the memsahib don't trouble him: she from Ozzland, you see.'

It wasn't the argument but the English that defeated Mother. She didn't know a word of it. Father, much to his advantage, had picked up his version of the language at the airport. And he used it to telling effect against his wife. Whenever, wherever he saw me, he would nod gravely and say:

'Englis hard labour, boy. But meself learning fasting, fast. Boy, you reading more and much. With Englis you go Ozzland, you see.'

From his tobacco-stained pocket, he would then bring out a crumpled page with which I had seen Lum Hop wrap bread, and say:

'Tek this gret noospaper and read, boy. Tell me worl noose. What happenin' in India? Gandhi king now? He gret man: too much reading he done. You read, boy, no look see me.'

How could you tell Father that Gandhi had died years ago, especially when, according to Birbal, Rama was still alive?

I think it was his job at the airport that made Father send me to school. He earned enough to pay the fees and buy my books. Otherwise, he had eggs for his yaqona, and everything else he needed grew on the farm on which my elder brother was now working.

My school years passed like planes across the blue sky. Night and day I wrestled with Dudley Stamp's *World Geography* and Brett's *History of the British Empire*. One night as I came out of my bure, a shaft of light hitting my eyes, I saw the door of Father's bure ajar. Seated next to him was Mother — a most unusual sight. Birbal was perched on a sack of rice, with his toadlike belly, looking very smug and snug. I knew at once that some matter of great importance was being discussed. I could just catch Birbal's words:

'Yes, yes, Bossie: Rama had *his* sandals. He leaving them behind when he gonna into exile. A noblest idea — already in the *Ramayana* . . .'

The rest I couldn't hear since Father sneezed rather loudly. I looked up at the groggy moon. Stars were flickering like the street lights of a distant city glimpsed only in pictures. Dudley Stamp looked more forbidding than ever.

Soon afterwards there was a loud howl: Father, marching towards my bure, had apparently stepped on Kallu's tail. 'Sorry, sorry, foolis doggy,' he mumbled as he entered. The kerosene lamp was burning with a single flame;

a few senseless moths lay around its oily edges. Father sat on the kerosene drum and gazed at the fat books on my table. His eyes were luminous pools of light. He was deeply happy. With the odour of grog exuding from his nostrils, he said that the family had decided to buy me a pair of shoes if I passed the Examination. With that message he walked out of my bure as though walking out of a temple.

A dream was coming true. My first pair of shoes!

I tried to read Brett's *History*, but my mind skipped the pages like a stone on the river's face. I'd always wanted a pair of shoes. I was the only village boy without shoes who went to a school in the town. It caused me hopeless humiliation. On special school occasions I would don Father's army boots, socks and newspaper stuffed in the toes . . . And now the promise of my *own* pair of shoes! When I finally fell asleep, a new day was breaking over the dark gaunt mountains.

I began to swot like one possessed — in the bus, in the school toilet, while grazing cows . . . almost anywhere and everywhere.

But then, a week before the Examination started, I was suddenly in the grip of a delirious fever. An octopus was exploring my brains with clammy tentacles.

Mother went to the village temple. A new red, holy flag went up on a bamboo pole. Village women came and whispered mantras in Mother's ears. Matalita, our Fijian neighbour from the koro across the river, came with bananas and coconuts. She talked only to Mother, and left with lots of rice and tea leaves. Sometimes Matalita stood by my bamboo bed and stared at me. Her eyes were pools of yaqona. A tear or two would trickle down her gnarled face. She had been the midwife when I was born.

Three days before the Examination, Father put me on his bicycle and pushed me to the airport medical centre. The vuniwai showed great concern and gave me a few tablets and a lemonade bottle full of a curd-like mixture.

'Finis the lot, boy. Too good for you,' smiled the medicine man, showing his missing teeth.

Father immediately promised him a rooster. At this the vuniwai, until now glued to his chair, arose and jabbed a needle into my boneless buttocks.

It did the trick, claimed Father. Mother and Birbal had other explanations for my sudden recovery.

One warm and sunless day, as I was twisting the tail of the bullocks while ploughing, I saw Father gesticulating from the top of the hill. He was frantically waving something and chasing my brother towards me.

I hurried home, scrabbling up the hill like a crab. Before I could reach him, Father threw the paper towards me saying: 'Look, see the *Fiji Tem* page et.'

On page eight of the *Fiji Times,* the Examination results were announced. For the first time I was seeing my name in print. I was overwhelmed: only two candidates from my school had passed and I was one of them.

Father ordered my brother to run and plough the field. He asked me to wash at once. I changed into my pink shirt and brown shorts, and we rode 'doublebank' on the bicycle.

After much panting and farting, we finally arrived at Lalla's shoe shop at the edge of the airport. Lalla, it appeared, knew Father. He was enormously fat, with an overfed belly and an undernourished face, and was extremely hairy — there was hair everywhere except on his head. His little nostrils were clogged with thick hair, and he seemed to breathe with great difficulty — reminding me of a bullock in the sullen heat.

'Mahajan, shoe for this boy,' Father announced.

Lalla looked at me and commanded 'Seated boy. Saw me your foots. Big ff . . . foots, eh?' Breathing heavily. His rancid breath warmed my nostrils.

Disappearing for a moment to the back of the shop, Lalla brought out two huge, shining black shoes. They glistened in the silent darkness. He asked me to put them on.

'How fit, boy?' he asked, a pudgy finger exploring one of his nostrils.

'Fit, fitum fit, Mahajan,' Father remarked.

'For you, Boss, price only three ponds,' Lalla muttered, scratching his sweaty left armpit.

'That plenty much cash.' Father said, getting up to go.

'Wokay, two ponds for you, Boss,' Lalla persuaded, shaking Father's hand.

Father gave him a pound and promised two roosters. Lalla looked pleased and wrapped the shoes for me. He also gave me a pair of red nylon socks free.

I walked all the way back home, carrying my shoes in cradled arms. As I arrived, the sun was setting over the sea, threading a golden lining to every cloud, which I had never noticed before. Mother was sitting alone under the raintree. Its leaves had closed like green oysters in the humid heat.

I went straight into my bure. The kerosene lamp had been lit, a few blundering moths were living to die. I placed the shoes on the table and then, with the corner of my shirt, began to wipe the dust that had surreptitiously settled on them. With a bit of spit, they shone again.

That night I placed the shoes on Brett's *History.* They glowed, black and beautiful idols.

Quietly I crept next to my brother to sleep. Only he wasn't asleep.

'Leave your shoes back when you going oversea,' he murmured, drowsily. 'You getting the scholarsheep,' he added as an afterthought, pointing to an OHMS brown envelope on the table.

I didn't reply.

Soon he was snoring like a peasant.

Years later as I sat in the Auckland autumn with a glass of beer, reading *Time* magazine, I chanced upon a little item printed in italics. It told the story of a young boy in the village of a war-torn country. When the journalist had asked him about his happiest day, the boy had replied:

'When my brother died.'

'Why?' enquired the man, disbelievingly.

'Because I could wear his shoes,' answered the boy, smiling.

The beer in the glass lost its autumnal glow. It tasted almost like yaqona, only infinitely more bitter.

Siddarth

I

Death makes its way
Day by day, cell by cell
Between the silences
In drops of blood!
The hibiscus blooms
Beyond desire;
We live from moment to moment
On the faith of Maya!

Rays of a burnt-out sun
Splinter the sea —
Twilight brightens another sky;
My father's dying;
No, not I.

A foetus tied in strings
Of sorrows —
What womb dare hold him now? —
The earth:
The first, the last mother!

There's no pain like this body
Nor no life like this death
The endless apotheosis
Of all living:

Arjuna's vision in Krishna
The nuclear fission of an atman:
Of darkness or illumination?
I cannot say,
The dying man will not tell.
Draw the curtain
Eyelids flicker:
'Open Sesame'.
Faces light up the landscape
Through battered hills, broken trees;
Men, women, behind the chariot wheels
Glow like memory-motes
In the last rays
Of a Kuruchetra sun.
A tear blinds the third eye;
The sea is broken by bits of rain.
Now all sorrows surcease!

'Waves are nothing but water.
So is the sea.'

II

Rain falls on dry grass
The Earth's smell fills the air
 Stones stir with drops
Voices tumble over dark waters
Waves become whales
In dry coconut skulls!
The Baitairni floods again;
Pundit has lopped Iali's tail
And I haven't even learnt to swim!

Siddarth, my son, my father —
Eyes lit with another life:
Of the Four Sights you've seen two
In your father's father:
A sick man, an old one, too.

The third they'll not let you see
A corpse cleaned like a salt-fish,

Powdered, scented, tinted
With marigolds, hibiscus petals
Burnt on the sea-sand.
A muthi of ashes
Enough for his roti.
Ants crawl on living stones
Worms live in the marrow of our bones.

The fourth, a monk, you may yet become
To know the helpless
Endlessness of our being.
No old paths lead to that knowledge
No other footfalls are heard
Nor even the sound of a tiny bird
Chirping the mantras of dead men:
'Oum', 'Amen', 'Close Sesame'!

Siddarth, once again,
Follow your own footsteps
Over ashes, blades of grass
And teach us to live
In life, from Life!

Ballet for a Sea-bird

in the blue lightning-lashed sea
the black wave-thrashed rock
entangle, entwine and mock
perhaps some common destiny!

the dark waters rise to fall:
the rock resists, bits crumble;
the waves hiss, boil over, tumble:
above it all, a lost bird's call!

from the green sea it rose —
an extension of the sea foam?
to rest its breast on a craggy home —
the immensity of death still so close!

it wobbles, flutters, loses its hold:
cries, crashes into the marbled ocean
an act larger than its last emotion:
the sleepless sea rocks it in its fold!

but in the cracks of the rock, moss
had seen the bird search for an answer
with the myriad movements of a dancer
touched by another life's tenderness!

the waves swirl to reach evermore
the infinity of a blind, birdless sky;
only in my heart, the tiny gull's cry
sings as I scuttle from shore to shore!

SOM PRAKASH

An Act of Love

Deepawali is still the favourite festival for Ramkrishna simply because it is the least commercialised — in spite of its having gained the dubious distinction of being a public holiday. Ramkrishna's eyes rest on the lone Diwali card on the bookshelf. He picks it up, and flips it over to read the message again: 'To Ramkrishna, May the Season's lights illumine your path. Wishing you a Happy Diwali and a Prosperous New Year, Love, Nina and Damu.' In the mirror fixed on the dresser in front of him he sees a wry smile forming on his face. The signatures are underlined!

Loud laughter from the neighbouring flat confirms his suspicion that the eyes and the nerves of Anand's family are glued to their video set, a gift Anand proudly gave to his family and himself last Christmas.

He has just returned from his solitary twilight walk along the celebration-conscious streets surrounding his flat. He is surprised how the electric bulbs are fast replacing the divas and the candles, even for religious festivals. The video audience cheers. He thinks of the commercial wasteland of television in Australia and New Zealand. In Fiji, the video is creeping in . . . next the television proper!

In this melancholic mood, he looks at the two burning candles sitting on what he likes to think of as 'the resurrected candlestand', a name he closely associates with Michelle. Sitting in his favourite chair, he wonders which channel his beautiful friend might be hooked into in the heart of Sydney tonight. His eyes vacantly rest on the occasionally wavering flames of the candles. Once in a while he notices beside the mirror in front of him the dimly illuminated official government calendar which, this month, celebrates the sugar industry in bloom. Then he looks in the mirror for the reflection of the oddly framed picture of virgin Fijian bush — placed as if to achieve balance just above his head on the wall behind him.

A light breeze blows through the room. The flames waver desperately and struggle hard to stay alive at first, but gradually begin reshaping, reaffirming their fragile strengths. His face relaxes into a smile. Then, shifting his head slightly, he is surprised by an eternity of images of one of the candle lights and the dimmer picture of the virgin bush vainly repeating themselves mysteriously, beautifully. A moment's reflection explains the illusion: the mirror and the framed picture glass placed opposite each other with the candlelight and the man caught in between. Just then the loud combined laughter of the live audience and the screen audience next door brings Ramkrishna down to earth.

Yes, that video set — a gift to oneself! Ramkrishna stares at his resurrected candlestand, something having suffered several transformations; this was also a gift, but of a different kind altogether . . .

Long, long he stares. He visualises Christmas approaching, and someone, without a name, faceless, arduously in search of an appropriate piece of sandalwood to be carved into a candlestand: a gift, for the Intended. Then the frantic rush to transform a dream into an actuality to meet the Christmas Eve deadline; the fears of possible disappointment; the slow, long, painstaking process of carving a particular meaning out of a silent log of wood — to transfigure it, with tenderness and love, into something like a piece of driftwood washed onto an unknown shore from many seas and years away.

Just before the finishing touches, the carver stands back in awe of his creation on the work-bench. Then in a wave of triumph, the final effort is exerted. The chisel misses its aim, tips the delicate candlestand onto the concrete floor and slits the palm of his left hand. He stands and stares. Slowly he bends over. A teardrop falls on the torn flesh, fusing with the blood that trickles down. And for a few moments there is a wonderful surprise; then a strange resolve of terrifying beauty . . .

Ramkrishna is startled out of this flight of fancy by the imagined smarting caused by the salty tear in the wound as if it was a personally felt pain. With an ironic smile, he looks at the candlestand with its two arms holding a candle each. It is indeed a beautiful thing. And beside it lies the Diwali card from Nina and Damu.

He met the couple eighteen months or so after their wedding and became very close to them. Damu was a tall, athletic man with dark fuzzy hair. He could play soccer, rugby or cricket with equal ease, as he was a born sportsman. His carefree attitude towards life and his sense of humour made him likeable among friends and irresistible to strangers. There were times, however, when Damu could become humourless. Moreover, underneath that tourist-hotel barman's smile, there lurked a sense of lethargic conventionality, which suggested a lack of concentration or ambition. Yet when it came to his wife, his jealousy and emotions could be fiery. He was unduly possessive, and took her for granted, which did little to enhance the growth of either Nina or their marriage — or Damu himself.

Nina, on the other hand, was charming, faithful, beautiful, understanding and long-suffering in spite of her husband's unpredictable nature. She could be as unfeelingly reserved as the earth she walked on while others around her lost their heads and hearts over her physical attractiveness. Like that of a forlorn child, her melancholy smile, cutting across all barriers of colour, creed or culture, seemed to speak of love and tenderness being withheld from her for a long time. And for all her angelic ways, she exuded an earthly beauty, a sensuality which was difficult to come to terms with either by directly grappling with it or by totally ignoring it. Sometimes she would remind Ramkrishna of a potentially fertile valley which yearned for much-needed rain, or a virtuous Cleopatra who ought to be ploughed so that she could crop.

In spite of her sensuousness, she appeared unfulfilled and incomplete — especially as she didn't have any children. But Ramkrishna had to be careful here. Maybe that is what she preferred, to be forever untrammelled, forever enticing. One thing he was sure of, though: she was an enchantress by nature, not by choice or design. But in spite of her inherently seductive quality, she paid undue attention to, and even encouraged, not only Ramkrishna, but anyone who flattered and pampered her. It made him extremely jealous at times, this lack of discrimination, this lapse of class.

Of course, Ramkrishna was hopelessly in love with her. Coming from a broken home, which at least in part resulted from his father's land being taken away by native reserves, he nursed a sense of rootlessness and insecurity which made him a perfect victim of such alluring charm. He unconsciously identified Nina's life without love with his own fate, and sometimes even deluded himself into believing that he could save her, perhaps rectify two, if not three, lives gone awry.

However, Ramkrishna knew that Damu was basically a good person and that they complemented and needed each other in many ways. He was at once moved by a strong, instinctive sense of justice, an unutterable love and a friendship that must remain intact at all costs. But what posed the greatest problem was a fear that even if he achieved what he secretly desired, he would become something like his friend, taking Nina for granted, loving her out of habit and nothing more. Although Ramkrishna had strong misgivings about marriages and friendships being made in heaven, he vaguely subscribed to the notion that they were priceless gifts to mankind.

But why such unevenness in these so-called gifts of friendship and love? Why so much fuss over gifts of any kind at all? Why were Nina and Damu, for example, so particular about conventional giving and receiving of gifts while apparently ignoring the greatest gift they had — their having each other in marriage? Such were the questions that at times troubled Ramkrishna. Sometimes he would react in strange ways. But more often he relied on his sense of humour (and his ability to act well) to cope with awkward situations.

One such awkward situation arose last Christmas, for example. In the evening, celebrating Anand's new video set, he approached the convivial barbecue scene with its opulence of sizzling steaks and piquant sauces, and Fiji Bitter flowing freely. For once Ramkrishna was not alone. With him came

Michelle, who was on another of her annual holidays with Ramkrishna, away from the bustle of life in Sydney. They party was in the basement flat of Nina and Damu.

Damu was minding the oversized steaks on the grill next to the tall, creeper-laden earthwall which served as a fence between neighbours. Nina, wearing a fawn and green floral dress, seemed part of the earthwall immediately behind her. Later on, a slight drizzle forced everyone inside. No sooner had Ramkrishna, Michelle and Nina settled in a small triangle on the crowded floor than Nina started that quizzical look which puzzled Michelle. Then the first of Nina's series of questions.

'Okay, Krishna, why did you do it?' Michelle noted the deliberate tone.

'Do what?' asked a puzzled-looking Ramkrishna.

'Oh, come off it! You know very well what I mean. Why did you give the gift that way?'

'Look, Nina, you know I don't give any gifts at Christmas. What on earth is the gift anyway? I don't know what you're talking about.'

Michelle searched Ramkrishna's face for any giveaway signs, but it reflected only a child's earnestness. With one hand pointing towards the top of the stereo cabinet and the other reaching into her dress pocket, Nina fired back, 'That candlestand and this note!'

Someone put on some music. Meanwhile, by the light of the two candles Michelle and Ramkrishna read the hand-written note. With a smile as imperceptible as the multiplying ironies, Michelle read the message once again: 'Nina and Damu, names don't matter; wishing you well does, from one who is occasionally a friend, love.'

'Krishna, your gift is very beautiful and we appreciate it.' Nina's voice trembled. 'But your crazy way of giving it spoils everything'.

'That's not my writing, and you know it,' he retorted simply, but with a strange finality. It was perfectly true.

Michelle scrutinised his face once again: no signs of acting. She understood in her woman's heart how Nina was dying to believe, against all odds, that the culprit was in fact none other than Krishna. Nothing further was said, as Damu grabbed his wife away for a dance.

Soon the music in the candle-lit atmosphere lured everyone. Ramkrishna danced mostly with Michelle and Nina and was happy for a change. Well after midnight and until she fell asleep, Michelle wrestled with a recurring impression of the evening: Damu and Nina dancing awkwardly because he was embracing her rather tightly.

At the late breakfast next day, Michelle asked whether the Indians had an equivalent of Christmas. Ramkrishna suggested Diwali and explained how it celebrated Ram's return from exile.

'Why was he exiled?'

'It was mainly because one of his stepmothers wanted her own son to accede to the throne instead of Ram, the rightful heir. Partly it was because of Ram's wish to obey the mother and do justice. A gift of love and sacrifice, if you like.'

'So that's the Ram you are named after?'

'And Krishna is really a repeat of Ram. Many Hindus believe that Krishna was born to atone for an indiscretion Ram had committed. Of course, you have the love and sacrifice symbolised by Christ: his body broken, his death on the cross, not to forget his resurrection.'

'Yes, Christians regard the resurrection as the greatest gift of love,' said Michelle with a thoughtful smile. 'Isn't it amazing how different religious ideas have reached these remote island?'

'You know, there's a story regarding Krishna. Once he subdued a powerful serpent which had tried to kill him. When it repented, Krishna pardoned it, and, as a favour, placed it in a land without eagles. Some people believe that serpent to be still alive in a mountain in Fiji!'

'How incredible! I suppose that's another gift of love. By the way, Ram, why are you so much against gift-giving?'

'Oh, I hate the fuss, the pretensions, the slavery to conventions. It's only an over-reaction. I am not really against gifts.'

'I know,' said Michelle teasingly. There was a knock on the door.

As Ramkrishna got up to answer the door, Michelle found herself resenting the intrusion. The visitor was apparently in a hurry and would not come in. That suited her fine. But when she heard raised voices she was drawn to the window facing the porch, where, to her amazement, stood Nina and Damu, who slightly obscured her.

With one hand gripping the ill-fated candlestand and the other gesturing angrily, Damu was doing all the talking this time, and loudly too.

'We have checked with all our friends. Like you, every one of them has denied giving it. We thought we'd give you a second chance. Now what do you say?'

'You know it isn't my handwriting,' appealed Ramkrishna softly.

'Did you or did you not give it?'

'No, I did not, if that satisfies you. But why do you have to lose your head over it, Damu?' Ramkrishna said reasonably. 'It can't do you any harm. Besides, it's so beautiful.'

'Look, we don't like someone just creeping in like a thief and leaving a gift under our Christmas tree without as much as signing his name. He must be a coward or a lunatic. We don't like his motives, whatever they are. We don't like such a mean trick. We don't *need* such a gift!'

'Damu, if you don't like it, give it to me. I'll keep it.'

'No, my friend, you won't get it. You didn't give it, did you?' pronounced

Damu viciously. Then, with anger surging beyond control, eyes red, he shouted, 'It's not yours. Neither is it mine!' and smashed the delicately carved thing on the concrete floor. The candlestand split into three ravaged pieces.

Michelle missed a heartbeat. She couldn't see the welling tears in the beautiful eyes of Nina, who had remained as silent as the landscape she was part of. Then Michelle saw Ramkrishna with clenched fists moving towards Damu, and for one mad moment thought of violence. But, to her relief, after a few steps he bent down before his friend only to gather the pieces together. Damu seized Nina's hand, stalked away to the fence gate, and banged it shut as a final gesture. Michelle witnessed a bent figure fenced in, felt Ram's banishment. But as she noticed her friend rise, his face almost a smile, his hands holding the broken pieces, joyous strength seeped through her being.

Back at the breakfast table Michelle continued from where they had left off.

'Why did you give that gift, Ram?'

'What gift?' The defensive instinct was that of a trapped animal.

'Ram,' said Michelle with soft, understanding eyes on the broken pieces in his hands, 'you forget that I wrote that note for you.'

'Oh, sorry, Michelle,' Ram said sheepishly. 'I forget myself at times. Too much acting, I guess. You see, I wanted to give them a gift, but not on their terms.'

'You really love Nina, don't you, Ram?'

'I love both of them,' he said simply. Then with a reminiscent smile, 'You know, originally this had three arms.'

'Really?'

'Yes, and when it was almost finished, there was an accident. It got knocked over onto the floor.'

'And one of the arms broke off?'

'No, not a scratch! It seemed a miracle then,' said Ramkrishna with a sigh. Michelle waited a long moment. 'But I decided to do the right thing for once. I thought it would be much better to do the sacrifice myself — to cut myself out of it — instead of leaving it to chance. In some ways it seemed perverse after so much effort, but I decided to cut off one of the arms finally.'

'So it was a sacrificial gift of love?'

'In a way it was an act of love. But you know, Michelle, a total sacrifice of the self is a pretty difficult thing. Even here, by dying one really wanted to live, by giving, receive and so on.'

'And what about not signing your name? A further act of self-effacement?'

'And don't forget the over-reaction!', and they both burst out laughing.

'What will you do with that?' Michelle asked, her eyes gesturing towards the broken candlestand.

'I will resurrect it,' said Ramkrishna with feigned seriousness.

'A resurrected candlestand!' endorsed Michelle joyfully. Again they laughed. A moment later, she moved over to him, held him tenderly and kissed him softly.

'What's that in honour of?' he asked, pleasantly surprised.

'A gift of love!'

Her innocent smile reminded Ramkrishna of the charm of a 'wave that breaches', a line recalled from a poem he particularly liked.

The Diwali night wears on as Ramkrishna sits in his room and watches the candles burning away. He turns on the radio for some music but instead catches the late-night news bulletin. Some politician is quoted as saying that the land is a gift of God to the Fijian people, and the Fijians will not brook any interference with that gift. He is amused by the timing of such a news item on Diwali night, especially when he himself has been preoccupied with the idea of gifts. He turns off the radio, glancing at the reflection of the virgin bush. He sits back and rests his eyes for a moment on the government calendar. Then, shifting his attention to his resurrected candlestand, he begins to admire the unyielding strength, the invincible hope, present in the light of the almost burnt-out candles.

SERI

Pigeon Park

Tankhead
    hi ya cous
it's me again
red with rum and feeling
like BBC English
(her England the protector of liberty
gave up sovereignty for a lb. of
EEC salami)
arseing when the three bad p's
of prostitution is seasoning
in Wellington Court-ney Place.

The gang came last night
at 12.22ish p.m.
jumping 100 or is it 2 cargo trains
on the crossing from Taumarunui
where our kid brother Dan Hohepapa
was shot
    the police   the weather
was fine . . .
shit! that's clearised stuff
that is/why would I start off these
lines to please literary justice
for games of rubbing snakes behind
large desks make these Pakehas speak
like kings. Git.

I say cous I
wrote cigarette poems
right on this bench — on the
underwear of some ciggies and vomit it
out in Wellington Police Station
then some angry poems lying
in a Mongrel Mob Petone flat
      for cycled house arrests
at least some scrubcutting months later.

It's the same ain't it cous
our uncles chasing after continental pin-ups
in the Great Wars
    and coming home to find
    lands legislatively stolen
and how you and I
wear leather like challenging slogans
on Parliament protesters
    and those in the marae
    beer and gin it away
    dammit.

Sione, God and a Railway Station

Last night I break bread
with tough-luck Sione
who kept on that there's no God
'men', Sione screeched, 'have
been victims of religious jazz
ever since day became flesh
they change quickly like
the weather outside'

Sione bragged that there's
no way, abracadabrally no way
he's going to believe in invisible
hosts — how can one see the
unseen he shot defensively
skyward

I told Sione of my new heart
and which repair shop it came
from, he took it bad, spat
jelly all the way to his homebound
train, spoke of killings . . .
that if the Pope and his wife
ever set foot on Aotearoa
he'd catch them both luxuriant
in bed with opossum trap
'Sione, tarry a jiff mate,'
I called stepping into the windy

Wellington night, 'why can't you tell
God that yourself, say to
Him you don't believe one grit'
—— J.C. heal con
buggers like us, all

Sione felt absolved by a soft
determined voice
ran to take a giant step for
the commuters, stared ahead
his hand tore through his pockets
and felt his innard
went to the mens
sank to his seat obviously shot-comed
through his middle.

From Tiata and Liz

Outside the flat Bob Dylan rained
as we sat heavily by the bed
and finished off the port which
Tiata had tucked away for this
special occasion
of going out into the big
world to show

his status quo tan
being of a high and confident
mind now
his last ebbs of downer
(a six-month seclusion)
gone before
he had popped the cork

Every step he took meant
a kicked can
aborted saturday virtues and
excited talks of great mana
to come

I just listened
as one who was meant to
listen

S U B R A M A N I

Tell Me Where the Train Goes

No. 3 skirted the foothills of Vunika and signalled its arrival with a loud roar. It thundered across the Vulovi bridge, the rumble growing louder and louder, and then groaned and hissed and came to a gradual halt with much collision and clanging of chains and metal. After disengaging the cane trucks, the train chuffed off again to its garage.

Manu waited for the barking of dogs and the familiar splashing of water from a bucket. The barracks precinct was strewn with dog dirt; it would be difficult to avoid though his father carried a lantern.

The paraffin lamp glowed dimly, casting wraith-like shadows which trembled and moved in the corner where Kunti slept. Manu clutched the old army blanket and curled himself inside. The floor was hard on his back. For a long while he listened to the whispers coming from the adjoining room through the wire mesh which was the upper end of the separating wall. Usually, toward midnight, talking died down in the barracks; after that all one heard was a chorus of snoring grunts. Manu felt terribly lonesome and afraid. Twelve o'clock was the hour of the earth-bound spirits (there were whispers of Tevoro in the lines). But more than these, he feared the villainy of men from the barracks.

The nights were fraught with danger. Even in the moonlit night there were threatening whispers in the rustle of coconut fronds and mango branches. Sometimes he experienced a sense of foreboding at noon on a hot day when there wasn't a breath of fresh air and the fields waited for some sort of strange eruption.

A rat chased some geckos across the cooking utensils. Manu felt a sudden chill run through his body; he uttered a hurried prayer, his gaze fixed on the quizzical expression on the countenance of exiled Rama. He was thankful for that picture which Jagannath had torn out of a calendar and pasted on the wall for him.

Almost imperceptibly the room was filled with an oppressive gloom; the oil was spent and the wick had burned itself out. He felt stifled by the mixed odour of kerosene and stale food. There was no ventilation; the only door had to be barricaded every night. He shifted close to the small opening in the wall which brought the draft in: the smell of dog dirt and urine was strong and nauseating. Except for the monotonous hum of mosquitos the night was still.

113

He peered through the crevice. Fear surged in his breast. He held his breath and looked intently: in the dark something sparkled like a firefly. Someone was smoking a bidi cigarette which glowed and receded, glowed and receded. At that moment, Tipo gave a yelp of fright, fled to a safe distance and growled. A whispering argument followed, and then a soft scurry of bare feet in the grass. Manu endeavoured to turn around and face his mother but he dared not move: he was paralysed with fear. His heart pounded frantically; he rallied all his strength and threw off the blanket and whirled around. Kunti was kneeling in a corner, sobbing.

In the morning, his father's body was discovered in the canefield. The women came out of their barracks, huddled together around Kunti and wept. Kunti clenched her teeth and tore her hair, beating her forehead and breaking her jewelry: it was the final display of frenzied emotions. After that, her sensibilities dried up again and she collapsed in a corner. Manu never saw her so emotional again.

In the simmering heat of the noonday, they took his father's body on a bamboo rack and buried him on Kanacagi Hills.

A restless and sickly wind blew across the barracks in the evenings. The land was parched, and many labourers stayed in bed with influenza. Manu watched the bats flitter in the dusk. He startled the flies which thronged the gutter in front of a detached shack where Kunti prepared a meal of rice and dhal and eggplant. She coughed and blew her nose, her eyes hurting in the smoke. Nowadays she seldom spoke. She answered curtly in a muffled voice when spoken to and then subsided in silence. Whenever someone called, she slinked quietly into the barrack. Now, more than ever, he wanted her to be open and confiding; instead she was self-effacing and secretive. He felt sadly unsupported and unclaimed.

After cleaning the dishes, she took the lantern from the kitchen into the barrack, and then barricaded the door. She made her bed quietly and sat despondently in a corner before falling off to sleep. Sometimes it frightened him the way she stared. She would gaze at him, her eyes abstracted, with such terrible intensity that he wanted to run away from her.

Manu pulled the blanket over him and listened to the bats circling the mango trees and swooping from branch to branch, chattering and fighting and gorging on ripe mangoes. He had seen Dhanai, pigmy-sized and misshapen, installed on a log in front of his barrack. Every evening he was there talking to Lakhan and Nekram and sharpening his cutlass. Manu noticed that Nanka no longer sought their company. This was not wholly surprising: here loyalties were transferred like the changing of one's dhoti. And new allegiances were made without much remorse.

What these men discussed he didn't know, but he was certain because of their sinister attention that in some horrible and insidious way they intended bringing harm upon him and Kunti. That evening, seeing him at the kitchen door, Dhanai grinned roguishly, baring his yellow fangs, and beckoned. Manu winced. Meanwhile, Lakhan was scrutinising him with his head tilted and his eyes screwed on him. Both these men inspired fear and revulsion. He was particularly frightened when Dhanai hopped about the barracks with the stump of his leg concealed under his dhoti.

There was a piercing cry from the adjoining room followed by wild exchanges of profanity and loud sobbing. Lakhan was beating his wife again. Ambika sulked and cursed her fortune and gradually worked herself into a frenzy. 'It's the engine driver's wife you want. Go to her then. She eat you like she eat her husband,' she shrieked. Lakhan's large and powerful hand came heavily upon her back and Ambika's sobs dried up into snivelling hiccups.

How Manu wanted to escape this nightmarish world where life seemed continually menaced! He hated the sugarcane (Jagannath said it was Karkotaka, one of the main serpents of the underworld) and grieved for the youths who were prematurely shunted into the fields together with the ragged labourers. His refuge was the cave. When the barracks were empty, he would saunter through thickets and reeds to the cave with Tipo leading the way. The dog would give a shrill yelp and rush into the guava shrubs, wagging his tail and forking his tongue in and out of his mouth. It was in this jungle he encountered the Fijian coconut seller whose leg was swollen with elephantiasis. He emerged quietly from the bushes, pursed his lips and ejaculated a loud explosive noise. Manu almost panicked. Later they laughed together.

The cave was on the other side of Kanacagi Hills. Jagannath discovered it when they were collecting firewood. 'It is Kailas,' his father said, 'the home of Shiva.' It was bowed and lined like the head of a gigantic cobra in repose. Once he dreamed that its mouth closed and he was sucked through a dark tunnel into a pool which glowed golden and orange in the sunset. He was afraid when he returned the following day, but it was safer here than in the barracks. Besides, he had Tipo. Here he rested, slept and allowed his untutored but precocious mind to wander. He surrendered himself to images and echoes, hoping they would fall into a pattern.

Sometimes, after a night of turbulent wind and rain, he would walk along the gullies where the grass had been twisted and combed by the overflowing water. From the cave he would follow the drift of fleecy clouds on the wet hills and wonder where the train went. He longed to find out if the 'mulk' that his father discussed with his friends was anywhere near the country where Mr Pepper's memsahib had gone with her children. Inevitably he would reflect upon the secret his father told him about Yama, his half-brother.

If life was restful and orderly in the cave, in the lines it was forever anarchic. During the week, tempers frayed and quarrels broke out. Whether in the fields or in the barracks, the labourers' passions seemed totally unchecked by any instinct for self-preservation. On Sunday they were calmer. One by one they emerged from their hovels clad in their dhotis and squatted on their haunches in the hot sun. Kasiram tinkered with his harmonium for the most part of the morning and when everyone had lost interest he sang his favourite bhajan. Others smoked bidi cigarettes and chattered while Ramsamujh, the barber, made his rounds with a small tin suitcase, the scowl on his face becoming graver and graver as he moved from one head to another.

These were the refugees from a depressed subcontinent, gnarled and weatherbeaten, and brutalised by ghetto life. Some had accepted their half-slave status, and a few seemed either bored or secretly dreaming of self-annihilation. There were others like Dhanai who were filled with destructive rage.

Almost unexpectedly, the uneasy stillness was ended when Kunti, her face veiled by her orhini, shuffled to the water pipe with her bucket. Nekram nudged Dhanai, and Dhanai's small rheumy eyes shot up in flames. Manu had observed that whenever Kunti passed there were catcalls from Nekram and Khelawan, and the women wrinkled up their noses insolently or gave disdainful sidelong glances. Ambika was already at the pipe and a quarrel ensued. Although Ambika was as ugly as she was sullen and no one really cared for her company, least of all Lakhan, the other women came out on her side, and Sukhdaiyya and Padma actively aligned themselves with her. Ambika heaved incestuous abuse on Kunti. Kunti at first made shrill bursts of protest and then, to mitigate the humiliation, became loud and assertive. The men intervened when Sukhdaiyya grabbed Kunti's hair and threatened to put the chamarin's tail on fire by thrusting red chillies up her rectum.

At the end of these meanderings Manu felt hopelessly violated and betrayed.

The dogs began to bark again under the mango trees.

Kunti was already up, her eyes fixed on Jagannath's cane knife.

For weeks they slept in snatches and woke up when the roosters began crowing. One morning Kunti found a ball of feathers — a dead myna — at the door. Another time it was Tipo. There was a deep wound gouged on his back; it opened like an ugly and festering mouth.

The garandilla bushes were filled with the warm fragrance of ripe fruits and garandilla flowers. Lacking his friend's energy and feel for adventure (Kalika had evaded the fields for two consecutive days), Manu rested under the canopy of a raintree overgrown with lianas and luxuriant garandilla vines while Kalika scampered, his curiosity flickering, from bush to bush collecting and discarding ripe fruits.

This was the closest Manu had come to the bungalow. From here the swooping curves of Kanacagi Hills, the sugarcane which resembled a series of playing fields and the breathtaking green of the golf course provided an incredible vista. The lines were twenty-odd rusty corrugated iron and timber hutments, a physical and spiritual ghetto, huddled together at the bottom of the hills.

Manu followed the way Kalika had entered the bushes. He was nowhere to be found. He searched through creepers and clumps of elephant grass and, before he realised it, he was halfway into the summer house. The light here was made green by the lush growth of coral vines which clambered the bamboo walls, and tree ferns and wax vine growing in earthen pots. The lawn was freshly cut and trimmed. It was cluttered with frangipani and acadia trees which shaded plots of anthurium lilies and ornamental begonias. The damp smell of earth and grass and the intoxicating odour of frangipani lingered everywhere.

Everything about the bungalow was large: a massive hall and an enormous verandah decked with giant wicker chairs. In the kitchen the furniture and the pots and pans and the cutlery looked as if they had never been used. It was hard to believe, looking through the wire gauze in the windows which revealed rooms, one as spacious as the other, that these housed real people.

The entire bungalow was wrapped in a heavy brooding silence. At the end room, which faced a gravel path shaded by a giant fig tree, he stopped almost instinctively and prostrated himself on the flower bed. His heart pounding against his ribs, he summoned what little courage he possessed and crept close to the window. There was someone inside in his underwear sprawled on a unmade bed. It was the Sahib. He had a cigarette perched on his lower lip from which he took occasional puffs while he gazed emptily at the wooden ceiling. Without his khaki tunic and topee, his sunburned body looked small and vulnerable. It was certainly not the Sahib who ran his truck over Dhanai's leg when the latter was resting in a mill garage after lunch. Manu recalled with awe how the labourers cringed and stood in disarray, like frightened myna birds, when Mr Pepper visited the barracks.

Manu was startled by a soft rustle of skirt behind him: a figure was moving through the hibiscus hedge, and then disappeared down the hill. He forced himself from the ground and followed her through the hidden pathway. He recognized her from the back: it was Kunti. Why wasn't she in the fields? What was she doing at the bungalow? He caught up with her at the pond. He hid behind some guava shrubs and watched. She loosened the knot of her long skirt and it fell on the ground around her. She stepped lithely over the tiny heap. Her hands moved to her small bodice. Naked, she looked taller than most women in the lines. She had a well-proportioned figure, and Manu noticed how attractive her face was in spite of the mournful expression. In those parts of her body where the sun hadn't touched she was golden brown; the rest was heavily tanned. She freed the braid of black silky hair; it fell loosely down to her thighs.

Manu felt a mingling of curiosity, excitement and guilt. He was entranced although he wanted to run away and hide himself with shame. He remembered his experience with Jumman's son when the latter tricked him into his barrack and exposed himself. There was a gentle tug in his own groin when Razak touched the ball of flesh nestled amid a tangle of hair. It had moved and become alive. He envied Razak's manhood and was ashamed of his small and shrunken body, and of pubes as bald as his skull which Ramsamujh had shaved after funeral.

Kunti waded into the deeper end of the pond where strands of moss spread like clumps of hair, and the water was littered with brown and yellow guava leaves and petals of bush flower. Kunti took a deep breath and disappeared under the water. When she emerged from the pond, Manu had gone.

Throughout the week there was a brooding smouldering rage in the canefields, the barracks and even in the movement of trucks and engines. Early Thursday morning Jumman came running breathlessly to the lines to fetch Murgan, the sirdar. There was trouble at the weighbridge. Manu heard the report with morbid foreboding.

The dancers arrived on Saturday. In the evening, he saw Dhanai and Lakhan talking to the dancers. The dancers shuffled and turned on the red earth. They held their long skirts and glided, waving the silken scarves they carried in their hands. Now and then one of them would gyrate his groin provocatively and make little circles in front of the women. This brought roars of delight from the men, and the women pulled their orhinis over their faces to conceal their enjoyment. The drums thumped louder and the clink of anklets became more persistent. The faces of the dancers gleamed in the light of the Coleman lamp. Someone from the spectators glided into the centre and wriggled his hip amid wild cheering. The crowd clapped and swayed and shouted, 'Wah wa! Wah wa!'

Dhanai and Lakhan were no longer in the crowd. Manu was alarmed by their furtive manoeuvres. He searched for Kunti among the women. Sukdaiyya was rebuking Padma for displaying her pleasure too overtly. Manu asked Somari: Kunti wasn't there. He hurried back to the barracks. The barracks were empty; there wasn't a soul around. He followed the path leading to the pond. Someone was urinating under a mango tree. Further on, a band of men were clambering up the hill. With their lathis and cutlasses they could have been mistaken for a bunch of thugs. One of them carried a lantern which lighted their black, shiny legs. They were scurrying toward the bungalow. When they reached the garandilla vines they halted and crouched on the ground. Only Lakhan climbed to the bungalow.

Manu wiped the sweat on his forehead with his shirt-tail, caught his breath and waited. He could hear the full thump-thump of the drums, which was now indistinguishable from the beating of his own heart. Minutes later Lakhan returned, followed by a figure in white. The men moved closer. Only the one holding the lantern remained under the bush. The Sahib had barely reached the hibiscus hedge when they descended on him like a swarm of locusts. He uttered a loud agonised shriek, tried to retreat, but stumbled and fell on the ground. 'The motherfucker is drunk,' someone cried, and kicked him in the stomach.

Manu gaped at this ritual of death and dissolution with muted panic. For the first time he noticed that the men were completely naked. Soon they were joined by a group of women who emerged from the bushes. They lifted their clothes and took their turns urinating on the wriggling figure who was pinned roughly on the ground by several pairs of rugged hands. A feeling of nausea was welling up: for a second, Manu thought he was going to be sick.

He struggled through thickets and elephant grass and threw himself headlong down the slope. In his mind he could see the men scramble to the pond to wash themselves. Then they would come for Kunti. He continued running, gasping for breath and throwing sidelong glances. He must find Murgan at the weighbridge. He came to a panting halt at the bottom of the hill, but was spurred on by the thought that he was being followed. When he reached the mill precincts he was thoroughly bruised and scratched.

Manu heard No. 3 rumble over the bridge. He ran along the railway track leaping from plank to plank. He was reassured by the smell of molasses and coal, by the mill lights and the crushers which moved furiously. No. 3 drew closer and closer. He could see the firebox glow and throw sparks through the funnel like an angry monster. The train disappeared behind rows of cane trucks. He must race past No. 3 and cross the tramline. If he waited it would be too late. He made a move, crossed the first track, and then faltered and tripped. Next instant he received a violent jolt and was thrown over the tramline into a heap of charcoal.

'We'll go away,' Kunti was saying. He could barely hear her. All night he drifted into waves of oblivion. Now the throbbing ache in the back of his head was becoming an agony. Afraid that he would sink again, he forced himself to create patterns in the ceiling, which was stained and splotched with smoke and dust. 'We'll ask for land and go,' she reiterated. This time he turned his face toward her. He knew she was lying. There was nowhere to go. They were simply shipwrecked in the barracks. Nevertheless, there was a dim consoling hope in her voice. He noted that the old anguish had vanished from her face as if something had snapped free. She squatted beside him, her hand caressing his forehead. It seemed to him for a moment that once again her life was entirely for his preservation.

He felt strangely exhilarated and safe.

JOSEPH C. VERAMO

Onisimo

Onisimo Viti closed his eyes; the music was too loud and the bar smelt too strongly of stale beer, which penetrated his nostrils and clogged his head, making him feel miserable. A mixture of deep voices, many slurred, congested the atmosphere. The bar was too crowded with the many labourers attired in faded shirts and khaki trousers. Onisimo Viti craved to consume beer to his heart's content. The previous night, Onisimo Viti had gone to Lucky Eddies, a nightclub he often frequented. The lass he had met there said that she didn't mind being with him. She said she knew he was old enough to be her father, but she didn't mind. Trust these lasses with their painted faces to be so tactical. She was too young and looked somewhat stupid and artificial in her make-up; her purple eye shadow, red blushes on her lean cheeks and her dark red lipstick made her look awful. The lass liked him and had been willing.

Onisimo hated the tall burly woman with rings around her eyes who came back to her flat in the early hours of the morning. She had two pugnacious brats, whom he pitied because their mother was a whore, but what could he do? Next to his flat was the Kasalu family who were forever begging for sugar, tea and other items from him. And couldn't those young people in the flat adjacent to his turn down the volume of their stereo? They were forever blasting up those awful songs, 'Sisili Mai Wainadoi' and 'Au Luveni Yali' which Onisimo hated on account of their being too sentimental. He was filled with revulsion for everything that occurred in the Block. But what could he do? The Housing Authority gave houses to whoever was in dire need and who could pay the meagre rent, irrespective of any of their traits, however eccentric. Onisimo wished he was not a primary school teacher. That was where the trouble had started. His darling ambition had been to be a lawyer, but fate had not been kind to him. He had wanted to go back to the university to get a degree in education. But at forty-four he had felt too old, with his energies leached from his body. He loathed his nagging wife who was forever complaining that she didn't have a new dress or that her fridge was getting old and couldn't he buy more furniture from Courts through hire-purchase. His mind had become so clogged up with her insatiable demands. It had compressed and stifled his thinking so that he felt imprisoned. Even his cronies in the school staffroom dubbed him a 'henpecked' husband who might as well be 'washing sulus and cooking'.

The only consolation he had was in teaching basic science to class six, seven and eight students. He felt a sense of usefulness, and the pupils respected him. It seemed to Onisimo that they held him in such high esteem as one who was omnipotent. The pupils loved him, like children loving their fathers. It pleased Onisimo Viti. But that was where Onisimo's trouble had started. The teachers had been making pointed remarks about how much time he devoted to his pupils during recess and lunch-hours on the pretext that he was helping them out with their weak points. Mr Vagabace, who disliked Onisimo (Onisimo was always at loggerheads with him during staff meetings), said that Onisimo could be in for trouble with some of the more precocious female students who grew like paragrass on a cleared farm. These pupils were easily encouraged by instincts that goaded them to satisfy their faculties for physical expression.

Onisimo Viti became obsessed with youth. It delighted him to reminisce over his youthful years when he had been so happy and carefree and had loved life. His pupils fired his imagination with his youthful longings, for their limbs were sprightly and charged with an inclination for vigorous sports and activities. Still in their early adolescence, they became strangely aware of their schoolmates of the opposite sexes. The boys would take great pains over their facial features and the girls would sometimes blush if boys smiled at them. But though there existed this liking for each other it remained closeted as if the expression of one's desire for another could not as yet take shape. Onisimo Viti observed all this and saw in youthfulness the beauty of life. But there was nothing he could do. He was old, lean, with an ugly protruding belly, the result of consuming too much beer. Onisimo knew that there was a barrier between him and his charges. He had longed to penetrate it. That had caused the trouble. He remembered when Akanisi had fainted in the classroom on a hot August day while he had been busy explaining a diagram. Onisimo had carried Akanisi to the staffroom and he had felt a strange feeling of elation. His conscience, so clogged up with his domestic worries, seemed to have its burden lifted. He felt intrigued by his awesome ability to identify with a sprightly youth. But all this was momentary, for as soon as he placed the lass on a couch he felt what he really was, old, lean and leached of energy. Staring at the sleeping lass, with her breathing soft and tender to the ears, it frightened him. For a long moment he stared at the child, using a folded newspaper to fan her, and gradually, deep inside his heart and inside his conscience, he felt an awesome burning sensation. It pained him. He breathed hard. He sat back on the chair cradling his head. Deep inside his head, he was weeping; weeping for all those futile years when they could have had children. She had always made excuses about their lack of finance (rearing children was agony and a burden without enough money), but as the years elapsed she became cynical about families. 'Look at the Kasalus or the Meredanis with their battalion of children. They are always in trouble. I'm not surprised if their children become delinquents.' She was too critical of others. Onisimo dared not protest. She had found a way to keep him quiet. 'A woman must decide, because it is she who will carry the burden.' But as the years raced by, she became more obese and no longer cared about her figure. Her tongue increased in causticity.

The previous night he hardly slept at all. The tall burly whore came back in the early hours of the morning screaming obscenities.

Onisimo Viti sipped his glass of beer. The bar was too noisy. It stank. But it gave him some comfort. If only he didn't have an ulcerated stomach he could make a fresh start, redeem himself and his fast ebbing spirit. That was the problem of being a failure, a lowly paid primary school teacher with an obese wife who possessed a caustic tongue. Dr Maciu had warned him, but he had ceased to care.

Onisimo Viti felt his heart burning as if eroded gradually but surely of its energies. His desire for existence was fast declining. Somehow, death seemed to enlighten his depressed imagination, sparking some optimism inside him. It seemed to him that in death he could find a chance to discover truth. It gave him a gratifying feeling. Onisimo Viti sipped his icy cold glass of beer feeling the awesome pain within his body. Then he slumped back in his chair and he became oblivious to the noisy stinking bar with its fair share of disillusioned men.

KIRIBATI

Vianney Kianteata Teabo

Abatekan

On an island called Abataningo, life was not so good for the islanders because the lands were overcrowded with people, animals and man-made things.

Its resources included coconut trees, pandanus, breadfruit and babai on the land, with fish in the sea.

In the old days there was only one tribe who were king of all the island. But as time passed, with the coupling and marriage between members of the tribe, it increased to five and yet more tribes.

After fifty years, the islanders were too many for their land resources and each family began to have problems cultivating the land and feeding themselves.

One of the tribes, known as Kaubai, had six nuclear families, but there were only five pieces of land for the tribe to share among themselves. The head of the tribe, when he was very ill, called all of his six sons to share the heritage, as was the tradition of Abataningo.

The five elder sons were given one patch of land each. When the sixth son, Kekeiaki, sat beside his father's bao, his dying father said this to him: 'My son, I have no other land to dedicate to you.' The father's eyes were full of tears, and Kekeiaki tried to hide his disappointment behind sadness for his dying father. 'My son, your elder brothers have got one piece of land each, but I can only give you an islet called Abatekan which is not very far from here. The island has only foliage and one big lake in the middle. Nobody has ever lived there because the soil is barren, there are no edible fruits and the water is salty. There are some secrets about Abatekan, only nobody has ever dared to explore the island. Go there my son and take care of the baby that your wife will bear. If it's a boy, name him Tebotu. Leave me, son. Be humble, and good luck.'

Kekeiaki cried 'Thank you' over the dying man and made his way out of the hut, feeling ashamed at his lack of a share in the family's heritage. What was he going to tell his pregnant wife?

On reaching the house he heard a baby crying. He ran into the house and saw his wife Baeao holding a baby in her arms. Smilingly she said, 'It's a boy!'

'Just as I hoped,' Kekeiaki shouted happily, but suddenly something changed his happiness into disappointment. There were tears in his eyes, and he hurried away.

'What's happened? Aren't you happy about having a son?' asked Baeao.

'It's not that, my love', Kekeiaki's voice shook. 'It's something else that I am too ashamed to tell you about.'

'Well, whatever it is, you've got to tell me,' his wife said. 'If it's your problem, it's mine also, isn't it? Please tell me and don't be ashamed. Remember, I wasn't ashamed when I told you that . . .'

'Stop it!'

Kekeiaki now remembered his father's final advice to be humble in heart. He walked to his wife and sat close to her, looking over the baby who was now asleep on Baeao's lap.

'Please tell me what makes you so sad,' she insisted.

'Okay, I've just come back from my dying father,' he paused, 'where I found out, to my embarrassment, that all the lands my father owned were given to my elder brothers, and none was left for me, only that islet,' he pointed to the west, 'which is without water, food or shelter.'

'That is good,' replied Baeao. 'At least we have somewhere to live. You are a man, I am a woman. We have both been brought up by our families' sweat. We could work the land, and plant germinating coconuts, breadfruit and pandanus.'

'But what about the baby, and the journey, and life on that remote islet? We could never enjoy our life out there,' Kekeiaki said.

But, as women often did, Baeao quickly calmed down her husband with sweet talk and encouragement. She explained how easy things can be if a couple have the will to work, determination and love to share between them.

Kekeiaki kept silent for a few minutes and finally nodded his head in agreement. He was now willing to live on Abatekan, and to explore its secrets.

'All right, we'll set out in a week's time. But first we've got to be able to take with us coconuts, breadfruit plants, pandanus . . .'

'And also kabubu, tuae, bero and kamaimai', added Baeao.

They laughed happily, forgetting the baby, whose sleep was interrupted. The baby on Baeao's lap cried with irritation, and this reminded Kekeiaki of the old man's wish for the baby. He took the baby in his hands, and whispered caressingly in its ear. 'Do not be disturbed, little boy. From now on your name is Tebotu. I could think of other fancy names for you as you are our prime treasure, but the will of your grandpa shall be done.'

'So his name is Tebotu,' said Baeao. 'I think it suits him.'

'What do you think about his future on that lifeless islet?' Kekeiaki asked.

'Well,' Baeao replied, 'to me, his future looks as bright as ours — as long as we work together to make Abatekan a resourceful and productive home.'

'For that island to be productive will take three years or more,' Kekeiaki put in, 'and for plants to bear fruit and nuts, even longer.'

But Baeao was still hopeful.

It was Sunday dawning. The baby cried loudly, awakening his father and mother, who had forgotten that the week had ended.

'Kekeiaki, Kekeiaki, wake up! It's Sunday, wake up,' the cry seemed to say.

Kekeiaki got up and went quickly out of the hut. He packed everything up and dragged it on his shoulder towards the sea.

Baeao took the baby in her arms and made her way out of the hut, following her husband. They both moved without making any noise. They did not want neighbours to know about their departure.

The canoe was ready, so they loaded everything and got ready to set out. On board the canoe were germinating fruits, bananas, breadfruit and pandanus, together with traditional long-lasting foods — bero, kabubu, tuae and kamaimai.

Kekeiaki and Baeao speculated that their food supply was just about enough for one year if they limited their eating. About the future, when their food would run out, they did not think. They left everything about the future to Time, God and Nature itself.

The sail was set and the canoe made its way through silent seas toward Abatekan, which stood in the distance.

Kekeiaki and Baeao, with their one-week-old baby, did not talk too much on the way. They both wondered if their happy memories of their old home on the main island would soon fade away. But they faced the future with patience, hope and determination. The baby, with his hands and feet curled up because of the cold of the trade winds and the dawn, clung to his mother's warm body.

Back on the mainland, people rose early as usual and went out collecting coconuts, but because it was the Sabbath day, they did only easy morning tasks. Part of the tradition of Abataningo was that there was a feast held in the maneaba after mass and prayers. Kekeiaki and Baeao attended mass and the feast regularly. Their absence that morning would surely give away their secret.

The couple reached Abatekan in the semi-darkness of early morning. Kekeiaki helped his wife carry Tebotu to the shore, then off-loaded everything onto the sandbank. When the canoe was cleared of their supplies, they dragged it ashore. The day was fine and the sun was now rising in the east. Kekeiaki explored the island.

Abatekan had salt bush, less than ten fruitless coconut trees, wedelia biflora trees covered with birds' nests, and a lake right in the middle. Kekeiaki studied the lake for some time. 'Is the lake fresh water or salty?' he thought. Finally, he decided to taste it. To his astonishment the water was not salty. He walked round the lake, tasting every part of it. There was something special about the lake. It seemed to have been divided into parts — the first division tasted partly salty, the second tasted like pure drinkable water and the third tasted salty.

'So this is the mysterious thing about the island,' Kekeiaki said to himself, and then he thought, 'We can have water from the lake and we can have salt.'

He was still looking down on the lake when he saw bubbles coming up from the water.

'There could be some living creatures down there,' he told himself.

Without thinking, he dived into the lake. Down, down, down he went, into a seemingly bottomless hole.

He kept going down, but he saw no sign of anything, except the bubbling that came up from the bottom.

He thought he heard his father talking to him: 'If you want to find something, don't give up.' So he kept on.

At last, he touched something solid and muddy. He picked the thing up, but because the water was muddy, he could not make out what it was. He knew that, whatever it was, it was down there in abundance.

Kekeiaki made his way to the surface of the lake and took a deep breath. He opened his eyes and found that he was holding babai in his arms.

'Oh what a mystery!' he shouted, and threw the babai corn to the bank. 'Now we can have fresh food from the lake.'

He was still contemplating the wonders of the lake when he saw something moving underwater. He waded through the water to the whirling objects. He went close and, to his amazement, found a huge school of milkfish. The fish were so close to him that he could touch them.

Kekeiaki could not begin to express his pleasure at what he had found in the lake. He called his discoveries 'miracles'. He ran back to where he had left his wife and son.

Tebotu's cry directed him, but on reaching the baby, he discovered that Baeao was not there.

'Now where's your mummy, boy?' he asked Tebotu.

'Baeao, Baeao-o,' he called out at the top of his voice.

'I'm here, Kekeiaki. Come over here,' was the faint answer from the other side of the islet.

Kekeiaki picked up the boy and made his way to where the voice came from.

'Well,' he started when he saw Baeao sitting with her face down to the sea, 'what are you doing there, dear, leaving the baby alone to cry?'

'Come and see,' she beckoned, 'there are fishes, red fishes in great number in this hole.'

'So you've also made a discovery?' he replied, and went to examine the hole.

There was something suspicious about the fishes and the hole itself. The hole seemed like a tunnel that led under the islet.

'Now I understand,' Kekeiaki nodded, 'this hole is a tunnel that ends up in the lake in the middle of the islet. Let's go back now and build our shelter.'

On the way Baeao still talked about the hole — 'Does it mean that sea-water makes the lake salty, darling?'

'Yes, but not all parts of the lake,' he replied. 'The lake itself is a secret that my old man told me about.'

They kept silent until they reached a spot that Kekeiaki thought was a suitable place to make a home.

Kekeiaki chopped wood and collected coconut leaves and built a small hut just big enough for the three of them. Baeao, after feeding the baby, laid the mats under the hut, comforted the baby to sleep and left him lying there.

It was about midday on Sunday, and Baeao decided to cook some food for their dinner and supper. She produced bero biscuits from one of their bags and cooked them in a pot. Then she took out three salt fish from a sack and fried them in a pan.

Kekeiaki built another hut for storing their supplies, and later dug holes in rows for planting their germinated nuts, pandanus and breadfruit. It was hard work, but he did not want his plants to die, and he had to do everything in one day, even though it was the Sabbath.

It had been said on the main island that Abatekan was a lifeless islet, with barren soil and bushes and a salty lake in the middle. Kekeiaki laughed at this now, as he came to realise that Abatekan was in fact a paradise.

'We have fish both in the sea and on land, we have babai, and most important of all, water, and after three years these plants will bear fruit and nuts. We have everything we need,' he shouted inwardly.

He laughed when he remembered how sad he had been when the old man had given him Abatekan.

For hours he thought about their bright future on Abatekan and about their fortunate discoveries.

But his thoughts vanished when he smelt the odour coming from Baeao's frying pan. He realised that he had not eaten since that morning. He turned back and followed the smell.

'What do we eat tonight, dear?' he asked.

'Oh, you're back,' Baeao answered in her soft voice. 'There is bero, and fried fish and boiled toddy. It is nearly cooked.'

'Tomorrow, we'll have some fresh food,' he boasted.

'What do you mean?' Baeao was suspicious about this. 'Where are we going to get fresh food from?'

'From the lake, of course.' He told her everything that he found when he explored the lake.

'Oh, how unbelievable,' Baeao exclaimed in wonder and pleasure.

'What is unbelievable,' Kekeiaki laughed and pointed to the cooking pan, 'that?'

Baeao looked down and saw that the fish was overcooked. She looked up at her husband and they both laughed, pointing the blame at each other. Tebotu, who had been sleeping, heard the noise and woke up crying. They both stopped laughing and Baeao took the baby in her arms whilst Kekeiaki lit the oil lamp, as it was getting dark.

In spite of the fish being overcooked, they both ate their supper eagerly.

After supper they went with Tebotu to bathe in the lake and then slept their first night on Abatekan. The night was glorious, with the sounds of the trade winds, the waves, and the songs of the birds slurring the tired persons soundly to sleep on the isolated, lonely but resourceful land.

In the morning, Kekeiaki woke up before the others and went out to chop down te buka trees to build a maneaba type of house for Tebotu. The birds were alarmed when their habitat was disturbed, and they soon filled the air with their cursing cries. Kekeiaki regretted what he was doing, but on the other hand, he needed those big trunks for the pillars of the maneaba, and branches for the frames.

'The birds won't mind what I'm doing since they have other trees to build their nests in,' he argued to himself. When the te buka trees fell, he cut off the branches and took all that he needed for the building.

Back in the hut, the sound of crashing made by the felled trees was enough to wake Baeao. She opened her eyes, wondering about the thrashing sound that she had heard just a while ago. Then she head the chopping, and guessed what it was. She felt ashamed of her laziness — it was not the right kind of behaviour for a woman. She knew that on the mainland the first to wake were the women, who prepared breakfast before their husbands set out for their morning tasks. Anyway, she argued, this was not her fault. Kekeiaki had woken up before the coldness of the night had left the land. There were still some stars visible in the sky.

Baeao crawled out of the hut, leaving Tebotu sleeping, and cooked food and boiled water. Kekeiaki, from the other side of the islet, noticed the fire and laughed proudly. When he finished chopping the wood, he piled up the sticks according to size and started clearing the site for building. He planned to build a bigger maneaba than on the mainland even though he knew that the bigger the building, the more the work that needed to be done. He had nearly finished clearing the bushes off the site when he heard his wife calling.

There was something in the call that made Kekeiaki forget his axe and run quickly to Baeao. She was standing and pointing to something near the lake.

'What is it?' he shouted.

'That thing there,' she began, 'it looks like . . . er . . . I can't believe it.'

Kekeiaki now knew what Baeao was trying to show him. 'But I believe it,' he shouted back, 'it's babai, isn't it? Babai in great numbers underwater.' He pointed down to the lake.

'And you're sure about that?' she asked.

'Of course I am. I discovered it myself yesterday. That's why I told you last night that we would be eating something fresh today.'

'Yes, but . . .'

She was still a bit overwhelmed, but Kekeiaki interrupted, 'Let's have breakfast now.' He laughed and led the way back to the house.

Baeao picked up the babai and followed, still in wonder at the discovery. On reaching the hut, she woke the baby up, while Kekeiaki fetched water for the baby's morning bath.

During breakfast, Baeao asked her husband to tell her about the lake, so Kekeiaki told her again everything he discovered the day before. He told her about babai, the salty and freshwater parts of the lake, including mention of the milkfish.

'So we have everything we need here. But why did you have to cut down those big trees?' she asked.

He explained, 'I shall not rest until we are well settled. I'm going to build a maneaba for Tebotu. But,' he added, 'only if you give me a hand, then the building may be completed within a month.'

Baeao, on hearing her husband talking about the maneaba, nearly choked. She knew the job was a tough one and that it needed up to twenty couples to build a maneaba in one month. But knowing their situation, she nodded in agreement.

'Both hands on the job — everything is easy,' she said.

After breakfast, Kekeiaki left Baeao and the baby to finish off his work in the bush. The sun was now shining on the land. He worked with determination and so did Baeao, who went to help her husband after finishing her cooking. After a few hours, the clearing of the site for the building was finished and they were now ready to start work on the maneaba's foundation.

Kekeiaki took a roll of string and marked out the shape of a rectangle on the ground. The maneaba measured thirty feet in length, and fifteen feet in width. Kekeiaki then dug four holes at each corner and fitted posts into them. He and Baeao both did the work as thoughtfully as possible. Kekeiaki knew how to build any kind of living-house — a dining-house or a store-house, but not a big public house like a maneaba.

He had no one to seek advice from, so he had to experiment in building the maneaba. He saw it in his mind's eye, while he and his wife worked tirelessly under the hot sun, with Tebotu crying among the grass. He felt pessimistic about their future. On the other hand, he saw pictures of his wife cooking all types of foods and serving them to a crowd of people in the maneaba. He saw Tebotu sitting beside a beautiful girl in the crowd. These thoughts gave him a strong urge to finish the building.

Baeao, in spite of her double burden with the baby and the housework, also concentrated most of her leisure moments making strings for the maneaba. And day by day, the maneaba gradually took shape.

Within a month, the building was completed. The only minor work to be done was the roof thatching.

Kekeiaki did not want to take rest, as he found if he did so he lost his determination to work, so he started collecting coconut leaves. Baeao taught her husband how to weave the thatch and they both wove thatch pieces at the rate of fifteen a day.

If Abatekan had had more coconut trees, they would not have kept running out of leaves, and the thatching would have been faster. It took them another four months to thatch the maneaba.

When it was finally completed, they were both proud of their work and decided to celebrate their achievement.

'Well, thanks to be to the one God of our Ancestors for the strength that he put into us,' Kekeiaki whispered in a prayer of thanksgiving. 'On this coming Sunday,' he told his wife, 'we shall have our prayer inside the maneaba.'

'And I will cook the foods from the lake to celebrate our settlement on Abatekan,' Baeao added.

So on Saturday, Kekeiaki got babai and two milkfish from the lake, so that everything would be ready for the feast. The following day they woke early to prepare for the feast. They said their Sunday prayers inside the maneaba, but the way Kekeiaki led the prayer made Baeao laugh, so they both laughed as they prayed. After their prayer, Baeao served the food and, as part of the custom, they held their plates up and shouted the words, 'Te mauri, te raoi ao te tabomoa'. Then they ate their meal and Baeao took out a garland of flowers and put it on Tebotu's head as a sign of dedicating the maneaba to their only son.

Tebotu was now six months old, and fit and well. Fortunately, he had never become sick. After their meal, Kekeiaki took the baby and hugged him to sleep on his chest. Because it was the Sabbath day, and everything they needed was within reach, and of course because they had no other people to socialise with, they spent the whole afternoon sleeping inside the new maneaba.

When they woke up, Kekeiaki went out with the baby for a walk around the island. They went to the hole, then to the lake and lastly to the plantations. 'These are all yours, baby,' he whispered to Tebotu. The plants were growing fast and Kekeiaki noticed that the bananas had borne fruit, and the breadfruit trees were tall enough to bear fruit within a few weeks, as were the pandanus trees. His mind looked forward to the future when the trees and plants would yield fruits and nuts. 'If only the coconut trees would bear nuts,' he said to himself, 'then we could start producing copra and get money from the traders.'

It was a long time after their settlement. Tebotu was eighteen years old, old enough to cut toddy, and he took over the job from his father. Kekeiaki was forty-five years old and Baeao was thirty-seven, but they were still strong enough to do their home tasks. Kekeiaki had built a big canoe for their copra, and had salted fish to sell on the mainland with Tebotu.

People on the mainland, the island of Abataningo, were very surprised to see Kekeiaki and Tebotu bringing foods from Abatekan, an islet long believed to be lifeless. Kekeiaki's brothers were amazed that their youngest brother seemed to be richer than them. They kept themselves away from Kekeiaki, because jealousy was beginning to haunt them.

Kekeiaki used the money obtained from his copra and salt fish to buy pots, cups, other utensils and more bags for copra.

One thing that he noticed on Abataningo was that the people were relying on imported materials, including food. The people became too lazy to work their lands, and on many occasion families did not have enough to eat. He thought how poor life was on Abataningo and how fortunate they were on Abatekan. The large storehouse near the maneaba was full of kamaimai in bottles, salt fish, kabwibwi and bero from breadfruit, tuae from pandanus, and green and yellow bananas.

Kekeiaki thought of helping his elder brothers on the mainland but they never talked to him when he passed their houses. He and his son made a trip to the mainland three times a week to sell their produce. Their successive trips created a change in mood in Tebotu. One day, when Kekeiaki was busy selling his salt fish and bananas and weighing copra, Tebotu decided to take a walk around the village. On his way he heard somebody singing the song that Baeao always sang back on Abatekan — 'I tei n taraa kaaboon te nang . . .'. It was a female voice and he was curious when he saw the young woman, younger than himself, singing while fetching water from the well.

The girl was singing and Tebotu whistled, following the tune. The girl stopped singing abruptly. Tebotu was still whistling, looking at the birds in the sky. He eventually realised that the girl had stopped singing. He looked down at the girl and scratched his head, laughing. The young woman stared at Tebotu, who was feeling rather awkward.

'The sky is pretty, isn't it?' he managed to ask.

'Oh, yes, it's lovely,' she replied.

'Ahm . . .' He was thinking of another phrase. 'Are you busy?' he asked.

'Yes, I'm fetching water for my old pa,' she answered.

Tebotu felt lost for a moment and then asked, 'Where do you live?'

The girl laughed and answered, 'I live here. And where do you live? I haven't seen you before.'

'Oh, I live on that islet, but I come here with my father to sell copra, bananas and salt fish,' he answered proudly.

'So you are the son of that rich man on Abatekan!' he said.

'How did you know about me?' Tebotu wondered.

'My pa is a storekeeper and he often meets your father at the store,' she replied.

'I see,' he nodded his head thoughtfully. 'By the way, my name is Tebotu. Would you mind telling me yours?'

'Teuee! Teuee!' came a call from a distance away.

'That's my grandpa calling me.' she said. 'I'd better go now or my elder sisters will come and scold me. See you round, Tebotu.'

'Oh, may I meet you again soon, beautiful girl,' Tebotu said, and he headed for the store.

On the way back to the islet, Tebotu kept silent. Kekeiaki noticed his son's silence and talked about his suspicions with Baeao.

'Well,' said Baeao, 'I am not surprised to hear that Tebotu might be falling in love with someone on the mainland but, to make sure our guess is true, why don't we call him and talk things over?'

So Tebotu was called to reveal his secret thoughts, but he refused to admit that he was in love with a girl on the mainland. Baeao insisted that he tell the truth, but Tebotu was too shy to tell his mother about his love. The parents then gave up being curious and left Tebotu alone with his thoughts, but they knew that a secret could not remain a secret for long.

The days were passing quickly and Tebotu maintained his contact with the girl on Abataningo. The more he saw her, the greater his love, and the greater his love, the more he wanted to see her. Tebotu kept his thoughts private, but not for long.

'What is the use of hiding things like this?' he asked himself. 'My parents want to help me, but I refused their help.' He thought for a few days, until at last he told Baeao everything, though he expected either a scolding or a frown from his mother.

'I've been waiting for you to tell me that, my son', she said. 'Kekeiaki, Kekeiaki,' she called out.

'I'm here. What is it?' came the answer from the lake.

'Come here,' she said, 'I have some good news for you. Quick.'

Kekeiaki swam to the bank with three milkfish and headed for the house.

'Now what is it, dear?' he asked, gasping for air.

Before Baeao could talk, Tebotu rushed out of the house, like any young man who was too shy to hear his secrets bring discussed. The couple talked things over. They planned Tebotu's proposal to the storekeeper's daughter on the mainland. A week later, Kekeiaki and Baeao sailed for Abataningo, bringing with them new mats, salt fish, fresh fish, boiled toddy in bottles and many more things to be presented to Teuee's family. They reached Abataningo at about midday, and anchored their canoe to a coconut tree near the local catechist's home. Kekeiaki went to the catechist and asked to stay till the day was over. The house next door belonged to Kekeiaki's brother, but they had to stay with the catechist because they were never invited to stay with any of the elder brothers.

When night came, Kekeiaki asked the catechist to accompany them to the storekeeper's home so that everything would be done according to the custom of Abataningo, and in line with the religious way of proposing marriage. The catechist was willing to help, and they made their way on foot to the storekeeper's residence. On the way they discussed what to say to the family, and who should speak first.

Kekeiaki left the first part to the catechist, Tetaake. He was to explain the unexpected visit. When they reached the storekeeper's home, they were welcomed into the house by the storekeeper's wife. In the house were the grandfather and grandmother, Teuee's father and mother, and five young women, Teuee's elder sisters. The sudden encounter between the two families created a lot of questions for Teuee's family. There was dead silence on both sides, but the local catechist broke in, explaining the purpose of their unexpected visit and giving an apology for coming without warning the family.

As was the custom of Abataningo, during the proposal those who came to propose were always seated on new mats. So Kekeiaki, Baeao, the catechist and his wife were seated on new mats and then the discussion started. Teuee's parents left the decision to the grandparents.

'Well,' said the old man, 'I fall in with whatever my youngest granddaughter has got to say. Every young woman should know what she is doing,' he added.

Teuee was called forth to give her opinion on the proposal. She sat down silently near her grandfather facing the expectant parents of Tebotu.

'The couple is here,' her father explained, 'proposing to have your hand in marriage for their son Tebotu, but you are called to give your answer to this.'

Teuee remained silent, as if she was afraid of saying anything. She looked at every member of her family and at Tebotu's parents and party, and then began to cry. Teuee did not know what to say, and at the age of seventeen she still did not know the full meaning of marriage.

'You don't have to cry, Teuee,' said her mother 'all you have to say is whether you want to take or leave the offer, or if you want to let one of your sisters take it up.'

The girl then thought of the many times she met Tebotu, and how they had talked of love. She even saw how lucky she would be to live on Abatekan and become the princess of that lovely enchanted islet. She finally found the courage to accept Tebotu's proposal.

'I accept it,' she whispered, crying.

Kekeiaki and Baeao were speechless for some moments, but the smile on their faces expressed their gratitude and happiness.

'That's that,' said the old man. 'Teuee has agreed to your proposal.'

'We thank you, Teuee, for accepting our only son, Tebotu,' said Baeao.

'Don't worry, we'll treat you well and try to make you happy.'

Then, to Teuee's family, Kekeiaki continued, 'We'll be back in a week's time to agree on a date for the marriage.'

Kekeiaki and the party then ate the food served by Teuee's family. The food had been served on their arrival, but they wanted to wait for the answer to their proposal before eating. If the answer had been no, according to custom they would not have eaten the food. After their meal, they returned happily to the catechist's home, and he ordered some boys to take the presents from Abatekan to the shopkeeper's home.

Early in the morning, Kekeiaki, after thanking the local catechist for letting them spend a night at his house, sailed back to Abatekan with a feeling of satisfaction. The wind blew directly from astern, thus making the canoe plunge speedily toward Abatekan. Tebotu was already on the shore to meet them. They lifted the canoe to its house, and in the maneaba, Baeao told Tebotu about how they had approached the family.

'We'll go back in a week's time, to make final arrangements for the wedding,' she told him.

The couple made their second trip to Abataningo when the week had ended. They were greeted on arrival by members of Teuee's family and the arrangements for the wedding were finalised. Both families agreed to hold the wedding on Abatekan as Kekeiaki and Baeao requested, so they went to tell the parish priest of their decision.

'God is everywhere,' said the priest. 'If your son and daughter are married in a church, in a maneaba or anywhere else, God is always there'.

The wedding was to take place within one month, but Teuee's family had not had to prepare anything because Tebotu gave his word to provide everything that was needed, including food, drink, wedding dress and ring, and presents for the priest. Teuee's family had only to bring new mats on their large canoes, and bring relatives and friends. Kekeiaki invited his five elder brothers, but the eldest brother ordered the other four not to attend the wedding as he had other plans already set. So only Baeao's relatives came to Abatekan and helped with the preparation.

The maneaba's floor was covered with new mats. Places of interest like the fishes' hole, the lake and the plantation were decorated, and the path from the shore to the maneaba was also to be decorated for Teuee's family and relatives to walk along when they arrived. Abatekan was to look as nice as possible because Kekeiaki wanted to show the natural beauty of the islet to the people from the main island.

The day was drawing near, and work for the wedding had already started. The pigs (very big ones) and roosters were ready for killing, and Tebotu and his father brought babai from the lake. Ripe banana bunches were cut down, together with ripe pandanus bunches, and all was made ready for the feast.

The wedding morning was fine, and the birds, knowing what was happening, flew around the islet singing songs for their prince. Ten large canoes loaded with Teuee's relatives and friends were sighted, and the birds flew in procession and led the canoes to Abatekan. The birds seemed to understand their part in the ceremony, and the people from the mainland were very surprised to see an islet so full of natural beauty.

The crowds were welcomed by Tebotu's grandfather (Baeao's father), and Teuee, with her father, mother and grandparents, was lifted on shoulders and arms to the decorated shore. From there, they walked on new mats towards the maneaba. The procession was long, but the people occupied only about half of the maneaba.

The visitors were told to take a short rest before the wedding took place at noon. The priest and the catechist were also among the crowd. Sweet drink was served, with yellow bananas. Thirty bunches were taken from the shed, but more yellow ones were still ready to be served. Then fried slices of breadfruit and cooked milkfish were served, and the mainland people helped themselves to these rare dishes Abatekan was offering.

Tebotu and Teuee were dressed in separate dressing-rooms, to be ready for the wedding ceremony. The cooking maids and helpers kept busy with their work. Baeao was their chief cook and she wanted everything to be boiling hot when it was served. The clock struck twelve, and the couple took their place in front of the priest inside the maneaba. The families and relatives remained silent.

'Do you take this woman Teuee to be your lawful spouse eternally?' read the priest.

'I do,' replied Tebotu, and this was also Teuee's reply. So the ring was slipped on the woman's finger and they became one in the sacrament of marriage.

The wedding was followed by feasting. Foods were served — pork, chicken, babai, sweetened babai and breadfruit, bananas, salt fish and many others. The new couple led the way, picking their food from the centre, followed by the priest, catechist, guests and relatives.

Everybody had had enough to eat, but food was still in abundance. In the afternoon, Tebotu, with Teuee, led the crowd around the islet. He led them to the hole which his mother had discovered. Reef fishes were still there in numbers. Some of the people put their hands in the hole, felt the fish and took them out. But Tebotu told them to put the fish back in their hole. He also showed them the mysterious lake that provided water, milkfish, babai and salt. The crowd then visited the plantations, admiring rows of bananas, pandanus, breadfruit and coconut trees covered with fruit. The trees were low and within reach. The people from Abataningo admired every living thing on Abatekan.

Abataningo had lost most of its natural beauty. It was now covered with modern buildings, and the people now depended solely on the cash economy.

Night came and everybody slept in the madeaba, except Tebotu and Teuee who were kept isolated in a house by the sea. The good news was broadcast when Teuee's mother danced madly outside the maneaba with a white sheet spotted with red. This was the custom of the people of Abataningo. The red colour on the white sheet was the sign of the woman's virginity. Everybody was agog with excitement and Teuee's family cried with pleasure. Everyone's eyes were fixed on the colouring on the white cloth.

The celebrations continued until morning, and Teuee's family persuaded Kekeiaki, Baeao and the new couple to come along with them to the mainland. Kekeiaki accepted the offer, but was worried about his toddy and his animals. However, Baeao's relatives offered to stay and to take care of everything until they returned from the mainland.

Ten canoes were loaded with food supplies and the other ten were crowded with people. Kekeiaki and the rest of the family sailed on their own canoe, and, as happened before, the birds filled the air with music.

While he was away, Kekeiaki's brothers came to the islet. They began to cut down trees and take all the food and nuts.

'Who are you and why are you chopping down those trees?' one of the men left to look after the islet asked.

'This is our land,' the eldest brother shouted back. 'Kekeiaki is the youngest in the family'.

The caretaker and family knew that the strangers were Kekeiaki's elder brothers. The man thought for a moment and then called to the five brothers again.

'But if Kekeiaki should go from Abatekan, then who will own this land?' he asked.

'Us,' they answered back, adding, 'We own this land by right of primogeniture.'

'So then it's no use cutting down those trees!' replied the clever caretaker.

The five brothers stopped their cutting and, because the sun was now up in the sky, they could see the beauties of Abatekan, the fruits, nuts, toddy, bunches of bananas, pandanus.

They spent two whole days picking the best fruits and nuts, and broke into the sheds and smuggled out the bags of salt fish and big bottles of kamaimai. They packed everything on their canoes ready for the return home.

Kekeiaki and Tebotu came to the end of their stay on Abataningo, and, after saying goodbye to Teuee's family, relatives and friends, they prepared for the return trip to the lonely, beautiful islet. Before they left, Teuee was called by her grandfather who gave her his final advice.

'My little girl, be a good wife to Tebotu, and remember that we will be praised only by your obedience and hard work.'

Teuee said goodbye to everybody and sailed away with her new parents. On their way, they were astounded to see five canoes sailing towards them from Abatekan.

'Daddy,' Tebotu pointed with his head at the canoes.

His father kept silent for a moment and then nodded.

'Those are your five uncles,' said Kekeiaki. 'I wonder what they have been doing on our land.'

Tebotu was now a man and his mind was suddenly filled with thoughts of revenge, but he tried to curb his anger.

The five canoes sailed at a slow speed because they were overloaded with smuggled goods, fruits, nuts and bags of salt fish and other long-lasting foods. Sea water would come into the canoe each time the waves bumped against the sides. When they got near, Kekeiaki shouted to his brothers, 'Where have you been?' but there was no answer from any of them.

When they passed the brothers, they heard cries, and, looking back, saw only two canoes with their sails up. The other three had sunk. The two canoes lowered their sails and waited for the three brothers to climb in, but these canoes also sank, with everything on them. The five brothers were eaten alive by sharks.

'Their greediness killed them,' said Kekeiaki.

When they reached the land, the caretaker explained everything to Kekeiaki.

'But before they left,' he added,' they said that they would be back to drive you away from Abatekan.'

They all laughed when they heard this.

FRANCIS TEKONNANG

Beia and Ioane

1

The bell rang. Desolate huts near the beach came alive with noise and laughter. The students were particularly excited that morning. It was the end of the school year. Ioane packed his books quickly in a cardboard box and followed his friends out of the classroom. It was a special end of term for Ioane and his classmates. It was the end of their primary education. They walked briskly out of their classroom with an air of freedom.

'We won't be bothered again by the sound of the bell,' Beia said to Teretia.

'Yes, but you'll miss *him* a lot,' Teretia replied teasingly, turning to a group of boys walking by.

Ioane heard her last words, and turned to them.

'Tia! Nei!' Beia slapped Teretia's shoulder in a friendly way, and turned away shyly when she met Ioane's eyes.

Ioane took his bike, which was leaning against the wall of one of the classrooms, put his cardboard box on the steering bar, and pushed it along a few metres to the main road.

'What about her?' Teretia called out to him as he pushed and hopped at the side of his bike preparing to get on it.

Ioane looked back at them, and smiled.

Ioane rode his bike quickly after the other cyclists. When he arrived home, his father, Maremare, was boiling some water for his tea.

'What are those?' Maremare asked him. He pushed a few more dry sticks into the fire.

'Why, my books!' Ioane replied.

'What's happening?' Maremare inquired. He pushed the wood into the fire.

'Why! Don't you know it's the end of the school year?' Ioane asked, surprised. 'And besides, we won't go back to school again next year. We are free,' he added.

Maremare only shook his head, as if to the fire. Ioane didn't know why he shook his head. 'Why care?' he asked himself as he pushed his cardboard box further in on the floor of their sleeping-house.

'What's for lunch, Father?' Ioane asked.

'There are pancakes left over from breakfast. They're in the cupboard. Make yourself some drink and take the pancakes,' Maremare told him.

Maremare was in his sixties. His wife had died many years before. He had a daughter named Birenrenga. She had married Toma and gone to live with him in another village. Birenrenga often came to wash Maremare and Ioane's laundry for them. When Maremare fell sick, she would come with her husband and stay beside her father for a week or more.

Ioane was fond of Beia, and he knew that Beia was also fond of him. However, they knew that they were still too young to be married.

When he had eaten, he had a rest. He tried to sleep, but he couldn't. He took his bike and rode off.

'Where are you going, son?' Maremare called after him.

'I'm going to look for coconuts,' he shouted back.

When he passed by Beia's home, Ioane looked around for her. He couldn't see her anywhere. Nobody was in her house. Beia's parents knew that some kind of romantic relationship was developing between her and Ioane. At times, Beia's older sister, Turia, used to tease them when she saw Ioane passing by.

'Where are you going?' she used to ask Ioane when she saw him.

'I'm going to look for coconuts,' Ioane would reply politely.

'Why don't you stop, and have a rest for a while? Come!' she would invite him teasingly.

'Thank you but I'm in a hurry,' Ioane would reply, laughing at the joke.

'Wait for Beia! She's going with you.' Turia would say to him at times.

Beia was embarrassed, and sometimes she threw stones at her sister.

'They must have all gone somewhere,' he sighed, as he rode on.

When he had bundled up many coconuts on the steering bar of his bike, Ioane rode home. When he came to Beia's house, he eyed it again. No one was there. He rode on. He came to the end of the village. He jumped down from his bike because the road was soft, and he couldn't ride his bike on it with a load of coconuts.

'Where are you coming from?' a familiar voice asked from one side of the road. Ioane turned, and smiled.

'I've been collecting coconuts. What are you doing here?' he asked Beia.

'I'm waiting for Turia,' she replied.

'I see,' he said, turning away reluctantly from her. He had nothing else to ask her, and so he said goodbye. He struggled, pushing his bike away over the soft road. She watched him go.

2

Christmas and New Year celebrations were important occasions for the people. Beside religious activities, many secular events also took place. People of different villages competed against each other in singing, dancing and sports. There were competitions in soccer and in netball. Other sports like canoe-racing and athletics were also often included in the competitions. Catholics and Protestants conducted their activities separately on these occasions. However, there were not many Protestants in Ioane's village, and they usually joined the Catholics in their secular activities.

People of each village were responsible for making arrangements to practise for the various competitions. The village catechist and some mature men usually organised the villagers. When the days for the festivals drew near, the people practised singing and dancing every night, and they played netball every afternoon. On Sunday afternoon, however, the men usually played soccer.

Ioane joined some of these activities. He attended soccer and netball most often. In the evenings, he joined his friends to watch the singing and dancing practices in the next village. They sat in the dark watching the people practising under the light of a pressure lamp.

People from other villages were usually unwelcome during these practices. Besides the dangers of love affairs at night with the girls of the host village, such visitors were often accused of being spies, come to hear the songs composed in the host village.

To avoid being detected easily, and to make for easy communication, people usually employed a go-between if their business was a love affair. Ioane employed Teretia as a go-between. Teretia was related to him, so he had no fear of being seen talking with her. Teretia often brought him flowers Beia had prepared for him.

One night, Ioane and his friends were chased away from the next village. They were accused of throwing stones on the roof of the maneaba where singing was going on. When they came back the next night, the catechist of the village approached them.

'What?' the catechist said angrily. 'You didn't do it? Then how could those stones hit the roof of the maneaba? Did they fly there by themselves?' he asked them.

'We don't know who did it,' Ioane replied.

'All right. But I don't want to see you here again. You must go. Otherwise, I'll call the police,' the catechist told them.

Ioane and his friends left.

After this, Ioane tried to keep away from the village at night. And when he joined his friends sometimes, they kept a safe distance away from the maneaba.

One afternoon, Beia and Teretia picked flowers in the bush. It was quiet except for the singing of the people from their toddy trees. The crowing of bush roosters echoed every now and then from a distance. The girls had gone their own way, picking up mao and uri flowers they found.

'Beia!' Teretia called.

'Oe!' answered Beia from the bush.

'Come here! There are many flowers here!' Teretia told her.

The uri tree Teretia was picking flowers from was a good-sized tree standing above kaura and kiaou plants, some distance from a babai pit. The tree was decked with small white round-headed flowers on long stalks. No one, it seemed, had spotted the tree before.

'Come,' Teretia hummed when Beia appeared. 'How is it? she asked her.

'I've got quite a few,' Beia answered, reaching out for flowers on the same tree.

Teretia glanced at her basket of flowers. 'Are you going to make one for *him*?' she asked, letting go of the branch she was holding.

Beia didn't answer. She took the flowers she had held between her teeth, and put them in her basket. She smiled, and looked around for more flowers to reach.

The girls continued to pick flowers, and when they had collected enough they returned home. As they walked back, they made jokes and laughed.

'Where are you coming from?' asked a middle-aged man standing at the foot of his toddy tree some distance from the track.

'We've been picking flowers,' Teretia answered.

'Garlands for your loved ones, hey?' the man teased them.

'Oh, no. For ourselves,' Teretia answered, laughing with Beia.

The girls walked on, following a snake-like carved track. There was a rattle of leaves in the undergrowth nearby.

'It's a pig,' Beia said as the pig ran away. 'It looks like Tato's pig,' she added.

'Are you going to make a garland for *him*?' Teretia asked as they hurried on.

'I'll make one for him, just in case he turns up,' Beia replied seriously, looking down at the track.

'That's true, he doesn't come regularly now,' Teretia sympathised. 'I'll look around for him tonight.'

'Thank you. And remember to give him my regards as usual,' Beia said as they parted.

Teretia hurried home.

Christmas drew nearer. Teretia hadn't met Ioane during the singing practices. When Beia met her, she always asked her about Ioane. One night, when they were walking home from the singing practice, Beia asked Teretia about him.

'No,' Teretia replied. 'He didn't come.'

'I see. My father has booked us on the boat coming tomorrow,' Beia broke the news. 'I'm going away with mum.'

'I see,' Teretia said, rather surprised.

'If I don't see him before then, give him my love,' Beia said. 'And tell him I'll write him a letter.'

'He might turn up at the harbour before you take the launch to the ship.'

'You may be right,' Beia answered.

They bid each other good night, and parted.

3

Nare, Beia's father, was waiting for the bus near the road. He had found a place to stay with his niece, Maria, who worked for an I-Matang family and was earning eight dollars a week. Nare had been looking for a job when he arrived, but he hadn't found one. His niece had also asked a number of people, but she couldn't find him a job either. There was a rumour that many people would be required to work on a water-scheme project starting early the following year. Nare decided to wait.

Since he arrived, he had built a small hut near Maria's house. Maria's house consisted of two small rooms in two separate buildings. The buildings were partitioned in the middle. The other half of each building was occupied by a girl also working for an I-Matang. One building was for sleeping, and the other was for cooking.

Nare had also planted a number of toddy trees. He was a good toddy cutter, and they had a lot of fresh toddy to drink. He had no fishing gear or canoe — he had left them back home. During low tides, however, he joined their neighbours to collect mussels in the lagoon.

Maria was very kind to him, though she hadn't much money herself. Every morning she boiled tea and prepared some sandwiches for him. She did his laundry for him, and she bought him tinned foods when she could afford it. That day she gave him three dollars for fares.

When the bus came, Nare got on it. There were many people on the bus, most of them civil servants and students. They looked neat and tidy. They wore ironed shirts and dresses. Nare felt like a stranger as he walked down the aisle. He wore a lavalava on top of his trousers. He found an empty seat near the back of the bus and sat down. One of the men sitting on the seat behind him recognised him, and tapped him on the shoulder. Nare looked back.

'Hey! Nanati!' Nare said, surprised. He shook hands.

'When did you come?' Nanati asked.

'Many weeks ago,' Nare told him.

The bus sped on, churning up dust. It bumped up and down, and it shivered. The passengers complained. The bus swung around a curve. Nare shifted on his seat, and nearly fell over. At last they came to what looked like a village.

'What's this village?' Nare asked Nanati.

'It's Eita,' Nanati told him.

The bell rang. The bus slowed down, and stopped. Some people got off. More people entered the bus. Some of them couldn't find empty seats, so they stood along the aisle. The bus conductor came to Nare.

'How much is it to Bairiki?' Nare asked.

'Thirty cents from Bikenibeu,' the bus conductor said.

Nare took out a dollar note from his pocket and gave it to him.

★

Ioane woke up late that morning. He had heard from Teretia that Beia had gone on the boat. He lay on his pillow awhile thinking. He rose up, collected the sides of his mosquito net together, and threw them up on top of the mosquito net. He shifted himself across and off his sleeping mats, and folded them.

'Come on. The sun is high up,' Maremare told him. He was sitting beside the fire. 'You haven't cut your toddy trees,' he reminded him.

Ioane tied on his lavalava and jumped to the floor. He washed his face, then took his toddy knife and sharpened it.

'What will you do after you've cut your toddy trees?' Maremare asked.

'I'll see,' Ioane replied. He took the special shells for collecting the toddy and rode away to the coconut trees that he had marked for cutting.

When the bus arrived at the wharf, Nare got off. The ferry which takes passengers back and forth between the islets of Betio and Tarawa was already in. He walked to the ferry. Many people were already there. He found an empty seat at the back, and sat down.

'Hey! Nare! When did you come?' a woman's voice asked him. The woman got up from where she sat and walked over to him.

'Several weeks ago,' Nare said, shaking her hand.

'And where is Nimanoa?' she asked him.

'She's coming this morning.' he told her.

The woman looked puzzled.

'She's coming with Beia on *Te Mauri*. It's due in at Betio this morning,' he told her.

'I see,' she said. 'You are an old man already,' she added.

'And you too,' Nare replied. 'How's Teaninga?'

'Thank you. He's well.'

'Sit down,' Nare invited her. He shifted to give her room. 'Is he working?'

'Yes,' she replied, 'he's working for the Council.'

'How's his drinking?'

'Aaa! He can't stop it. And that's why I'm going after him now. When he

144

gets his pay this afternoon he'll spend it all at the bar.'

'I see,' Nare said sympathetically.

'The only way for me to get some of his money is to go to him immediately after he's received his pay,' she said, shaking her head.

'I see,' Nare said. 'What time is the ferry going to Betio?' he asked.

'At eight o'clock,' the woman replied.

The purr of the engine became louder, and the ferry began to move.

'It's going now,' the woman told him.

Nare leaned back and looked down at the back of the ferry. The water below moved forwards, swishing loudly under the ferry.

When Ioane returned, he hung his toddy shells on the side of the house, washed his toddy knife with water and put it away. He climbed onto the floor of their sleeping-house, and stretched himself out.

'Are you going back to bed?' Maremare asked. He was tying two long sticks together.

'No, I'm taking a rest.'

'Why don't you cut open those coconuts? It's only a week more to go before Christmas.'

'That's right, Father,' said Ioane. 'I'll go and look for more, when I come back.'

Ioane jumped down from the house made himself a cup of fresh toddy to drink and rode away on his bicycle.

4

After Mass, the people flocked out of the church. They were smartly dressed. Most of them withdrew to the maneaba, the meeting-house where all the people met together to discuss church matters. Those who had come some distance to attend the services brought their lunches in woven baskets. Maremare, too, withdrew to the maneaba. Birenrenga had boiled some rice for them before Mass and she had packed their food and utensils in a basket. Ioane took the basket with him on his bike to the maneaba when he came for the morning service.

Maremare withdrew to his usual place in the maneaba. There he spread out a pandanus mat and stretched himself out on it. After a while Birenrenga came with some hot water in a pot and began to prepare some tea. A whistle shrieked sharply. The president of the Church Committee blew it to get people's attention.

'Women! Prepare the plates,' he called out loudly.

Birenrenga spooned some rice on one plate, and opened a tin of corned beef. She spooned about a half of the meat onto the plate. Then she put some sugar in the tea.

'When the plates are ready, take them up to your men,' the president announced loudly.

Birenrenga spooned some tea and tasted it.

'Maremare!' she called her father softly.

Maremare turned back to her.

'Take those,' she told him as she pushed the plate and the teapot towards him.

Maremare took them. The old men sat in a rectangle with their plates of food in front of them.

'Let's say our grace,' the president told them. 'In the name' — he raised his hand to make the sign of the cross. '. . . of the Father and of the Son and of the Holy Spirit, Amen,' the old men joined in.

'Bless us, Lord . . .,' the president began. '. . . for these gifts we are about to receive through Christ our Lord, Amen,' the old men added.

'In the name . . . ,' the president began. '. . . of the Father and of the Son and of the Holy Spirit, Amen,' the old men joined in.

'Help yourselves,' the president told them.

Maria had gone to Betio to visit her friends. She left on Friday morning. Before she left, she gave Nare a two-dollar note.

'I'll be back on Monday,' she told Nare before she left. 'That's all I have on me.'

She took her handbag and left.

While Maria was away, Nare tried to spend as little of the money as possible. He bought five pounds of flour. Nimanoa and Beia mixed it up with scraped coconut and water, patted the mixture into small balls and boiled them. These lasted them until Saturday morning. Nare bought some more flour. In the afternoon a cart of fish passed by.

'Dad! Fish!' Beia called out to Nare.

'Dear, I haven't got any money to buy any,' he told her .

Beia walked away. She stood by the cart and watched the people buying fish. She complained to her parents for not buying some fish. 'We also are dying to eat fish,' Nare said to her.

On Christmas day, the family went to mass. Beia sat beside her mother, and Nare sat among the men. The old priest gave a long sermon. They found the way the priest spoke strange. Beia thought it was funny. She laughed a lot in the church and her mother looked at her threateningly. When the service was over, the people flocked out. Nare walked away with his family.

At Tabiteuea the singing competition had begun. The people of different villages grouped in their usual places, forming a rectangular pattern.

'Thank you, Eita,' the president said to Eita, or to whoever had just finished singing. 'It's your turn now,' he announced to the next choir.

After singing a number of songs, the choir members had warmed up. Girls and boys began to stand up and shake to the rhythm of the music of their choirs. At times they made abusive joking gestures to the choirs of other villages.

On Tarawa, Nare stood some distance away from the maneaba, under the shade of coconut fronds, watching what was going on and listening to the competing choirs. The maneaba was packed full, and many people were standing crowded under the verandah. The president and members of the Church Committee sat on a long bench. The choirs were almost indistinct from one another. Beia had met up with two girls from home, and they were watching the choir from under the verandah of the maneaba.

'Thank you, Nei Kaue,' the president of the Church Committee said at the end of the song. 'It's your turn now, Ueen Meei,' he announced .

While Te Kaibangaki choir was singing, one of the women stood up shaking and screaming fanatically. Two men supported her as she shook. She continued to shake and scream as if possessed. One of the men helped her to sit down. The people laughed.

Ioane felt tired of listening and watching the choirs. He walked slowly away through the crowd, excusing himself to a number of people who sat in his way. Some of his schoolmates were under the shade of a breadfruit tree. He took his bike and pushed it along to them.

'Where are you going?' they asked him.

'I'm going back home,' he told them.

'Let's go with him!' Romi suggested to his friends.

They took their bikes and cycled after him. They raced through the village making a lot of noise as they sped on.

When Ioane thought the singing was nearly over, he hurried back to the maneaba. He picked up his basket, and took it home. He then prepared his toddy knife and the coconut-shell toddy containers.

On the atoll of Tarawa, Nimanoa was sleeping in the hut Nare had built. Nare crawled over to her and woke her up.

'Nimanoa! Nimanoa!' Nare called, shaking her by the shoulder.

'Ooo!' Nimanoa murmured.

'Wake up,' Nare told her.

'What?' she asked him sleepily.

'Go and see what's in that parcel,' Nare told her.

'What is it?' Nimanoa asked him, crawling over to a parcel of green coconut leaves woven together. She loosened the knots of the parcel. 'Crabs!' she

147

exclaimed, pushing the parcel towards Nare.

'And what about you?' Nimanoa asked.

'I've had some.'

Beia, who was standing outside the hut, hurried in when she heard her mother.

'What are those, Mother?' she asked.

'Beach crabs,' Nimanoa answered.

The crabs had been roasted, and the smell was tempting. Beia fingered them gingerly.

'We've never eaten these back home,' Beia said, looking at her father for a long time.

5

Maria knew the person well who was going to manage the water-scheme project, and she inquired about a job for Nare. One evening Nare and his family were retiring to their hut. They had a small radio turned on. Nimanoa and Beia were arguing bitterly. Beia wanted to go to the cinema. Her friends had invited her, and they were going to pay for her ticket.

'No, dear,' Nare said. 'When you have money to pay for yourself, you can go.'

Beia insisted on going. She squatted beside her mother sobbing.

'Mmm . . . I'm going,' she mumbled.

'You can't go. If you do . . . ,' Nimanoa said angrily.

'Stop arguing,' Nare cut in, 'and listen to this.' They listened to the radio.

'Those who have given their names to work in the water-scheme project must report to the office tomorrow,' the radio announcer read.

'That's the job I've been waiting for,' Nare told them. 'Dear, you see,' he told Beia, 'I'll soon have a job. When I get my first pay, I'll give you money to go to the cinema.'

In the morning, men like Nare gathered around the office. Many of the men were about the same age as he. A lot more were much younger.

'Hey! Nare! When did you come?' Taburi called to Nare. He walked up to greet him. They shook hands.

'Several weeks ago,' Nare answered.

An officer, smartly dressed, came out to the men. They flocked around him.

'Right,' the officer began when the men had gathered around, 'I'll read out the names on my list.' The officer unfolded his list. Some of the men who stood by his side poked their heads in to look at the list, while he read out the names.

'The work will start tomorrow. So those whose names are on my list, please come back tomorrow morning. Be here at eight o'clock. The truck will take us to where we are going to work,' the officer announced.

When Nare arrived home, Beia ran up to him.

'Dad!' she called. 'You won't forget what you promised me, will you?'

Nare held her tightly.

'My dear, I didn't get the job,' he told her, smoothing down her hair. 'It'll work out, though. They said that work on the telephone cable will start soon.'

Ioane woke up that morning feeling happy. He had received Beia's letter. He hoped that one day he would see the things for himself that she wrote about. However, he had made arrangements with some boys to help each other in turns in collecting coconuts. It was his turn first to be helped. He cut his toddy trees quickly that morning, and had some scraped coconut with fresh toddy. Then, while he waited for the boys to arrive, he made catch-sticks for a trap he had constructed for catching bush fowls. He had collected a number of straight mid-ribs of coconut fronds for the trap, cut them carefully into lengths and tied them up neatly with a string, forming a kind of pyramid shape. Ioane liked his work and was proud of the craftsmanship he had put into it. He found two pieces of uri branch, cut them to the right length and shaped them carefully with a sharp knife. After trimming the sticks for a while, he tested them.

'They are not as sensitive as they should be,' he thought.

He scraped off the rough surfaces with his knife and tried them again. They were more sensitive this time, and yet he was not satisfied. He shaped and smoothed them again and tried them once more. Some of the boys had arrived and were standing beside him admiring his work.

'What's that?' they asked.

'Ah!' Ioane said, 'my bush-fowl trap.'

He placed the catch-sticks in position and set the trap. He wanted to test how good they would be when a bush fowl happened to sneak into the trap, and stepped on the strings attached to the catch sticks.

'They are far better now,' he said to himself.

He set his trap again. He found some scraped coconuts and spread them inside the trap.

'It's beautiful,' one of the boys said.

'Yes, and it's mine,' Ioane replied.

He walked back to the house with his friends.

The rest of the gang came when the sun was high in the sky. They rested for a while, then he took them to his family's piece of land, a long way from his home. The piece of land was small, and there were few coconut trees on it. He had never visited it before. He showed them the boundaries of the land, and the boys collected dry nuts that had fallen. Many of the nuts had

149

germinated. Ioane studied the nuts on the trees.

'Anybody want to climb a tree?' Ioane asked.

'Yep,' Teinging and Tetabo replied.

'Try that one,' Ioane said to Teinging, pointing out a tree. 'And you can try that one,' he told Tetabo, pointing out another.

Teinging and Tetabo walked to the trees.

'How about you, Tonga and Ibeatabu ?' Ioane asked.

'I got a sore foot,' Tonga replied, nursing his wound.

'I don't feel like climbing,' said Ibeatabu.

'All right,' Ioane said. 'Drop the green nuts too,' he told the boys up the trees.

They piled the nuts together in one place. Some of them drank from the green nuts while others tied up the dry ones.

When Maria returned home from her work, she asked Nare about the job.

'I didn't get it,' Nare replied.

'Anyway, it doesn't matter,' she sighed heavily. 'I've asked a number of I-Matanga if they could give you odd jobs. I'll have something to eat first, then I'll take you to the one I know would like someone to work for him.'

When she had eaten, he followed her to a big house. Maria knocked on the door.

'You told me once that you needed someone to do odd jobs for you. I've brought a man with me who can work for you,' she told the man.

'Come in,' the man said

Nare admired the room. There were paintings, salusalus and artefacts fixed on the walls of the room. The room was furnished neatly with armchairs and small tables.

'Please sit down,' the man invited them.

Maria sat on an armchair opposite the man. Nare was going to sit on the carpeted floor when the man asked him not to.

'Sit here,' Maria told Nare, pointing to an armchair near hers.

Nare sat uncomfortably on the chair. He squeezed his hands together between his closed thighs as if he was cold.

'Are you the man Maria has been telling me about?' the man asked. He gave his hand to Nare. Nare, accustomed to this gesture, shook it.

'Can he speak English?' the man asked Maria.

'He can't,' Maria replied.

'I see,' the man said. 'I would like someone to build a coconut-leaf fence around my house. Can he do that for me?'

Maria asked Nare. He nodded his head.

'All right. Come! I'll show you where and how I want it built,' the man said to Maria, rising from his chair.

Maria explained to Nare everything the man wanted. Nare nodded again.
'How much does he want for the job?' the man asked Maria.
'Whatever amount you are willing to pay him,' Maria answered for him.
'A dollar a day?' the man suggested.
Maria asked Nare. Nare nodded like an obedient child.
'Good. He can start whenever he likes,' the man said.

6

Nare was anxious to commence his work, and to earn the money quickly. The
school year would start soon. He had heard about St Louise School where his
daughter could go. That very day, he collected dry coconut leaves in the bush,
dragged them along the road and piled them up together near the I-Matang's
house. Every day during that week, he woke up early, cut his toddy trees and
had some scraped coconuts with fresh toddy. Then he went to the bush to
gather more dry coconut leaves for the fence. When he thought he had enough
leaves, he cut some wood to hold the fence together. He carried these on his
shoulder to the house.

When the I-Matang returned from his work in the afternoons, he admired
Nare's efforts. The man's neighbours liked it too, and they thought about
asking Nare to do the same thing for them. After four days of hard work, the
fence was completed.

In the morning the I-Matang stopped at Maria's house on his way to work.
Maria had already gone to work. Nimanoa saw the man coming towards the
house.

'Nare! Your friend is coming,' Nimanoa told Nare.

Nare saw the I-Matang, and hurried to meet him.

'Where's Maria?' the man asked.

'Maria?' Nare said with an embarrassed look. He guessed what the I-
Matang wanted, and motioned with his hands indicating that she had gone.

'Ooh,' the man nodded.

He took out a few dollar notes, and ran through them quickly with his
fingers. He picked out two and gave them to Nare.

'Thank you very much,' the man said. 'It's beautiful.'

'Ko bati n raba,' Nare thanked the man as he turned to go. He walked back
to Nimanoa.

'What did he want?' Nimanoa asked him.

'He paid for the work I did for him,' Nare told her. He threw the notes to her.

'How much will you have to pay for school fees?' Nimanoa asked.

'Twelve dollars, I think,' Nare told her.

'Why don't you go and pay them now?' Nimanoa suggested.

'I will,' Nare told her.

When Nare arrived at Teaoraereke, he asked the people he met to whom he should talk regarding the school.

'Go to Father Martin or to Viane,' they told him.

'Thank you,' he said.

He walked towards a group of children playing marbles under the shade of a breadfruit tree.

'Where is Viane's house?' he asked the children.

'There!' The children pointed it out to him.

Nare walked towards the house.

'Come,' a middle-aged man invited him smilingly.

'Are you Viane?' Nare asked.

'That's right,' Viane assured him. 'Come and sit here.'

Nare got up from the floor and sat beside him.

'I want to ask you to enrol my daughter in your school. Do you still have room for more?' Nare asked.

'Oh yes. Where did she attend school before?'

'She went to school at Teabike in Tabiteuea North,' Nare told him.

'What was the class she completed?'

'She completed her primary school,' Nare replied.

'Good. She's all right then,' Viane told him.

'To whom shall I pay her school fees?' Nare asked.

'To Father, but you can give them to me, and I'll give them to him. What's her name?' he asked.

'Beia,' Nare told him.

Nare gave him the money. He thanked Viane, and left.

When the school year began, Beia attended classes at the school every day. She liked to please her father, and she liked to mix with her new friends. However, she knew she had failed to be selected for secondary education. The school she was attending, she realised, was a kind of school for people like her. They didn't have to sit any public exams. The teachers were not the kind of teachers in other secondary schools.

The school consisted of three rooms in a grimy old building. There were four teachers: two old nuns and a middle-aged man, and a young man who, she learnt from her friends, had completed fifth form and was waiting to go on with priestly studies.

Beia liked her teachers, though she often found the things taught in the school difficult. Many times it didn't make sense to her. During the first few weeks, she learnt about sines and cosines and was introduced to the trial balance. The school was co-educational, and the students came from all the islands of Kiribati. Most of them were staying with their parents or relatives on Tarawa. Some were from as far away as Betio and Buota.

One day, she accompanied her friends to a store. A number of boys and girls were there buying refreshments. A boy came walking along towards them. He pulled the hair of one of her friends and they exchanged slaps. The boy slapped her friend particularly hard on the shoulder. Miriana complained, nursing her shoulder.

'You are rough on her,' Anna rebuked him.

'It's only play,' the boy replied.

'For your punishment, buy us drinks,' Anna told him.

The others echoed her request.

The boy bought some drinks and distributed them among the girls. He gave one of the tins to Beia and winked at her.

'Tia . . . ! Nao . . .!' Anna and Miriana rebuked him. 'You are bad,' they called after him as he hurried away.

When the boy was out of earshot, Beia asked about him.

'The boy is from Marakei. He is working at the Chief Minister's office,' Miriana told her.

'He is her cousin,' Miriana added, pointing to Anna.

Beia remembered that she had seen the boy somewhere, but she couldn't remember where.

A few days later, she was on the bus on her way to school. She was sitting by herself in a double seat looking out of the window. The bus halted at a bus-stop and the people waiting crowded in, squeezing themselves through the door. A boy was squatting like a frog on the beach. The people on the bus stared at him and giggled. The boy hid his face with his lavalava, and the people on the bus laughed . . .

Beia fell back in her seat, shyly.

'Do you live around here?' Beia asked Anna's cousin as the bus staggered on slowly.

'Yes,' Tenten replied.

'Oooo!' Beia mumbled. She remembered.

'I haven't seen you at island nights,' Tenten said.

'No. I don't go to island nights,' Beia told him.

'How about attending one with me?' Tenten suggested.

'I'm afraid,' Beia told him.

The bus conductor asked them for their fares. Tenten paid for them.

'Thank you,' Beia said.

'How about going to the pictures with me during the weekend?' Tenten suggested.

'I don't know,' Beia replied.

'I'll take you there with Miriana and Anna,' Tenten assured her.

The bus shook violently as it ran over a wavy surface. The passengers complained. Tenten consoled Beia, stretching out his arm to hold her.

153

When the school year started again, Ioane didn't go back to school. Sometimes he went fishing, and at other times, when he felt like it, he helped his father in their babai pit. Otherwise he would join his friends to look for coconuts or he would look for dry leaves for compost.

One morning he didn't bother to get up early. His father disturbed him a number of times, waking him up to cut his toddy trees before he went to the bush, but he refused to stir. He stayed in bed for quite a while after sunrise. When he couldn't go back to sleep, he lay on his back, staring at the top of his mosquito net. He tried to figure out what day of the week it was. A mosquito hopped across the inside top of his net. He jerked himself up quickly, and clapped it. He examined the palms of his hands for blood stains. He smeared the stain on the palm of his left hand with his right finger to examine it. He looked around for more mosquitoes in his net. He found a couple of others. When he had killed them all, he lay down again.

'What's wrong with Beia? She hasn't written me a letter yet,' he thought. He looked around again for mosquitoes. There were none. He collected the sides of his net together and bundled them up on top. He folded his sleeping mats together and climbed down from the house.

7

A few more months lapsed. Ioane had not received a letter from Beia though he continued to write to her. He had heard news about her from Teretia and from people who had just returned from Tarawa. He couldn't believe it. He waited anxiously a while longer. He didn't receive any letters from her.

'Father, I want to go to Tarawa,' he told his father one evening.

'Why, son?' Maremare asked.

'I want to go and look for a job.'

Maremare shook his head. Ioane understood. Maremare was not an old man to be left on his own.

'I'll come back quickly if I can't find one,' Ioane assured him.

'Where will you find the money? You can find relatives to stay with there, but where will you find the money to pay for your fare?' Maremare asked.

'I'll make copra and I'll ask my brother-in-law to lend me the money.'

Ioane worked hard to find coconuts. He cut them open and dried them under the sun. When the copra was dry, he put it in a bag and took it to the local co-operative store. He got four dollars for the copra. When he returned from the store, he gave the money to his father to look after. He learnt that a boat was coming in a couple of days. Just before the boat arrived, he asked his brother-in-law for a loan.

'Do you have any cash?' Toma asked his wife, Birenrenga.

'How much does he want?' Birenrenga asked.

154

'Six dollars,' Toma replied.

Birenrenga searched around for the money in their boxes.

'Here. Four dollars only,' Birenrenga told Toma as she handed him the money.

Toma gave the notes to Ioane.

'Wait. I'll go and ask Toromon for a loan of two dollars. We'll pay it back when that copra of ours is dry,' he said to Ioane as he jumped off the floor.

Ioane waited for him.

Beia had received Ioane's latest letter. She was worried. Tenten had taken her and her friends out a number of times to the pictures, to island nights and to balls at the Otintai Hotel. She had had a lot of fun with Tenten. She had grown to know him well and she thought he was wonderful. She had also learnt from Anna that Tenten would be sent on a course with others to New Zealand. Tenten had gone to school and completed the fifth form, and she had seen his certificates. The government would pay for him and the others. At times he took her to official parties. She never liked these, but Tenten had always persuaded her to go with him.

When the boat arrived, Ioane was there at the landing waiting for the launch. Many people were there. Maremare came to see him off. Birenrenga and Toma were also there. When the launch from the boat arrived, the people walked down to it. Many of them grouped around a neatly dressed officer. The officer wore a smart marine cap, a white shirt and a pair of white shorts. He wore striped ribbons on the sleeves.

'Yes, your name is on the list,' the officer told one of the young men in the crowd when he jumped down from the launch.

Ioane recognised the man. He was a civil servant working at Tarawa. The man had returned for a holiday at home. He had attended St Joseph's College many years before.

The officer pushed his way into the crowd. The people followed him up the beach.

'You are booked for a saloon,' the officer told the civil servant.

'Have you got room for more passengers?' a middle-aged man asked the officer when he had sat down on some coconut leaves.

Yes,' the officer told him. 'But let me see first whether the people who are on my list are here.'

The officer read out the names. When he had finished, he took the names of other people who wanted to travel on the boat and collected their fares. Ioane gave him his name. The officer wrote his name down on his list among the names of deck passengers.

'Ten dollars, please,' the officer said to Ioane.

Ioane put a bundle of notes on the palm of his hand. The officer counted it. It was exactly ten dollars. The officer was not surprised. It was the custom for ordinary outer-island people travelling by boat to ask for a space on deck. Saloons were recognised as being for government officials and people of social standing.

Ioane walked back to Maremare and Birenrenga.

'Did you get a place on the boat?' Birenrenga asked him.

'Yes,' Ioane replied.

Toma arrived. He was carrying husked green coconuts and a ripe pandanus fruit for Ioane.

They were silent for a while, watching the men carrying cargo up the beach. The officer walked back to the boat, waving his hand to the passengers to follow. Ioane bid Birenrenga goodbye.

'Come back quickly, son,' Maremare mumbled to him. 'You won't be happy there.'

Ioane sobbed for a while, then hurried away. Toma helped him to carry his luggage down to the launch. He found a place among the passengers from Tabiteuea. After a supper of rice and tinned fish, he spread his mats on deck and stretched out. Not long after, however, the wind blew cold and the boat began to sway from side to side. The waves beat against the bow of the boat, and occasionally they splashed through the openings on the side. Ioane folded his mats together quickly and carried them away, looking for a safer place. The passengers complained about the water. The ship continued to wade through the night.

Tenten and Beia were watching a film show at Galu's theatre that evening. The film was about a poor, handsome young man who saved peasant people from a dragon. The dragon wouldn't kill them if they offered him their daughters. The people were waiting fearfully for the dragon to come. Beia was leaning against Tenten's chest. Tenten had his arms around her. When the film was over, Tenten took her home. Anna and Miriana walked ahead of them. When they arrived at Beia's place, Tenten kissed her. It was the first time that she had allowed herself to be kissed. She bid goodnight and hurried away.

On the boat, Ioane found a place between two other men sleeping at the bottom of the boat. He felt around with his hand. The bottom of the boat was slimy. He pulled his lavalava off and spread it out. He lay on his side. His lavalava was soon soaked with water. He felt his wet side with his hand. He tried to think of somewhere else to go. He didn't know many people on the boat. He felt around for a better place.

'Go to sleep,' one of the men told him. The man had been awakened by his moves. 'It'll be all right in the morning,' the man assured him.

Ioane returned to his place. The boat continued to sway from side to side. At times, it would momentarily stop and shake when it collided with a big wave. Memories of warm mats flashed into his mind. He tried not to think about home. The boat continued to sway and dive into the night.

8

The boat arrived at Betio some time in the morning. It moved slowly down the harbour to the wharf. Ioane didn't know where he would find his uncle who, he had been told, was working on Betio. Some of the sailors ran about throwing ropes to the people ashore as they moored the boat beside the wharf. Ioane carried his things and followed the other passengers. Many people were there to meet their relatives. Ioane looked around for faces he might recognise. He took his things and carried them towards the gangway. He stopped momentarily and joined the queue. A girl on a motorcycle had her back to them. He wanted to shout out to her. He bumped into a woman in front of him. The woman dropped the basket she was carrying.

'Come on, boy, look where you're going,' the woman said angrily.

'Excuse me,' he apologised, staring at the girl on the motorcycle. He hurried to her. A man, who was walking past the girl, pointed out something to her, in the direction of the boat. The girl looked back and saw Ioane coming towards her. Ioane hurried up to her. The girl drove away. Ioane wanted to call her back, but he was afraid it might not be her. The girl drove to the main road, turned to the right, and disappeared.

'I knew she wouldn't come,' he thought.

He carried his things aimlessly across the road, and put them down a few feet away from the tar-sealed road under casuarina trees. A number of motorcyclists were getting petrol in a small shed near by. Ioane seated himself on a root of one of the trees and decided to wait for people he might recognise. He waited there for a long time.

'Katarina!' he called to a woman walking towards the ferry shed with a number of friends.

Katarina didn't hear him. She was talking with her companions.

'Katarina!' he called again.

Katarina bid her friends goodbye, and hurried towards the ferry shed.

After a while, a boy of about his age drove past on his motorcycle. The boy saw a suitcase and a couple of things beside the road and looked around for the owner. He saw Ioane sitting under the tree.

'Hey! Ioane!' the boy called out, stepping on his brakes. His motorcycle slid across the road and came to a stop.

Ioane rose and hurried forward to greet him. They shook hands.

Beto was his classmate. When they sat the entrance exam years ago, Beto was the only one selected from their group for secondary education. Then he went to work in the Post Office.

'When did you arrive?' Beto asked.

'I came on the *Tautunu* this morning,' Ioane replied.

'I see,' the boy said. 'Are you coming to look for a job, or are you coming after Beia?' the boy asked him teasingly.

'I came to visit my uncle,' Ioane told him.

Beto switched off the key of his bike.

'She's attending school at Teaoraereke,' Beto told Ioane teasingly. 'And how's Tabiteuea?'

'It's the same as ever,' Ioane replied.

A group of girls about their age walked by. Beto whistled to them.

'Shut up,' the girls said angrily.

'They're beautiful, aren't they?' Beto commented. Ioane nodded.

'Does your uncle know you're coming?' Beto asked.

'No,' Ioane told him.

'I'll go and deliver these letters to a friend of mine. He's going on the ferry now. Then I'll come back and take you to his house,' he told Ioane.

Ioane went back to the tree, and sat on the roots, waiting. A number of girls walked by. One of them whistled at Ioane. He looked down shyly at the tangled roots.

When Beto came back, he took Ioane's suitcase and put it across the steering bar and petrol tank.

Ioane sat behind him and held the rest of his luggage on his knees. They drove away. The road was hard and had a rough surface. They passed a number of buildings. A policeman, dressed in a dark grey uniform, hurried into a small, square-faced building.

'That's a police station,' Beto told him.

'Yes,' Ioane assured him.

They drove slowly on, making way for a car coming around the corner.

'That's the Lands and Survey Office,' Beto told Ioane.

Ioane murmured, not knowing what the words meant.

'Those are the Courthouse buildings,' Beto told Ioane, looking at the buildings on his left. They drove to the main road.

'That's a Japanese bomb shelter, built during the war,' Beto told Ioane. They turned left, and came to a number of houses under casuarina trees.

'Whose houses are those?' Ioane asked

'They are I-Matang houses. Some are occupied by local officers.'

A number of motorcycles passed them.

'That's the Marine Training School,' Beto indicated. 'Why don't you try that?' he asked.

They came to another road and stopped for a while to allow a motorcar and a motorcyclist to pass. They turned to their right and sped on.

'That is Takoronga Labour Line,' Beto told Ioane.

They turned off the road to their left and came to a row of concrete-block houses.

'He lives here,' Beto told him.

Beto slowed down the motorcycle and stopped outside one of the doors. Ioane dropped his things on the ground and Beto put the suitcase on the ground.

'There seems to be no one around,' Beto commented.

He knocked on the door.

A middle-aged woman appeared, filling up the door. She looked at the boys for a while.

'Ooo! Ioane!' the woman said, stepping down from the door and opening her arms out to embrace him. 'You are an old man already. When did you arrive?' She led him to the house. 'Come in,' she invited Beto.

'Thank you, but I'm in a hurry,' Beto told the woman.

'Really?' the woman asked. 'Well thank you. Where did you find this man?' the woman asked.

'I saw him standing under the casuarina trees at the wharf,' Beto explained.

'Thank you,' Ioane said to him when he turned his motorcycle around and started it.

'You naughty boy, why didn't you or your father let us know you were coming?' the woman asked. 'This is your cousin, Bikiniki, and this is your niece, Terira.' The woman introduced a boy and a girl who were looking at Ioane from the doorway.

They carried his things inside the house.

'Your uncle won't be here until lunchtime,' the woman told him, 'so have a shower first.'

The woman gave a two-dollar note to the girl and told her to buy a tin of meat at the store. Ioane looked for his change of clothes in his suitcase and went to have a bath.

9

Ioane stayed with his uncle Tiaoni and his aunt for several weeks. Though they were kind to him, he knew that he couldn't depend on them all his life. One day, he would have a family of his own. Besides, though his uncle gave him money for entertainment, he was aware that they couldn't quite afford the money most of the time. Nevertheless, his uncle and aunt treated him as if he was their eldest son. Ioane often thought about his father too. He wanted to send him money as often as he could. And, of course, Ioane considered himself old enough and able enough to contribute to the economy of the family.

Since arriving on Tarawa, he had tried to contact Beia. He knew some of her schoolmates and he had asked them to deliver messages to her. One afternoon he met her at the Nanotasi Co-operative Store at Bairiki. They talked for a while under the shade of the mango trees, and he noticed that she had changed a lot. He bought drinks and they drank together. He was not happy when they parted. However, he knew he would win her back. When he met her again on the bus to Bikenibeu during one weekend, he sat with her. They talked about their school days, and he talked about her letters and the things she had told him, which he had now seen for himself.

After a while he asked his uncle to help him look for a job. One day his uncle told him about a salesman's job. Nei Ranran Co-operative Store was advertising the job by posters. Ioane sent in an application. A few days later his uncle told him that the applicants were wanted for an interview at the office at eight o'clock the next day.

In the morning, Ioane dressed himself up smartly and ran through in his mind some of the things he was likely to be asked at the interview. He walked to the office where the interviews were to take place. Many boys and girls were already there sitting or talking in groups. The committee that was conducting the interviews was already talking to one of the girls. Ioane waited anxiously for a long time for his turn. At last he was called in. He followed the assistant to the room where five men sat around the table.

'Sit down there.' One of the men indicated an empty chair.

Ioane sat uncomfortably on the chair.

'I understand that you are interested in the job we advertised,' the man said.

'Yes,' Ioane replied, lifting his head to look at the man.

'What's your name?' the man asked.

'My name is Ioane.'

'What island do you come from?' another man asked him.

'I come from Tabiteuea,' Ioane replied quickly.

'Oo! The knife island,' one of the men said.

The men laughed. Ioane was a bit embarrassed.

'What's your father's name?' the first man asked.

'My father's name is Maremare.'

'And your mother's name?' one of the other men asked.

'My mother's name is Eritabeta. She died many year ago,' Ioane replied.

'Well Ioane, thank you for coming. We'll let you know the result of our interview when we've finished talking to all the applicants. I suppose that you went to school at Tabiteuea too before you came here?' the man added.

Ioane nodded. The assistant opened the door for Ioane. He rose to his feet, thanked the men, and walked out of the room happily.

'The questions were very easy to answer,' he thought.

The interviews were completed some time late in the afternoon. The applicants flocked around the chairman of the committee when he came out to announce the decision. After he had learnt the result, Ioane walked away quickly.

When he arrived home, his uncle asked him what had happened.

'Someone else was appointed.' Iaone told about the interview.

'I see,' Tiaoni nodded. 'Yes, Ioane. There are very many people like you. But there are not many jobs around the place for them. The same thing is happening in the Service now. When I first started working, there were not as many educated people. Now we have graduates, and the government is sending more and more students overseas to study at universities and technical colleges. From the beginning until now, I've managed to move up to an executive position.' Tiani paused. 'And I don't think I'll be given a higher post than that. There are already many educated people in the Service.' He lit his cigarette and thought to himself, 'The number of personnel required decreases as you go up the hierarchy.' He knew Ioane wouldn't understand. 'Anyway,' he continued, 'I've inquired at the wharf for you. They told me that they would need casual labour when the boat arrives next week. Would you like that?'

'There's nothing else, is there?' .

'No.'

When the boat arrived, Ioane was hired as an extra labourer. At the wharf, he sweated, all day carrying and moving things here and there. He enjoyed working with his gang. However, they were constantly being told what to do and very often how to do the tasks they were given. On Friday afternoon, they were paid. Most of the members of his gang disappeared after they received their pay. When their boss saw that Ioane was all by himself, he told him he could go home. He also promised him that he would allow him to work on at the wharf after the boat left. The other boys would not be continuing in their jobs. Ioane went to the Post Office. There he asked Beto to send home ten dollars to his father.

'There's a ball at the hotel tonight,' Beto told him. 'Would you like to come with me?'

'True?' Ioane asked him. Beia came to his mind.

'We can take the seven o'clock ferry,' Beto explained to him.

'Good. I'll go with you.'

'I'll come for you tonight some time before seven.'

A bit before seven Beto arrived at the house. Ioane was ready and waiting.

'You can't enter the hotel like that,' Beto told him. 'Wear your uncle's long trousers.'

Ioane looked around for his uncle's trousers and put them on. They were too big and looked loose on him. He shook his head.

'It doesn't matter. The ferry will soon leave,' Beto warned him.

At the hotel they bought tickets at the door. Ioane looked around for Beia. He paid for another ticket and told the students at the table to give it to her when she arrived.

They went in. Many people were already there, scattered at a number of tables. Ioane looked around for Beia.

They found a small table around the corner, and sat down.

'What do you want to drink?' a waiter asked them. He was carrying a tray.

'Can we have two cans of beer,' Beto told him. 'Do you have any VB?'

'No. I'm not drinking beer. A soft drink, please,' Ioane interrupted.

'All right, one VB and one soft drink,' Beto said to the waiter.

'Orange?' the waiter suggested.

'Yes,' Ioane replied, not knowing what to ask for.

The waiter noted down their order.

'How much are they?' Beto asked the waiter.

'A dollar twenty cents,' the waiter told him.

Beto gave him the money.

People continued to come in. The band boys were tuning their electric guitars.

'Hey! Beto!' Ioane said to Beto. 'There's Beia.'

The waiter came with their drinks, and he gave Beto his change. Ioane stood up to go and meet Beia. Beto held him back.

'She's with a friend,' Beto told him. 'Drink, man,' he urged him. He gave him his orange, and opened his can of beer.

'Cheers!' Beto motioned him to lift up his can.

The music started and the stage lights were switched off. The seats and tables were fully occupied. An I-Matang and a local girl and a couple of others had joined Ioane and Beto at their table. At first a number of rock songs were played. Only a few people danced to start with, but after a few numbers the floor was packed full. The dancers found it difficult to move without touching each other. Ioane was watching Beia and her friend at the end table. Tenten was facing Ioane and Beto. Beia had her back to them.

'Shall I go and drag Beia here for you?' Beto asked Ioane when he returned to the table.

'No, leave her alone. They are enjoying it,' Ioane said to him.

Another rock number was played. Beto ordered another can of VB and looked around for a partner.

'Come on, boy,' Beto said to Ioane when he returned. 'Come off it.'

Another number began.

'Let's go,' Beto invited Ioane. 'There are many girls around.'

Ioane shook his head.

The music was slow and emotional. Ioane watched Tenten and Beia rise together and walk to the dance floor. Tenten held her by the waist, close to him. They were whispering to each other. Tenten was looking down at Beia, and she was looking up at him. Beia laughed at something Tenten said and turned away. She met Ioane's gaze, and looked away quickly.

At the end of the number, Beto took his partner back to her table. When he returned to his table, Ioane was not there. He hurried to the toilet. He was not there. He looked for him outside the hotel. He went back in and asked the people he knew if they had seen him. They hadn't. He drank his beer quickly and left.

When the dance was over, Beia followed Tenten out of the hotel. They walked hand in hand to his motorbike.

'You are coming with me tonight, aren't you?' Tenten asked.

'I'm afraid,' Beia replied.

Tenten looked at her. She was pale under the dim light of the street lamp.

'What are you afraid of? I've told you many times already that we can deal with your parents later,' Tenten reminded her.

They got on the bike and rode away.

'Good night, Beia,' her friends called out to her as they drove past.

'Good night,' she replied waving back.

Tenten drove past a couple of motor cyclists. Beia clung to his waist firmly.

A few days after the ball Ioane learnt from Beia's schoolmates that Beia had never gone back to school after that night.

It's difficult to know what Ioane did or how he felt when he heard the news about her. Nevertheless, tonight he was sitting leisurely with his uncle and aunt on some mats spread out between the sleeping-house and the kitchen. They were listening to a radio request programme. One of the requests had just been sung, and the announcer was reading the next one. Ioane got up quickly and walked away.

'Where are you going?' Tiaoni asked him.

'I'll be back soon,' Ioane replied.

The request was played.

Ngaia bon ataei n te rerei i PST / *She is a student at PST*
Ae babaina naba te kewe / *Who also knows how to lie*
E bia uringa n ana tai ni kaotibure / *May she remember for confession*
Ngke e keweai n te airan naite / *Her lie to me at the island night*

I a bora kangara nangi ni kakariariako / *How tired was I waiting for you*
N te tabo are ko bon ataia ne / *At the place you know, dear*

Sixty second, sixty minutes	*Sixty seconds, sixty minutes,*
And how many more over time	*And how many more over time*

Nei Tenanou ko a boom irau ngkai nei	*Dear, what form are you in now?*
Ani keiakina reken te rabakau O	*Learn as much as you can*
Ba kakabaiara ma kakatongara	*For it is our hope and pride*
Ngkana ko a reke nei n te mein aobiti	*When you are asked to work at the main office*

Nei Beia ko a bon takamainaina ne	*Dear Beia, you are fair*
Ao ko a bon tiribaea nanou	*My heart yearns for you*
Taran matam a bakarereai ao a kakang	*Your eyes pierce through me*
A nimtai man tautauai	*Stick and hold me fast*
Bon tei meang ae kani manemane riban	*It's me, the man from the north*
Ao an te ririka ae am ririkan	*Who loves you.*
Am bai n akoi am bai ni kaeabea	*Something to remember you by*
Ao bon raom n am tai ni bane.	*To serve you and your friend always.*

Some time later, Ioane returned. Another request was read. The announcer paused for a while.

'I've booked myself on the boat leaving next week.' Ioane broke the news to his uncle and aunt.

His uncle looked at him, and lowered the volume of the radio.

'Yes, go back home, son,' Tiaoni said quietly. 'You'll be happier and freer to do things the way you like it.'

Ioane raised his head and looked at him for a long time.

NIUE

JOHN PULE

from *The Shark That Ate the Sun*

At evening when the sea is low and the waves haunted by infinity, the dark gives stars, shattering the silence. I recite to your eyes; those large perpetual pupils signify two boats in the distance, the clandestine sleep of birds that you wrote meet in the aspect of secular dreams.

I want you to always look upon me, to cast shadows of islanders a few miles off the American site. Maybe just to beautify the image in tourist magazines, put a little colour in the mothers' yellow eyes. Paint a hotdog in the child's hand and, if the original picture has Kwajalein in the background, instead have them posing in front of a travel agent. Show the reef at night when the sea is sparkling and hide the missiles that fly from California. Show the coconut trees swaying in the wind that carries the pollution, and to really hide the mysterious death have a church built or better still say amen and every time there is an atomic test give Christ back so we don't confuse the people who are black or olive. Christ is white.

I go now into a sad evening, go with meaning, regret and love. If I was to fall asleep in an ocean's tide, I would not dream again if you have been blinded by my violent ideology, you now know I am buried in sadness. If love was born on earth for every soul to immigrate into, I have then failed. For who judges? You go and I stay? I would very much like to avoid cities, and crowds. I would seek desolate shores. Be distant and apologise.

Golden one, my life is a net caught in nocturnal water that comes to be lost with the tears that fall when in your presence I dream. I want to wander for a while. Where shadows cast their moonless nights into Platonic estuaries and change every time their emotion awakes. To be sleeping inside paradisaical thoughts, drink a lake and recite a thousand lyrics to whoever comes to listen, or, when the word death is mentioned and scatters the people that heard the name, they can go and burn to the socket.

And we gave things a new world to suffer in, forgetting that it is only an illusion. The days go on. Whatever wearies me blackens my countenance. My thoughts ebb and dry quickly when the night folds the sharks away. I have fled from life's meaningless joys, now I understand how bright stars never cease to lose their luminosity; even storms cannot lift their eyes out.

That night we drove around the city with a red spray-can. While we are

spraying on the American Embassy WHEREVER AMERICA GOES DEATH FOLLOWS
an audience from the local pubs stroll over and form a circle as I entertain
them. Who gives a damn? — Bravo, Bravo, Bravo, shouts the captain. Let
me recite a poem, but before I do, let me say this. This is where the strength
of love begins; over its clear and celebrated flood I swim, swim from lost
and dreamy people to sweep the frost and piously beg.

Earth. Time's curfew desires only our attention
the landscape mirrors another reflection of
the other sorrow known on earth as life

the ocean is left behind as we walk to a dream
war is not known on earth but in the isolated
image human beings once ran naked in caves
carved out a history of a new birth
embellishing art to become blood and beauty
when mysteries poked at our brain, leaving holes,
and we dropped whatever we had in our hearts to
look at each other in amazement, and whoever possessed
the desire to live forever will never die, but we die, and suffer,
and the shock has long been forgotten
because the word death is only a gossip

and not when we carelessly describe to our
children how we love on earth, which ceases to
fascinate, and falls about our bodies like confetti

and standing naked to surmise a tranquil field
a city appeared to haunt the waterhole where
animals browse and drink. Years later
the remains of that lone figure are dug up
the position odd, the hands covered the eyes as if to
hide from some horrific vision, maybe a
revelation of what was seen is what we now live in
did the vision kill whatever his name and tribe is
staring out over the tranquil field?

the question glittered as centuries battled
in iron and the rain washed the blood away to
settle in small dark cities, which we tasted and
the smell caused a strange evolution to take
place in our emotions, and the change dressed
us in miraculous nights, the stars challenged
our answers

if they could glimpse into this present day
they would die in the presence of hate and confusion
that sleeps in every country

we contemplate distant illuminations,
yet the difficulty remains in
recognising the true human
which is a dream the firstborn forgot and hopes
this earth will never feel

goodbye, said the captain. Goodbye, said the islander.
Next time test in your own country
perhaps New York or Paris

So it goes on and on in that little state house, whose occupants are usually up all night drinking until the morning calls them to work and Kau staggers over to the next-door neighbour to use the phone to call a cab which appears in the misty hour like a single torch wading through the morn. Lila is by the fire staring into the flames, potatoes cooking, and the smell of gin, beer is swift in the air.

I part the torn curtains, 60s, colours of flowers, yellow petals scattered around the stem. My room is full of clothes, they touch the roof. Leather cases stacked with coats and suits carelessly tucked away. The rooster skins the silence alive with a crow that wakes up the sun.

I go out down the silly path towards the sea just to talk to the geology of land, and architectural trees win the first light bouncing off the windows; a dog barks from far away, and where the street meets the bleak coast, so dark, and dark mossy seaweed whose hair is as lovely as dolls' hair.

I collect driftwood and the fragrance of rocks together with the sour caves taking in the pollution foam keeps my senses tuned. The boats swing in the waves. Gulls cry to Sisyphus. The sun is bright like cars. Can I compare cars to the sun? Here comes the triumphant soul of Jack, one-armed, well balanced on his bike with the long rifle cradled on his lap, the shoes torn at the foot, holes in the pants and the woolly threads of the brown jersey drag in the breeze.

I arrive home arms full of wet wood. Lila is up, saying something to the spiders. She cups a passing queen bee and throws it down into her breasts. The muffled sound of tiny fans is a great act and I wait for the sting. Lila opens her clothes and the bee flies away. Lila replies, — Done, and is off to the kitchen where food from two weeks ago rots in the pots and the stove is greasy, so brown I draw patterns in it.

Ants have formed a black line from the cupboard to the floor across the tiles into the bathroom and out the back door into the garden stones.

Bread is rock-hard and the fridge door hangs on one hinge, the light inside shines onto the floor; it is empty except for a shrivelled onion. Outside, the entire back yard is like the gardens back home. Talo and corn cover from fence to fence. The shed is full of clothes.

By the tiny fire Lila teases the coal. On the table stand empty bottles of beer, ashtray full of lipstick butts.

The main road today is full of cars going down to Point England, the neat row of brick houses and the roses hang listlessly over the fence. Lila throws a pot of crabs once again onto the fire and soon it is bubbling in dead excitement, this is our lunch as long as there are crabs in the sea and two burnt-out potatoes. In the afternoon Kau arrives home and prepares raw fish, talo and chicken for dinner, also out of the taxi he carries in a crate of booze and two bottles of sherry.

Every morning Kau gets ready for work about 4.30a.m. He opens a bottle of red and drinks until his mate from down the road hoots and off Kau goes at 5.30. Sometimes he manages two bottles and his cough is disastrous and mean like two cars crashing.

One thing about my uncle Kau is he is a fantastic cook. I am by the fire, Lila is with a bottle and Kau is drinking too. The room is soon a smoky place and the front door is kept open and the sound of cars is louder and Lila saying, — Done. The atmosphere is durable, sometimes so supple that I take a swig of froth. When they retire to their beds, they never sleep together. I wonder when the last time was they had each other, as I have never felt their pangs of pain for each other nor love nor affection.

A grunt from Kau when he disapproves. From Lila — Done.

Simple as that. The back of the house is stacked with empty bottles, bottles everywhere. When no one is home I push the armchair to the window that faces the main road that goes to ruins in paradise. Stare at the stars and the cars, bright lights, and there I used to fall asleep and be woken up by the damn bang of a bottle hitting the table. Cough, cough, smoke. The same routine with Kau. I spend my days down at the coast, watching families fish off the wharf or explore the caves.

Sometimes I spend a weekend at Lani's house, my sister's in Mount Roskill. Lani is married to a taxi-driver, Leo. They ain't together any more. Lani followed Leo one night to a party, and found his honest face between the thighs of a skinny palagi, and to this day she is bitter.

Before that incident their home was their castle, consisting of two beautiful children, Tina and Lance.

I liked being around these two, but for some reason my sister, who is my half-sister, my father's daughter from his second marriage, keeps asking me questions, as if my family had no food to eat. You see, Puhia had a reputation for not feeding his family, which includes me. He just drinks, works, drinks, in that famous order.

At the table over dinner with a plate of veges and meat under my chin, she would say — Do you eat like this at home? Does Puhia buy food as good as this? Fuck you, I thought, what's so shit-hot about this meal, what I steal beats this piece of skin. Soon after I walk out of the house while everyone goes to have a siesta. I know when the air is tangible and rejection surfaces. So I walk out (it runs in our blood down to the sea), and find my way back to Crummer Road. No one is home. I experience no fear, only rejoice and know the freedom by its filthy shoes and empty stomach.

The spirit climbs down from the tree smiling. I climb into the house through an open window. Tiptoe through the house as if an intruder.

No food in the kitchen. I go walkabout on the streets, stopped by a taxi-driver who is a friend of Leo's. Leo turns up and takes me back home. While Lani is hitting me I just look at her and want to deck her. The house in Mount Roskill is another shed that I don't want to be in.

It will be a while before Puhia takes me home.

Goodbye.

LET'S DANCE

the poet does not know whether he is earth's fruit or a
dream blazing like a star

rain in my hands
rain in my mouth
cups on my body
my eyes are empty

after a good night's sleep with trees they give me advice
what this advice is I must ask the poet who writes his
lyrics in sand, especially black coastal sand
littoral areas are the best, he said, they are soft and
easy to read

drunk again on wine
while rain gently falls
the wind's song is rough
mixed with wine and rain

the streets shining like the sun
although water masks the surface

as a face lost in pain
as words cannot say goodbye

pray to god so all sensation
at least sleeps till love reigns
your beauty drifts like driftwood
in another dream I crawl to the altar that means peace

another drunk night in the mud
beer and gin
the switched-on bombs
bopping to dark dancing
music rain ripped shirt

that lonely chair
electric sorrow told me so
on red sheet you spread
yourself out my love

all in one burst
love you love you love you
is that action a

lion tamer's whip?
or did I see you hidden
by guilt although enjoying
everything?

early morning and darkness music rebounds
universe stars new moons
touch perpendicular notes
is sound parallel to time? vast void for my words to
travel like light through silence. Collide with
meteors and suns
then pass into human coma where
horizons cover me. And seagulls scatter the reflection
of broken mirrors of the city.

I sing your name, music, sweet one,
you stagger like I do. When you stagger to the clouds
stagger like I do.

— I don't know if swans died in their final song, said the poet, — but when I glance into an overcast distance I sing to myself a sad tune, sing, for example: How can I approach her? On clear nights like tonight I dream of a ballad to quieten my burning soul, a ballad voiced to the sound of solitude. I am waiting. Every time I leave this woman I always try and see her once more because if I don't my soul becomes unbearable to carry around. I walk along the shore deserted by gulls, slowly and wearily, and the stars shatter the night as if to imitate certain illusion. The love I carry, I carry in contempt. Because love is perfumed in anxiety I go out of my way to find what is godly and kneel, because I know love is like the waves, eternally in flight. It will reach the waiting heart. It is about this time I stop and talk to the stars, who also try to become part of the one I speak so highly of, the one I love so dearly, the one I will die for.

I said — Do you know who I speak of?

And one star looked around meekly at his brothers and sisters in the same predicament; all answered —Yes. We know who you speak of, her light shines all the way into heaven, and the angels talk all evening about her, they keep saying things like: Surely she belongs to the divine intelligence that keeps all unique entities in holy embrace, and one who abides on earth must surely be of noble lineage. And we, we want to be her eyes, which are of oceanic beauty. We dare not interfere or approach her, as the colours are too traumatic, they are of sublime creation, we feel belittled.

The poet paused and poured a glass of whisky, lit a cig, emptied the fire into his mouth, said cheers and continued.

— You see, I'm a Romantic. I'd rather be a Romantic than a Modernist, those boring farts whose reality bores the shit out of me. A poet must travel towards God. Our God. A poet's god is healthy and knows every detail of our suffering. This god can also be merciless, mad and dangerous. When this god touches you, it is death. Any poet who has had a life of misery knows this. That is why we damn the white hope, white factories, the intellectualisation of the white death.

— But you yourself are white?

—Yes; sometimes I wish I was black. Black is the colour in our dreams. Black is the colour of reality.

I pour myself a sincere glass of whisky. Cheers! Outside, the moon is fat and delicious like the insides of love. There is one lit candle that flings bulbous shapes of objects across the room. The floor is blue and slowly we will make our way to the oblivion to recite our poems.

For the past two and a half years all I've been doing with great gusto and with the piousness of a priest and the dignity of Prince Charles is to get myself totally, horrendously drunk. My friends tell me I'm revolting, selfish and destructive. What's so selfish about ringing someone up at 2 a.m? Well, I still keep my integrity intact. Spend my dole money every week on alcohol. Alcohol is a gift wrapped in clouds. Clouds that could be the eyes of gods, for all I care. This habit of getting drunk is as soluble as the wind.

Remorse and guilt is the morning's chant. Trying to fuck a Greek woman who danced for me to the music of three Samoans. One woman at our table outdrank four fat-bellied men. Beer bottles shine like diamond flowers that sweetly soak the mouth in satanic honey. Love's bullet shoots at the heart and not succeeding he hangs himself in the band's practice room. The days never looked so bleak. I'm drunk.

The poet then stood up and downed a glass of whisky and recited a poem.

tonight when waves
crash against desire
and the wild slaves
of the heart's fire

turn up to sing
what is their song?
I, Poet, have wings,
I can do no wrong,

His eyes begin to roll. His lips are dangerously red. His white hair drops like dew over the forehead. His blue eyes are shining.

It is not yet over.

I empty the last drop of whisky and reach under the kauri table for a bottle of port. Black Ruby.

We both go out and piss against the night. It is starry. The wealthy houses that live in the private world are difficult to understand.

Back at the table I stand up and recite a poem. Although I feel the groggy litany circle in my mouth, I still manage a poem.

it is after 3 a.m.
I cannot sleep
a river is fierce
I go out
sit quietly
under Jupiter's head
until a wave has passed over
worried about reality
sane memory
I am sleepy
holding a clear vision of a road's
crooked speech
while in my head

sings tomorrow's festival
while in my head
cries a bitter youth
famous as cut talo leaves
faulty as a light bulb
I remember too much
repetitive images
I ask myself again
what is it slapping you senseless?
the shadow in the city?
the poet's story of life?
stand firm, says love
I carry my guitar
lugged on my shoulder
cast a crane-like shadow
onto another's property

manic man
in your troubled house
in your segregated land
your people forget your name
drowsy, lost, no star

burns, no rain falls
and don't you love rain?
no truth heard
I hate your god, your factories, your systems
I hate your doors, your roads, your words
I hate your cars

my father fell down twenty-five steps
I dig up the past
ahead of me is the angel of gaiety
shitting beside the statue of war heroes
oak trees sway
the sun is lukewarm
I grab a handful of stars

We are both drunk. My poet friend, eyes closed, more like in prayer. There is silence. I take a swig of black port, shake my throat, my senses are deranged. My friend looks at me, holds his glass and sings out, — Cheers! It is my turn to recite. I will recite a love poem, may I? We drink and fill our glass.

He stands up. Takes a swig. Burps. Closes his eyes.

I bring you baskets of roses and doves
I bring you handfuls of nuts and raspberries
I lay these before you
bursting forth ants that tremble
I'll dream for you Venus and Athens
the remains of an alchemist's vision
I'll dream for you sunflowers and potatoes
fields, parish and paintings, plough and seeds
colours red, yellow, blue, pink and green
I'll show you my home. It is surrounded
by laughing children, Polynesians that
liven the street up with colour and laughter,
with their bags full of food
from the market. We can live among them.
I'll lead you across bridges to botanical gardens
where sun sets, moon sets and daisies blossom

where there are parks whose trees blot out the sun
in a brilliant cup of green luscious leaves
where horses, heifer, and goats graze
together we will walk the metal country roads
past deserted houses, broken fences and barns
the melancholic distance of hills and gum trees
that resemble swollen oranges

I'll show you fields of solitude of winsome tranquillity
I'll show the fence where I often sat with
my stubborn sadness. The paths I walked
along to hide my misfortune, where
I listened to the lament of the wind
that often carried me beyond Cape Te Reinga Wairua
where my soul is lost

My friend slumps down awkwardly in his chair. — Let's see now. Any other
poems we can sing to each other? He falls asleep, and I go off to sleep.
Somewhere until the morning.
  Goodnight.

PAPUA NEW GUINEA

NORA VAGI BRASH

Mass Media, Mass Mania

Yummy, sweet marie, tea cake
KO kraka, PK, KK
Tic tac Fanta tango
Toothache, decoy, decay
koikoi anyway
Fall out, pull em out
Strong teeth? No way!

Talking about lime fresh
Blue Omo for brightness
Palmolive, brighter soap, white soap
Soft soap, dope soap
Whiter wash, wash wash, brain wash
Brain blank, blank cheque, blank bank
Check out!

Buy now, buy new, buy big, buy bulk
Buy more, buy me, buy now, Dinau
Buy! Buy! Goodbye self-reliance
Sell! Sell! sell self, sell soil
Sell soul, sell out, sell bottles
Sell empty promises
SOLD OUT.

APISAI ENOS

Moon

Nothing is tender and soft
like a handful of glittering grass
cuddling my back with gentle fairy fingers.

The mountains, packed onto each other,
sit with mighty bottoms and golden heads
puffing blue clouds from bamboo pipes;
they cast dark shadows
on the sloping kunai grass.

The river Fly flows to the sea,
not chattering like starlings do around their nests
nor giggling quietly like midnight lovers,
but silently; like a bracelet of silver
it seems to encircle the earth.

The scent of frangipani
is heavy under the coconut palms
and bats play the love games
against the moon.

Steal away, then,
steal away tonight
to the dance of the fireflies.
Fly away,
let me love you
with moonlight touch.

JOHN KASAIPWALOVA

From *Sail the Midnight Sun*

I am the midnight sun
My soul conceived to body
The love embrace of that night
When my Bwalai turned monster of the depths
Trembling for blood revenge on mankind
But instead summoned with burning desires
My naked Libra in her virgin love
Ecstasying the tender patience of the stars.

The waters raged like earthquake mountains
To couch the love bed of my parent blood
While the heavens throughout smoked their blackness
To weave a marriage-curtain of lover's secrets
As my Libra plunges into the ocean
Into the thrashing arms of my Bwalai erect with eagerness
For her open flesh craved of untold hunger
Of nights and days that never meet as one
On that loving night my ocean depths flashed
In unison with the openness of my heavens
To join night with day as one lovers body soul
And through the crescent peaks they whispered my name
The midnight sun.

In the heat of passioned love kisses
That smashes the chains of loneliness
And the barren emptiness of waiting so long
Bwalai shivers to thrust his oceaned sperms
From which come my limbs filled with currents to flow
And in answer Libra shakes in soaring flights
To born my mind out of heavenly flashes of delights
Till the stars and ocean depths make one their flowing currents
To shape my heart a fountain of love
The heart of the midnight sun.

The midnight sun born of love

Came forth with tears of life apart
As the star and the ocean in the bliss of after-loving
Smiled their baby the unknown secrets of his course
Horizon wedged to part the two
When Libra caressed their farewell with mother's chant
The blanket of heavens is torn apart
To show the glimmering joys of the midnight stars
And in praise in his lover's glistening flesh
Bwalai prostrates the turbulent waves
Into a soft cradle for their love child
To wait the charge of breaking dawn.

The birth of the midnight sun
Has rippled the heavens and the seas
With tidings of their blood,
With currents of their soul, so fast and loud
A battle raged between night and dawn
To decide the home for the midnight sun
The love child of their dreams
To grow and flourish the barren soils
So often tracked by their lonely steps.

Dawn came blooded from the fight
Her twilight fingers stretched in delight
To kiss in adoration her newborn son
The love fleshed of the midnight sun
She took the baby in her soft arms
She straddled the east with her open legs
To bid her smiling day shine forth
As she turns away to below the horizons
They travelled many days
They sailed many nights
First to the skies, then through the seas
In search of Tutauna
The land long written by the stars
To be the home of the midnight sun.

One hundred days lined the paths of the travellers
Two hundred nights fed them food and water
While Dawn flowed her breasts with milk of tenderness
For the growing midnight sun.
The currents of the ocean depths have long commanded
That the journey to the land of Tutauna

Must swell like the rising tide
The shadows of many currents to come
Whose seeds the rays of Dawn
Must pierce the mind of the midnight sun.

Sopi magic of the seas being seeded
Dawn smiled to see a handsome body grown
Tempered by their travels to the land of Tutauna.
So the last day wiped away
The hazy shrouds of landless horizons
Black oceans blushed to green their waters
As towering mountains beckon the land of Tutauna
Dawn pointed to the midnight sun
To look the soils that must feed his flesh and blood
Till the currents of sopi seeds
Break their waters to flow beyond
Their magic and their tide.

Dawn stooped forward with countless tears in her eyes
To shore the midnight sun on human soils
His land of youth Tutauna.
The golden sands danced their joys
Green waters sent their feathered palms
Mountains burst downward their waterfalls
To greet and quench their dreams
Long long promised by the moons.

Never has Tutauna seen such welcome feast
Breezes trembling with music everywhere
To carpet the steps of the midnight sun
Women skirted their passioned waists with rainbows
Men raised their flesh with conch-shell blasts
Children drummed their restless youths in tune
To the seas, the mountains and the skies
While drifting smoke marked the hundred pigs slain
To sizzle the tongues of feasting dancers
Mother earth spared no fruit from riping trees
Left behind no foods in their swollen mounds
To feast all feasts

The coming of the midnight sun.
Time slept with the passing moons and rains
The midnight sun soon grew a man

His limbs flow like ocean currents
His mind opened like the heavens above
And where the rivers of his body
Meet the twinkling flashes of his mind
His heart grew a fountain of love
Flowing through the land of Tutauna.

Into the youthful fountain river
The women soothed their burning flesh
While the men sought in their wild wild dreams
To be themselves the flowing waters
With no currents to make new rivers
Only lustful rolling in and out
Between the fleshy folds of crying desires
Till the frolicking swims and futile dreamings
Turn to arrows of pain and loneliness
For wanton fame and magic richness in themselves
Are but solid rocks unmoving
Against the melting point, against the flowing current
The sad crying of the midnight sun.

The midnight sun grew full man
Always giving but never receiving
The loving desires of his heart.
Days stretched like endless plains
He spoke no words to the men
Nights covered so cold like needles
No woman wanted to share the pains of his loneliness
That seem no end to sleepless torments
But a sea of fear for the midnight sun.

One night when Tutauna had fallen deep asleep
The midnight sun weary from crying
Fell to his knees on the empty sandshore of desperation
His heart feeble with no one to love
He lay his limbs naked before the pillowing winds
To let sleep of nowhere gate his mind
Against the pain of empty frustrations.
Soft and silent so not to wake the sleeping lover
The virgin moon rose naked from the seas
Her golden hair sparkling as they kiss the ocean
Her soul angered to break those gates of nowhere
Her flesh shyly trembling with desires

183

To make love and let the currents of her passions
Melt the heart of the midnight sun.

He woke as if she was but a dream
She blushed her desires for his naked body
Her beauty and her flesh set fires
To the heart and blood of midnight sun.
The moon melted her soft body into his
The lovers' currents making one river
With not a word spoken to waste
Their flesh, their minds and their hearts
Speaking their longing years of separation.

No sooner would their mountain waves crash foaming
The rising tide of their desires would swell again
Till their loving carried them near the break of dawn.
The cocks crowed in Tutauna
To strike a silent fear between the lovers
The midnight sun cried for her to stay
Her fears dressed a shame around her naked flesh
Her heart begged to stay but past memories
Struck their pains of fear like thunderbolts
Till again her virgin heart she cried
'I have seen too many women laugh and swim
In the currents of your river flows.'
And as Tutauna stirred new day
The sad moon sank crying to the west.

Sadness clouded Tutauna
Like monsoon rains before they fall
The women frolicked no more
The men silent with dreams
The midnight sun grew thinner
Loss his food, sadness his drink
He searched the seas, he flew the mountains
No leaf of the forests left unturned
But nowhere could the midnight sun reach
His lover, the flesh of moons.

Tutauna grew sadder still until one day
They begged the midnight sun to hear
The magic tales of the old old man
Who lives lonely in the caves where the waterfall breaks.
Taking gifts the midnight sun set for the caves

'Lonely mirror, your hair whitened by your journeys,
Tell me which way to the land of my lost lover.'
His eyes sparkled to see the gifts of the midnight sun
'Young lover, I too am the corpse of once a dream
But the seagulls sing the loveliest of the women
Waiting sadly for their lover across the seas
In the far distant land to the east
Where the evening star has named her Imdeduya.'

The midnight sun took the tallest of the forest trees
Night and day Tutauna shuddered
To his sweat and skills
As the fallen woods turned to shape
His canoe like the rainbow curves.
The women wove his gifts
The men basketed the garden harvest
The winds tensed ready to search
The lost gone lover of the midnight sun.

Farewell tears of Tutauna rolled
Like the breaking ocean reefs
To anchor forever the sail of the midnight sun
But he rose to his prows with tears in his eyes
And the currents of his heart burst their longings
    Imdeduyo — Imdeduyo — Imdeduyo — Imdeduyo . . .
    Kwanuwedi bakenu
    Yegu Yolina
    Newawegu Kesai
    Nemtemata uwogu
    Naluveyamu Naluvebogi Kamdoyoyu
    Imdeduyo — Imdeduyo — Imdeduyo . . .
The spells of anchoring weight broke free
The midnight sun set sail his back to Tutauna.

Blue waters parted to stream foams of white
Before the jutting canoe of the midnight sun
Flying fishes leapt from the depths
To catch sight of the pregnant sail
A lonely steersman in the landless seas.
Into the winds he threw his scented leaves
Towards the land of seagulls now rising from the haze
Fluttering hearts rose in flying salutations
To conch the searching lover sails down to shore.

After feasting their joys the seagulls cried
'Why torment your soul sleepless in search of love
So illusive and bitter pain
When freely you can roam like the oceans and the gales?'
Their host cried to break their magic
    Imdeduyo — Imdeduyo — Imdeduyo — Imdeduyo . . .
    Let me lie against your breasts
    I am the midnight sun
    Thrashed by the ocean waves
    My body frail
    By night, by day I long for you
    Imdeduyo — Imdeduyo — Imdeduyo . . .
His canoe broke loose the ties of the seagulls
To sail east to the Land of Happiness.

Many days sailed past
Many nights compassed the stars
To steer the passage clearly laid
By the old old man of the caves
Till the twenty morning brought to shore
The Land of Happiness he sought.
Dancing and music floated like gentle breeze everywhere
As beautiful women danced to sleep with the midnight sun
To fill his sorrowed heart with happiness.

In their happy feastings the chief pleaded
'Why sadden your heart by the one night love
That has but filled your heart with sorrows?
Take this land to fill you happiness all your days instead!'
The midnight sun cried the memory of that happy night
    Imdeduyo — Imdeduyo — Imdeduyo — Imdeduyo . . .
    Let me dance in your flesh again
    I am the midnight sun
    Music and song without you water my eyes
    Sorrows burden my lonely heart
    And passing stars only steep my desires for you
    Imdeduyo — Imdeduyo — Imdeduyo . . .
No happiness can tie down his sails
The midnight sun parted for the Land of Beauty.

At every feast the solitary seaman rained his hosts
Gifts laden from Tutauna to lighten his searchings
But they packed his leave with new gifts

To weight heavy his sinking heart
Yet between the crimson sunsets
And volcanic sunrises
The midnight sun sailed further east
Rainbow shores the Land of Beauty.

In tranquil beauty they feasted and begged
'Why blemish your youthful blood with dreams of love
Whose ugliness surrounds you when you wake?
Let your flesh and blood glory the beauty
Solid rainbows at your touch and sight!'
The midnight sun cannot answer the shapes of that night
Embedded like glowing fires in the depths of his eyes
    Imdeduyo — Imdeduyo — Imdeduyo — Imdeduyo . . .
    Let your burning eyes sparkle my sights
    I am the midnight sun
    Golden sunsets touch my dream
    Your face mirrored in the skies
    Darkness cannot make you blemish
    Imdeduyo — Imdeduyo — Imdeduyo . . .
Once more the holding spell is broken
To set sail to the Land of Truth.

For many days the midnight sun fought the tossing seas
Angry waves turn to tender calmness
Many nights the skies shrieked with fury
Cyclones break into whispering breezes
Blackness of nights couch the light of day
Creatureless ocean surface harbours million fishes below
Unbroken circling horizons of emptiness
Turn rugged by peaks haloed with clouds
The rising mountains shoring the Land of Truth.

In the midst of their innocent feastings they asked
'What truth is there in love
That has no constancy but a fading memory?
Learn the truth of mountains unmoving
Constant and firm throughout the days!'
The midnight sun cannot show the valleys in his heart
Carved by the flowing currents of that night
    Imdeduyo — Imdeduyo — Imdeduyo — Imdeduyo . . .
    Let your river flood my streams
    I am the midnight sun

The valleys we have shaped
Crush me restless in pains
Crying for our currents to meet again
Imdeduyo — Imdeduyo — Imdeduyo . . .'
His steer untied their tangling words.
To set sail for the Land of Hope.

To sail the open seas alone
Has no friendship laughter to comfort
While silent men sleep below their roofs
Madness hunts the fearful mind
Of the midnight sun fevered on the seas.
His sails strain in shaking obedience
Tempted so often by the shores of ease
To lie folded in restful despairs
Against the shadows of the Land of Hope.

They heard his dreams and cried to comfort
'Why wrack your limbs to hope
The love that is your desperation?
Take the unbroken heavenly hopes
That carry no pains to flesh and blood!'
He searched to capture the jealous tears of that night
That seeded his hopes amidst the spears of despair.
    Imdeduyo — Imdeduyo — Imdeduyo — Imdeduyo . . .
    Let me kiss those fears away
    I am the midnight sun
    My hopes breed a madness
    From the jeering laughter of crowds
    Your jealous tears burn me alive
    Imdeduyo — Imdeduyo — Imdeduyo . . .
Their gifts changed hands to break their magic
The midnight sun sailed for the Land of Leisure.

Weariness of toil spurned by mockeries
Numbs the soul the think of death
To end the cares of fruitless search
For the woman whose love the seagulls sing
Whose beauty is shaped in the old man's dream
Doubting fears ice the thoughts of the midnight sun
Can she be the woman same
As the shores of Leisure rise to greet him

Luxurious was the feast to greet the weary steersman
'But why tire your sweat and toils
To the misty tales of the old man alone?
Take the honey sweetness of leisure unconcerned
Trusting not another's words!'
Yet how can the midnight sun abandon now
When one sea away lies the Land of Love
    Imdeduyo — Imdeduyo — Imdeduyo — Imdeduyo . . .
    Return to me your waking touches
    I am the midnight sun
    On your bed the scented leaves
    Bathe your oils shiny
    My flesh to touch and rest
    Imdeduyo — Imdeduyo — Imdeduyo . . .
Fear of treachery fights the yearning tides of nearness
As the midnight sun sets his sails for the Land of Love
Where lives the loveliest of all women.

Two years have passed since the land of Tutauna
Raging seas and star-filled nights
Have sinewed the midnight sun
Till the soft palms of untried youth
Have turned to manhood bristled hands
His song of search knotted to his music of love
Have flung the turbulent cyclone clouds high
Have dipped amidst the ocean currents wide.

In the Land of East, the Land of Love
Dressed in laughter and shining smiles
She sits impatient longing her lover across the seas.
Many a man has sought to comfort her bed
But none can quench her dream by the seagulls flown
Till the breaking waves sing out their load
Music song from currents afar
    'Imdeduyo — Imdeduyo — Imdeduyo — Imdeduyo . . .
    Kwanuwedi bakenu
    Yegu Yolina
    Newawegu Kesai
    Nemtemata Uwogu
    Naluveyamu naluvebogi kamdoyoyu
    Imdeduyo — Imdeduyo — Imdeduyo . . .'
The midnight sun shook the shores with his magic conches

His canoe laden full of gifts of love.

Five monsoons flooded their waters
Five harvests filled their yam houses
Yolina grew his legs and arms
By day the midnight sun seeded their gardens
By night the fishes filled his nets
Till his sweat and skills
Brought them fame and riches
The envy of the Eastern lands.

One night as Imdeduya sat lonely
Waiting for the fisherman midnight sun
Their son asleep to the furtive footsteps
Of her once lover near long-forgotten
'Why wait in lonely tears of a husband
Who can no longer comfort your bed?'
The secret lover smiled
As the silent truth opened her closed lips
'I beg you leave with our memories past
I have shared my husband's sleep
To flower our beautiful son.'
The secret love poured his poisoned farewell
'The midnight sun catches not fish alone at night'
As he crawled away his angered bitterness.

Who can measure the heights of treachery fears
Who can count the spears of suspicions
When waiting loneliness mattresses a marriage bed
And the doors of vanity secrets
Open to the knocking of fork-tongued gossips
Imdeduya cannot sleep in peace
Imdeduya cannot eat in laughter
As the poisoned drink trickled down her veins.

On a second night the secret lover came again
'Are you blind to your husband's daily absence
Have you not seen the twinkle for other women's eyes
While you sit dying with age?'
Imdeduya weakened her reply
'My honour is my husband
My son is my love
Whose house must stand before the neighbour's eyes.'

The fires of old love began to stir their hate
'What fool you are in all our eyes
To lie trampled by your husband's wanderings
A stepping-stone where once a morning star
Whose dignity none can equal.'

When the heart of vanity takes eyes
Upon a fallen dignity once held high
By faceless neighbours seeking comfort false
Flowers begin to wither
As the roots of anchoring love leave their soils
To writhe upwards to the blistering heat
Till cloudy storms become her face
A wall to fence her crying heart.

Imdeduyo begged the words of the secret lover's third climb
'If your tongue carries a flowering innocence
Why do you plant the seeds of falsehoods
When my husband stands unshaken
With tears for my pains
And crying for my shyly withdrawing love?'
The secret lover laughed to feel
The waited bait taken at last
'Let not your son cloud your eyes
To see the secrets of your husband's yearnings
Night after night to fish the empty waters
For his long-gone lover a woman of the moons
Who once loved him naked from the seas.'

The midnight sun woke next day to see
The footprints of the secret lover beside their house
Like fence stakes jagged and sharp
But when secret discoveries shake hands
With vanity dressed in fears and loneliness
Humble truths fall chained and imprisoned
And in their place like rotting graves opening their stench
Profusing lies spread like the forest creepers.

How can Imdeduya kill the angered pains of rejection
To ask him the naked woman from the seas
How can she face the fears of another more beautiful
Who will but trample her dignity and pride
Throughout the eyes of the Eastern lands.

So she masked her beautiful face
To let her steeled heart weep dry tears
'These are but footprints of our neighbours come
To gossip away the hours till you shore your nets!'
The midnight sun saw the tears dry
But how can he tear the masks apart
Without making his wife cry more feeble lies
To turn the hate of countless suspicions
Into wedges oceaning their island separations.

The midnight sun fished at night no more
To keep company his wife's suspicions
She smiled to all their neighbours' asking
Shutting away the silent yearning of her husband
To open his dreams of the long-lost lover
Till sunsets closed their doors
Locking their limbs in shivering coldness
As they sailed apart in their dreams.

Their gardens ceased to grow
Their nets raked seaweed and crabs
The midnight sun cannot speak before his fellow crowds
Without the haunting jeers of his emptiness
Imdeduya cannot smile to all the women
Without the fears of her silent separation
Taking flesh and blood to smear
Her once beauty which seagulls sing.
Where once their son swam in laughter and love
Yolina sat silent and rejected like ocean driftwood
While pretentious smiles and careless concerns
Dried their rivers to make no currents flow
Against their pains of bridging the chasms so deep
A sad withdrawing love.

One day the midnight sun left to fish at the break of dawn
Imdeduya took her son to the gardens alone
And as the garden grasshoppers led Yolina around
She met the secret lover near the bushes' edge
'This naked woman of the seas has robbed my love
No more my husband but my shame for all eyes to see!
Sleep with me to quell my hurts
My revenge against his treacherous lies!'

192

The evening brought them like gathering stormy clouds
The fish lay rotting beside the pots
Their throats lumped to hate the sight of foods
While silence haunted them like a ghost
Till Yolina cried out his ignorant innocence
'My father, you promised to be at sea all day
Why did you come to the gardens at morning noon
To fight my mother near the bushes' edge?'
His seeking tongue struck her face like lightning bolts
To leave no words that can blanket the day
As her angered palm slapped to shut the truth between his lips
'My son, the open waters have shared my loneliness all day
My veins have cried and cried to share their painful currents
But vanity and revenge have drifted us so far apart
I have no strength to fight your mother's fears!'

When failure and sadness fight their wars
Against the urchin spikes of determined revenge
There is no turning back
As eagle eyes of hatred pluck the eyes of love
The midnight sun cannot breathe and flow
In the barren fields of the Eastern lands
Nor can he face retelling the tears of broken love
In the waiting lands of Tutauna
Yet he must set sail, he must set sail with tears in his eyes.

The setting sun reddened her tears before parting the skies
The midnight sun untied his sails to set free his heart
Yolina cried desperately to beg his father return
But as the sandshores disappeared Imdeduyo cast her hatred loss
'Witches of mountain tops take your meal his flesh and blood
The midnight sun has burnt my beauty, my pride
Take him dead that I may laugh again!'
The horrid witches swooped down with hungry fangs to kill
He snatched his scented leaves: their magic into the wind
To cloud their eyes to flying blindness
'Imdeduyo — Imdeduyo — Imdeduyo . . .'
Your current is killed and dried by vanity
I leave behind the fruits of the Eastern lands!'
He shook the dress of the parting shores
He threw them into the seas.

Having shed the leaves of his marriage lands
The midnight sun trembled his fears of leaving
With memories to chase him sleepless
Throughout the nights in the open seas
But the dancing waves washed anew his nakedness
To melt his timid and frozen heart
Embittered by the five seasons passed
So he must set sail, he must set sail even with tears in his eyes.

Twilight began her watch like a placid judge
Yolina sobbed his orphan tears
Never to see again his mother's face
As her voice filtered behind disappearing tree tops
'Demon sharks of my waters around
The midnight sun has robbed my heart
Cut his veins that he may never love again!'
They snapped their teeth with blood revenge in their eyes
He snatched the ashing fire logs
To feed their warrior gaping mouths
'Imdeduyo — Imdeduyo — Imdeduyo . . .
Your memories fill me with shame
Tutauna shall not see my face!'
The midnight sun tossed away his sleeping mats
To drown behind the parting waves.

As the mats of bedded nights vanish
Last traces of once tender moments drift forever
Like sea mists before the morning breeze
The heart of the midnight sun began to stir again
The once currents for the naked woman of the seas
The deadening weight of his seasoned limbs
Began to flow their youthful blood
His urge to set sail, his set sail to wipe his tears.

Darkness fell behind the parting twilight
To fade away the distant mountains of Eastern lands
Yolina cried and cried and cried
The last remorsing of his mother's fading voice
'Avenging monsters of the ocean graves
Take four weapons into my son's limbs
To strangle the neck of the midnight sun!'
The dark oceans began to flash their thousand neon eyes

Leaping their slimes of greenery upward so high
Their snaky arms seeking to swell Yolina's limbs
'Imdeduyo — Imdeduyo — Imdeduyo . . .
The currents of my heart flow wild and free
To seek my lover in our new land!'
The midnight sun broke Yolina's neck
To smear the ocean monsters with his blood.

When yesterday is forever killed dead
Her flesh and blood turn to shying spirits
That must hide in the limbs of the midnight sun
As lessons learnt but unsure to teach
The far-away tomorrow that no one sees
While lonely cry the hours of between
With fears of destruction foretold to wreck
The sail of the midnight sun.

Never was the night so blackest
The stars so deeply buried by the tempest wild
The skies opened their gates of terror
To sanction loose their cyclone dragons
Screaming their fury against the riggings
Burning to tear apieces the midnight sun
The summoned oceans rolled into mountains
Their peaks so jagged and sharp always crashing
To spit their thundering foam against his prows
Tearing apart the canoe now lost in storm
The midnight sun jumped into the hungry boiling seas
Clutching only his steer and bwalai stone to his heart
As the ocean monsters devoured his broken sails.

A splintered canoe sunk in midst of stormy seas
Brings tears and wailings to the loved ones on shore
Who weep their despairs with suspicious blames
To lose their hopes of the battered seed of truth
While the enemies of the midnight sun dance their joys
Claiming their magic falsehoods to be so true
Vowing with the cyclone storms their success to sink forever
The flesh, the blood, the soul of the midnight sun.

The smell of blood summoned the witches again
Bwalai stone swelled to a mountain cliff-face
To shield the drowning seaman from their greedy eyes

The sharks attacked again their slighted revenge
His steer spread between the raging waters and their teeth
To send their gaping mouths grumbling away
The ugly monsters of the ocean graves leapt up again
Hoping to chain him to their prison depths
But their eyes and searching tentacles could only see
A bwalai stone afloat a wooden steering oar
While the midnight sun fought the screaming gales above
And the lashing waves with stinging froth all around
A shipwreck in the wild wild ocean storm.

Who has not stood petrified and hopeless
When wrathful destruction reeks all around
And inevitable death swings down to kill?
The weak of heart die before their deaths
The foolish smile to hide what their eyes behold
But cool and lithe are the waiting sinews
Of the midnight sun who carries a dream of love
A heart of fountain strength no wave can swamp.

In anger the shooting tempest waves would gush
The wreckaged sailor upward, upward like flying fish
Into the giddying spiral twists of screaming gales
Always biting, always tearing to break apart
The midnight sun from his steer and bwalai stone
And from the heights of heaven like a falling star
The gales would plunge their hoped carrion downward, downward
Back into the tumbling mountain waves so deep and dark
Always crushing, always suffocating to wash apart
The midnight sun from his steer and bwalai stone
Yet the armies of swirling skies and angry seas
Cannot dislodge the welded clench between the three
As he fought to see which way they flowed
The tangling currents of cloud and frothing waves.

Trembling fears of waiting unknown cease
Stunning moments of collision death withdraw
For the lonely warrior who poises to return their blows
And in their place the clouded mind is crystalled sharp
The tired limbs swell the beating rhythm of the heart
And as the gales swirled him through the skies
His open hand traced their eddying currents
While through the tumbling depths of crashing seas

His hair screened the magnet ocean current flows.

Time disappears
The midnight sun makes his home among the danger deaths
And with his right he drops farewell the bwalai stone
Down, down, down into the darkened seas
In a flash the ocean depths shuddered awake
The mother of swordfishes summoned at last
By the knocking magic of bwalai stone at her doors
She rose upward with swelling tides at her sides
To search the call, her son the wreckaged midnight sun
 He leapt from the clutches of the tossing waves
His feet firmly planted upon her back
To ride the tides through the angry storms to shore
His steer thrust beside the swordfish fins.

His steer fluttered taut their scented pendants
Music quivered his lips with the rushing fish
'Ride the tide, my tide let me ride
Darkness my bride, my darkness always at my side
Break, breaks, break you covering mists break
Break away the fog in my eyes
Tide away my darkness bride
And where the dark ocean currents cry
Come my love, my naked woman from the seas!'

Lightning bolts flashed from east to west
Thunder quakes split in half the carrion darkness so deep
And out of the angry seas broke the radiant moon
She came so full, beautiful and so tender
To meet her lover long-remembered night
Now erect beside the swordfish tide
They touched their bodies one, the burning hunger of so long
She cried to hold forever their trembling kisses
'My love, my love, my soul, my flesh
My tears, my fears, my silent yearnings
Have locked me barren and sad so long
The countless years I have wasted us apart
Waiting for you where the dark ocean currents cry!'

Into the raging storms he sang the happiness tears
'My love, my beautiful woman from the seas
I have walked the face of every soil

Shame and blood scar my hands to retell
My angry searchings to share you my flowing heart
I have snatched the twisted currents of the skies
To bind together the currents of swamping waves
To know love where dark ocean currents cry!'

There is no freshness to compare the eyes
Discovering each moment deeper still the mysteries
Of beauty in touch, the smile, the dream
When the currents of two hearts make one river flow
'I have cried to see avenging death so close
To rob me my silent longings all these years
So short are the hours that remain
To share our love, our cravings deep
See my soul the flowing beauty of love at our feet
The heavenly currents alone destroy with wrath
Water currents alone swamp out the breath of life
But our searching steer must link the separate passions
To flow one river riding the swordfish tide
A loving dream where dark ocean currents cry.'

No riches can measure the treasures of love
Searching to flourish new lands ahead
As the midnight sun steered the swordfish tide
'Ride the tide, our tide let us ride
Before sunrise breaks new day
Let Yakeba shores catch your waves
Yoyu caves to shelter our fires
Bweka waters to wash away our salty tears
Our love currents to turn a mountain spring!'

In the night and through the dangerous storms
The swordfish shored the lovers on land
The shifting sands of Yakeba cliffs
Where the midnight sun embraced his lover afresh
To dance the firmness of his feet
To end the many years on ocean waves.
Then hand in hand their hearts as one
They rested first at Yoyu caves
To melt away the journey's stiffness
Till they came to Bweka waters cool and sparkling
To wash away forever their salty tears
And there in love embrace they bore

A yelu dream where dark ocean currents cry.

Today the rock of the midnight sun sleeps at rest
With thousand secrets buried deep inside
Whose back has carved many an ocean steer
The silent passage through Yakeba beach
Yoyu shall gape open and mossed with age
The shelter for warming fires
While Bweka waters is haunted filled
With the dream of the midnight sun

    Yes a dream
    A restless flowing dream
    Whose sopi was seeded
    Where dark ocean currents cry
    Whose waters I have drunk
    To love you today
    With the longings for the tomorrow
    Sunshine and flowers
    The flow of the mountain spring.

IGNATIUS KILAGE

from My Mother Calls Me Yaltep

Introduction

My name is Yaltep. I am a Simbu, from the Kuman-speaking group of the upper Simbu. I was born a bit too early to go to school but I am old enough to see and try to understand and keep up with the tremendous changes that are taking place in my beloved Simbu and all over our country.

You may not be able to understand the confused state of my mind as you may have been spared the painful experience of trying to understand two diametrically opposed cultures at once.

Since I had the privilege of a peculiar and unique experience, I wish to tell the story of my life in my own way. I can only hope that you will get a glimpse of, and experience, my bewilderment at such stupendous progress in a lifetime.

Many of my ancestors give me the imagination and descriptive words to express my thoughts and feelings, which I hope will represent the experiences and feelings of the thousands of Simbus who have gone through the same confusing period. May this prove to be a humble story of events for the Simbu sons and daughters of tomorrow. May I request the pleasure of your company to accompany me through my life and experience with me the events that took place in my life. Since it's my journey, let us begin at the beginning of my life. Let us hear from the person from whom I got my being, my mother. Let my mother tell her story.

Early Childhood

'It was one of those rare, cloudless nights, when the moon was full. It had already glided over Mondia, and was heading for the western hills. At that moment it was directly over our little hut nestled by the banks of Gowe River. The broad smile of the moon was chilly, so was the river as you know.

'I was sick, and wanted to stay near the fire, but there was too much smoke from the green wood that was burning, so I came out to watch the moon and listen to the songs of the insects and birds, and the croaking of frogs.

'Also, in the crystal clear waters of Gowe, I watched our little home reflected, and it looked as if it was dancing in time with the ripples of the river, it looked as if a wind was shaking our little home from its foundations.

'Watching these and sitting in the cold, crisp mountain air made me feel momentarily quiet, but then a wave of sudden pain engulfed me. I gave a cry at which your aunties came to my rescue and brought me into the house!

'After what seemed an everlasting agony of pain, I was conscious and unconscious in turns, and at one moment the pain stopped, and I heard a sharp wailing cry. That was the end.

'When I came to, in the early hours of the next day, your aunties placed you in my arms. I remember saying, Boy or girl? They answered me in the traditional indirect way, saying, "Kua si nenga", in other words they said that I killed a bird, or that you were a boy!'

If you will bear with me, we shall pause to hear about the society into which I was born. This will give us the total picture of the people from whom I got what I have. The following are descriptions of my people from whom I got what I have, about a decade before my arrival.

My birth, even though insignificant in itself, was preceded by an extraordinary event. As it was related to me, an extraordinary white bird making thunderous and booming sounds suddenly appeared over the eastern horizon, and disappeared into the west.

The timid ran for cover while a few tried to shoot it down, but the strange bird went so fast and flew so high that everyone was baffled.

After a little while they heard the noise again. They stood on the hillside watching it disappear in the eastern horizon whence it came. That strange bird was the first aeroplane that flew over the Highlands. Tradition also has it that for months after that strange bird came and went there were rumours that the Gende people of Bundi were about to perform one of their famous magic spells, known as Kimagl, on the Mitnandi people. The fearsome Gerigl or Gende people over the other side of Mondia were notorious for their Kimagl. The rumours were spreading everywhere. The Mitnandi people did not venture far from home, for it was also said that the predicted catastrophe would fall on them in the form of floods or slides.

However, the rumours were soon forgotten, for the people were busy trying to eke out an existence in the already overcrowded Mitnandi valley.

But fate was not to allow these people peace of mind, for fresh rumours had it, this time from the lower Simbu, that Nigl Kande the gigl yomba was seen walking into Simbu and behaving strangely.

People were casting counter-spells, putting up strong posts in front of their houses to ensure that those strange beings would not follow the river up to its source.

The endi yombuglo and the binga ceremony were the signs of powerful spells cast at the main gates of men's houses, to ward off evil influences and protect those who were within the fence.

However, in spite of the binga ceremony or endi yombuglo, some of these strange people suddenly appeared over the Mondia pass and crossed the Gowe–Kualke river junction and settled at Kangrie.

So you can imagine: strange events followed by sudden arrivals of white men with their funny ways, trying to communicate amidst the general confusion and social turmoil. This was the society I was born into.

The white people who arrived from upper Simbu were a gentle crowd; our people took them to be the spirits of our ancestors, and treated them with respect.

But there was a misunderstanding at Womatne. A Kulkane man shot one of those men, then suddenly a much tougher and dangerous looking white man and his black men arrived on the scene. These latecomers were called kiaps and the former ones were called batres.

These two groups of people were instrumental in bringing about the confusion and sudden changes that we are going to sense and experience through this narrative.

The usual tribal wars, fought with bows and arrows, sharp spears and blackened shields were suddenly halted by these 'good spirits' with the help of their polished sticks. These magic sticks of the white men were so powerful, that the people came to fear them more than anything else. Here is an account given by a man who saw a magic stick at work.

'That stick spoke like thunder and spat fire and smoke when it was pointed at something. Even the birds in flight were brought low by it.'

Fortunately, the people had enough sense to see that swarms of arrows and sharp spears were no match for a single magic stick, for even one of these sticks was capable of wiping the entire tribe from the face of the earth, whereas an expert archer could kill no more than one at a time. The long range of the magic stick was the deciding factor in overcoming the former, conquering swarm of arrows.

The Kuman people and their warriors were surprised to see that the kiaps, with their sharp-headed black men from the Coast, were always on the move, ready to go wherever there was trouble. With the aid of their thundering sticks, they could put fighting warriors to flight. In this way, they gradually established peace in the Highlands of New Guinea. Ultimately, an era of peace and previously unknown quiet prevailed in the Simbu valley!

A few days after my arrival, there was much discussion among the men of my clan — almost ending in clan war.

The cause of the dispute was the question of my future name. As I was the first child, everybody in the clan who had contributed towards my mother's bride price wanted me to be named after him. My mother, of a cooler temperament than my father, solved the problem and averted the impending war. The consequence was that everybody was pleased and nobody disappointed. Hence my future was guarded against the poison of jealous clans.

This was how my mother solved the problem — she decided to ask the batre to give me a name. They had already given high-sounding and pleasant names to the children who lived near their house. Furthermore, she wanted me to wear one of those shining things that the children named by the batres wore around their necks — Mother took them to be charms to ward off evil influences. Besides, she was convinced that the batres were the good spirits, so, if they favoured me with a name and gave me the shining object as a sign of their good will, then the whole family would be fortified against any misfortune that might come along. Apart from these lofty reasons, she wanted to get some of the white crystals which the batres gave to women and children when they named them. When put on food, the crystals gave it a tasty flavour. My mother brought me, after many moons, to the white men at Kangrie to be named. The good batres were not too willing to name me at first, but, after many and fervent requests from my mother, they gave their consent and the following is the account of the ceremony in her own words.

'The batre, dressed in black and white, told me and the other women with their babies to follow him into the huge house, at the far end of which there was a high, smooth table on four legs.

'In the centre of this table, there was a small box, and on each side of it beautiful flowers were growing which were always in bloom. These extraordinary flowers were growing on shining bamboo. In between the flowers there were smaller shining bamboo on which there were tall white sticks that the white man burnt when he came to do his mysterious rites at the table. In that place of loveliness, there was a small red light burning all the time — it stood on the left side of the table and not far from the box. I was thrilled to see such a beautiful place, and was till gazing at it when the lady next to me told me to sit down. So we sat down at the end of the long house.

'The batre and some of his men who stood behind us exchanged some words. The batre always spoke first and the men spoke something to him in return. The batre put some white crystals into the mouths of the babies, in turn. I saw you lick your tongue, so I knew it to be mundi, which we used to get from the batre in return for the food we gave him. Then the Batre and his boys recited a very long and complicated formula, and we were made to march up the huge building. Half way to the door, we were halted, and there were more conversations between the batre and his boys. When they came to the end, the batre made many more signs with his white, lighted stick. After that the boy at our back held your head up and the batre poured some water over your head while uttering some formulas — he went down the line washing all the babies in turn and saying more of the formulas. When that was over, the batre said some words while holding his hands over us all in a graceful manner. Then we were told to go out, for the ceremony was over.

'At the door of his house, the batre asked us if we still remembered the names of the babies. I thought that there had been a mistake and told the batre that you had no name, even though I had brought you to him so that he could name you. The batre laughed. I thought it was not funny, but he composed himself and told us that each of the babies had been already named in the big house. So, to make us understand, and to remember your name, he made me repeat it after him, over and over, until I got used to it, then he put a shining metar on your neck, and gave each one of us a parcel of salt.

'Full of joy, I brought you home and the people asked me what your new name was, and I told them that your name was Yaltep, and all were satisfied.'

So from that day all my people called me Yaltep. I discovered afterwards that my baptismal name Yaltep was equivalent to Joseph.

My early days were spent in the beautiful valley of Gowe. I grew up under the verdant canopy of pointed yara trees and disported myself at will among the water lilies, known locally as nulai maine and korara.

With long sticks and twinkling eyes, my companions and I would shake the colourful shrubs and out of them would jump the green frogs — they would make for the river, but our watchful eyes would see them land and, falling on them, we would grab them and roast them on the fire. Their white meat was delicious, so delicious that you would even turn your back on your dear tambu, as the people would say.

Our timekeeper was a certain willie wagtail. When it was time for us to go home, he would fly by with his mate — they would chatter to each other in a most intimate manner, and we would follow them at once. In front of our house there was an ancient yara tree, huge and mossy, and, on its loftiest branch, the two willie wagtails built their nest, which looked like a tennis ball chopped in two and turned hollow-side-up (a perfect semi-circular nest built out of twigs and mud from the river). Each morning they would come down and perch in front of our house and twitter to each other as they flitted from branch to branch. They sang the same old tune, which became familiar to us. We would shout to the two of them 'Teck da tala tala' as a morning greeting and they would respond and fly to the river. We took their example and followed them to the river, but not until we had been given something to eat and the sun was up in the sky, for it was very cold in the Gowe valley in the early morning.

Every day, when the sun was high in the sky, I would run to my mates who lived next door. There we would decide our movements for the day — whether to go to the river to frighten the little frogs, or to roam in the mountains with our bows and arrows and hunt the little birds. One thing that could spoil our rambling, was the rain, as its soft touch was so cold we had to keep indoors and usually we would eat up whatever our good mothers had preserved for future use, such as dry beans and corn.

These were usually hard and our young teeth were no match for them. The good ladies would punish us, but we accepted that as a mere trifle. On fine days we roamed and played at will, with the little creatures of the bush, and came home in the evening with downcast faces to demand food from our tired mothers. Instead of reproving us, the good Kuman mothers usually had something prepared before we came stumbling in, either sugarcane or cucumber or some sweet potatoes hurriedly placed under the hot ashes to satisfy the little tyrants back from their mighty tasks in the jungle. Only when we were satisfied would the main meal be prepared for the family.

The First Census

One day, when I was about five, there came a sharp clamour from the mountain top. This was the usual way the people in the Highlands communicated messages, from mountain top to mountain top. The messenger that day announced in his gruffest voice that the white batre who had been stationed as Kangrie had some visitors who were coming to Waimambuno and the people were asked to come and assemble there early in the morning to see them.

Early the next morning, my mother dressed me up with okan, wagia and map. Okan was an interwoven wristband, while the wagia were made of similar string, and were for the legs. When they were worn they looked like a pair of long socks such as modern youths wear. Map was a broad interwoven cloth with pigtails hanging from it — it was meant for the front. Then she put some precious beads around my neck and some strings of tambu shells were slung over my shoulders. When I was done up, I felt very proud of my appearance and I was eager to start at once, but I had to wait for my mother to get ready.

At last mother was ready, so we started. At the junction of the road and the two rivers known nowadays as Watabung, my hopes were frustrated, for I did not receive the attention that I had expected. My fellow rascals were done up too, and some of them had even put on bird of paradise feathers. In comparison to these lucky chaps, I was inferior. When the last of the women had arrived at the junction of the Gowe and Kualke rivers, we went to the kiaps' rest-house at Waimambuno to await the newcomers. But the kiaps took their time and did not arrive until the sun was over the left ear (after noon).

The visitors came at last with the batre — the one who had given me my name. These kiaps came with more black men with sharp heads from the coast. The black fellows were all dressed up in black with red borders, their polished magic sticks over their left shoulders and their covered knives suspended at their sides. Their red-bordered clothes and their belts made a great impression on me, and I came to like and admire them. But all too soon I was to fear them and hide from them with all the cunning I was capable of.

They were much more than watchdogs — a word from one of the white men would make them freeze and stand stiff as a post, and when they had their orders, they would handle the people most roughly.

These black men lined us up in a row according to our small clans and families, and then we were marched in front of the white men who asked us our names. But, as they spoke in a strange tongue, we did not know what was wanted until batre came to our rescue.

'Ene kagin daglo', he said, so we understood that they wanted our names. Most of the people gave them their real names, but others with more imagination gave them any word that came into their heads at the moment. Only after the names had been given did the wise sages scold the silly ones for being fooled into giving their real names, for the wise of the land had other ideas about it.

When the census was over, the women and children were sent home and the men settled into the shade to discuss the meaning of this peculiar problem of giving their names to the strangers.

As the sun grew hotter, there issued from the kiap's house a fragrant odour — its fascination drove the white men indoors, so the old men discussed the question. One of the newcomers among the kiaps was a young man whose looks resembled those of a man from our tribe who was killed during the tribal war. The brother of the dead man was convinced that his brother had returned to revenge his foes, so he told the people that, since his brother was among the new group, they did well in giving their real names, for then he would be able to send them goods in their real names and the others would lose theirs because of their false information. All agreed that this was the only sensible solution to the question, for after all why should the white men come all the way from lower Simbu to get names unless they had some genuine reason like the one just revealed?

While the old man was still speaking, something remarkable happened — an episode that brought amazement to the whole crowd. A shining object thrown from the white men's house landed in the middle of the group and rolled around for a while and finally came to rest at the feet of the old man who thought his brother had just returned. Was not this shining object the testimony thereof and a sure means of settling doubt? The old man collected the shining object and reverently put it in his bag. The men went home shouting and rejoicing and spread the news of the marvel of Waimambuno.

On the next day, the entire tribe contributed pigs, which they slaughtered on the grave of the dead man, in order to make peace with him and to welcome him back to the land of his fathers. According to the custom, the meat was cooked in a huge hole in the ground with hot stones. Normally other foodstuffs were placed in the lower part of the hole and the greasy part of the meat placed on the top, so that when the grease melted it could go through the food, making it very tasty. This time, however, the shining object was placed on top of the hole so that its charm might penetrate the food and the meat; in that way its good charm might be shared by all the participants of the big feast. After the feast, the old man was encouraged to bring some meat to this long-lost but returned brother — but to his dismay, on arriving at the station, his 'brother' and his companions were gone. The old man kept the shining object in a small string bag and always carried it during the day and put it near his bed during the night. Often he prayed that his brother would soon return to stay and bring all the good things that the people down the lower Simbu, who had some contacts with the Europeans, enjoyed, but he was not to see him again. The famous shining object which stimulated speculation and was an object of so much veneration was in reality an empty tobacco tin.

The old sages of the tribe came to realise that we young people hated and feared the kiaps and their black boys. The most effective means used to silence us in those days was the mere mention of the word kiap or kimbri nem. If we happened to be too noisy, then some imaginative members of the community would go out and whistle or shout some potent words such as 'hoi', 'sarap' or 'yesa'. These had their intended effect on us, for they were the words used by the kiaps, and we would be silenced at once. At other times, when we saw somebody with a laplap with walking stick approaching, we would rush to the nearest bush for cover until the intruder was out of sight.

Some of those old Kumans were so imaginative, and such good actors, that not only did they molest us, and interrupt our games, but sometimes they fooled the newly discovered people of other tribes. One of the actors would dress himself as a policeman, while others would act as his servants and interpreters.

They would go to an out-station and stay there for months, judging cases and settling disputes. The people, meanwhile, had to feed them, so that they returned home rich with booty. We hated them for their intrusions. Later, however, we discovered that they were good at heart, but, sensing the winds of change in the social structure, they had decided to have some adventures of their own before growing too old to enjoy them.

The First School

Our happy and carefree state did not last long. Our regular rambles amid the evergreens were soon stopped, and we were left to pine for our lost liberty. The cause of the sudden change in our daily lives was that the batre thought he had been with us long enough to introduce some changes, so he decided to make us youngsters stop roaming and become serious, just like the grown-up people. Early every morning we were marched to the place where there was a big building, unlike any around our homes, and there we were placed on rows of planks and indoctrinated with all kinds of signs and words which meant nothing to us. We came to call the house 'the house of seriousness', but later on we were told to call the serious place 'shule', which nowadays has come to be known as school.

Our teacher was a man from the Coast who knew not a single word of our language, and we knew none of his, so there was real confusion in this place of 'seriousness'. He was trying to do the impossible, by putting some complicated signs on the blackened board and making some sounds which he encouraged us to imitate. While he was speaking, we had to keep quiet, but, given a chance to shout, we did it with a terrific noise; we were just like a flock of parrots, uttering sounds which meant nothing.

However, as you might guess, our hearts were roaming the cool Gowe, but there was nothing doing. The teacher might just as well have tried to teach the wild tree kangaroos to keep still. The only thing in this house of seriousness which gave us some interest was a picture of a small boy, comely of countenance and with a joyful smile. Other than that smiling boy, nothing went into our heads. We were given something to learn by heart, such as our Kumbu Kaman, which we rattled off without understanding what we were talking about.

After we had been going on in this way for five days, the teacher told us not to come to school the next day, so that afternoon we rushed to our usual reserve in the valley.

Early the next day, and on the days following, we made for the bush, thinking that the shule was over and done with. So we had a good time in the bush, as formerly, but the unfortunate ones who lived near the house of seriousness were hustled to be taught by a chap named Batre Bosuai, who was something like a village policeman and who saw to it that the young boys and girls went to the man from the Coast to be taught and kept in idleness. My comrades and I who lived far away from that place of idleness, kept out of it for a long time — but others were made to go and sit like lifeless posts on rows of planks.

One day, however, the man came very early in the morning while we were still snoring on our mats. On wakening, we were surprised to find the hated rascal waiting patiently in the doorway. There was no hope of escape, so the old people, who were afraid of an influential man like the Batre Bosuai, told us to go with him and not to run away — if we did, we may as well sleep in the bush, for we would be punished. We followed him to school on that fatal morning. The other children made faces at us and the shule yagl was stricter than usual. He wanted us to keep unduly quiet, but to me that was ridiculous. If somebody pricked his companion and happened to be seen by the teacher, the culprit would be given five lashes on the centre of gravity — making it impossible to sit down.

One day, as our teacher was in this mood, I whispered to my friend what a nasty fellow he was. My friend grinned, just when the teacher was looking in our direction. The man wanted to know what was amusing us, but the answer was 'nothing'. Furiously, he came down and dragged my pal from the desk and began belabouring him. After the second blow, my grandfather's advice, and the words of an old man of our village, came to me like an inspiration: 'Never stand by and see your friend put at bay' — so without thinking, I acted. The teacher was so intent on the poor boy that he did not know what was happening. I looked around and my eyes lighted on a little round stone. Picking it up, I hurled the stone at the back of the teacher and, without seeing the consequence, I shot out of the door like a wild cat, into the open, and went flying down the hill as fast as my little feet could carry me.

In the meantime, the teacher straightened up and wanted to know who was the 'daring devil'. There followed a chorus of 'Yaltep' from the children. While they were in confusion, I reached the bend of the road.

Once out of sight at the bend of the road, a leap landed me into thick grass. There I tried to compose myself, but the grass above me shook violently, as if an earthquake was smashing everything to pieces. My heart throbbed so wildly that I thought it would jump out of my breast at any moment. In my hiding place, I could hear the great tumult — the people were shouting on top of the mountains that the young Yaltep had almost killed the teacher. Gradually, the tumult died down, but I dared not stir from my hiding place. I stayed in that position till darkness had settled over the entire valley.

When at last I rose, my limbs were stiff and cold, but I dragged myself along, hiding when I heard somebody coming and taking cover in the bushes to avoid being caught. This time I avoided the men's house, knowing full well that their comment would not be too encouraging, considering that the victim was the friend of the white batre. I headed for my mother's house. There I peeped in and saw her anxious face, so I ran and fell into her warm embrace and sobbed out my sorrow and shame. My mother comforted me and told me to eat something. Usually so thoughtless, I felt then how wonderful it was to have a mother who could comfort me in trouble. She told me that it was manly of me to defend my friend, and she agreed with me that it was not reasonable that children should be shut up and expected to behave like grown-ups.

Early in the morning, when everybody was still in bed, my mother took me to her parents' home in the lower Simbu. There she left me with my grandparents at Womatne and went back. She managed it in such a way that even my father did not know what was afoot. The search for me was on, but there was no sign of Yaltep. When father came to mother, she told him to go and see her parents, for she thought I might have gone there. So father came and found me there and was happy, but I could not be persuaded to return with him.

LOUJAYA KOUZA

The Expatriate

He was what folks called
an expat-ri-ate
And when he came to visit
chose to sit on Mother's mat
And called it ex-qui-site.

He didn't eat taro, fish or rice
Just sat and said
'The food looks nice.'

He refused every drop
of what we gave him to drink
He doesn't take water
I solemnly think.

Until at last it was time to go
he bowed and said Thank you
for so and so.

Mother quietly whispered and said
'He didn't touch a thing I cooked
nor take a drop to drink
There's something awful queer
about these expat-ri-ates
I think.'

JOYCE KUMBELI

Caught Up

(For those who try their luck)

I dream of a Mercedes
so I buy a raffle ticket
I dream of going places
so I buy another raffle ticket

I dream of money
so I buy a Coke
I dream of more money
so I buy a win moni ticket

But alas!
when the top falls
I find gazing up at me
'Sorry try again'

And when I scratch
the last square
I find that there is
one ten thousand less

I curse myself
for having spent
the last toea I had
and shout *Finish*
this is the last!

But then I dream again

So I buy one more raffle ticket
then I buy one more Coke
and yet one more win moni ticket

Is there an end to all this!

JACK LAHUI

We Are Tukes

It was not very often that the Tukes drank beer. Karoho and Kokoro had little money to spare. Since the formation of the band two years before, they had had only two opportunities for drinks.

Even then the drinks were provided by friends. The first was during an end-of-the-season village-league social and the second was during the birthday party for a girl who claimed to have turned twenty-one. For reasons unknown to Kokoro, she was a girl Karoho fancied from a distance. So the drinking was an excuse for Karoho to get within talking distance. But nothing resulted from that initiative.

Karoho, sitting on his bed in the dark of his bedroom, thought and thought. The problem was getting the carton of beer through the living room without raising Baru's suspicions. He realised the great odds, with so many relatives seated in the outer room, in particular his brother Pune and his uncle Vagi. Their immediate view was none other than the entrance to his own room. And there was the more risky problem of the ever-pressing milling relatives inside, outside and down on the landing. One way was to wait until the crowd had eased a bit, but then that might mean keeping to his room until it was too late. Karoho gradually grew tired of sitting and letting time pass, so he rose and opened the door. He had to talk to Kokoro and tell him his plan.

The layout of the Baru residence was such that Karoho's room formed one wing. The only windows were on the eastern side. They were the push-out type without mesh. There was an immediate drop from the window of about seven feet to the sand below.

Karoho found Kokoro and gave his instructions. 'I will return to my room while you loiter and bide time hereabouts near the landing. I will find an old rice bag, place the carton in it, tie it to a rope and lower the bag down to you. You know what I mean?' Karoho gave a low whistle, to be used as a signal and, when Kokoro had no more questions, he assumed it was 'all systems go'.

After finding a rice bag, Karoho entered his room and set to work silently pushing the carton into it. That done, he pierced the two top ends and inserted a rolled end of his bed sheet, and then bent out the window to study the movement of the crowds below. All seemed well, so he sounded the low whistle.

Moments later, Kokoro silently materialised out of the dark and stood directly below the window, straining his eyes upward as Karoho spoke. 'Ready, Tukes?'

'Yes, I'm ready. You?'

'Here it comes. Nurse it good,' said Karoho.

Kokoro received the carton and quickly undid the end of the sheet, and then made for the darker area away from the glare of the Coleman lamps. In a moment, he became one and the same with the street crowd.

Karoho found Kokoro in the open street some twenty minutes later and the two left in the direction of the unfenced school beach-front, some hundred metres short of the boundary to the old village cemetery. Both were in a good mood for talking. They passed through the village primary-school yard in silence. 'You didn't think we'd make it, did you?' asked Karoho, to break the silence.

'We could've done this hours ago,' said Kokoro.

'But? You were the hardest person to find this afternoon, and why did you have to fight?'

'Ha! ha! ha! Tukes,' Karoho laughed. 'I needed exercise.'

'Say, what was that fight over?'

'I don't know exactly. All I know is that Meabo's sister, Kaia, was trying to humbug with our nakimi Morea but Lucy found her out.'

'My word, that's not right, Tukes. Morea is now married to our sister Lucy. What does Kaia want anyway?'

'Yes, shame on her. What do they all want? My main reason was to give Merabo a good knockout,' Karoho said bitterly, and he demonstrated with a balled right fist and melodious laugh.

From accounts of the fight, Karoho had not got a chance to even touch Merabo, although his vicious heckling was of such intensity it would have tired any man of average build. It was unfortunate for Karoho that the intervening man was none other than the solidly built eighteen-stone Kohu Gaudi of Gunina clan. Karoho was dwarfed by the Goliath Kohu. Kohu felt the need for peace, so held Karoho in an armlock until the worst of the struggling was over, and then he led him home.

Koroho and Kokoro reached the beach-front and found a grassy spot beside a beached canoe. Kokoro unfurled the top of the carton, revealing a neat row of bottles. He reached for one and tried to open it with his teeth. He had it open with little effort, and passed it to Karoho while he collected another for himself. Then he held his own towards Karoho in the manner of a good toast. 'Very good cheers to you my Tukes bro,' cracked the enlivened Kokoro.

'Cheers to you, Tuke. Good luck to you my bro forever,' toasted Karoho in return.

'Merry Christmas to you, which is one month away,' replied Kokoro.

213

They started to drink noisily and voraciously. Their day-long thirst made it easy for them to go through their first bottle. They then had their second. After drinking two bottles each, the earlier quiet of their settling-in now gave way to noise. Kokoro was narrowing in on the subject of genealogies and family ties. Now it was Karoho's turn.

'You see, Tukes, my father is Baru Mataio. You know, he's a deacon, very important. He's one of the powers in the village. He's also one of the family heads in our Botai number-one clan of Porebada. My grandfather was known as Mataio Vaburi and my great-grandfather was also called Baru, but his other name was Karoho, my namesake. He was Baru the Terrible, and for that they gave him the name Karoho. My great-aunt was Kone Baru, who, my mother told me, married your great-grandfather Kauna Gau or somebody by that name, and he begat your grandfather who in turn begat your mother Manoka.'

'Very clever, my bro,' Kokoro said, surprised.

'Yes, Tukes. So what I mean is that you are really my brother properly.'

'Momokani, Tuke! You are sure that is the way we were born?'

'Honest.'

'But I did not know.'

'Didn't you ask your mother or father?'

'Put it here, my brother. We are brothers.'

They shook hands.

'No wonder my father came to your house once for the dava kara hebouna many months ago. I do remember that, Tuke. But today they just paid the bride price, eh? Tuke, you are very lucky and rich.'

'You think so? But no. No. I think you are wrong. I think my father Baru is wrong in calling many relatives and friends. I know tomorrow they will come and collect everything, the toeas and moni. I fear I may not get the bus I marked.' said Karoho sadly.

The mention of a bus sounded most interesting to Kokoro. 'A bus, hey? Like the one we climbed into some moons ago? That was a long, long time ago. Somebody has probably bought it finish.'

'Then I will get another. If Father does not get it, I'm going to get it some way. You know that.'

'No, Tukes. It's all right for small cars, but buses, they are like houses. You cannot easily hide them in bushes. By the way, you ought to be thinking of finding a partner rather than a bus'.

'A partner? Definitely not. I'm still a boy. I'm only twenty now. I know one thing, though. When you marry, you become a slave to Woman. I've seen it. I'm not joking.'

'But, Tuke, what I'm saying is that you will eventually get married. You must get ready while you have some money. And, of course, when you are ready, tell me so that we can make a muramura to hook her very quickly,' said Kokoro, boastfully.

'Ah ha, I don't think I'll need any help in that. I've got a plan. As soon as I'm ready, I will tell Bubu Virobo to let me try the most powerful muramura she has!'

With that Karoho reached for his third bottle and passed one over to Kokoro.

'This is a very beautiful night for animase, honestly. Very quiet, and not a sound coming this way. But keep your voice down. This is a schoolyard. We should have brought the other carton too.'

'Shut up. Leave it for tomorrow, Tukes,' Kororo said as he reached for a fourth beer. He was trying to get the note for the start of a song. He started singing the song the two had composed for their band, the Tukes of Porebada.

Ihareha ogogami. Emai orea
binai. Mai hemaraimi ida
anemu, a lolo isimu Tukes.

The song ran into a second stanza with a slight variation, which went:
Tukes of Pore, lalo namo,
hetura dainai,
Emai orea binai mai mainomai
ida anemu, a lolo isimu Tukes.

The last stanza was an extended version of the second stanza, worded as follows:

Tukes memero of Porebada,
ihareha, ogogami,
Emai orea binai, mai lalo namo
ida a anemu,
a lolo isimu tuke
A lolo isumu hosana!

Mr Taravatu Bodibo, the deputy headmaster of Porebada Primary School, heard singing from his study in his staff residence while finishing off Monday's lessons. Mr Bodibo had just completed the write-up and was preparing to retire for the night. He usually remained in the school over weekends. It was his fashion to ensure that no strangers were on the school grounds. The headmaster often entrusted this duty to him when he himself went away. The singing sounded too close to neglect. Mr Bodibo put out the Coleman and lit the storm lamp. He took it into the bedroom where his family, his wife and two children, lay fast asleep.

Outside, the duo were repeating the last stanza. Bodibo, who had taught two years in Porebada, knew the song well, but could not identify the singers.

It was a very popular song, one that village youths had on their lips everywhere they went. My Bodibo stood on his verandah to accustom his eyes to the sudden darkness, and for some time tried to figure out who owned the voices. When Karoho and Kokoro reached the finale, Mr Bodibo ascertained the direction and the distance of the singers. Bodibo felt duty-bound to make the celebrants establish their business.

He set off in the direction of the singing. The school area was cast in pre-moonrise darkness. The heavens were star-cast and lit the way ahead. After some twenty metres, Mr Bodibo noticed the flicker of a naked flame as a match was struck and held ready before a face. The glowing embers of a lit cigarette appeared as the flame went out.

A voice shattered the silence with a shout of 'Smaha!' Mr Bodibo was now five metres away and an audience for the dark forms ahead. There was an exchange by the Tukes, followed by a clash of bottles. Mr Bodibo spoke: 'Hey, dahaka . . .'

Karoho dropped the newly lit cigarette, turned and shot up as he saw the dark, wide figure approaching, He made a hasty grab at the carton, but snatched only two bottles while Kokoro shot up with a drink in his hand and went off, already in full flight.

'What do you villagers think you are doing here disturbing the peace!' shouted Bodibo behind the disappearing forms.

'Hey, you! You! You!' Bodibo made as if in hot pursuit of the scurrying shadows, but then felt something against his leg. He stopped and looked at the spot where the two had sat. There was the carton! He bent low and looked inside. He saw the glowing yellowish tops and the intactness of at least ten bottles of beer. As many as ten empty bottles were strewn about carelessly. He collected the empties and tried to fill the carton but found it four short. Bodibo carried the carton toward the main assembly ground. He could see from the village the distant glare of as many as five pressure lamps. He felt a little frightened, even though he had his earlier daring. He turned and carried the carton to his residence.

Karoho and Kokoro ran into the street at full speed, heavily panting from the strenuous sprint. They settled down to recover but could not talk.

Karoho finally spoke. 'Tukes, can you guess who that was?'

'I dunno, could've been a vada tauna or an evil spirit. Remember the school is not far from the old cemetery. Or it could've been the headmaster. Who knows? If it was the headmaster, he would've carried a torch or something. I'm sure he was not an ordinary person. You know, perhaps we were sitting above some old grave.'

'The beer. Shall we return and collect it?'

'I'm afraid, Tukes! I still feel my legs shivering. I don't dare!'

'We should have been more daring, like the way Homoka and Tara acted to

Councillor Nohokau. The old councillor was returning from his garden at Taurama and saw Homoka in a coconut tree. It was a very hot day and the old man fancied a drink. He thought he'd chase the youngsters away and help himself to what they'd gathered. Homoka, who was up in the tree, saw the intention of the old man. By then he was near and was in a rage. Homoka climbed down quickly to tell Tara of his observations. The whole thing did not happen the way the old man expected. Homoka and Tara stayed put and drank as if the old man did not exist. Councillor Hohokau pelted the two with all the merciless Motuan curses he could think of, calling them thieves, crooks, trash and dogs. He emptied his mind and left, warning them of the consequences of their stubbornness in later years.

'This is not funny. Whoever that was, a spirit, a vada tauna or the headmaster, is going to have a good night with those beers.'

'Forget it, Tukes. We mustn't think too much about it. I have the last beer still in my room. We must select a better place next time.'

'Oh, well,' said Kokoro. 'I managed to collect two bottles in our hasty retreat.'

The wide sandy windswept street of Porebada is one which experiences a peak traffic hour between 7 p.m. and midnight. At weekends the traffic goes on into the late hours, especially when the moon is full. It is then that the young people start to roam, sing and walk the full length of the oval-shaped street. By midnight a few daring youths remain to keep the vigil. After midnight the street is left to the ghosts and the dogs to patrol until the next sunrise.

For this Saturday night, the normal pattern had been broken. There was some traffic of late-night socialising from aivara makers in different parts of the village. With the shift of the lahara into a mirigini from the Kokoro mountains, there were families taking full advantage of the cool inland breeze. Karoho and Kokoro had finished their beer and found themselves in the quiet mood of the village. They too rose and made for their separate houses. It was well past midnight. The smell of Sunday was already in the late night air.

STEVEN THOMAS LYADALE

The Frost

It was May and the dry season was only two months away.

Kambi Tofeu was only ten, and lived in Kandep, a village high in the mountains of Enga. Nothing new ever happened. But he was eager to see the white man again. He had seen him once three years before. At first he was scared of this man, but now that he was older he wasn't scared of anything.

The other boys were not like him. They spent most of their time playing games, doing nothing. Parents didn't expect young boys like Kambi to do very much, but they appreciated it when they did. They were expected to fetch water, look after younger children and such things. But Kambi did more difficult tasks as well. He enjoyed working hard.

In his family, his older brother Kasa was twelve, and his sister Lino was eight. The family had a good life; there was lots of food to eat and in great variety too. There were kaukau, taro, beans, potatoes, sugarcane, bananas, fish and sometimes even rice, which was brought to them by wantoks from a place called Laigam. Occasionally tinned fish was eaten with the rice. There were no trade stores in Kandep because it was high in the bush and there were no road links.

'White-man's goods', as they were called, were sold at Laigam, many miles away. The only white man's thing that Kambi's family owned was a thick woollen blanket which Kambi shared with his mother. It kept them warm at night, and they took good care of it. The blanket had been given to Kambi's mother by a white man's cook-boy in exchange for a fat piglet. Kambi wished that another white man would come to his area with a cook-boy, because now he had a big fat pig. He would ask for two blankets in exchange for the pig. He had asked his mother many times if the Europeans would come again, but she always replied that she didn't know when they would come. He had also asked her many times if she would allow him to exchange his pig for a blanket. She said yes, but he knew that his father had the final authority over all the pigs. Father used pigs in the moka exchange and also for paying bride-price. He knew his father would never let him trade a big fat pig for a blanket. The men would never allow their wives or children to use the pigs in trade, although they were the ones who looked after the pigs. Kambi told himself that he would secretly trade his pig and his father would know nothing about it. However, time went by and the white man and his cook-boy never came. The pig just stayed in the village and grew fatter.

Kambi enjoyed fishing so much that he called it his 'kaikai', like the other children. Anything they liked doing and were good at was called kaikai. Kambi loved to fish in Kandep Lake, which wasn't far from his home. He liked the lake because he caught fish easily, and usually they were big ones. There were lots of rivers around with lots of fish in them, but the fish were hard to catch. However, many of the boys fished in the rivers because they had trout in them.

Trout are delicious, mainly white meat with few bones. Once a trout was caught, the boys made a fire on the bank and then waited until the flames had died down. Then, when only the hot glowing embers were left, the boys would throw the fish on the red charcoal and wait until it was cooked. They used a long stick to turn the fish over and over to make sure it was properly cooked. Then they pulled it out of the fire, removed the backbone and had a feast.

Kambi didn't spend much time at the river because he didn't have much luck there. When he did catch something the older boys forced him to share, and when he didn't catch anything they wouldn't share with him. So he often sat with his mouth watering as he watched the others eating.

His brother, Kasa, spent a lot of time fishing along the river banks. Often he was lucky to catch one or two fat trout, but if he wasn't he would threaten the other boys and sometimes steal their fish to eat himself. He was very big for his age and he was a bully. But in doing general duties and helping his parents he was just the opposite of Kambi. He had to be told what to do. He was a very disobedient boy and Father often had to spank him. Kambi called him a mad dog because even little things would make him angry quickly. He would spring at you and hit you. He did this to younger children, especially Kambi. Very often Kasa would become very jealous of Kambi. When everybody else had gone he would beat up Kambi for no reason and then warn him not to report to their parents what had happened. At other times he would prevent Kambi doing the jobs his parents had told him to do. Later, when their parents returned, they were very angry with Kambi for not doing what he was told. It wasn't his fault. He wanted to tell his parents, but he was frightened of his brother. If he did, Kasa would beat him up the next day.

Kambi returned home from fishing, late one afternoon. He was very happy because he had caught many fish. He knew that his mother and sister would be pleased with him. He loved to hear Mother praise him. His sister had said many times that Kambi was the best fisherman in the whole world. Although he knew this wasn't true, it made him very happy and proud.

He'd pushed a piece of bush-rope through the lower jaw of each fish and hung them on the end of a stick. It was quite a heavy load for a small boy. Soon he was tired. On the track home he met his brother who was crying. He asked him what the matter was. Without even answering, Kasa jumped up and bashed him on the mouth. It was a mistake to ask Kasa questions when he was angry.

As usual, Kasa had been naughty, but this time Mother had caught him. During the day, when everyone was out, he and some friends had slipped into the house and taken all the kaukau Mother had saved for the night's dinner. They had cooked and eaten all the kaukau and they had also stolen and eaten all the dried pandanus nuts that mother had in a bilum at the back of the house. Mother was furious when she found out and had thrashed Kasa soundly for being so greedy. Kasa was feeling sore and angry, but since he couldn't hit his mother he had taken it out on his younger brother.

Kambi was confused and surprised at his action. Why was Kasa beating him this time? He was too tired to fight back and anyway he wasn't strong enough to beat his brother, so he just started to cry. This made Kasa even angrier. He grabbed Kambi's fishing pole and shook him violently. Kambi almost fell. The load of fish slipped down the pole and the sharp fins stuck into Kambi's back. He cried out in pain. Just then they heard someone calling to them from the house. Kasa was afraid Mother had heard Kambi's cries. If she saw what he was doing he would be punished again. Quickly he put his hand over Kambi's mouth and told him to stop crying.

Kambi looked up at Kasas with big brown eyes full of tears. His back was bleeding badly where the fish had scratched him. Kasa suddenly felt very sorry for what he had done. He wrapped his arms around Kambi and held him tightly to his chest. Using some leaves, he wiped away the blood and tried to clear the tears from his eyes and nose. He kissed Kambi and promised he wouldn't beat him again. Kambi wiped his nose and looked at Kasa. He didn't know whether to believe him or not. Kasa now begged him not to tell his parents what happened. Kambi didn't say anything. He just picked up his fish and walked towards the house.

Kasa wasn't always bad to Kambi. Sometimes he helped him, and he always protected him when other big boys wanted to beat him up. Kasa was big and tough for his age, and the other boys knew that and respected him. Often he went hunting in the bush with Father. Sometimes when they killed opossums, he would bring the baby ones home as pets for Kambi. So far none had lived more than a month; some escaped, others were killed by dogs, but most just died.

More than anyone else Kambi loved his little sister Lino. Kambi always tried to please Lino. Often Lino got wet when coming from the garden during the rainy season. So Kambi decided to make an umbrella for her. He went into the bush and cut down some broad pandanus leaves. He took them home and left them for some time until they were dry. Next he gave them to Mother to sew together. She sewed many of them together until she had made a big square. Then she folded it in two and the umbrella was complete. When Kambi gave it to Lino she was delighted. She felt grown-up when she had her own umbrella. Now she wouldn't have to share any more with Mother when it rained. She could now walk at her own speed when coming or going to the garden, and she wouldn't have to run all the time to keep up with her mother's big steps. She put her arms round Kambi and thanked him.

It had been raining for the past few months. Soon it would be the dry season. All the children enjoyed that season because they had plenty of free time to play all sorts of games. One of Kambi's favourite games was called Saka Yanda, which is a fighting game. The boys used tender young pitpit shoots to try and spear each other. The children divided into two groups, each representing a different tribe or clan. These clans were supposed to be enemies. The make-believe fight would follow the same rules as a real fight.

First one group would accuse the other group of doing something wrong. That group would deny it and call back some insults to the first group. Then more insulting words would be exchanged. One boy would pretend to lose his temper and throw a pitpit spear at the enemy. The fight then started. Each side would start shouting war cries and make charges against the other. The pitpit spears flew, and boys had to jump quickly to avoid being hit. As they ran they threw their pitpit spears.

Usually the girls stood at the side and watched, but sometimes the really brave ones joined in. If someone was hit by a shoot it didn't really hurt because the soft part would smash against the skin, leaving a wet mark. Some boys dipped their spears in mud so that when they landed on someone the mud would splash all over his body making him really dirty.

When the fight was over, the wounded on both sides were counted to see who'd won. It was easy to see a wounded person because the splashed mud had dried on his skin. After the fight, the groups would dance in a circle singing war songs. They sang about how strong they were and how badly they had beaten the other side. After the singing and dancing, speeches were made on both sides and compensation was claimed from the enemy clan. Usually the biggest and most talkative boys made the speeches while the girls and the smaller boys just listened.

Instead of pigs as compensation, the children used ferns. They went into the bush and collected bundles of soft ferns. They used the fern shoots because they were hairy, like pigs. The children then returned to make their exchange. The boy who had collected the most ferns was recognised as the big man of the tribe. The ferns were all laid out in a long line. Each one was tied with a special kind of reed and tethered to a stake in the ground, just like a pig. The 'pigs' were now counted, and the enemy clan were called over to inspect the wonderful pigs. They were counted again in front of the enemy clan. Now the leader of that clan could start distributing all the pigs given in compensation. He called out someone's name in a loud voice. The person came over, untied the rope from the stake in the ground and led the pig away. As he walked past someone said, 'Grrnn! Grrn! Grrn!', imitating the grunting sound of pigs. Some children laughed at this, but most of the children were silent and treated it seriously. When the compensation was over and peace was made all the children went home.

The rainy season was over and the dry season had come. The days were clear and bright. At night it was very cold. In the village there were two separate houses for each family; one for the men and the other for the women and children. It was against the people's custom for men and women to sleep in the same house. It was believed if men slept in the same house as women they would not become tough and strong. They would become weak and would lose most of their fights and they would be easily killed in battle.

Kambi still stayed in the women's house with his mother and sister while his father and brother slept in the men's house. He was old enough now to stay in the men's house, but it was terribly cold there. Unlike the women's house, there were no blankets in the men's house. Kambi used to shiver when he visited the men's house. Men had to get used to the cold so that their bodies would become hard and tough and they would grow up to be strong fighters: so even young boys were encouraged to sleep in the men's house.

Kambi's father and brother often made fun of him because he slept with the women. They said he would always be weak like a girl and would never grow up to be a great warrior. This upset Kambi, so he decided to spend a night in the men's house. That night he went with Kasa and Father to sleep with them. At first everything was fine, but as the night went by it became colder and colder. Kambi was shaking all over and his teeth started chattering. He just couldn't sleep at all because it was so cold. About midnight when the other men were asleep, Kambi crept out of the house and hurried back to the women's house. He slipped quietly under his mother's blanket and held her tight to let some warmth into his bones. From then on, he never went to the men's house, no matter what they said.

As the days passed, the nights became colder. Usually their blanket kept them warm at night, but now it wasn't enough. Kambi still felt cold. Sometimes his mother would have to get up and make up the fire again to keep them warm. One particular night he was lying curled up beside his mother, trying to get as much heat as he could. But it kept getting colder and colder. Mother had to get up three times to light the fire again to get some warmth. Kambi would then be warm for a short time, but as soon as the fire burned down he was cold again. So he didn't sleep at all that night. He just lay there waiting for morning to come, but the night seemed longer than usual. Finally, the sky began to lighten. A few grey fingers of light came through the door. The first bird called, then the next. It was dawn, but the sun hadn't risen yet. Everyone was wide awake and Mother had the fire going again. Kambi was grateful for its warmth, but soon the house was full of smoke. It was in his eyes. He went out to stretch himself and breathe some fresh air.

He stood on the verandah and breathed the cool crisp air. Then he saw it. It looked as if white ashes had been sprinkled over everything. It was on the ground, on the leaves, on the trees. Perhaps it was salt. He had never seen anything like it before. He jumped down off the verandah and ran across the yard to have a closer look. It was all over the place. He bent down to look at it. He tried to pick some up and bring it in to Mother. Perhaps some silly fellow had spilled salt all over their yard. He touched the white sparkling stuff, but quickly pulled his hand away. It was as if he had touched hot coals. His fingers felt as if they were burnt. He looked at them, but they weren't burnt, just wet. How strange! He felt frightened, so he called out to Mother to come quick. Maybe some kind of sickness was coming to the village.

Mother came out and looked around. She shivered a bit with the cold and then told Kambi not to be afraid. It was only ice. Ice only falls on the ground during the dry season when it is very cold. People call it frost. It is formed high up in the sky. The air becomes very, very cold and all the water turns to ice and falls on the ground during the night. Soon the sun will come and turn it back into water when it warms up.

The ice was seen for the next four days. Every morning it covered the clearing, the yards and all the gardens. Kambi thought it was very beautiful as it sparkled in the sunshine. But the old people didn't like it. They were worried and spoke against the frost. Kambi couldn't understand until his mother explained that heavy frost can kill all the plants, including their crops. If that happened there would soon be no food in the village. Now he understood why the people were anxious.

Next day Kambi went to his own little garden and examined the crops. They seemed all right, but when he returned two days later he saw something strange was happening. The leaves of all the plants were beginning to wither, just as if someone had uprooted the plants and left them in the sun to dry. In a few days all the leaves, including those of the kaukau, had dried up. All the food plants had been killed by the frost. Not only in his family's garden but those of their neighbours as well. All over Kandep the gardens had been killed. There were no fresh vines for replanting. Only the bare mounds, like graves, could be seen. Even if they could get vines from somewhere, it would take another six months before harvest. Meanwhile there was nothing to eat. They must move out or die of hunger.

With a sad heart, Father decided they would have to leave their mountain home and go to live with a distant relation in one of the valleys lower down, until times got better. Father had visited the place once or twice before. He knew a path across the mountains. The journey would take two or three days, so they must start preparations. They decided to take only a few necessary things and their pigs. They had five pigs in all. Kambi didn't want to leave his beloved homeland. He didn't know anybody in the new place. There was no lake, and so he was going to miss his fishing. He hid his fishing gear in the house, and he pushed his canoe under a tree, hiding it under dry leaves.

They planned to leave the next day. Everything they could carry was already packed. It was still cold, but not as bad as the nights of frost. Kambi lay under his mother's blanket thinking for a long time before he fell asleep. That night Lino became terribly sick. Her skin was hot and she complained of having pains all over her body. Then she began to shiver and her mother lit the fire again. But it was no good. Lino's sickness got worse; her body was covered in sweat and she seemed to be talking nonsense.

Morning came and Lino was no better. She was too weak to stand. She lay on her mat, unable to get up. The family had to make a decision. There wasn't any food left to eat and everything was packed up. All the other villagers were leaving. Father decided they must go too.

He asked his wife for one of her biggest bilums. He put the blanket on the bottom and then very gently placed Lino in the bilum. He would carry her to the place of safety. Kambi picked up his own small bilum and went outside. Mother untied the ropes from the pigs and led them outside. Kasa carried his father's bow and arrows, his bilum and some other things. Mother closed the door tightly and put a big log across it. She set out on the track calling the pigs as she went. They squealed and grunted, but followed her very closely, like pets.

Kambi knew he would miss his best friends because they were all going off to live with wantoks in different parts. Perhaps he would never see them again. He stood by the side of the road and started crying. Suddenly he heard his father calling him and telling him to hurry up or he would be left behind. Quickly he wiped his eyes. Then he grabbed some red clay from the road side. This clay was used for decorating the body. He rubbed some on his face. He didn't want others to know that he had been crying. He ran down the hill to catch up with them.

The first night of the journey was spent in a small hut by the roadside. Mother lit a fire and cooked a few kaukau in the ashes. The hut wasn't very comfortable, but, since it wasn't their home, Kambi couldn't complain. That night Lino was sick again with a high fever. Mother stayed awake all night trying to comfort her. The others didn't sleep either. They just sat around the dying fire and watched the sick girl.

It was nearly morning. Lino's fever seemed to have gone down a bit and now she was sleeping peacefully. The sun was already lighting the high mountains. There was no food, but at least they could get something to drink. Further down there was a little creek. Kambi picked up the bamboo water-container and went off to fill it.

The hut was built right on top of the ridge. From the top Kambi had a clear view of Kandep. In fact, it was the last place from which he could see Kandep before descending into the valley. He stood and looked at it for a long time. The sun was shining on the roofs of the little houses. It looked very peaceful. Then he hurried on down to the bed of the creek to fill the container with water. The water felt cool and fresh. He let it trickle down his throat and some poured down his face and chest. It was refreshing.

He rinsed the container out and began to fill it again for his family. Perhaps some cool water would help Lino. The container was about half-full when he heard his mother scream; a loud high piercing scream that echoed through the trees and ripped into his ears. He didn't wait. He rushed up the steep bank and raced across the grass to the hut. He didn't have to ask what had happened. Now his mother was moaning; a deep, low moan as if there was a deep wound in her heart. His brother was crying too. Mother was holding Lino and rocking her in her arms. She didn't move.

The water container slipped from his hand and smashed on the ground. Lino's eyes were closed and her body was limp. Kambi would never hear her laugh again or see her running up the hill to tell him some secret. He threw himself on the ground and rested his head against her body. But it was silent; no moving, no breathing.

How unfair, he thought, to die in such a lonely place. There was nobody to mourn or make a funeral feast. There were no other women to help Mother prepare the body. No one to share her grief. No one to help Father dig the grave or say prayers for Lino's soul. They had no friends, no relatives to call on for help. They were alone in their sorrow.

All afternoon and all that night they stayed with Lino's body. They watched and cried. Father kept a big fire burning all night to keep them warm and chase away the ghosts. Next morning Father and Kasa dug a grave by the roadside and placed Lino's body in it. When all the earth was filled in Father placed some heavy rocks on top of it. It was terrible to think of little Lino all alone in that lonely place. Kambi's mother held him tightly against her breast as the sobs shook his body.

It was time to go. Father picked up the bilum and slung it across his shoulder. Although the bilum was empty he was now carrying a much heavier burden. Mother released Kambi from her embrace and called all the pigs. Together they set of down the road after Father.

Kambi turned round to take one last look at his sister's grave. He plucked a flower and some leaves and stuck them into the grave. Then he turned and followed his family to the new land.

RUSSELL SOABA

from *Maiba*

Maiba steps out of the ring of her fallen garments and walks down the yellowish sandy beach of Tubuga Bay to the edge of the sea water. The tide is low. The coral reef before her is a long strip of opalescent consolation.

Before the reef, which spreads in imitation of Tubuga Bay from one point to the other, is a brief depression that forms a lagoon. Schools of small fish, abandoned by the outgoing tide, leap here and there, giving the surrounding atmosphere the sound of grains of sand being sprinkled on water. Then the lagoon is calm again, only constantly wrinkled at irregular places by slight sprays of breeze.

Beyond the reef is the vast expanse of deep blue, its surface corrugated by timid ocean waves, slowly creeping in past the reef to meet the land at Maiba's feet. Behind Maiba is the dark presence of tropical greenery, with its streams and rivers further inland, its densely forested hills, more hills and mountains, clouds, sky.

A few coconut trees grow along the beach, some of which lean over the sea in snaky and slender poses. Some more much-younger coconut trees grow in a row along a sandy path that leads immediately behind Maiba to her family's gardens and garden house.

On her left is a dead tree which has fallen into the sea, its branches partly buried in the sand under the water, and its roots reaching aimlessly for the sky. Its arching trunk enables fishermen to walk along it at high tide with their spears and stand in wait for fish or cast their fishing lines out toward the reef.

Past the dead tree the yellowish sand thins out, giving way to white coral, rocks and dead sea-shells, sea-worn or smoothened clam shells and random debris washed ashore by the waves. In windy seasons the angry waves storm past the defending reef and beat the mangroves and the land the hardest there, until all that is left of the landmark, which is also the point that forms one end of Tubuga Bay, is tired and wounded mangrove trees that shoot their roots straight into the raging sea. Off that point and along the reef, clam-shells are harvested often in plenty.

On her right, where the sea waves have been less angry, the sand retains its own sense of hope, and spreads further up to the other end of Tubuga Bay. The coconut palms grow along that beach and the lush green with all its creepers holds the sand firm, turning it the colour of grey and making it offer pleasant shade and sitting resorts on hot days. The creepers with all sense of freedom snake their way hungrily to the edge of the water. The lagoon is calmer at that end of the bay.

Tubuga Bay isn't really big enough to be called a bay. It is just an inlet, an ordinary leeway or harbour that can be seen and not marvelled about by anyone passing through. But the chiefly Wawaya-Magura family members called it Tubuga Bay, once upon a time, for it protected their canoes against rough sea winds, even cyclones, and, in all its mysteriousness, it gave them also the sense of belonging, the feeling of home.

Maiba is standing down at the heart of the bay, further away from the dead tree, the coral and rocks and the wounded mangroves on her left, and away from the thick sand and the lush green on her right, viewing the open world of rainbowish blue before her. The constant sprays of sea breeze that brush against her flesh are light and pleasantly soothing. The sun overhead is tepid, not yet passing any form of judgement on her presence.

The traditional name given her by her father was Yawasa Maibina, meaning the Parable of Life. Her father, the late Chief Komeroana Magura, had chosen that name for Maiba probably out of the necessity of concealing his fears and guilt (which were vague, and the suggestion that the chief had suffered any guilt at all came only from those villagers who could not see the point in having a chief when Makawana village had no need for one, including the chief's brother's wife who could not win his fancy): Yawasa Maibina, for instance, had never understood the meaning of having to wear clothes until she was nine or ten years old or at least on the verge of puberty; and this indeed aroused much gossip among the villagers.

Each morning of her five years at the Posa Bay Primary School, Maiba's aunt, Mrs Veronica Wawaya, had Maiba properly clothed, gave her her share of puata wrapped in banana leaves and sent her off with her cousins and other Makawana village children. The Posa Bay Mission Station, with its primary and high schools, its general hospital, its expensively built Anglican chapel, which was three-quarters smaller than Dogura's St Peter-and-St Paul's Cathedral, and itself serving as a district headquarters for the Milne Bay Provincial Government, was six kilometres away from Makawana village. Apart from the salaried government and mission workers, much of the station's population, including the villagers of the surrounding areas, did not have much material wealth or even food.

The people who inhabited the land after the semi-savanna Posa Bay Mission Station and further on along the northwest coast and into the heart of the Great Kuburabasu Savanna Country were subsistence farmers. Only the mission station enjoyed a wealth of food and other forms of luxury that came through trade-store supplies ordered from Samarai and Alotau. Otherwise, and before Elder Yaraga and the others had acquired the licences to run trade stores in the district, one could never expect to see an empty tinfis lying under a Makawana village house and those of other villages that surrounded the Posa Bay Mission Station, or even a broken bicycle wheel (whose rubbers would be removed for manufacturing diving spears) rusting by the wayside.

There were no trucks or buses or even village boats and motor canoes in this remote district — the whole district (the Great Kuburabasu Country included) offered nothing for venturesome businessmen or land developers of any sort. The students from the surrounding villages walked to and from their respective schools, enjoying the odour of the bush on the wayside, or alternatively walking home along the coastal road, which offered them the beauty of the sea at low tide, the reefs, the long stretches of yellowish beaches, golden sunsets behind purplish swaying palms, and rocks and exciting cliff faces on which the sea birds perched or under which the gentle waves — the long voyagers from oceans afar — reached the land with prolonged gurgles and tired sighs. Returning home from school along these roads upon such evenings the other children jeered at Maiba, addressing her as 'Satan's daughter' or 'Number eleven' because of the two vertical droopings of thick mucus from her nostrils, and the bigger boys from the high school teased her even to the point of encouraging and finally forcing a primary-school boy to seize her roughly, push her onto the sharp rocky earth and attempt to make love to her. These attempts by the small boys (each afternoon there was always a new boy for Maiba) were never successful, however, since Maiba's cousin, Siril, had often come to her rescue by threatening to report the high-school boys to Mr Wawaya. Maiba came home each evening, her eyes swollen with silent weepings and carrying her skirt over her shoulders.

'There, there now,' Mrs Wawaya had often comforted the child, 'that's the price little girls pay for not wearing clothes and looking tidy.'

By the time Maiba had completed her primary and moved into the high school these incidents became rare, and some of her student enemies began to respect her, though for what reason they themselves could never explain. One afternoon, straight after Miss Baker and most of the Grade 9s had left the classroom, Maiba was confronted by a thirteen-year-old student. She knew him very well. It was Mikhail, the quiet Kuburabasu mixed-race boarding student who was very popular at the school because of his keen participation in Expressive Arts exercises. Before Maiba opened her mouth to ask what was wrong Mikhail was already on his knees in front of her and, weeping quietly, cried, 'Forgive me, Maiba.'

'Forgive you? But what have you done to me, Mikhail?' Maiba asked, more shocked than bewildered.

'I have betrayed you, Maiba, my elder. Please forgive me.'

'You have betrayed me?' Maiba returned, and laughed because she could not, for one moment, believe her ears. 'Mikhail,' she then said, 'not only do you have a very strange name, which is Russian according to Sister Macormack, but you must be the best actor I have come across, because I can't ever recall a time when you've done me wrong. But to tell the truth, I admire you for the kind of person that you are, very quiet, a good reader of poetry and, as well as that, Mikhail, everything about you is very, very creative indeed.' She went over to him and took hold of him by the shoulders. 'Get up,' she said, 'you have no right to kneel in front of a woman. And that's the only wrong you are doing me now.' Mikhail rose, still weeping quietly. Slowly he walked away without looking at her, and Maiba felt deserted.

They were strange students, these Kuburabasu boarders, Maiba realised, but very helpful indeed to others. They rarely argued with others, even among themselves, and whenever they lost a hot argument or felt that they were totally misunderstood they broke down and wept. And they had been baptised with the most incredible names: there was a Kuburabasu girl in Grade 1 who was called Anastasia; there was a boy in Grade 8 called Anaximenes (who was nicknamed 'Anux the tedi', meaning 'the liar', for his reputation as 'the greatest teller of fibs'); and many more.

Any associations she had with these Kuburabasu students and their 'foreign names' (Sister Macormack's words), which were through brief encounters such as the one with Mikhail, Maiba found baffling. The more she had endeavoured to get close to one of them the further away he or she drifted from her reach. That very night, several solitary hours after he had asked for Maiba's forgiveness, Mikhail groped his way down to the mouth of Wakoko River, carefully measured the thick rope he had stolen from Miss Baker's tool shed and freed himself from the bough of a mangrove that overhung the deepest part of the water. When the half-past-seven morning sun cast its glory over the calm ocean, children walking to school from the nearby village saw from the Posa Bay Bridge the remainder of Mikhail's corpse. Everything from the waist down was missing, and the base of the remaining part of his body was lightly touching the surface of the water. The smallest children fainted at the sight of the intermingling colours of tan, sunlit green and blood red. Thus died Maiba's first love and her sense of respect.

From the day of her birth to the time she had first started walking four years later, Yawasa Maibina was paralysed from the buttocks down. In such a state and particularly at the time when normal babies are first expected to walk, Yawasa Maibina could not move a fair distance, and had to spend her days either lying down or just sitting, having only to cry to be fed or cleaned. At the earliest stages of Maiba's infancy, Mrs Wawaya fed her with green coconut juice in place of breast milk and later, as she grew older, with potato soup mashed beforehand with rich coconut oil, then later still with over-boiled yams, until the child was old enough to grip a hard cooking banana in her own hands and start chewing away. A year before his daughter had actually started walking, Chief Magura's bronchitis grew worse. For this reason his visits to his only daughter at his brother's house grew fewer and fewer. It became clear then, both to the chief and the rest of the Makawana villagers, that the child would grow up as an abandoned orphan.

Chief Magura's contemporaries were worried, or pretended to be, about the child's condition. They had gone so far as to claim that the child might be suffering the consequences of her father's wrongs. The mother died while bearing Maiba, mind you, cautioned some of the Makawana ogababada. Father Gabriel Kedaboda, the priest in charge of Posa Bay Mission Station, had morally supported such an opinion. The rest of the Makawana villagers insisted that the fate of the child lay in the soul of their chief.

'If you feel that you are entirely free of impurities,' Father Kedaboda had remarked in the face of the chief during one of his parish patrols, 'then what of the warnings expounded in the Bible that it is your children who will suffer the consequences of that deliberately hidden mote in your eye?'

The villagers then, particularly Mrs Wawaya and those who could not for their own satisfaction see the practical realities of their chief's role as the leader of the Makawana village, loathed Chief Komeroana Magura and his paralysed daughter.

In April of the year when Maiba was four years old, Chief Komeroana Magura died of phlegmatics at the dissatisfied age of thirty-two and, heeding his pre-mortem request, the villagers of Makawana dutifully carried his body in a coffin of pandanus mats down to Tubuga Bay where he was buried without a funeral service. Three days later, Maiba, or Yawasa Maibina, surprised everyone in the village by running round and round her uncle's house like any other healthy child.

Until she was eleven years old, when not only the people around her but the whole of Posa Bay district began avoiding her, Yawasa Maibina was something of an ill omen to people who came in contact with her. Royal Bob Rabobo often took her out fishing on his father's canoe. Maiba sat on the platform as Royal cast his line overboard and waited. He rarely caught anything — not even a sea snake. He became convinced that Makawana and all its surroundings no longer bred any fish; he would sadly paddle home at duskfall with his half-sister. One evening Royal took Siril with him instead. He couldn't believe the amount of fish that fluttered inside their canoe. Royal carried out an experiment by alternating fishing trips with Maiba and Siril; with Maiba he caught nothing and with Siril he reluctantly accepted the villagers' compliments that he was the best fisherman in Makawana. One evening, Mrs Wawaya advised Royal Bob Radobo not to take Maiba out fishing again. The expert fishermen of Makawana found out why for themselves.

At the early stages of her adolescence, Maiba didn't quite possess the looks which could enable those around her to readily accept, appreciate or gossip about as beauty in a growing girl. Not one male passerby, with the exception of Mikhail, for cryptic reasons perhaps, looked at her twice. Thick layers of yellowish-green mucus, her 'number eleven', dripped down each of her nostrils. Her red tongue licked at the phlegm wherever she went, and she sniffed noisily like a neglected child. Healed tropical skin diseases such as borobe and those skin disorders caused by sandfly and mosquito bites showed out clearly from each ball of her light brown buttocks like faded ancient tattoos on an old woman's thighs. Her back, her belly and the fresh buds of her virgin breasts were always muddy, due to so much labour in her foster parents' gardens and around the cooking fires at home.

She stole away from Makawana village one afternoon and ran down to Tubuga Bay for a solitary brooding over her father's grave, and a dusk-blest solemn swim afterward. Her underarms stank eternally and her hair was wiry, knotted in a tangled, fuzzy mess. ('The truth is I am bored with everything by now,' she had once explained casually to Royal and Siril; Siril said nothing then, while Royal nodded with a fixed stare at her calm face.) Dark-red blood from an unexpected menstrual discharge trickled painlessly down one of her legs. She sniffed loudly, then brought up the back of a hand to wipe away the mucous. Honey bees, blood-sucking sandflies and buzzing mosquitoes from the nearby swamps swarmed her perspiring nakedness.

A slight breeze tickles the hairs on her flesh and she grins when she smells perfume in the air about her. The sun above her has changed position slightly. The tide is coming in, she notices; the reef before her is slowly being submerged, and she feels the weight of the whole world pressing down hard on her. Calmly, and without looking around her in search of other presences, Maiba enters the ocean.

From *Naked Thoughts*

1

A medley of tall wood distorts
streaks of light into the floorbeds
of this vast virgin jungle.
Weak sunlight
dances lazily 'gainst the illusive downflow
of falling lianas. Birds of paradise

sing at brief intervals,
yet, as time would destine
this to be, vanish into the depths of massy
green, into the depths of some dark ocean.
Somewhere a lonely
bird whistles. Or is it a bird, really?
A hunter perhaps, perhaps just the wind,
even a tune, and echoey. Or simply a call, a scream, in fact?
Still, a sound,
maybe some dialectical utterance —
a message.

2

Come to my village
one day
and you will see that . . .
No, what
you see are two eyes
stilled
and a smile falsified. Here,
let me
move an inch, and there,
right before you is the red curtain
falling
into streams of dreams.

3

Those men who are now completely lost
could command the wind to blow my house down.
Sure, the wind would come, these timber walls would fall
the iron roofing would fly, leaving only I
at this table, writing.

4

I was on my way down to the bottom
of an abandoned water-well.
I've been crawling downwards for years
and I've known my movements well in the dark.
Some youngster trying to be funny, I think,
slipped and fell upon my shoulders.
Slipped again off my shoulders and

fell head first to the bottom.
(He should at least have asked for advice.)

5

heavy windows of mucous red
long tall storeys of orange buildings
fading yellow as the day wears on
would there be green parks below?
in the ice of this city
rainbows
are never complete

6

anxiety stares
waiting for the world
to define

happiness

is a rainbow
where waters leap
and fall red

7

what a pity
you have asked me to speak
at this time

I would rather sing

Looking thru Those Eyeholes

Once an artist went overseas
His father died in his absence
and was buried in the village

He followed a rainbow upon his return
and came to a cemetery
He dug in search of reality
till he broke his father's skull
to wear it's fore-half as a mask

Try it/look thru those eyeholes
see the old painting/view the world
in the way the dead had done.

Kuburabasu

Da kuburabasu green,
Over the years of your poets' dreams
You patched up each fragment of green
From the broken kwamra that everywhere
Held to keep the country green.

Then it was time to cultivate the savanna,
To speak of green things in mystic chambers,
Of voices holding out in the low savanna
And of kindling found among dying embers
For the baking of clay in the high savanna.

The hiri would come with its winds
And you would be troubled by its echoings
Of voices not of the laurabada winds,
Wondering if it too in such undertakings
Would build towers out of trade winds.

The sand will see its first morning
Of thatched castles, airborne as islands
Along cliff-faces this morning
And the city will be stone with multiple hands,
Juggling severed roofs on a skyless morning.
So you leave us, kuburabasu green,
Tropical ruins across this savanna,
Hamlets blown ablaze by the winds,
And for the morning
Ondobondo on the green.

KUMALAU TAWALI

The Song of the Rower
(Dedicated to OPM)

The son said to his mother
The monster is defeated
Let there be a sign
That I your son
Your blood, your flesh
Have destroyed
The terror the monster's rule

Tie now, mother of my flesh
Mother of earth and liberty
The intestines of the monster
To this log and send
Across the ocean
To the refugees, among them my uncles
Your brothers

That they may know
That I your son
Am the master of the vanishing island
That they may know
The little streams flow quietly here
And return
To rejoice and flourish in the valleys

The seagulls shall fly like before
The storm of the northwest
The rower to row as it was
Before the northwest storm
And the tyranny of the monster
The rower shall swim among the crocodiles
The dolphins shake hands with the sharks
The seagulls fed by the tuna
The rower shall leave his canoe unanchored

Yet currents nor tides dare
To take it away

Dreams come true often
Solids melt in the heat of the noon sun
Action often is wasteful and fruitless
Rationalisation void and murdering
But dreams often come true
Dreams walking on two legs
Dreams walking on a million legs

Dreams bursting like dynamite
In a thousand million beating hearts
The dream of the ancient rower
The dream of the present rower
Whose ears are even listening
To the flopping of the seagulls' wings
To the rowing and marching songs
The songs of islands and continents.

THOMAS TUMAN

Kum Koimb

There was a great sorrow and loud wailing among the people of Dondua village. Dark shadows settled like sediments in every heart. Kipiye, a great warrior in the dark days, a luluai and leader of the Kumga people had died. It was the second day of mourning, and Kipiye's corpse was due for burial that afternoon.

Kipiye had been a man to be remembered. He had been a man who was feared by all the hostile tribes. The very mention of his name sent cold shivers through anybody who heard it.

Now he lay lifeless in a bed of blankets. People from far and near, both enemies and friends, came to mourn over the death of a tribal leader. This was one of the rare occasions when all tribal barriers were put aside.

All the fierceness had abandoned his face. What were once powerful hands now lay by his side, stiff and cold. His head rested on two pillows which were coated with talcum powder. Covered in mud, his three wives and the other women of Dondua village sat around the body, weeping loudly, while the men stood weeping silently.

In a house some distance away, a group of ten young men, all relatives of the late Kipiye, sat quietly, ears cocked in the direction of the wailing. They were the night guards. They were to guard the grave of Kipiye lest evil Sangumas came to steal the body.

It was a rule not to go out of the house as there may be some Sangumas among the crowd who, by evil powers, may take their sense of sight away, thus enabling the Sangumas to steal the body without being seen. The men could not afford to lose their sight if they were to thwart the evildoers.

The wailing grew louder, and the ten knew that dusk was around the corner and Kipiye's body was ready for burial. It was a couple of hours before sunset. Kipiye's body, wrapped up in thick blankets covered with sweet-scented talcum powder, was laid in a wooden box and the lid closed tightly. Four young men, two on each end, lifted the box onto their shoulders to be carried to the graveyard.

It was now about an hour before the sun went down over the western horizon. People made their way home heavy-hearted, leaving the procession of close relatives bearing Kipiye's body.

Ans, one of the ten guards, tiptoed to the door and peeped out. Satisfied that no one was in the immediate area, he went out to scout. He came back some minutes later and armed himself with bow and arrows. The nine others did likewise. Each had an axe tucked into his belt as they moved out into the grey twilight of dusk to take their posts.

They placed themselves quietly under the cover of some bushes, equidistant from each other, surrounding the grave and about twenty-five metres away. With their axes laid in front of them, for immediate action, they fitted arrows to their bows and waited at the ready, eyes and ears peering in the direction of the grave.

In the fading light, not knowing where, but conscious of the hidden guards, the relatives watched sadly as the coffin-bearers finished covering the grave. Such was the end of Kipiye, one-time warrior and leader of the Kumga people.

The relatives stood with bowed heads for a few moments to pay their last respects before they made their way home. The last to leave, Kipiye's wife, lit up a kerosene lamp and left it burning by the graveyard before she also departed.

Except for a few campfires glowing in the distance and the lamp at the graveyard, complete darkness once again claimed the earth. The ten guards waited patiently, each busy with his own thoughts in his own location. It was one of those dark nights when the moon wasn't in the sky. A silent breeze started to blow and the leaves rustled as if singing a soft farewell hymn. The breeze brought with it cold, and the men began to feel the bitterness entering their system.

The small flame in the lamp was dancing to the breeze, casting huge, monstrous shadows on the bushes near the grave. In the very early hours of dawn, the men's eyes were heavy laden with sleep, but the bitterness of the cold kept them awake. They threw down their weapons and relaxed.

Then, from a tree near the grave, an owl hooted loudly. As if this was a signal, the earth sent a small tremor and then the world became alive, with the slight breeze developing into a strong wind hollering through the leaves.

Both creatures of the air and the earth seemed to come out of their sleep, making ghostly noises. Every single hair on the guards stood on end. Each man knew too well: the hour had come for the sons of man to turn evil and try to eat their own kind.

Each in his own little hiding spot, the men trembled like leaves. They fitted arrows to their bows and waited, eyes fixed on the graveyard.

The owl hooted again, and this time it was followed by a movement near the grave. The loose soil began to fall in and the ten pairs of horrified eyes beheld the body of Kipiye coming out of the grave.

Voices could be heard around the grave, but they could see no one. There were sounds of footsteps, but nothing was visible except the body of Kipiye.

Both of his hands were now out of the grave. The body kept coming out, stripped naked of the covering of clothing and blankets in which it had been wrapped.

Then he was there, standing upright on his grave. The ten men were now shaking heaps of boneless flesh, soaking in their own urine.

A commanding voice shattered the night, although the owner was invisible: 'All you men of the mountain tribes, you Doms, Bandis, Kambugls, Kewas; you men from the valley tribes, you Dagles, Numans, Kumais; and all from far and near, far, as far as the eye can see, and near, as near as the hand can reach.

'Tonight is a moment of history for our secret lives. A great feast shall we have and a feast to be remembered. Hark thee to my words, all you comrades of the secret life I live; for the hour has come for us to destroy and devour the body of Kipiye!

'The body that once was a fear to us and our fathers. The body that once molested us and sent terror through every living soul. Ha! Ha! It is now ours. Am I not right, all you fellow comrades of Kipe Kangi?'

'Siu-u-u-u-u Sip-u-u-u-u Ha!' they cheered. A loud roar bellowed from a thousand voices, shaking every leaf and shrub in the vicinity.

There was complete silence for a while, and the ten could still hear the roar of the multitude of invisible Sangumas ringing in their ears.

They were the guards, to protect the body of Kipiye from Sangumas, but how could they fight people they couldn't see?

Despite their precautions, and although no one saw them in the house preparing or hiding in the bushes, there was a leak somewhere in their proceedings that caused the theft to go unchallenged.

Then there came a sudden burst of rain, and thick fog dominated the graveyard. Amidst the fog, they could see Kipiye's body ascend and then stand in the air a few feet off the ground.

The bewildered men could hear voices as Kipiye's body, now lying on its back in mid-air, moved across the bushes. It was too obvious. Kipiye's body was being carried away by invisible hands.

The men were too scared to follow in pursuit as they watched the body float away into the darkness. The faint voices of the Sangumas, the wind and the rustling of leaves settled like sediments of sorrow on the earth, bringing complete quietness.

For a while the men sat in silence, a thousand thoughts forming in their minds. There was only one who grinned to himself and sat at ease. Then Ans disturbed the stillness.

'Yekomba, woia woia,' he called, as he walked towards the empty grave. 'Come out, comrades.' He stood looking at the hole, while large beads of tears rolled down his cheeks. The other nine men were soon by his side. All swallowed lumps in their throats and found it hard to talk as tears streamed down their cheeks.

The magic of evil had outwitted them. It had outfired the weapons of their forefathers. Under the watchful eyes of ten able human beings, the once-honoured body of Kipiye the great was stolen without challenge, to be devoured by lawless creatures of Kipe Kangi.

Despite their precautions, and despite their careful planning, there was a leak somewhere; someone had betrayed them.

They stood in silent concentration for a while and then moved off into the darkness in single file. In the darkness one man smiled to himself as a cock announced the coming of dawn.

The morning was bright, and the promise of a good day hung in the air. Taie, the old tultul or messenger of the Kumga tribe stood alone in the meeting-ground. Soon, people of Dondua village began to pour in. Stirring restlessly, they had been wondering why the meeting had been called so abruptly during their sleep.

Taie, his face revealing nothing, stood meditating for a while and looked up at the people. The women had taken to one corner and were silent while the men talked in low murmurs.

The sorrow at the death of Kipiye was still around the corner of their hearts. Seated at the back of the conversing men were the ten guards of the night, looking grave and very much shaken after their experience.

Taie looked up and all held their breath. His eyes, glassy with tears, but fierce underneath, betrayed the purpose of the meeting. Pointing towards the ten guards of the night, he boomed, 'All you sons and daughters of Kipe Kangi: a great injustice has been done, and it must be avenged! Last night the body of Kipiye was removed by lawless, heartless followers of Kipe Kangi.'

It seemed as if the fury of a demon had suddenly seized him and he knew himself no longer. Shaking his head, he continued. 'Under the very watchful eyes of ten guards last night, Kipiye's body was removed without challenge. Do you know why? Do you know how? Those who did it were invisible. Now there is only one conclusion. One of us here, in this very congregation, is a Sanguma, a heartless Kum Koimb who has spied on the guards and by the power acquired from the evil Kipe Kangi has upset their vision.'

There was a sigh of disbelief. Heated arguments followed. Some young men wanted to seek out the lawless Sanguma and avenge the theft of Kipiye's body, while others disagreed. Then Ans spoke out.

'Before it is too late, a search party must be organised and the body recovered.' There was general agreement and the men prepared themselves.

A group of twenty young men were picked. They armed themselves with bows and arrows and tucked axes under their bark belts. The women went to their houses and came back a few minutes later with what food they could find. This they gave to the twenty.

The men, having eaten, made their way out of Dondua. Those remaining watched the column until it disappeared into the bushes, and then made their way to their houses.

Taie stood for a while longer and then, uttering a curse on the Sangumas, the Kum Koimb, he too left for his hut.

The sun was overhead now, and the people went about their normal routine, the women to their gardens, while the men went about collecting firewood and fetching water. Some of the younger men, who were employed by the Administrative Station, went to work.

Taie sat in his tent, making arrowheads for his arrows. He had just completed sharpening his axe. He was an old man who had lived during the dark days and he still had a strong belief in superstition, sorcery and the payback system. No white man was going to make him change.

The search party had split up into ten groups of two. Each group took a small creek, and starting where they joined up with the mighty Waghi River, searched upwards towards the mountains. It is a belief that Sangumas always ate their prey near a creek so as to drown the juicy flesh with water. The search continued all day and the men became weary.

It was late afternoon and dusk was around the corner. They were now about the same distance from the Waghi River as Dondua village, and they could see it in the distance, a mile or two away.

Ans and his comrade, Wagl, were just about to quit when Wagl noticed some footprints. He place his foot on one, but found that it did not fit. Surveying the area, he noticed more prints. Following them, he came to a dark spot where the canopy of the leaves and vines overhead concealed the sunlight. He could see the remnants of a feast. He scanned the area for a while and then, brushing aside a hump of leaves, he exclaimed, 'Ans! Ans! Come over here.'

Ans ran over and stood motionless at what he saw. It was an arm cut off from the shoulder. The fingers had been gnawed off. It was hidden under the leaves which Wagl had brushed aside. Kipiye's arm! The two men stood silent for a short while, and then Wagl called the other groups.

In the quiet, early stages of dusk, the other groups distinctly heard Wagl's voice. They quickly arrived at the scene. They surveyed the area for more remnants, but found to their disappointment only dying grass, from the flow of fat, and a few bits of flesh strewn here and there.

They collected what they could find and, finally, with heavy hearts and forcing their voices through lumps in their throats, cheered aloud at the finding.

Taie, who had just finished his meal, was reaching for his bamboo pipe and some brus when he heard the cheering in the distance. He walked out into the twilight and called for the people to gather at the meeting-place. With difficulty, he rolled a stone stool into the middle, where he sat smoking his pipe and waited for the people to gather.

The search party, carrying the remnants of Kipiye's body, made their way home, followed by a multitude of flies. The cicadas had ceased and night met them halfway. There was a gentle breeze and the night air was cool.

Nearing the village, they could see campfires blazing, revealing the crowd around them. They walked forward at a slow and quiet pace.

They entered the meeting-ground from the entrance and placed their findings in front of Taie.

'Ah! Woia woia,' he shouted, jumping. 'What! Come, come.'

The people stood horror-stricken at the sight. It thrilled every fibre of their frames. Some of the elders, age-mates of the late Kipiye, started weeping.

Taie's aged frame was rocking violently as he straightened to address the congregation.

'Good people of Dondua, the white man hasn't taken away all our tribal customs. Our old judiciary system still remains. Hark thee, my people! From tonight onwards, keep your eyes and ears open at all times. The thieves must be sought and dealt with according to our tribal laws. An eye for an eye, and a tooth for a tooth. My good people, go now and rest your tired frames.'

In the quiet, moonless night, their hearts burdened with sorrow, the people made their way home. There was only one man who pondered over the tribal laws and shivered in his blanket.

The morning was bright. The sun's rays broke through the partitions of leaves and tree barks, waking the Dondua villagers. It was a market-day and the women-folk were already on their way. The elders, who had had their share of the pleasures life offers, slept long on their wooden beds.

It was a special occasion for the young men, a time of social pleasure. This was a day when they met all the young girls from the neighbouring tribes, the day of mating after long hibernation.

It was one of the special days when a girl could invite a girlfriend to her house for a social evening. A chance not to miss. The young men washed and put on their Sunday best.

Along all the roads around the Kup administrative centre, the people were coming towards the market. Some women led a pig or a piglet by a cord. Their sons, walking behind the animal, whipped its haunches with a leafy branch to hasten progress.

At the market there was a throng of human beings, animals and food all mixed together. Ans and Wagl had just arrived at the market and were directing their steps towards some of their age-mates from neighbouring tribes when they saw some young girls sitting in one corner. They changed their course and walked towards them.

'Hot day today, eh! Do you reckon so, girls?' began Ans, always good at beating around the bush, 'On such a day as this, it's glorious to end it by pairing off. Am I not right, Wagl?'

A grinning shrug from Wagl brought an angry retort from one of the girls, 'Get out, old rascals!'

Ans was quick to respond 'Apa'ah, pi amb kawi, enz kembigl nond wa.' He patted her on the bottom. 'Come on good girls. You know you possess the best stuff in the world, bottom and all!'

Irritated at being touched, the girls stood. This was an opening, and the whole lot got ready to leave. Ans and Wagl watched as they melted away into the crowd.

Wagl turned on Ans and was just going to let him have it for his behaviour when a small boy interrupted them. The boy looked about him and then in a shaky voice said, 'Come to the girls' house over there tonight,' pointing in the direction of the house.

Before they could ask questions, the child left as quietly as he had come, walking delicately, as though his feet would harm the grass. Ans called after him, but the boy took to his heels and disappeared into the crowd.

They had come to the market with one aim and that aim was achieved. Lack of sleep and sorrow had deepened their sexual frustrations and tonight was a time they didn't want to miss.

Night came. Ans and Wagl left for the girls' house. All along the road they spoke of the kind of night they would have. Wagl wore a big khaki laplap and a T-shirt, and Ans, baggy trousers and a singlet.

They entered the house to find the girls fast asleep. They were a bit late, but that was better still. There was no rule saying one had to be early. To be early was an honour, but to be late meant throwing yourselves beside the girls without further ado. Ans and Wagl did so without waking the sleeping girls.

They had been asleep for about an hour when Wagl detected a strange noise coming from Ans. Taking it to be Ans on business with his girl, Wagl dozed off again.

In the pitch darkness Wagl came awake again to the same noise. This time Wagl, sitting on his sleeping mat, listened attentively. The sound was more distinct now. Teeth rubbing bone and tough flesh being torn off and chewed. He listened for some time, when he heard Ans whispering in low murmurs.

'Kum Koimb, we have fooled the stupid people of Dondua. Who now would know that I am a Kum Koimb? I, Ans, am the one who betrayed them. There is no man, not even the stupid Wagl and the two girls sleeping here like logs who would know I am a Kum Koimb.

'What do you say, my little pussy cat, my Kum Koimb?' There was a small meow. A sign of contentedness. The evil possessed had to be in their Kum Koimb's favour at all times, lest it took their lives away.

Wagl let out a loud yawn, as if awakening from a deep sleep.

'Ans! Ans!' he whispered. 'I haven't had a proper meal the whole day, and I feel as if my stomach is going to dump out bitter acid. Have you anything with you that can help me?'

Oo'o, Ans thought, that is bad. Why wasn't the bastard asleep? What a mess. Had Wagl heard him? No, it must be no. Was his girl awake too? He shook her quietly. No, she was dead asleep. He had to think fast. Thank God, the girl would never know of his possession.

Thinking Wagl would eat without bothering to examine the food, he said hurriedly, 'You couldn't have asked at a better time. I brought a piece of pork for you but had quite forgotten about it until just a while ago. Curse my deep pockets, I am halfway through it, but if you want to help . . .' Ans tried to sound normal as he handed something cold and soft to Wagl.

Wagl's hand trembled a little as he received the cold, tough and jelly-like flesh. Human flesh! Cold shivers ran through his body. So Ans was the double-crossing Kum Koimb who had a pussy cat. The heartless traitor who upset their vision and took an active part in the theft.

Wagl sat for a long while, allowing Ans to fall fast asleep. He then woke his girl quietly and whispered to her all that had happened. He told her to remain quiet and not reveal anything until he met her again.

Then as the cock announced the coming of dawn, Wagl slipped out quietly with the flesh still in his hands and made at breakneck speed for Dondua. Twice he stumbled and fell, hurting his foot, but he kept on running.

He raced into the men's house. 'Wake up, all you sleepy heads of Dondua. The traitor has been found.'

With the past still fresh in their minds, the mention of it was enough to set the brains awake and soon a crowd of naked men surrounded Wagl.

'Make the fire,' he bellowed. In the bright firelight, the men beheld the human flesh, the torn bit from what had once been a magnificent body.

'Who is the culprit? Who is this Kum Koimb?' A volley of questions were thrown at Wagl.

'None other than Ans,' came the reply. A silence followed in which the men prepared a 'welcome' for Ans. A council was held.

'Ans shall die. The yetom's son shall be killed and thrown into the bush. Let us bury this low-class villager,' Taie began.

'But we can't kill him. The white kiap at the station will be angry with us for killing him and put us in the kalabus. And if we tell him about the theft, his white head won't believe us,' one objected.

'Yes, that's true. We cannot kill him because we'll also end up in the kalabus.'

'The white man has a thick skull. He is a longlong, insane. We cannot convince him. Therefore, we'll denounce Ans and make him a bomblam. An outcast,' Taie concluded. The men nodded in general agreement.

Ans woke up early to find Wagl gone. He woke Wagl's girl and asked where Wagl had gone. She stared at him for a short while. The early mist in her eyes concealed the sheer hate she had for Ans.

She answered, 'He left very early, he said he had to go somewhere.'

Ans hastened home, thinking he could catch up with Wagl on the way.

Entering the gates of Dondua village, he called for Wagl.

'Come here and have a puff, Ans,' came the cool reply from the men's house. 'You were fast asleep, all curled up and wrapped like a cocoon around your girl's huge breasts, so I decided to leave you alone.'

Ans hastened to the men's house but never entered it. A mighty blow from old Taie's club took him on his back and felled him. It was the rule. When enough evidence was found against a man, action came first and any explaining came later.

The women and others of Dondua heard the commotion and rushed out, some of them still wrapped in their blankets. Taie told them what had happened and the punishment decided upon. Some of the women broke through the crowd and into Ans's house. They threw all his belongings out and set his house on fire.

The people were gathered in the meeting-ground when Ans came to. Taie stood up and addressed the crowd: 'A great injustice has been done and the punishment shall be bitter. Ans! You would be a dead man now . . . Thank your white man friend, we can't kill you.

'I therefore banish Ans from our tribe and announce that from now on, he is a bomblam, an outcast.'

Then, turning to Ans, 'Go, therefore, you Kipe Kangi's son, to wander to the four corners of the earth, until you come to rest your body somewhere.

'You will see no more of your inheritance. Your property and land will be shared among us. You shall no more steal our people. Get out of here with your little Kum Koimb, and if you show your face here again, kiap or no kiap, "Peng-nim kule geu nal".'

The people cheered and pushed Ans forward to hasten his wandering.

In the late afternoon, a miserable Ans left Dondua village forever.

VINCENT WARAKAI

Dancing Yet to the Dim Dim's Beat

We have been dancing
Yes, our anklets and
Amulets now are
Yes, grinding into our skin
No longer are they a decor
Yes, they are our chains

We have been dancing
Yes, but the euphoria has died
It is now the dull drumming
Yes, of the flat drums
Thud dada thud da thud dada thud
Yes, it is signalling, not the bliss
But the impending crisis.

PETER WATLAKAS

Speak Up

the ornamental birth
the long road
the unknown steps
the little feet
the locked doors the rusting locks
the fenced knowledge

the dark mind
the black paths
the blank gifts
the unexplored leaps
the curious winds the stubborn keeper
the valve questions

the final burst the talking flame
the first truth the first song
the cheering crowd the singing artist
the visual harmony the real colours
the beautiful words the broken tomb

the second birth
the long road the black paths
the unknown steps the blank gifts
the little feet the unexplored leaps
the locked doors the rusting locks
the curious winds the stubborn keeper
the fenced knowledge the value questions

the enlightened orator
the short road the white paths
the learned steps the written gifts
the enormous feet the explored leaps
the open doors the new keys
the knowing winds willing keeper
the freed knowledge the valve realised

alas

the new morning the singing words

STEVEN EDMUND WINDUO

The Dancer

In solitude with the spirits
A silhouette
Dances against the blaze
Letting words and chants re-echo.
Fingertips of flames
Race to every part
Calling the sleepers to return
To life with the dancer.

As the fingers of flame
Returned to the beat of the drum
The dancer sweated and panted.
Sweat fire, breathe smoke.
Sleepers awake! Join the dance.

The Mother and Child

This is the story of a woman
Her first child she left on a canoe
To sail downstream to the open sea
The canoe was lost in the flowing stream

Having reached the open sea
Still he had not learned to paddle
Weathered and battered
The child forgot his mother
Not knowing he would drown
He never returned to his mother

For years the woman waited for her child
She believed his return would rescue her
From the hardship and labour of her years
The woman died in her mournful tears
Without satisfying her dreams

Nuigo Market

Each day that she lived
she made the Nuigo market her survival
And after a day's earning would march
into the local trade store by the road
on her way home or up to the mission bulk-store
by the old airstrip for a packet of rice
and a tin of mackerel
She would never buy mutton-flaps,
lamb chops or chicken pieces
as the others do, but knew her family
cared less about such imported goods
Better buy a dried tilapia or the wasted beef ribs
down by the Wirui Catholic convent,
at least if there was enough money
from the sale of betelnut, coconuts,
ripe bananas and vegetables from her gardens.

Different Histories

I once returned to the place of my blessed cord
Buried in the black earth.
I stood silent at the wonder of those
Birds that flew day in and out from their nests
Below the blue sky which drops to earth somewhere.

I remember those years of my childhood
Papa in front with his piece of firewood
Me in the centre
And Mama at the rear loaded
With string bags of wood, food and water.
Each day I returned home earlier than Papa and Mama
To find the evenings of fun and games frolicking
In the cool evening breeze.

But watching the sky again
I realise the clouds have moved
So has my childhood Buk'nholi life
Which has drifted
Into a different world.

Making different histories.
My people no longer to me
Are the people of my childhood's history
My Papa and Mama are no longer to me
The protectors of my life
My home no longer to me
My place of being
But a mere reference of my whole history.

SAMOA

A P E L U   A I A V A O
Translated by Tili Afamasaga

The Married Couple

Tapale and his wife, Tumua, live in a small faleoo not far from where the pigs are fed in the guava grove. The mosooi and fuafua floor of the faleoo stands about four feet off the ground. Through the spaces between the floorboards can be seen Tapale's pet sow which sleeps under the faleoo. The floorboards are pocked with burn marks, evidence that the couple do not have matches and that Tapale has to resort to the traditional method of rubbing dry sticks together to make a fire.

The western end of the faleoo does not have a floor. Instead, an earth fireplace for cooking stands there. Beside it is a table-like structure made of sticks on which are stored baskets of uncooked taro and bananas, an axe, a bush-knife, an iron pot and kettle, and an empty four-gallon kerosene drum open at one end which is used for cooking taro and bananas. From one beam of the faleoo hang three metal hooks that are used to hang baskets of cooked food on. At the opposite end of the faleoo is a wooden glory-box with a curved lid and a lock that rings a bell when the key is turned. A red-checkered cloth covers the box, and a roll of sleeping-mats and pillows lie on top of it. In front of the glory-box is another stack of mats. A mosquito net lies on top of these mats. This mosquito net used to be white but is now quite brown from constant use and from the wood smoke that rises from the fireplace. The mosquito net tells the sad story of Tumua's unsuccessful attempts to mend the tears that plague it. Some of these tears have been covered with breadfruit leaves when Tumua has been unable to get a needle to mend them. The breadfruit leaves keep out the mosquitoes at night. Tapale often tries to borrow a needle from Simoli, Tapale's mother, but the old lady refuses, saying that if Tumua wants a needle then she should go back to Savai'i to her aiga to get herself a needle! This logic is incomprehensible to Tumua. After all, how can she travel all the way from Safata to Apia, then catch another bus to Mulifanua where she has to get a boat to Savai'i, just to get a mean little needle. Tumua can get a needle from Sanitoa, the itinerant Chinese salesman, but he only comes round to their village once a month. With the last harvest of copra Tapale sold to the store, Tumua had wanted only a needle from the money they got, but Tapale forgot about it and gave all of the money to his parents, and the matai of their aiga. So Tumua does not have a needle.

Simoli, Tapale's mother, does not like Tumua. As far as Simoli was concerned Tapale had married below his station, and because Tumua's family is far away in Savai'i their family cannot get any material goods from them. Every day, Simoli harps on this theme. On this particular day, Tapale has just returned from fishing. Tumua is in the process of giving Tapale's parents their midday meal, which consists of faalifu and koko. According to Simoli, the koko was not properly brewed, and she really makes sure that Tumua gets the brunt of her anger. Tapale, as usual, gets the tail end of the tirade which more often than not goes something to this effect: Had Tapale obeyed his parents and married the girl they had chosen for him they would never have had any of these troubles.

Tapale listens to his mother, without comment. He puts on his dry lavalava and walks towards the fireplace where Tumua has been cooking. He sits down facing the guava trees. Tumua sits down beside him after giving Simoli the wash bowl for washing her hands.

'Was the koko brewed properly?' he asks Tumua. Tumua does not answer, so he asks again, 'Did you brew the koko properly?' Silence. Tapale glances at Tumua, who is flicking the remaining embers in the fireplace into a heap. The glow from the embers lights up the tears that are sliding down Tumua's cheeks as she gazes dejectedly into the fireplace. Tapale gazes at his wife: he feels love and tenderness well up in him. A strong feeling of protectiveness rises in him when he remembers that Tumua is expecting their first child. His parents do not know this yet.

Tumua feels her husband's eyes on her, so she begins to speak softly, as tears continue to trickle down her cheeks: 'Your mother has never accepted that we are married. She has refused to accept that I am your wife. It would have been better if you had married . . .'

Her voice trails off as she blows her nose with one corner of her lavalava. Tapale says nothing. Tumua continues in an even lower voice, 'I've always taken great care when I prepare their food, but whatever I do she always has something to complain about.'

Tumua stops speaking for a while as her tears increase, then says, 'My mother warned me about this, but I refused to listen because I loved you so much.'

Still Tapale does not speak. He stands up and, taking the glass cover for the kerosene lamp, he cleans it with a corner of his lavalava. It is not time yet for this chore, but he has to do something to check his rising anger against his mother. His wife is right, of course: his mother had never tried to like his wife or accept that Tapale loves her.

Right then, Simoli calls out from their fale, 'Why doesn't one of you come to take back the wash bowl? What are you doing talking over there when you should be here waiting on us?' Tumua gets up quickly and runs to the house, but Tapale gets up slowly, takes down the lamp and throws it out savagely onto the stones. He takes the metal pot and kettle and throws them after the lamp. He kicks at his pet sow as it grunts up to him. Then, taking his bush-knife and yoke, he makes to go off to his plantation, but Tumua runs after him and tries to detain him. He throws the knife down violently, sits down behind the glory-box and faces the guava grove.

For a while there is shocked silence in the main fale. The old lady is nonplussed. The sounds of the splintering lamp, the pot and kettle hang heavily in the air. After a while, as Tapale's anger cools, he says to his wife, 'This is it. You and I are going to Savai'i to look after your parents. When the men leave to work at the wharves in Apia, we'll join them, and get some transport from there to Savai'i.'

Tumua does not want to add to Simoli's store of grievances against her, so she persuades Tapale to stay with his family. The only time she wants to go to Savai'i to her family is when it is time for her to have her baby. Tumua likes Tapale's village and she likes his family, except his mother, but she puts up with her for Tapale's sake. As for the old lady, she becomes less domineering and critical of Tumua after the incidents of that particular day; she tells Tapale that they should not mind her when she criticises Tumua, as most of the time she does not mean what she says, and if they go to Savai'i, who will look after them? The people of their village will laugh at them if Tapale and Tumua go to Savai'i. Simoli's outward change of face belies what is in her heart.

Before Tapale married Tumua there was a girl in his village that his parents wanted him to marry. The girl's name was Penina, daughter of Moliaga. Moliaga was the best fisherman in their village. Penina used to bring fish to Simoli and Tafa every time her father came home with a good catch. Those frequent visits enabled Tapale to get to know her quite well. He came to like her. She was a pretty girl, virtuous, and she had long, straight hair which was not unlike Tumua's hair except that Tumua's hair had a slight tinge of brown in it. Sometimes when Penina delivered fish, Simoli would detain her to cook the fish, then he would praise her saying that no one in Safata knew how to cook fish on hot charcoal as Penina did. Sometimes when Penina went by to get water from the village pool, Simoli would invite her into the house to eat with Tapale. Penina's father knew and approved of Penina's visits to Simoli's house. Simoli was known in the village as a strict lady, but she liked Penina and would look after her; and if something came of the friendship between Tapale and Penina, Penina's father would give his blessing to their marriage.

The whole village expected Tapale and Penina to get married. Penina waited, sure that it would only be a matter of time before Tapale asked her father for permission to marry her. Sometimes Penina daydreamed about such a night, wondering how she should look at Tapale: she would probably be shy and gauche, and he would also be awkward and hesitant. Penina was sure that, even though there had not been any declaration of love between them, Tapale loved her.

Tapale had thought about marrying Penina, but there were two factors which made him hesitate. Firstly, if he married Penina, the day would come when people would say to him that if it had not been for his mother he would never have obtained a wife. Secondly, she was of the same village. He doubted the wisdom of taking a wife who was of the same village. He wondered about the malaga that usually resulted in marriages between their young men and girls from other villages. If their young men went on a malaga to another village, he often heard the older men say to them, 'Tautuana ma outou se ai o le malaga.'

Tapale still had not made up his mind about Penina when the village prepared to go to Savai'i on a fa'afailelega tama trip. Tapale decided to go too.

When they got to Savai'i, the young men heard that there was a beautiful young girl in the village after whom all the taule'ale'a pined. The only trouble was that the girl lived at the pastor's house and was not allowed to join in the poula which would be put on for the entertainment of the visitors. In fact, Tumua was not allowed to go anywhere without the company of other girls. Tumua's father had put his daughter in the care of the pastor quite deliberately. She was a beautiful girl, but she had not had the benefits of a formal education. She had been through the pastor's school and, even though she had not gone on to Papauta Girls School, Tumua's father felt she had all the graces which a pastor's wife should have. His dearest wish was that Tumua should marry a pastor. In the village he was only a taule'ale'a and he did not possess much material wealth, but he wanted to give his daughter the best, and this best, he felt sure, Tumua could get from living in the pastor's house.

Even at sixteen years of age, Tumua had had several offers from theological students who visited the village. The pastor turned down all these offers, saying that Tumua was still very young. The pastor wanted, as a husband for Tumua, a theological student who was in the top five at Malua Theological College; someone good and intelligent.

Tumua was nineteen years old when the malaga from Safata arrived. There were two alii, four tulafale, five girls, four women and ten unmarried men. When the visitors arrived at ten in the morning the family to which they were taking the fa'afailelega tama were already gathered in their guest fale. The visitors were welcomed by an usu; a lavish feast followed. After it, there was the exchange of gifts between the visitors and the hosts. The visiting women and girls took turns to cuddle and admire the newborn baby. The baby's bed, which consisted of about one hundred and fifty baby mats, was replaced by just as many baby mats from his father's family. There were, in addition, gifts of kerosene lamps, cakes of toilet soap, mosquito nets, baby napkins and tapa. All these gifts were given by the baby's father's family to his mother's family. The mother was of Tumua's family.

While the exchange of gifts was taking place, the young unmarried men of Safata and the girls of Tumua's village took every opportunity to mingle and get to know each other. Some did the cooking together while others waited on the matai in the main guest fale or went to the pool to fetch water. While this went on, the taule'ale'a from Safata kept in mind what the older men had said: 'Ia maua se ai o le malaga.' The Safata young men liked what they saw of the girls, especially Siniva, daughter of the highest alii of the village.

On Saturday night, the poula was held. Never did Siniva shine more brightly as she did that night. Her mother clothed her in red velvet and, when Siniva danced, the mother sprinkled perfumed talcum where she danced, all the while proclaiming that her daughter was the best dancer in the village. The young men from Safata looked and marvelled at Siniva's beauty and skilful dancing. Tumua was not at the poula that night. The pastor had forbidden any young girls in his care to attend such gatherings: he wanted to protect their virtue until they could be properly married off to suitable theological students. As well, the pastor knew that at gatherings at which Tumua was present fights occurred. This happened because the other girls and their mothers disliked having Tumua around: she took all the limelight as she was the best dancer in the village. Siniva's mother disliked Tumua intensely.

Filemoni, the pastor, was glad that Tumua had not attended the poula on Saturday night. He forgot, however, that both Siniva and Tumua were in the church choir and they sat opposite each other. The next morning in church the fact that Tumua outshone Siniva in beauty was made obvious when Tumua arrived. The eyes of all the Safata taule'ale'a followed her as she made her way to her place in the choir. Siniva's mother saw this and her anger burned.

Tapale was in church and, like all the young men, he had seen Tumua arrive. His heart was thudding wildly as Tumua sat down and threw her plaited hair over one shoulder. He felt jealous when he saw that all the other taule'ale'a were gazing at her. All that Tapale wanted to do was to meet and talk to Tumua. But how to meet her?

A few pews away, Siniva's mother seethed. She turned her side to the pulpit and gazed at the graves in the cemetery outside the window. She waved her fan, savagely. The pastor knew that she was angry, and he was sad that she could be so foolish as to despise a young girl who could not help looking the way she did. He went on with his sermon '. . . and there is faith, trust and charity . . .' 'Liar!' hissed Siniva's mother at the graves. '. . . but the best of them all is charity.' 'Favouritism! Lying old man!'

Before the last prayer ended, all the girls from Siniva's family were outside waiting for Tumua. They were angry, saying that Tumua should not have worn silk to church as she was not a taupou, not even the daughter of an alii.

Even before the pastor got outside, his girls and those from Siniva's family were fighting. People tried to prise the fighters apart. It was only through the efforts of the visitors that the fight was finally quelled. This was the opportunity Tapale had been looking for. He had rushed into the fight as soon as he had seen that Tumua was the target of the other girls' jealousy. He managed to get Tumua away from them.

That evening, Tumua left the pastor's house and went back to her parents' house. Tumua's father told the pastor that if the other women in the village did not change their attitude to his daughter then he and his family were not returning to church. Tumua's father did not want to run the risk of another fight at church.

That night at the guest fale, where the visitors from Safata were housed, Tapale could not sleep. He wanted to marry Tumua, and he was wondering what his mother's reaction would be when he told her of this. His father would not mind because he had made it clear that whoever his son chose as his wife would be acceptable to him.

His mother would not like the fact that Tumua's father was only a taule'ale'a. Tumua did not have any high connections and her family was in Savai'i, but to Tapale she was the pearl he had been looking for. Her voice, when he spoke with her the previous morning, was like music to his ears. She was shy and retiring. Let his mother look for a genealogy that stretched from the earth to the sky, as far as he was concerned Tumua would be his wife. He would elicit a promise from her to be his wife before he returned to Upolu.

'Tumua! Tumua!' her mother whispered from where she lay with her father in their old mosquito net. 'Are you not asleep yet? What's the matter? Do you want to go back to the pastor's house?'

'Oh, no. I'm thinking about the fight today. I'm also thinking about our small faleoo. It will probably fit ten times into the pastor's house, but I really like it here. The pastor's house is too large and filled with furniture, all given by the congregation. There are other big houses — those of the tamalii with their high paepae and elaborate decoration, but I do not want to live in those houses. I prefer our small faleoo and the fact that there is just us.' Her mother heard her voice catch in what sounded suspiciously like a sob.

'What is the matter? Are you all right?' Ruta, Tumua's mother, sat up quickly and moved outside the mosquito net and peered into Tumua's net. 'Why are you crying?'

It took quite a while before Tumua replied, 'I've been thinking of your wishes to give me the best. That is why you wanted me to live at the pastor's house, but I know people have been saying that I did not want to tell the world that you are my parents and that you are poor. They have been saying that I am an impostor who does not want to live with her parents. That is not true. I love both of you and I do not want to live anywhere else again.'

Posi, Tumua's father, heard them talking; he sat up and said, 'Tumua, do not think about the fight ever again, and forget what people say about you. It's not worth worrying about. That is the way of the world. People need to have something to talk about. Even though our house is not a big one, we are quite happy here with you.'

They continued talking about other things. They even joked about the fight that day. Ruta got into their mosquito net first. Posi was just lifting the flap to get in, without letting in the mosquitoes, when someone whispered from outside the house, 'Posi?'

'Sole! Ruta, where are the matches so that I can light the lamp?' Posi felt in the dark for the matches. He struck a match and lit the lamp. Ruta sat up, while Tumua turned over and tried to make out who the intruder was.

Posi saw the young man and said, 'Come closer, here, and please sit on the mat. This is only a small house. Tumua', he called to his daughter, 'get up and pull back the mosquito net so that there is enough room for Tapale to sit.'

The young man said, ' I apologise for disturbing you at this time when you are ready for sleep.'

'It is all right,' Posi said. 'We were not asleep. We have been talking. How did you get here?'

'I came with some other boys, who showed me your house,' Tapale replied.

After this brief exchange, there was a long silence when neither Posi nor Tapale said anything. Posi got a leaf of tobacco, dried it over the lamp, and then rolled it in a dry piece of banana leaf. He lit his smoke, put it in his mouth, and waited. Ruta tried to break the silence by inquiring whether Posi had got his fishing gear back from the neighbour who had borrowed it. Tumua waited in her mosquito net.

'Well, Posi and Ruta,' Tapale started hesitantly, 'I know we have not known each other long. I am in your house but I am very much afraid. Even though we do not really know each other . . . I thought of going to the pastor, but I know you are the real parents . . . I hope you don't have any doubts of my love for . . . I have not known her long but when I saw her at church this morning . . . I can't tell you how I felt . . .' Tapale babbled on incoherently. The couple heard his frequent stops and starts and guessed that Tapale was asking for their daughter's hand in marriage. The fact that he had not tried to enlist the help of someone else to talk for him appealed to Tumua's parents

When the visitors from Upolu returned to Safata, the word spread that Tapale had proposed to a girl in Savai'i and that his proposal had been accepted. Simoli heard this and from that day on, she nagged Tapale as to why he wanted a girl from Savai'i when he was already promised to Penina.

Simoli only consented to the wedding when she discovered that Tumua's mother came from a family who were just as proud as she was.

Litia Alaelua

Ghosting

Red roses. Rampant at the bottom of the front stairs and through the borders on either side of the path. Profuse in summer and defiant even to the first frosts of winter. Heady in fragrance and, when spent, headier — a swan song. As a child, I could not wait for the petals to free themselves and fall. I would shake a loosened head to expose a thrusting, perfectly formed crown of spun gold.

On long, hot evenings, Mum cut them in bloody swathes for church while Dad cleaned and swept the paths. They sang Samoan hymns in two parts while dark fell, and my mother's voice soared, liquid air, while Dad's would rumble and boom away. Years later, I understood implicitly that music was physics, but at the time, I hoped the neighbours did not hear. They took the flowers to church and I stayed home with the others, thought things about the glory of God and wondered why Mum never cut flowers for the house like I had seen in pictures in the *Woman's Weekly*. 'In Samoa,' she told me one day, 'these do not grow.' She was final on this point. Surprised that New Zealand could offer her something she didn't already have.

It is my grandfather I think of, though, when I recall those roses. I knew him briefly, but his image is placed firmly, permeated by their scent. After he had bathed and dressed for church — and this was a ritual of meticulous order that kept my aunts busy in a hallway suddenly misty with steam and the smell of Old Spice — he would pace the front path slowly. Austere and tall, he was oddly Victorian in his formal grey lavalava, tweed jacket and white shirt. My mother laboured over these shirts on Saturday night with a swiftly administered iron. I remember the almost scorched smell of steam and heat, and the gentle thud-thud of water drops she would scatter from long fingertips that flew like birds.

Through a film of netted lace, I watched my grandfather as my hair or my sister's was being braided for church. Torture! The weight of our hair was lifted off our backs and necks, then patted, smoothed and combed by my mother's hands, made liquid and warm from oil kept in a Jucy bottle and stopped with a frayed wad of fibre. Our hair was then woven tightly onto our scalps, accompanied by my mother's words — warnings, and hidden messages of love and belonging, reinforced frequently by the sudden and strategic tugging of hair. From the temples down, the skin around our eyes and cheek-bones was pulled taut as strands of hair were gathered so that we looked at each other when finished and grinned. 'You look chichi.' 'You do.' 'No, you do!' Ever resourceful, and in final insult, our mother would bind the ends of our hair with white sheeny-shiny bows. These sessions were a kind of mental agony, but when she had finished my sister's head and mine were perfectly sculptured.

Grandpa kept his head shaved, and Mum did this with an electric razor. A Remington. This fact was stamped in tiny silver letters on its grainy black case. It was a Father's Day present to Dad, who never used it, preferring the drama of a razor. I watched one day as Mum shaved Grandpa's head while directing a young aunt who sat in another part of the room, cross-legged and neat before the wide-open glory-box. From this slid the quick scent of camphor as my aunt layered and sorted linen with smooth, sure movements, the quiet slope of her back intent on private inventories. They spoke evenly in Samoan, and Grandpa called to me, cupped his hand-span over my head and smiled so that a myriad of wrinkles patterned his eyes and included me.

At ten I was made up of eyes and ears. At some signal each evening, family lotu would begin after the closing off of curtains and doors, and the deferential sound of feet on mats as bodies arranged themselves appropriately to Grandpa's seating place and to each other. Not having learnt how to 'look without looking', I gazed carefully at and around Grandpa as he prayed, and having my thigh pinched surreptitiously between the thumb and forefinger of some all-seeing aunt did not stop me. I really felt that he was talking to someone. The bristles that covered his head in a silvery cap would glisten and nod under the yellow light, as his words fell like small polished stones into the still room. He would often call for me to sit near him and turn the pages of his Bible while he read, and I would do this with great care, listening for the papery rustle of something old and rare. I looked for the small pinked snapshots that had been placed carefully as markers. People who covered themselves from neck to wrist to ankle in strange textures looked back at me, unsmiling and sure. And on their backs, the feltish, blue-black smudge of some other person's memories. Firmly rounded copperplate script that I traced with my finger — 'My dearest brother in Christ . . . until it is God's Will . . . that we see one another . . . 1953.' Quaint Victorianisms from a colonial missionary upbringing.

To Grandpa's way of thinking, everything that was important was within walking distance, so on Sunday we all walked to church. The Valiant, or what Mum called 'your father's prideful joy', remained inside the garage, in all its glinting, blue-green entirety. Mum and Dad walked behind with my aunts, and Grandpa walked in front with us. In one hand he held his Bible — bound black, with gold-rimmed leaves edged in small, script-filled half moons. It was rare for Grandpa to look at or speak to us directly, but he sometimes cautioned us against 'spoiling the hard work of our mother', or smiled as we quested him daringly in our shy child-jabber. Walking to church, the grown-ups were all gods and goddesses, and we, their offspring. I understood their presence of mind. They were all larger than anything around us, because in this land there was nothing that could contain them.

On Fridays, Grandpa fasted until midday. If Dad was on night shift, he stopped at the markets on the way home and bought taro, fish and green bananas. Mum worked the early morning shift, so he made our school lunches, heated the milk for our Weet-Bix, fixed our hair, then cooked an elaborate meal to break Grandpa's fast. Before this, though, he showered and bathed himself scrupulously. One of us had to run to the washing-line for the pulu when he shouted for it above the noise of crashing water. Without the shower, he always said, he never felt himself to be truly clean. Fresh and glistening, in a clean lavalava and work-shirt, he began to cook. We ate breakfast and watched a rapidly spreading mound of brown peel on newspaper, as Dad knife-flicked the taro deftly to expose the hard white-speckled flesh beneath. With the point of a knife held like a pen, he slit the emerald-green bananas open and discarded their skins, then sent tiny, opaque mirrors skidding damply over the sink as he cleaned and scraped the milky-eyed fish. Soon the kitchen would be filled with the clatter of steaming pots.

Grandpa always had his own food. My parents served him from different dishes which they arranged around his eating-place in a neat semi-circle of steam and pleasing odours. When lotu had finished, Grandpa would look over at us and call us to bring our plates, on which he would place a portion from each of his dishes — despite my parents' efforts to scold us away. Grandpa ate fastidiously, savouring each mouthful as though it were his last. His fingers never got messy. This interested me. To my uncles, eating was serious business too, but they ate hunched over their plates, looking neither left or right, ending their meals quickly and with fingers shiny from grease.

As the oldest daughter, it was my chore to bring Grandpa a thick white china bowl of warm water and a small embroidered hand-towel when he had finished eating. This moment had to be chosen carefully, because if I got it wrong my parents would be unsparing in their rebuke. But it was hard to know when he would be finished. At some point, he would simply cease to eat, place his hands on either side of his plate with fingers curved carefully and look ahead. I liked to watch the way Grandpa would wash his hands with care, touch at his mouth briefly with wet fingers, then dry them with the towel I gave him. He would look ahead and smile, then thank me gravely in Samoan, 'the daughter of Alaelua'. I listened for this same patterning of words when my own father died, many years later.

Grandpa went back to Samoa a few months later, and not long after this, he died. I remember feeling no sadness when I knew, only the need to comfort my parents in their grief.

The roses still come every summer. My mother's voice tends them alone now or sometimes mingled with the sound of my own daughter's in child-play. Sometimes I sit on the stairs, close my eyes against a long, shimmering dusk, and listen to my mother's voice as it shifts the perfumed silence around us. I can recall my grandfather's image with clarity and sudden love. But the ghost of the ten-year-old girl is lost to me.

My grandfather left an understanding, and this came to me through my mother. People do not die, for this would be too hard. They are merely transposed, etched indelibly on the hearts and minds of those they choose to love.

PASITALE FALEILEMILO

Funeral in Savai'i

'The bus will be full as usual,' Ioane said to the huge man next to him.

'Yeah,' he replied, 'as long as we get to Mulifanua before that last boat goes. Otherwise we'll have to sleep there and have nothing to eat.'

'Don't worry. The driver's a good man and he'll get us there.'

Ioane stared out the window and caught a glimpse of an old girlfriend. He whistled to her. She turned, then disappeared inside a shop, not wanting to remember him.

The bus raced along. Fast. At a halt, three hundred metres on, a large cooked pig was put in the back. Three matai with briefcases got on, their women and mats coming after. Children stood and moved back. Three or four to each seat now. Jammed. But no change in speed because Mulifana had to be reached.

'Malo faauli,' yelled Ioane. A pig scuttled out of the way of the bus. Lucky. 'This bus is really full,' continued Ioane as the bus bumped over the potholes.

'Ah,' replied Seli, his wife. 'Let's get our boat tickets.'

Across the water, Savai'i's mist hid the coconuts on the lowland and the rich tropical forest higher inland. Ioane's and Seli's home village was tucked in there somewhere. They'd left only six months before to work in Apia. Having for several years planted a plantation of taro and taamu for themselves and their matai, they'd decided to break with that life. In Apia they could work for their own money. The matai, their family leader, took too much.

So, with three children, they became part of Seli's father's family, close to the main street in Apia. Seli's three and four dollar baskets were popular with the tourists. Ioane was a good strong worker labouring at a big, new building in town. They liked the town. New people, money, movies, food, no matai, freedom. And going back to Savai'i now for Ioane's mother's funeral . . .

'How much money did you say you'd brought to help the family with this death?' asked Seli, as the boat chugged through the dynamite-blasted passage in the reef.

'Selau tala. That and those six fine mats will have to do. See what we get back from it, eh!'

'What about some money for your brother with his eleven children to feed? He's always short.'

'Not this time. They've got the plantation and sea to eat from. Also, his daughter's school fees in Apia are expensive. I paid forty tala last week for this term's fees. And boy, she eats a lot around our place.'

'Let's not start talking about that again. I'll weave a few more baskets next week to make up for it.'

'Pepelo,' Ioane snorted, and he stared across at Manono where his first wife's family lived; she now had another husband to look after their two beautiful young girls. Savai'i was still clouded and the sun at the far end of the island was going down fast.

'We'll make it tonight,' thought Ioane. 'I hope our village bus is waiting at the wharf. If it is, we'll get there well after dark, but at least we'll be there for tomorrow. The quicker this funeral is over, the quicker we'll get back to Apia. Since the boss doesn't know where I am we should get back as quick as possible anyway.'

Seli, fast asleep beside him, was far away. All her baskets sold, and the children safely in the hands of her mum; no hurry at all for her. A good chance to get some lau paogo for her baskets.

A tall white steepled church cleared the coconut trees in Salelologa. From the sea, this and the houses clustered along the foreshore looked peaceful and silent. Smoky Toyota buses at the wharf altered this picture as the drivers waited impatiently to hurry away from the quiet town to an even quieter village. Perhaps a rush to get home for some taro, breadfruit, coconut milk and fresh fish. The wharf bustled as the boat came in. Buses revved up. People swarmed onto them. Racing off, they left a handful of bags and people waiting for another.

'Are you coming back for the funeral?' asked Sia, the local late-night girl of Ioane's village.

'Yeah. How's everything there? Found yourself a husband yet?'

Sia laughed, 'My two kids are enough of a problem without a husband too. Your family seems pretty sad now. She died on Tuesday night you know.'

'What are you up to tonight? How about us meeting?'

'You're still up to your old tricks,' hinted Sia. 'But Seli'd beat me up.' They laughed loudly together and Ioane knew things were the same in the village.

The bus raced along the new Australian-aid road. The green bush swept by. A young man with a loaded horse veered to the side of the road. The horse and man moved twenty years slower than the new road. The man cursed the bus. Having come all the way from the taro plantation he was tired, but not too tired to shout and wave his knife angrily at the bus.

'Fa,' yelled Ioane to an old friend from a neighbouring village. His friend paid the forty sene fare and jumped down. Again the bus stopped, and the three matai and women paid their fares, got off, took their pig out of the back, and the bus took off again.

The road running along the coast gave a great view of the calm lagoon, with its few men paddling back from their fishing. Waves broke sharply on the reef. White froth swept into the calm waters. Darkness was on them.

'How long are you staying for? What did you bring? Where's my cousin Nu'utai? What boat? Grandma's dead. She left a note I think. What's in that? Where are you living now?' Ioane pondered his family's greetings.

The bus had come off the seal and onto the gravel. At the end of the gravel it turned around. Ioane and Seli got off. A few children came running to meet them, took their hands and grabbed the bags. The house was the same; standing open and proud beside the rocky coast. And on the malae it stood prominently in the village.

Children put a clean mat out for them. They sat and leaned against a post, and Ioane's brother, Viko, the matai of the family, welcomed them. Ioane replied. The children scrambled for the Twisties, and the box of food he had bought in Salelologa was taken by Viko's wife, Pam, out to the cook-house.

Then the questions started. Ioane knew his brother was interested in Apia. They hadn't seen each other since he'd left the village, but had only heard news of each other when Viko's daughter came back for the school holidays.

Ioane respected Viko as the matai of the family and for carrying out his matai duties. He especially respected him for his ability to give a lauga. Viko was good at this. Though only forty-one he often spoke first for his village at celebrations, in front of older matai.

In turn, Viko respected Ioane for breaking out to earn a wage in Apia, and thus help the family; as in helping in his daughter's education.

'You should come back more often,' said Viko.

'I'd like to,' Ioane lied, 'but there's no time off from work.' He knew Viko liked him to visit and to bring money, and that's why he didn't want to visit too often. He'd never have any money for his and his wife's and children's needs. Things were expensive in Apia now. Two tala for only two or three taro.

The conversation moved onto the death. Ioane was tired, especially after eating Pam's delicious food, which the children obediently served to him and Seli. Ioane presented to his brother his contributions for their fa'alavelave. His words were brief since other members of their family had just come, and they needed to have words with Viko in preparation for the next day.

' . . . and here we have six ietoga, our small contribution to you, Viko, and our family in this time when we are together. Also one hundred tala.'

A pretty young girl showed each mat in turn before Viko and the others in the house. Thanks were expressed by different people. The hundred tala was taken by Viko, who slipped it into a briefcase placed behind him.

Viko quickly replied to Ioane. He saw their tiredness. It was well past midnight. Seli and Ioane were told their sleeping-mats and sheets were in the smaller house to the left and closer to the sea.

265

The waves slapping on the rocks in front of the house were noisy.

'No waves like this in Apia,' thought Ioane. 'I hope they won't keep us awake or come into the house and wash us away. Although our mother's gone, it's not time yet for us to be swept out to sea.'

But the waves didn't keep them awake. It had been a long day. Nothing could stop them from sleeping. Not the waves, nor the sound of the women of the village mourning two houses away.

Ioane woke up as the sun's first rays came over the lagoon. The sea was calm. The waves had receded. Altogether, about twelve adults and several children were sleeping in the house. Ioane had no idea who they were as they hid under their sheets from night-wandering mosquitoes. He saw several people already in the cook-house. He knew it was going to be a very busy day preparing food, the umu, pigs, and killing the two cows tied under the pulu trees. These would be a few of the jobs, but at least he knew many people from the village would lend a hand.

Indeed, the morning was busy. It was good also to be greeted by his friends, people he'd been brought up with.

'You'll be staying for good, won't you?' asked Farani, an old friend.

'We'll see. But when are you coming to Apia yourself, to work or tafao?' he answered.

'Maybe next Independence Celebrations. But now I have no money, and the village duties use any money that we get from our copra.'

So it was really the same. Matai using the money. People working for the matai. He was glad he'd left.

Different buses arrived bringing relatives with mats, and then left with an assortment of mats, pigs, boxes of biscuits and money, depending on how many mats the people had brought and who they were.

Ioane had seen it before but this was different, for it was his mother who had died. He felt sadder and sadder as the day wore on and as he went about his tasks. It was tiring dealing with people. Everyone was busy.

'If only I could go to sleep,' he thought. But he knew he couldn't.

After the church service the body was buried in front of the house. The women of the village, all dressed in black, congregated together in one house. Pork and beef were distributed. It was a big funeral.

Many speeches were heard on the malae that day. People from all parts of Savai'i came, and some, too, from Upolu. As the sun fell near the horizon, things slowed down. It had been a long day. Night came and groups clustered together in different houses to retell the day's happenings.

His family was there but Ioane's heart had left. His thoughts wandered back to his new life in Apia. He and Seli would get on that bus out tomorrow.

Epi Enari

The Olomatua

Tia eased herself out from behind the steering wheel of her pick-up truck. The back of her maternity top was sticky with sweat; she waved it back and forth at the hem in a fanning motion. She would fold up her cumbersome ankle-length lavalava to knee-level except that Tu, her mother-in-law for whom she was waiting, might come out any minute now from the Filiola Law Office and condemn her for it. A matai, and the only female in the village council, Tu was a noted orator who, though better known as the olomatua, was, in Tia's regard, a brutal dictator. Although her children had protested, the dictator filed a complaint against Tolo who, like her, was a matai with a clan in the same aiga potopoto. Tolo had registered the Silia title in his name without consulting anyone, and the dictator was in Fifiola's office to retain him as her legal counsel in the case.

Going to the back of the truck, Tia stiffened as the baby's kicks churned her insides. Sione, her husband, who worked as a loan officer in the Bank of Hawaii, had asked her to wait there in the air-conditioning, but she'd preferred to be alone. Once perched on the pick-up bed, she brought her legs up to ease the tension from the swelling.

A taxi backed out from the Black Ace Stand, sending up spurts of water from a puddle. The newly built fale fono stood imposing against the blue of the Pacific Ocean behind and the green of Rainmaker Mountain across the bay. Its glass walls, through which people peeked for a glimpse into the much-rumoured gambling and ribald activities of the law-makers, and which served as mirrors for passers-by, glistened dazzlingly in the mid-morning sun. To the left, the Amerika Samoa Bank bustled with customers going in and out. A few stragglers passing by the police station and along the malae were either on their way east toward Scanlan's, Annesley's, and Burns Philp's or up the rise to the residential area.

Beyond the Amerika Samoa Bank and to the right a crowd waited as the *Salamasina*, on its weekly trips from the neighbouring Western Samoa, glided in to dock. Watching the stern of the boat loom larger by the minute, Tia remembered her own trip across on it four years ago.

The daughter of the faife'au, she had become bored with having to watch her every move because, as her mother nagged, 'the village was watching'.

Her teaching job in the village school didn't promise an exciting future either and marriage prospects were limited by her parents' strict censorship — a process that eliminated almost all males except theological students from Malua. Determined not to be sent to New Zealand like her older sister, Tia had secretly arranged for a permit to American Samoa through a girlfriend's sister who lived there and whose husband worked in the immigration office.

Upon arrival, Tia waitressed at a local bar which, because of her immigration status, paid her under the table. The owner, an elderly man, docked her pay cheque. 'I've rented a room at the hotel,' he said. 'Come with me and get the rest of your pay, plus a bonus.' Dying to yank the gray hairs from the man's eyebrows and ears and stuff them in his nose, she stormed out. 'I'd rather sleep with a dog!' she called from the safety of the outside. Leaving that job, she waitressed at another bar until the St Francis School, to which she'd taken her teaching credentials, sponsored her.

It was a year after Tia's arrival that she met Sione. Having taught her to play tennis, he'd then registered them both in the exclusive Tafuna Tennis Club. He also introduced her to golf, and wined and dined her at Soli's Restaurant, Ramona Lee's and at the Rainmaker Hotel. They married a year and a half later, at which time she got a teaching job in the public school system. Sione had a three-bedroom home on his family's land and, except for his occasional night out with the boys, life with him was quiet and satisfying. That is, until the dictator returned from Hawaii where she'd stayed with Sione's oldest sister. 'Tu's like any army general,' Tia warned repeatedly. 'She'll demand every ounce of you.'

On the day she arrived, the dictator, short and plump and with the voice of a man, demanded that Tia know her place. The matai of the village had come for the welcome-back ritual and the exchange of gifts: they bearing sticks of dried kava roots, she, money. Some were leaving while a few still sat around the fale posts talking when Tia, beside Sione at the back, found herself under the dictator's hard stare. 'You should be in the umu!' barked the dictator, pointing to the cooking fale. Broad shoulders slightly stooped, she sat at one of the front posts, her legs partly crossed and hands at her hips. 'You should have seen to the food and now the clean up.' Coughing up phlegm, she spat on the rock foundation outside. 'If your mother didn't tell you, *I* will! You came to this family to burn your eyes out, not drape yourself around Sione all the time.'

Tia held her breath. Surely Sione would defend her. But in the air was only the echo of the dictator's bellow. Aching to scream in his face, Tia swallowed, almost choking on the explosion stuck in her throat. And the events of the next two weeks were testimony that Sione couldn't be counted on when it came to his mother. In one argument with him, she butchered the Tu title (which literally means 'to stand') with derogatory extensions.

'Her name should have been Tu ma le fana!' Tia shouted. 'She's more deadly than a gun.' In another, she extended the name to Tu a le ai tae — 'Because,' she berated him, 'only a shit-eater can be so cruel.' Tia also loathed being referred to as le fafine. 'Do I have to carve my name on my forehead?' she would rave. Once in a while Sione was sympathetic, but mostly he'd say, 'You know that's how it usually is.' Now, more than two years since first meeting the dictator, Tia, about ready to have a baby, found herself entertaining other possible lives — away from the dictator. Perhaps even away from the three-bedroom home, the two-year-old car, and Sione, who was probably oblivious to how he'd redeemed himself the night before.

The two of them were having supper when the phone rang. Scooping another spoon of beef gravy into her mouth, Tia was still chewing when she picked up the receiver. 'Hello.'

'Aue,' bellowed the dictator. 'Didn't your parents teach you not to talk with your mouth full? I'll never know what my son saw in you.'

My gorgeous body, the beautiful organ between my legs, and a nicer personality than yours! Tia wanted to shout. Instead she mumbled, 'I'm sorry.'

'I need to be at Filiola's Law Office tomorrow at 10.30,' the dictator continued. 'Pick me up at ten.'

No! It'll be too hot and I can barely fit behind the wheel now and you can just go to hell! But again she only said, 'I'll be there.'

Having hung up, Tia went outside. The pebbles dug into her bare feet, but if she were to get her slippers, Sione would see the tears. Clad only in the lavalava hitched under her arms - her dress code around the house now - she was easy prey for mosquitoes; but she eased herself onto the bench under the mango tree to indulge in the fragrance from the plumerias and gardenias in the garden. The quiet of the night also promised solace. A flying fox glided away from the breadfruit tree. A star fell in the sky. 'My baby! My husband!' she wished fiercely.

Then Sione was coming to her. 'I thought you'd be here. Remember, they say you can't be in the dark alone?' He sat beside her. 'Who was that on the phone?'

Hitler! she wanted to reply, but protecting herself against a loyal defense of his mother, she answered in her most casual voice, 'Your mother.'

'And?'

She relayed the exchange in as few words as she could, leaving out the fury eating away at her. Breathing deeply to stifle her sobs, she was startled when he kissed her cheek.

'You're crying.' he observed. 'I'm sorry.'

An arm around her shoulders, he moved closer, and though she stiffened at first, she eventually slumped against him. She wept softly now, from time to time undoing from above her right breast the flap of her lavalava to wipe her face. And it was several minutes before either of them moved.

'Thank you,' he whispered.

'For what?'

'For putting up with my family, my mother especially.'

'You're the reason I try.'

Tightening his hold on her, he whispered, 'The reason is the three of us.'

'I . . . I guess,' she'd whispered.

A slim girl in a black skirt and red silk blouse who, Tia thought, had to be holding her breath so as not to bust her skintight clothes, was coming toward the truck now, the clippety-clop of her shoes grating in an irritating way. She lived in Pago Pago, two villages from Sione's. 'Talofa,' she said flashing a toothy smile. 'Filiola wants you to come inside, please. He wants you to explain something to the old lady.'

Tia heard the dictator's rattling cough from outside the door. As she entered, Filiola rose to shake her hand before reporting on the progress of his son whom Tia had in her classroom the year before. Then he asked, partly in English and partly in Samoan, if she understood the concept of ethics. 'I know what the word means,' she answered in kind, 'but I don't know what you're getting at.'

'You see,' he said, 'Tulou, Tolo's wife, is my cousin so I can't be involved in the case. Tu doesn't understand that.'

Filiola was the third lawyer the dictator had tried to hire and Tia didn't welcome the job of crushing her hopes. She turned to the dictator who, meanwhile, was watching intently.

'Tu,' Tia started. 'The legal profession doesn't allow . . . '

'He won't be my lawyer, will he?' the dictator interrupted.

'I'm afraid not,' Tia answered

'Then let's get out of here! These greedy lawyers are interested only in corporate cases.' Too embarrassed to apologise, Tia followed her. The next morning, the dictator went to court without a lawyer. Sione and his sisters, reinforcing their disagreement, went to work as usual, leaving Tia once again to drive their mother and wait to take her back home.

Tolo came towards Tia and the dictator as they stood in the corner of the courtroom lobby. In a white shirt tucked into a red lavalava, he walked in short quick steps. His sister, brother, and several cousins remained in the opposite corner. Tulou, his wife, was trying to pacify her whining baby. 'So, Auntie,' he said to the dictator. 'We're going to face each other in court?'

Tia eased backward and sat on the rail. Pack of Winstons in hand, the dictator took out a cigarette, put it in her mouth and flicked a lighter.

'I said relatives don't face each other in court,' persisted Tolo.

'Well, did you think that having gone to school in America gives you the right to the aiga's highest title without consulting it?'

Tolo said it would have required a meeting of all member clans, would have taken more than one meeting, wasted too much time, let in too many vaguely qualified people. 'Being the direct heir,' he announced, 'I have fifty per cent right through blood. I was only trying to save everyone a lot of trouble.'

Anxious for everyone to be inside so she could go to the car, recline the seat, and relax, Tia bunned up her braided hair. Coughing, the dictator went to the side and spat the phlegm into the hibiscus hedge alongside the building. The back of her dress was damp with sweat and Tia knew she'd soon want the box of tissues in the bag she held. Then a clerk was summoning them inside.

The baby kicked. Standing up, Tia felt as if one of its limbs had been drawn up then extended into her right hip joint. Handing over the bag with the tissues and the extra cigarette pack, Tia wished the dictator luck. But the older woman invited her in. 'Tolo has almost his entire clan here; you might as well come with me.'

Tia sat on the bench behind the dictator at one side of the aisle. At the other, Tolo sat with Watson, his lawyer, in the front bench while his supporters sat behind him. A female clerk in a red and white floral puletasi announced the arrival of the judges. In black gowns, the men, four Samoans and a palagi, sat themselves at the long table to the clerk's left, the American flanked on both sides by two of his counterparts. Below the palagi's gown, black leather shoes, dark brown socks, and the legs of gray pants showed. As for the Samoans, three wore brown leather slippers while one wore black ones.

'This is a preliminary hearing,' the clerk announced. 'The court asks if the two parties have tried to reach an agreement through the fa'a Samoa.' After the translation, the clerk looked at Tolo's side.

'My client suggested that to the plaintiff,' said Watson. His Samoan was colloquial: not only unflowery, but also using *k* instead of the more official *t* and incorrectly interchanging the *ng* and *n* sounds in several places. As the translator spoke, all eyes turned to Tu who mopped her face lingeringly without a response. Wondering at the ever-vocal woman, Tia peered at her from the side. The olomatua was sweating profusely, the back of her light blue dress now a shade darker than the rest of it.

Tia knew she was going to engage Sione in another bitter argument tonight: about why he was letting her become the family chauffeur, why didn't he spare her this and many other situations, why he wasn't here with his mother. She wished she could enjoy the olomatua's difficulty, but she didn't feel her usual anger. In its place was a painful awareness that the next few moments were crucial to what the olomatua stood for, and to the future of Sione and his sisters.

The clerk asked the olomatua if she would consider withdrawing her complaint. Tia repeated the question in a fierce whisper and when there was still no response, she moved up to the front bench.

'They're waiting for you to say something, Tu,' she whispered intensely. 'You have to defend yourself or the case will be dismissed.'

'They're speaking English so fast I can't keep up,' said the olomatua.

'Tell them to slow down the proceedings, and concentrate on the Samoan translations.'

Inhaling deeply, the olomatua looked at Tia. 'Please stand up for me,' she said. 'I get dizzy when everyone babbles in English. I'll tell you what to say.'

Looking at the judges, Tia cursed her own lack of foresight: she should have stayed in the car. There was a commotion from Tolo's side. Interlocking her shaking fingers, she gripped them tight. Her throat was dry, yet her armpits were damp and felt like they might drip any minute now. Her right hip-joint throbbed and her bra, cutting into her, felt as if it would bust when she next breathed out. But she stood up.

'My husband's mother,' she said, 'cannot speak for herself today. But she will help me tell you her wishes.'

'This woman's an outsider!' protested Tolo. 'She has no right speaking on family matters.'

But the olomatua was whispering her address to the court now. Straining to catch every word, Tia repeated, recognising genealogies, yet not able to distinguish which was for whom of the four Samoan judges. At the olomatua's next word, Tia gasped before she could repeat them.

'I,' she said, 'soon-to-be-mother of an heir to the Silia title, am not such an outsider any more.' Stretching a hand toward the olomatua, Tia continued, 'She has granted me that!'

The olomatua's coaching was getting louder. 'The last one to hold the Silia title was Tolo's father,' she said. 'Now the title should be held by a member of another clan. As head of one clan in the aiga potopoto, I have come to fight for the title. My great grandfather was the first holder of the title. Tolo has nothing to compare with my years in the matai council and the length of my service in the aiga.' She was rising now, and when she stood steady, Tia went back to her place on the second bench.

Breathing hard, the baby's kicks and the throbbing in her right hip not helping, Tia sat back rubbing both sides of her stomach. The olomatua was still standing, her rhetoric ringing in the courtroom. Looking back at Tia, she asked, 'Are you all right?' With a momentary smile, Tia nodded.

SANO MALIFA

Rain

(Washington DC)

The wind comes and the rain.
Now I remember everything that happened,
everything that mattered,
because at that moment when the rain comes,
a huge door opens out,
and I see through it glittering crystals in
all their marvellous colours,
in all their different shapes,
like a nude family united and underground.

And in that moment, I see why everything that happened
happened, and why it mattered so much,
because there is the truth in the rain,
and depth, the numbness of the cold thought,
when memory opens like an old wound,
yet there is no pain.
Although the wind is strong and bold,
it sweeps away nothing but dead leaves, sadness,
everything lifeless.

But the rain,
which throttles the earth and dresses it up like a corpse,
walks with me home,
and in her arms, slender and strong,
there is strength, sustained warmth
for a man alone, difficult to hate.

Night

(State College)

The sidewalk is buried in ice, slippery.
Icicles hanging from branches illuminated

273

in the neon light like silver dead vines.
If you walk on the snow, you hear snapping noises
as though of knuckles cracking.
The tracks through campus are empty
and quiet.
No one about.
No one.

A stray Labrador is whining on the snow, homeless.
A wail of siren going off to a mugging
somewhere.
Must be a reason I'm walking in the night
instead of sleeping.
Must be an end somewhere to all this wandering!

But an evil decadence, insomnia-like, dreamlike,
ephemeral, follows the scent to its burrow.

I know there's a reason for all this!
Why the mountain slope is forever mauled under
the avalanche of snow,
why the ice sheet is a warm blanket under which
the earth sleeps,
why the mind opens and shuts,
refusing to sleep.

from Midnight Sonnets

3

The heart has one door which opens and shuts, an
Enormous arch made of happiness and pain, and
My mind travels through it, back and forth,
      searching for a reason.

Life has very little meaning in times like now.
I'm afraid — the terror of guessing the limit from the
Limit as though everything would fall apart
      at that incredible moment.

It is as if God has given up everything, even refusing
To decide where happiness ends and sadness begins.
I have a terrible fear of the inscrutable, the unknown —

Why must sad thoughts rule over the whole?
Today I plant poems that may one day to life bloom,
And tomorrow I shall wear my heart on the sleeve of hope.

My wish for your sake, young man,
Is that God has not turned his back in shame on this world.

5

The moon is a distant red glow in the dark heavens,
A sad woman, light of foot, weeping among the stars.
Dawning, and the lonely dark thought of belonging,

The yearning, this incredible desire to unravel
    completely on a straight line.
Now two birds have woken up singing
As the house next door is still without light,

As the poems' cage has flung open —
The barren thought has become swampy all of a sudden.
These hours of solitude when vision is opening up,

And the thudding heartbeat vibrates aimlessly along
    the sleepy dawn light,
I think of that time in the cold city when the cruel
Fist of winter shattered open the box of dreams,

And the beggar's dogmatic prayer
Could heal even Lazarus's wounds.

TASI MALIFA

Christmas in Samoa, 1978

Coming home, I am expected to live according to some people's lies and scheme!

Sorry brother, that's not my line — not even for a Christmas vacation. I cannot carry another man's burden nor contain his freedom in the palms of my hands. It's all trash in the wind!

Consider, instead, why the young get stoned on disco slit and boiled mushroom brew fed on cow-shit — their quest for freedom high is their only escape from society's stale and dying conception God is just, and the government is not corrupt. Can you blame them?

Consider, too, why they seek shelter on the banks of the Vaisigano, where the river eats into the turmoil and the wound, while their fathers, in the company of other men's wives, ride the town length in flash American cars; build mansions up Vailima, dictate the flow of blood and waste into Vaiusu Bay to kill my brother tomorrow.

Man, Christ this Christmas did not die on top of Mt Vaea!

We celebrate merely dates: the true and real meaning is forever lost in our futile attempt to construct another tower of Babel!

Cheers, lady, our hypocrisy speaks to us even from these stone marbles beneath our feet!

The pebble thrown into the sea settles not on the ocean bed, nor can the wound heal without the hands that feel the heart. I cannot foretell the future. But one thing is certain: I shall come back. Samoa is the only place I can call home.

More Bacardi, please; blood runs more freely when the wound opens up wide and clear. And when you ask me about where it'll all end, I sense you, like the others who have put some measure into my line, really want stability for a gift.

Well, sorry, lady, I have nothing to offer.

Not even the wish for the Midas golden touch to turn our myth 'nobody starves' into bloated bellies, or the dim hope Samoa grows out of her lust for power and corruption

to love her own people.

For now, come close my love.

Let the pebble feed on the turmoil and the wound.

Let the end come divinely on Cupid's arrow fling.

I have you this Christmas, even if without Christ.

Ruperake Petaia

Poems in the Rain

In the rain,
people like chickens
cluster under the wings
of buildings; and

trees like old men
hang their bones
lazy with wetness.

In the rain,
fale like sick-bays
droop their blinds
in isolation; and

green mountains
in the skies
sleep like giants
with grey beards.

Looking
        down
on a rainy day
I see
careless
        feet
shatter my face
rippling in the water.

Freedom Day

This day
I see
On a stage
A small group of
Big Men,
These so-called liberators.

Up on a pole
The national flag waves,
That say of Freedom.

This day
I will hear once more
Solemn promises
Reassurances
Of Freedom and Unity
Of Prosperity and Satisfaction
Of Toleration and Peace.

I see
On the malae
A people misled,
With more flags and
Fancy uniformed marches
And brass-band parades.
I see their weary faces
Marked with bright-coloured
Images of the liberators.

I see them made
To sing and dance
In the sun's pain,
Lured to
Compete for the prize money
Of the Big Men.

The people
Assume this day
Will last forever.
But soon,
Too soon,
The darkness will return
The people to their villages,
And I will join them
Chanting
Their evening rituals
In prayers of hope
For another today
Tomorrow.

And Freedom flies on,
Way up on a pole,
Unreachable.

Papeete by Night

The bitching breeze is caressing me,
on a villa, looking down the inviting
crotch of Papeete bay by night;

Each evening I watch the smiling
sun turn;
her golden buttocks swaying
to the blazing beat
of the waves' clap;
the breeze is always around;

nothing ever sleeps it seems
in Papeete by night;

Even the soulless sand
whispers in the beating darkness,
as we run the crazy highways and
byways to the heart of Tahiti-Iti;

Ia Manuia; as we poured through the
slippery throat of Pearl Farm Swamp
breathing down our drunken faces
like silly French gendarmes
testing drunken drivers
on a pouring night;

Papeete by night,
your face, your bronze face
tells the tale of a proud
Polynesian dynasty;

mixed to the bone
in blood flesh and culture.

CLARA REID

Island

The rain falls
on an island
a bowl in the ocean
and it seems miles
pass beyond the tiny bowl
clouds that drift and drain rain
and keep with every morning star
the glow of sand from midnight
stars falling or climbing
beyond the bowl horizon
the morning resting upon the green
of the island trees
drenching hilltops
webs of a spider
resting on a ceiling of the cold
the rain falls on an island
a bowl in one ocean . . .

Violent Storm

dear Dino
trusting you
has lost me
my reputation
as a taupou
there is talk
in my village
of importing chickens
from Tahiti
and killing them
for my wedding
sheet

ETI SA'AGA

Birthday Present

It was the eve
of the new moon
that my daughter
gave me a pebble
for my birthday.
It was gift-wrapped
with tiny fingers,
sticky with mango juice.

Of Butterflies and Bubbles

Last night,
I watched my son
catching moments
that I missed.
With rompish care,
he tossed my
fears and regrets
into the air,
shrieking with laughter
as they bounced
on the floor
bursting into
brilliant sunshines
of butterflies and bubbles.

For hours
he frolicked
with my awkwardness
through the rainbow vapour
and dancing smiles
while I,
in discomfort,

sprouted impossible wings
only to find that
I was too heavy
for the butterflies
and too clumsy
for the bubbles.

Noumea Simi

Peace

The sleepy-eyed sun
ascends to peel away
the membranous shroud-haze
of ashen grey Sunday morning umu
Somewhere in the horizon
the flying fish is anxious
that Vaea has not awoken
to guide the sails of dawn
to the safety of Apia harbour
Somewhere the spirits have risen
for the flight to Pulotu
leaving us in fleeting momentary
peace

In Life

(For my father, Gatoloai Peseta)

I wish I could write a book
compose a song a note or two
or even capture in a line
the wealth of your life

I've seen the statesman politician
in the tattered leaves of photo albums
and ribboned medallions of mildew-stained
colonial times

I've traced your life of public service
in seventy years of diary entries
and well-preserved proficiency
in framed certificates

I've remembered that we sat UE together
your resolve to let your children know
that education did not leave you
one generation behind

283

I've admired your many talents
in the lyrics of song
and the production of musical drama
and the creativity of dance

I've followed with awe your cultural finesse
in value-imbued customs and sacred norms
You often chided but did not decry
the shortcomings of my time

What Are We?

(On the Mead/Freeman debate)

Do we know what we are
Mebbe mebbe not
Some palagi wommin
say we the chilrun of free luv
shud be examples to prudish societies
But some palagi man
calls hisself a Free man
says NO!
we the chilrun of violence
cause we play war on criket pitches
Dis Free man even say
we are liars
but only to Mead and not to him
and dat is why his word is god's
for he alone know what we are
So com on bruddah and me sister
your fuddah and me muddah
may ave bin guinea fowls
for naive academics
and slit-minded brainwashers
to make a name
and make proof
dat Samoan andropology is a miff
Leave us alone palagi man
we will bare to the world
our dents and flats
our blues and blacks
when it comes to us

TATE SIMI

Birdcall I

(To Ofa)*

This morning there was
no birdcall in the tree
Was it because
in the cyclone's wake
the bird had
no more cause to sing
Or because having bared
its soul to the wind
the tree had no more appeal
to the bird?

*The Tongan word for love; also the name of the tropical cyclone which
devastated Samoa in early 1990

Poem to My Father

Thank you father
for causing
me so much pain
for it opened my eyes
to the pain in others;
it made me see
how painful it is
to love

Taumeasina

(A poem for my grandmother, Saara)

They have reclaimed Taumeasina
the hoarding-place of our primitive wealth
where the ocean washed our dreams ashore
dead shells that your delicate fingers

stringed into ulas of hope
They have buried the beach
the sanctuary of my nostalgia
where the Taumeasina stream once
met the sea in a soothing embrace
as they rolled in aquatic bliss
in the shallows of our watery path
as we carted our simple wares
and simple smiles to Aggie's for sale

They have destroyed our monument
to simplicity and love — Taumeasina
where a grandmother and child once
shared so much joy and happiness
in the discovery of a simple sea shell

One more bead in our search
for our rosary dream . . .

CAROLINE SINAVAIANA

Ianeta's Dance

the young girl treads
   on grandfather's ailing legs.
   lying belly down on the coarse woven mat
   Grandpa murmurs & dreams
                 of a time before his leg got big
                 with mosquito sickness.

ianeta of six years
kneads with her feet & toes
   that veined and buckled path of
   the old man's legs
   that still after seventy years haul
      coconut/taro/every day
      fish from the sea every day.
      they bend to coax earth oven, umu
      they kneel to lift the baby, aua le tagi
      then fold to sit for evening prayer,
      Lo matou Tama e, o i le lagi . . .

while Grandpa dozes,
Ianeta walks his legs,
dancing with her shadow on the wall.

War News

small flag of white lace
hangs from barbed-wire
fence, which keeps the ducks in
all safe among teuila /
red ginger, and banana trees.

at the lagoon, i wash clothes
on black rocks, bowled lava,
glad for small discoveries:

if you fold them into quarters first,
your blue jeans won't trail
in the muddy pebble bed.

radio voice drifts down the early morning breeze:

LAST NIGHT, AN AMERICAN WARSHIP SHOT DOWN
A PASSENGER AIRLINER OVER THE PERSIAN GULF.

beyond the clothesline, a congress of chickens
mill about pecking grass seeds,
one brown hen teaching wee chicks
the art of pecking coconut from the half-shell;
two offspring listen rapt / one foot each
planted *in* today's   lesson

290 PEOPLE DEAD. PRESIDENT REAGAN DECLINES TO
COMMENT. VICE-PRESIDENT BUSH DECLINES TO
ISSUE APOLOGY.

in the mangrove swamp, shadowy wings
disturb the dark air:
    matu'u / reef heron,   and once
    god of war,   now ascending /
    his ablutions   complete,
        to survey the day's grim business
        out   across the mudflats,   where pigs
        love to root at low tide.

Talosaga Tolovae

Polynesian Old Man

I wonder why
   old man
when I went away in an expensive suit
and steel-heeled pair of Italian boots,
your bloodshot eyes looked away
      hopeful.

I wonder why
   old man
when I came back to you
with a three-year white-man's degree,
you still wore those anxious hopeful
      bloodshot eyes.

I wonder why
   old man
before you were gone refused
black Italian boots, a new black suit,
silver coins for your bloodshot eyes, a present
      from your educated son.

I wonder why
   old man
I guess you feared meeting a pale shade
of your brown Polynesian son
with a white-man's stride.

Crucifixion on Sunday

You have talked
      about your Christ
      with a bleeding heart
      a face aged with pity

crucified on the calico sheets
on cool rafters
of your place of worship
for my sake.
But I've seen
 my father
 eyes bloodshot
 skin cracked and blackened
 by hours of labour in the sun
 to keep his children in school
 and provide for a family.
Still you talked
 of the sacrifice
 your Christ
 made on Golgotha
 to earn for us
 a one-way ticket
 to his place of residence
But I've seen
 the black-robed priests
 of your Christ
 crucifying my father
 on Sundays
 with loaded scripts for his wages
 to aid heal your Christ's
 injury to his heart.

EMMA KRUSE VA'AI

Ta Tatau

I was eight years old when my father came home quite late one evening. As he came through the door, I noticed that he stooped a little and that his shirt had been rolled up and was stuck under his armpits. Hiding my curiosity, I went back to doing my homework, but noticed that when he sat down he winced and didn't lean back and stretch out in the comfortable and easy way he usually did.

'Are you all right, Manu?' I asked.

'Ia,' he replied haltingly.

I kept watching him until, apparently impatient, he said, 'Be a good girl, Sarona, and get Mama's fan. OK?'

'Now,' he said, 'just fan my back. Ah! No, no — more gently!' And I wondered what terrible thing could have happened that caused a little fanning to give him so much pain. I slowed down my fanning and soon had it right.

'Good, good,' he said. He breathed in deeply, and then out very slowly, as if letting the air leave too quickly might hurt him. As he did this, I thought to move round him and look at his back where I was fanning him.

'Uola — it's a picture!' I said, staring open-mouthed and feeling very confused at the lines and patterns. You know, we were always being told not to draw on anything — not on the walls, not on books — nor on bodies, for that matter.

'Who did it? Who drew the lines, Manu? Who put the picture on your back?' I asked him.

'Oh — just another — man,' he breathed.

'Why did he do it — and did he use a ruler? Will it rub off?'

'No it will never come off,' he told me, wincing, 'and keep the fan going, my daughter — it eases the pain.'

At that moment my mother, Sala, appeared, carrying my little brother wrapped up in a towel. 'There's your father, there's your sister,' she sang to the laughing Fatu as she came towards us. Then she paused as she realised my father was not responding to her. Two more steps, and then she knew.

'Why?' she asked, tight-lipped. Fatu was quiet, and peeped out from the towel with one wide eye, almost as if he were frightened. 'Why have you made yourself suffer — why must you make me suffer?' she asked my father.

'I've begun it now and have to finish it.'

Nothing more was said between them that night, nor did they speak to each other throughout the rest of what became a very long month.

The following morning I woke late and felt mad with myself because my father had already left. I knew my mother was also mad with him, but unlike other times when she had been angry with the whole world, she seemed quiet and gently tired, and I very much wanted to put my arms around her.

'After school, come home quickly, Rona,' she said.

'I'll run all the way, Mama,' I told her as I reached up to kiss her, and then stooped to kiss Fatu, who pulled my hair as Mama hugged me and pretended to straighten the back pleats of my school uniform.

After school my mother sent me to collect gogu and ti leaves. I collected quite a few from my Aunty Mele's tree and some from our old Fofo down the road. No one asked any questions — which made me feel a bit disappointed. I suppose everyone knew why I was collecting the gogu and ti leaves.

That evening my father was actually limping when he was brought home by his older brother. In fact, he could hardly stand up, and had to be supported. My uncle said, 'Malo, Sala, be brave — it will be over soon.'

My mother's eyes filled with tears, but they didn't melt. She smiled stonily and thanked him for helping my father.

'Lots of cold water and leaves,' my uncle said, 'and don't dry his clothes in the sun; dry them in the shade. And don't sleep with him either!' he laughed.

My mother didn't laugh. She already had a bowl of ice water and a cloth ready to ease the pain. 'He'll try to sleep, and I'll stay awake,' she told my uncle, who kissed Fatu and me goodbye, then left.

That night, wearing nothing but his lavalava, my father slept on the floor on a bed of leaves. He slept face downwards and my mother sat beside him, spreading cold cloths across his back, pressing them gently, peeling them off, dipping them into cold water, and starting all over again. The only sounds that could be heard were my father's suppressed wincing and drawn-out breathing, and water trickling into a bowl when a cloth was squeezed.

For two weeks our lives revolved around my father. I gathered leaves and my mother kept the refrigerator well stocked with water. Of course, we lived in town and didn't have a proper Samoan fale which would have been cooler and better suited to my father's condition. As the days passed his tatau spread steadily and increasingly across his back, then moved forward and round his ribs, across his buttocks and down onto his legs until it was just below his knees. His legs were tattooed one at a time, and there wasn't much design on the front of them — which meant that in these places the tatau was mainly black and the needle pricks which drove in the ink were very close together.

For a while, when his knees were being tattooed, my father could scarcely walk because the skin thickened into a tight, wet, sticky seal. Each step he took broke the skin and the whole process looked as if it were pure agony. As the tatau grew, so did the pain. He lost weight and strength, and he seemed to need support all the time — even for as simple a thing as getting up from a chair. I fanned him whenever I could. I wasn't used to seeing him so weak and helpless, and it was the least I could do. But I had to admit to myself that the designs were beautifully symmetrical — even if they did keep oozing, and had to be wiped with a cold sponge.

One day when my uncle had been called away to a meeting, Mama and I went to pick my father up. The car stopped about ten metres away from the fale. There were about six men there and my mother told me not to look, but just to talk to Fatu — but I looked as well. One man sat away from the rest, leaning against one of the posts. He was strumming a guitar and singing. The others sat in a kind of circle around someone they leaned over and looked down at. It reminded me of the day when my family was visiting my mother's village, and we sneaked over to the Women's Committee house to see a woman giving birth. We never saw anything — just a lot of women round the mother-to-be.

I said, 'Where's Manu, Mama?'

'He's coming soon, Rona,' she told me. 'Now be patient.' And then I saw a foot sticking out from the group. It was my father's foot, and the men were holding him down. I started to cry, and Fatu started to cry too.

'Oi, Rona, stop crying,' my mother said, as tears began to well up in her eyes too. 'Those men aren't just holding him down — they're helping him because of the pain the tattooing causes.'

'Then why doesn't he stop having it done? Why does he hurt himself so much?'

'Because he wants to have a pe'a,' Sala said slowly.

'Why?' I insisted.

'Because it's important to him,' she said quietly. 'Because if something's important to you, then you have to be prepared to endure all the pain and suffering that's necessary in order to get it and keep it.' I didn't really understand this, because getting the salu from my mother for my various escapades was quite sufficient, and I couldn't see that any more pain was necessary.

The last part of the tatau was around the navel, and by that time the healing process had started in the areas where the tattooing had begun. The patterns across my father's back now looked like grey welts because of the scabs forming on the cut skin. There was also a noticeable and distinctive smell — not unpleasant, but not entirely fresh either. It was the smell of a healing tatau.

Because the scabs were very dry and very itchy, the cold-water treatment was abandoned and, instead, grated coconut was roasted until it was hot and then it was scooped onto a thin cloth which was tied securely into ball. When hot oil started seeping through the cloth, the ball was pressed firmly onto the healing parts. This procedure seemed to give my father a great deal of relief.

After a while, everyone could see that between us we didn't have enough hands to look after my father, and that because of its European style, our house wasn't cool enough. My father decided to go home to his village where he could get better treatment. Once he was there, swimming in the salt water sped up the healing process, and his many young cousins sat with him in the airy and open fale. Some of them fanned him. Others kept a small fire going and roasted the shredded coconut over it. Because it was more comfortable for him not to wear any clothes, I knew the fale was no place for me, and I made the most of the sea and my extended family until I had to return to our house with my mother and go back to school.

When my father returned to us ten days later, he was so much stronger that he gave me a big hug and a kiss, and swung Fatu up into the air. After he had greeted us, he went into the kitchen and turned Mama round to face him. He held her very gently, and she seemed to cry very quietly for a long time.

MAKERITA VA'AI

Song of Discovery

Your card
reached me today
I read it with joy.
The atua have been kind
helped overcome
difficult
turbulent times.

I was amazed
by your discovery
of another life
interspersed with trials
tribulations
woven in a web
entwined round
faith and the senses.

Every event teaches a lesson
each beginning reaches an ending
every problem seeks a solution
a pain finds a healing
an ailment brings a cure
a crisis opens a new world
with every death a new life is born.

We experience
a rebirth
of the self
an awakening
of the dead
buried in us
ready to be born
guided by the spirits
aitu
the trustees
of our heritage.

I Thought of You

I looked in the rice pot
spotted many holes
I thought of you.
A big man.
I wondered,
When will you grow up?

I woke up this morning
found disappointment
staring me in the face.
Last night
I dreamt
I was sleeping in a fale

I looked in the glass
saw clouds
gathered at the rim.
They beckoned to warn against
believing
hearing and
accepting the lies.

I looked in the mirror
saw many flaws.
I remembered
it was time
to get some sleep.

⋆

Your ghost
my shadow
haunt me
in dreams.
They smile
as I search
in vain
to recall
the events
of yesterday.

I thought of you
all alone
not a soul
but four grey walls
four ceiling fans
witnessing
your every move.

At Claire's Place

It is raining heavily in Suva
dampness hangs in the air
water everywhere
luxurious growth abounds
in greenness.
The essentials of life
often taken for granted.

The night brings quiet
interrupted by Heloise's scratching on the screen.
The music of the crying cicadas
adds dignity to the peace
surrounding the night

MOMOE MALIETOA VON REICHE

Solaua, a Secret Embryo

She can smell
Cowdung in the mist of
Solaua, where her heart
Is suspended
From a rubber tree
Telling her of German tyranny
And Chinese indentured labour.
She lusts for the earth so
Completely there,
For he, unknowingly, showed her
A naked picture of surrealist
Beauty in eerie stumps
And ancient banyans,
Flying foxes and white ginger.

My House Idea

I'd like a house
With windows that
Face the horizon.
Big enough to fit
Me and my five children,
Small enough to contain
Warmth and hold my
Ideas.

I'd like a garden
Where the colours
I paint will become real
And where the stories
In my pictures will come alive.

I'd also like a man,
An ugly one with
Broad shoulders and a
Big heart. Who will love me,
Me and what's mine,
Share my thoughts and discuss
An idea,
And hopefully no piss-offs
About the past.

My Guest

You flaunt your pretty
Dresses in my face,
Your perfume spoils the
Dinner I cook for my husband.
My children look on while
You bat your false lashes
And smile your
Thirty-year-old seductiveness
At the master of my house.
You drag your words
Pointedly, and turn your
Nose in the light so that
Your bottle-beauty catches.
You spread your red fingertips
On the table-mat,
And give him the long looks.

I feel like bloody Cinderella
In my tattered shorts
And torn shirt. My hair smells like
A garlic shop, and my nails
Are chipped to the core.
I look at him and the
Bastard sits forward eagerly
Langouring in all your femininity.

The dinner tastes like dog-shit.

Nostalgia

My son said
I smell like New Zealand
This morning.
Do I?
Do Nina Ricci fumes
Remind him
Of a crisp winter morning
In Nelson?
Or the deep red roses of
Cathedral Hill, or the
White snows of Mt Arthur,
Or the apple-orchard blossoms
In spring at Moutere,
Or the old-fashioned
Pear trees in Mrs Potter's garden,
Or the wide stretches of
Tahuna beach?

Does it bring back
Strains of the
College orchestra at
Prize-giving,
Or the yellow of Golden Downs poplars
In autumn,
Or the small daisies
And the lazy Maitai River in summer?

Who Is Lili Tunu?

If you ask me
To describe her to you,
This is how I remembered her:

Every morning
She was like a freshly opened
Teuila bloom —
Full of red vibrancy and deep flame,
Fresh with an elusive dewy fragrance.

She was like an elegant touch of
Green in cool tropical afternoons,
Or the softly mysterious mists
In deep river-beds that are rarely seen.
Her laughter was the brilliance
Of sandy days with the sun beating
Down on blue and white waves,
Her love as all-consuming.
She was faithful and forgiving,
Wise, poised, charming, classy, humorous,
With style and sophistication.
But in her profound beauty,
Like a soft sunset,
Or a gentle moonlit night,
Or a quietly crying rain,
You could have touched her
Sadness.

A L B E R T   W E N D T

I Will Be Our Saviour from the Bad Smell

On Wednesday morning, we woke in our humble village, Saula, to find ourselves caught nauseatingly in the grasp of what we would later call the Bad Smell. Immediately, I approximated it to the stench of a coral reef that is drying above water level, but after rushing to the beach and scrutinising the reef, I knew it wasn't — the reef was aswirl with fierce waves.

Slowly I strolled back to our main house, trying to identify the ingredients of the evil concoction that was the Bad Smell: rotten fruit, decaying flesh, rancid cheese (I've never tasted that), brackish water and swamp mud, the list was limitless. All around me, I could see that our people were excitedly discussing the evil invader in their houses and fale while preparing their morning meal.

I didn't want to alarm my aiga unnecessarily, so when I entered our house, and my children, hands grasped firmly to their noses, attacked me with their shrill questions, I pretended it wasn't *that* bad by saying, 'It won't last, it'll go away, just a dead little something somewhere!'"

Meleane, my mother, who was helping the children get dressed for school, said, 'It is like death!'

'The children are listening!' I cautioned her. She got the message immediately.

'Well, it is like decaying breadfruit!' Less alarming.

I nodded and smiled, noticing that my wife, our children and our other numerous relatives were now unclenching their fingers from their noses. (We all prefer dead fruit to dead people!)

Soon we were all gathered in our back fale for our morning meal.

'It must be coming in from the sea,' my wife theorised. (My wife thinks a lot and expresses her views, opinions and prejudices openly and often.)

'Maybe,' I murmured, still pretending the Bad Smell was a harmless nothing.

'She is correct,' my mother agreed with my wife. (My mother, now in her insecure seventies and not blessed with white-haired wisdom, is very cautious and rarely offers any views whether commonplace or controversial.) And with that affirmation, I watched my whole aiga — there were about twenty people in the fale — turn their noses seawards and take long sniffs, trying to confirm my wife's claim. The sea was a slowly shifting mass of dull silver glimpsed through the tangle of palms and fau on the shore.

'Don't think it's the sea!' my brother Siaki, the always provocative but useless dissenter, attacked everyone, who then looked at him. 'It can't be the sea!' Siaki, as usual, was sitting at the back of the fale beside the young people who were serving our meal; he is never far from any food source, and he looks it, being what my wife has described as 'a solid tune of fat'. 'Must be a dead animal somewhere,' Siaki added. Siaki, though older than me, had not been given our aiga's highest matai title (that was conferred on me), because according to our mother, who still spoils him, 'He is too delicate and weak to assume the heavy responsibilities of a matai.' He is fifty-five years old and, as far as I am aware, has never been sick (seriously) in all those years.

'The smell of one dead animal can't fill he whole air of our village!' I insisted, knowing Siaki wasn't going to contradict me — he rarely does, because he owes his comfortable life to me. Siaki started to sulk immediately.

'And it isn't the smell of a dead animal,' my wife whipped Siaki a bit more. Siaki opened his mouth to speak. 'It *can't* be the smell of a dead animal!' She closed his mouth.

Because we, the elders of our aiga, were disagreeing about the source of the Bad Smell, the others were now visibly confused: some had their noses fixed on the sea, others on the malae and others on the sky.

'What is it, then?' My mother tried to rescue Siaki, her favourite.

Excrement! The word ballooned in my mind like a pink bubble, but I wasn't going to release the bubble publicly and before our innocent children. No one else was going to either, though I sensed that at least half of them were thinking the same thing. It isn't moral or aristocratic to mention excrement (in any form) in public, even though *tae* is the first word most children learn to utter.

'Could be the smell of trees drying in the bush,' I side-tracked them.

'Yes, could be.' My wife took our aiga's thoughts farther away from excrement. Most of us now focused our silent sniffing on the plantations, the bush and hills.

'Bring our food now,' my mother instructed. The young people served us, the elders, with fa'alifu and mugs of hot cocoa.

While we ate, we tried not to inhale the Bad Smell. But it attacked us relentlessly, as if It now filled every crevice and space in Saula.

Our village, as I have said, is small. We have only about thirty matai, and we meet as a council, a fono, at our tu'ua's main fale every Thursday morning starting at 10 a.m.

We met the day after the Bad Smell had arrived. For a frantic while we tried discussing village affairs, such as repairing our school and inspecting our plantations, but the Bad Smell's omnipotent presence became our only topic of discussion.

Our tu'ua, the venerable Pesemalie, who is about eighty and married to my father's sister and the wisest human being I know, opened the heated discussion with the question, 'This Bad Smell, where is It coming from?' (His polite name for the stench, in time, became *our* name for the invisible insidious invader.)

Each matai in turn explained his theory about the Bad Smell, using long, ornate and elaborate speeches. (Need, so a papalagi proverb goes, is the mother of invention and poetry!)

Those among us whose tempers are short-fused like dynamite found ourselves raving frenziedly about the Bad Smell. For instance, Moefalo Ioane, a good friend but an impatient man who always acts before he thinks, declared: 'It is the Devil who has sent this curse. We have to locate Its source and burn It, exorcise It . . .' His whole face and body inflated visibly with an angry frustration. 'My wife and aiga can't stand it any more. We must act, drive the Devil away! We must slay It!'

After the speeches, Pesemalie summed up our views thus, 'We all agree that we must find the evil source of the Bad Smell and kill It. We will appoint a committee to explore the land, sea and air . . .'

A committee of four was duly appointed and Pesemalie, my wise mentor, appointed me committee chairman. I was the only matai who had undergone a good science education at the district high school, and I was fluent in English, Pesemalie justified my important appointment.

'You are to lead the army that is to save our village from Evil!' Pesemalie exhorted our committee. Full almost to bursting with pride, I began to understand for the first time why I had felt, throughout my life, that I had been born for a special mission and that one lucid day that mission would be revealed to me.

After our council meeting, our committee of four assembled in the sitting-room of my house.

Tila, the oldest, is blind in his left eye (a cricket-game accident in his boyhood); his skin is splotched with enormous continents of tinea; a little formal education, acquired at pastor's school, inhabits his head. He usually talks fluently and poetically, but mostly about nothing. His powers of oratory were, I surmised, his main qualification for our investigating committee.

Our second investigator was Fa'afofoga, a middle-aged fisherman who says little and whose brooding silence is interpreted by most Saulaeans as a sign of profound intelligence. He was to be our special sea investigator. I was glad of this because I am, to put it mildly, *afraid* of the sea.

Fiamuamua, our third investigator, had, as usual, manoeuvred his clever way onto our committee. He considers himself the most educated among us, having finished fifth form at Samoa College. However, we all know that his qualifications couldn't get him an office job in town, and he had returned to

Saula to pester us with his arrogant pretensions.

'What if the Bad Smell is being caused by *other* things?' Fiamuamua asked as soon as we were seated. He was already trying to take the leadership.

'What do you mean by *other*?' Tila asked.

'If it's *others*,' I interjected, 'we can deal with those too.' Fiamuamua tried to speak, but I kept talking. 'But, firstly we will assume that the cause, or causes, of the Bad Smell are of this world.'

'As I see it,' Fiamuamua continued to attempt to usurp my leadership role, 'we should search the whole village first.' He stopped abruptly when he noted that the others weren't bothering to look at him, let alone listen to him.

'We will assemble all the taule'ale'a, divide them into four groups, each to be led by one of us, divide the village into specific areas and assign each of them to the groups to search thoroughly,' I explained. Tila and Fa'afofoga nodded. Fiamuamua opened his mouth — and he had ugly teeth — to speak again. 'Do you agree?' I stopped his mouth.

I sent three of my sons to summon our men, and within thirty minutes they were in my large sitting-room and I had divided them into four groups. (The group I assigned to Fiamuamua groaned audibly when I did so.)

I have a large blackboard which I use for teaching my children in the evenings. (I'm not a qualified teacher, but my father and his father had been, so I am pursuing an aiga tradition.)

Quickly I drew a sketch map of our village on the blackboard. (Geography had been one of my strong subjects at high school.)

'That map isn't *quite* correct,' Fiamuamua said. No one paid him any attention.

On the map, I drew straight lines from the seashore through the village and into the plantations, dividing the village into four areas.

'We'll take one of the middle sections,' Fiamuamua offered — it was the least crowded area. No one looked at him. I chose his group to search the western area which is the rockiest and inhabited by rows of pigsties and latrines. My group was allotted the middle area — after all, I *was* chairman.

'We'll all start in a line from the beach and work inland,' I instructed. Fiamuamua didn't nod; all the others did. 'As soon as you find a possible source, send someone to inform me.'

As we were leaving my house, we observed Fiamuamua folding a large red handkerchief and tying it around his nose and mouth — like a bandit in a cowboy film. 'To stop the Bad Smell,' he said through his mask. Some of us chuckled. 'It might be poisonous!' he argued. Suddenly, we considered him wise for once, but, courageous men that we were, we refused to wear masks.

'If we get poisoned, we *get* poisoned!' Tila challenged the Bad Smell and Fiamuamua.

We searched every corner of our village for two futile, tiring hours. As was to be expected, Fiamuamua raised three false alarms that nearly choked us with heart-thundering hope as we all dashed to his sector to confront, firstly, a stand of dying banana trees, secondly, an almost dry pile of turds (pardon the impoliteness), and lastly, with murder in our hearts, the almost fully decayed skeleton of a dog. The usually silent Fa'afofoga, his blazing eyes aimed like newly sharpened bush-knives at Fiamuamua, uttered his only comment for that afternoon: 'You do that again . . . and . . . and I will murder you!'

As we retreated tiredly to our respective homes, the Bad Smell smelled more infuriatingly nasty. We cursed It to ourselves, and like one of King Arthur's knights — I had read about them at high school — I swore a sacred vow that I would defeat the Bad Smell, even if it killed me.

After my aiga had gone to sleep, I circled, on my blackboard map, the area we had searched that afternoon. All around me the Bad Smell was a bristling thick sea of rottenness. The members of my aiga tossed and turned in their mosquito nets, and occasionally spat out their nausea. Most of them slept with their sleeping sheets covering their faces.

The next morning, as arranged, our men gathered again at my house, after our morning meal. Many of them, like Fiamuamua, wore handkerchiefs as masks; most of them coughed constantly and spat out the phlegm; some looked sick. It was obvious that the Bad Smell was having detrimental effects on all of us.

Using my blackboard map, I divided the plantations into four equal areas, and assigned them to our groups. My group got the flat fertile plain, which was green with large patches of taro and bananas.

'We will find its source today!' Fiamuamua vowed but no one else was *that* enthusiastically sure; we forgave him, though: he had always been an optimist, though a tactlessly stupid one.

Reverend Lua, our revered pastor, was weeding in front of his house as my group and I went by.

'May God lead you to It today!' he called. We tried to smile hopefully and politely.

'Yes, I am sure God *will* lead us to It!' I replied.

We entered our assigned area, spread out in a straight line and started moving inland slowly, searching every tree, stone, stand of crops. Everything. Methodically.

'No one is to rest until I say so!' I ordered my men. 'No one!'

An hour or so later, our bodies sleek with sweat, our skins stinging from the heat, two of my men — elderly, admittedly — sat down in the shade of a mango tree.

'We must not rest!' I called. 'Stand up!' Reluctantly, they followed me.

I noticed, slowly, that the Bad Smell was of an equal density everywhere, even when we penetrated deeper and deeper into the plantations. Within enclosed spaces, such as banana stands, the stinking thickness was the same. East, west, south, north — It was of equal nastiness, a thick transparent syrup.

Later, I experimented. I sent a youth up a tall palm tree. Every ten paces up the trunk, I asked him if the smell was the same. All the way to the top he kept informing us that the Bad Smell was neither increasing nor decreasing in density. Even the soft breeze, which varied in strength and flow, was having no effect on that density.

Late that afternoon, too exhausted and hungry to be angry about the Bad Smell, whose source we had once again failed to find, we assembled in my house. No one, not even the usually loquacious Fiamuamua, said anything as we ate the meal of stewed tinned herrings and umu-cooked taro and bananas that my aiga served us. No one was bothering with masks either. We didn't care if the offensive Smell was attacking us: only our empty bellies were important.

Afterwards, before my men could escape to their homes and inevitable sleep, I drew the inland boundary of that day's search on our blackboard map.

'Tomorrow we will search the bush immediately behind the plantations,' I instructed them. Silence. No one seemed to care.

'Sir, I can't come tomorrow, I have aiga problems to attend to,' said Tila, our most poetic group leader. Before I could push him back into line, three others were offering excuses.

'The council has entrusted us with a most important mission,' I threatened them. 'You, Tila, must *not* disappoint them. For the sake of our village, we *must* find the source of the Bad Smell!' Immediately, Tila re-offered his services; the others did too. I decided to be more vigilant (and ruthless) about any signs of indiscipline.

During our evening meal, I noted, with relief, that my children ate, laughed and argued as if the Bad Smell wasn't troubling them any more. I remembered my wise but strict father telling me one day, while we were out fishing for bonito, that we people got used, imperceptibly, to even the worst things given enough time and our need to survive. Were we getting accustomed to the Bad Smell?

We were about half a mile into the dense bush, the next morning, when my breath caught itself in my nostrils — the air was brilliantly fresh. I stepped two paces back, breathed in, the Bad Smell almost choked me. I stumbled two paces forward and was once again through the perimeter of the Bad Smell into the cool, laughing, invigorating freshness of the bush and hills.

We laughed and danced as we poked our heads in and out of the Bad Smell, telling one another about the Edge, the dividing line between the Bad Smell and Freedom.

For about five hundred yards we traced the Edge and decided that it ran in a line through the bush northwards and southwards.

I have always been blessed with a very astute, sometimes profound intuitive insight, which in unexpected moments brought me lucid glimpses into the so-called mysteries of ordinary life. Such a glimpse opened my mind as we were hurrying back to our village to tell everyone about the Bad Smell's inland Edge. The Bad Smell has a corresponding sea perimeter, the message registered in my head. That being so, It must therefore have northern and southern boundaries.

I didn't tell anyone, though.

That night, I drew the bush perimeter on our blackboard map.

'What does it mean?' my mother asked me after I had explained the Edge.

'Yes, what?' my wife asked, equally afraid.

'Must be like the film I saw last year at the Tivoli in Apia,' Siaki stirred their fear. '*The Blob*, it was called. About this huge horrible blob that settled over a whole town in America and sucked up all the electricity, houses, people. Everything into its evil body!'

'What happened to it?' our mother asked him, giving me the opportunity to cure their fear.

'It died!' I laughed, and our children laughed too.

Using a fleet of alia with outboard motors we searched the sea within the reef the next morning, and, as I had expected, we found that the Bad Smell had a sea perimeter. Beyond it, the air smelled of tingling salt and brisk sun and wind. 'Like a willing, fertile woman!' Fa'afofoga described it.

We sucked it in as we lay in our canoes, our hands trailing in the diamond-blue water, chuckling, sighing, gazing up into heavens as huge as a child's imagination.

Strangely, we didn't mind returning into the Bad Smell and our village, knowing now that there were limits to our prison, out of which we could escape any moment we chose to.

During lotu that night, my mother thanked the Almighty for having revealed to us, His helpless children, the dividing line between Evil (the Bad Smell) and the saving air of Goodness. I hadn't thought of it that way, but I had to agree with her. Confronted with our common problem and adversary, my mother was acquiring *some* wisdom.

I waited until my aiga were asleep, then I drew in the sea perimeter and sat down in front of our blackboard and contemplated my map. Mentally, I filled in the northern and southern perimeters. The insight blinked like the opening of a bright eye, and I saw it: the whole area *occupied* (that was the appropriate description) by the Bad Smell was oval-shaped and our church was its centre.

Silently, I made my way through the still darkness and our sleeping village, which came alive periodically with the familiar sucking sound of the cicadas, to our church, expecting the up-thrusting currents of the Bad Smell to be streaming up from its foundations and the very earth on which it stood, knowing from what my grandfather had told me as a boy that the missionaries had deliberately sited the church on the centre of our malae, where, during pagan times, prisoners of war had been killed and sometimes cooked and eaten.

I found no up-surging fountain of foulness. Just the massive sinews of concrete and stone and corrugated iron caught in the ocean that was the Bad Smell.

In the next two days we located, and drew on our map, the northern and southern boundaries.

'An oval!' exclaimed Fiamuamua before I could tell everyone that I knew *that* already.

'Like a gigantic egg!' Tila said, poetically. 'Like the egg of the Roc, which Sinbad the Sailor discovered.' And before I could distract him, he was telling that tale to an attentive audience, who had demanded that he tell it.

I tried to be patient: leaders *have* to be patient with the weaknesses of their followers. There was no way, short of an angry demand from me, to break Tila's spell. We were all suckers, so a papalagi would say, for fantastic stories, fairy tales; and Sinbad's adventures were a rich strand of our village's mythology.

While Tila wove his magic, I realised that we didn't really care any more about the Bad Smell's source: we had been preoccupied almost totally with mapping It. Perhaps there was no source? But It must have come from somewhere? Another lucid insight opened in the centre of my head: perhaps It has always been here in our village in another dimension, and some slight alteration in our existence had sucked that dimension into our daily lives? My imagination was running away with me; I stopped my thoughts. You may as well believe in Siaki's incredible story of the Blob!

'How high is the Bad Smell's outer perimeter?' The usually silent Fa'afofoga fished me out of my head.

'If we had a plane, we could find out!' said Fiamuamua.

'A helicopter!' added someone else.

'What's that?' someone asked.

Before the fickle imaginations of my men could be distracted again, I said firmly, 'Here is what we have discovered so far about our friend the Bad Smell!' I now had their attention. 'Firstly, we still don't know Its source.' Pause. Pointed at the map. 'Secondly, we don't know, because we don't have a helicopter, how high It rises.' Pause. 'Thirdly, we don't know if It penetrates into the ground and, if It does, how far down it goes,' I was surprised by that sudden insight. 'Yes,' I re-emphasised, 'It *must* have a downward perimeter!' Even Fiamuamua nodded. 'So, if we are all agreed on the boundaries of the Bad Smell, this is how It might look.'

I went up to the blackboard and, with bold yellow chalk, drew these diagrams:

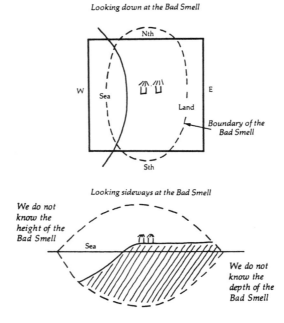

The geography and maths I had studied at high school had come in useful, I concluded, admiring my diagrams.

'Perhaps It extends right up to Heaven where our God dwells.' The profound Fa'afofoga eased his wise presence into our contemplation.

'Perhaps It also extends down to Hell where Satan dwells,' Fiamuamua speculated pessimistically, and frightened us.

'Our village is the yellow of the Roc's Egg that is the shape and form of the Bad Smell,' Tila described slowly. Looking again at my diagrams we had to agree with Tila — and I resented him somewhat for having seen that symbolic truth before I had.

In every community there is always that hard-hearted realist who, whenever our imaginations lift us up into dizzy poetic speculations, drags us back down to our body odour and juices and pain.

'That is all very well,' my wife's intimidating voice started clipping off our dazzling, speculative wings, 'but do you yet know what the Bad Smell is, why It is here and how you are going to get rid of It?' Before I could stop her interference, she added, 'In short, how are we, the bright yellow of the Roc's Egg, going to hatch ourselves out of that Egg and breathe fresh air again?'

All my men looked at me to save them from my wife's large, unwelcomed truth. Blank spaces punched at my frantic search for an answer.

'It's time we fed these hungry men!' I ordered her. As she whirled to go and bring our meal, I caught an infuriating glint of triumph in her eyes. My men tried not to look at me; they didn't envy me my brilliantly perceptive spouse and the defeat she had just inflicted on me without justification. Right then, I envied them their extremely obedient wives who never revealed — at least in public — how dumb (or otherwise) their husbands were. Not the time for senseless domestic quarrels, we had a formidable enemy to defeat, I soothed my pride.

Sunday. Reverend Lua's particularly forceful sermon in the morning service can be summed up thus:

Text: The Bad Smell is punishment from our wrathful, just God because we have sinned!

Body: For almost one arduous, trying year, he, Lua, had tried his humble, utmost best to warn us of our wicked, sinful ways. For instance, on New Year's Day, ten disobedient, hypocritical matai and fifteen wicked, greedy taule'ale'a had spent the day carousing at one of Apia's sinful, expensive beer clubs; eleven of them had been jailed after the huge, violent brawl which had wrecked that heathen, unchristian club; and he, God's humble, worthless servant had been forced to plead with the police to release the worthless, licentious brawlers. (Licentious because unmentionable, wanton sisters of Salome had featured prominently in the brawl.) (*Aside*: I note here, as I report this, that the learned Reverend Lua uses double adjectives to describe almost every noun he uses; I must learn that.) A slow, restful month later, a shameless, aigaless matai, who was to remain anonymous, brought irreparable, painful shame to our peaceful, honest village by going to jail for stealing food from an important, innocent papalagi's house in Apia. Lo and behold, just as we were recovering from that unpardonable, disgraceful disgrace, three of our youths were gaoled for killing and eating someone else's well-looked-after, well-fed pig.

Reverend Lua, a small man whose crisp speech and jerky, tense movements remind me of a fit rooster with gas in its belly, then proceeded to enumerate and condemn another gallery of rogues, criminals and sinners. The most colourful cases concerned: a hinted-at adultery between an unnamed but satanic matai and an unnamed but promiscuous girl who was now living in another unnamed village; a stone-hearted, pagan aiga (which had since converted to that unholy, unmentionable sect called Mormonism — a sin in itself!) which had, in a satan-inspired, blind anger almost castrated ('operated on' was Lua's polite term) a youth who had, secretly, but knowingly, impregnated one of their innocent, godly daughters; and most revolting of all

311

was the beastly act between an obviously insane, two-legged beast and an innocent, unaware four-legged one.

Though the rogues were not named by the honest, forthright Reverend Lua, he knew that we all knew who they were.

Conclusion of Rev. Lua's Sermon: 'So because of all our unpardonable, vicious sins, God, who is a just and loving Father, has now shrouded us in an invisible, strangling shroud of Rottenness and Decay. To be free from It we must repent, ask Him for His boundless, all-embracing forgiveness . . .'

He finished by encouraging us to pray fervently to God for His forgiveness that night, which all our aiga did, then we slept soundly, expecting God's forgiveness to descend on Monday morning.

At dawn I woke; we were still in the embrace of the Bad Smell, and I cursed myself and our people for not having repented genuinely enough. The Almighty, I am sure, would have forgiven us otherwise.

On Wednesday, I spent a long time mentally composing the verbal report I was expected to give to the matai council the next day. I would also show them my neat blackboard map and diagrams.

For half an hour or so I mesmerised the council like the cobras I had seen in an Indian film. 'We are living in the Roc's Egg,' I concluded my speech, using Tila's imagery. 'Soon we will, with God's help, hatch from It!'

Obviously impressed, Pesemalie, our tu'ua, thanked me and my men profusely, then in his practical wisdom, he said, 'You have mapped out the Enemy, now tell us Its source and how we are going to rid ourselves of It.'

'We do not, as yet, know the source,' I apologised, 'and, because of that, we cannot recommend ways of destroying it.'

Fiamuamua recommended a further fervent appeal to God, for his divine intervention.

'And if prayers don't work again?' Pesemalie asked. For once, the loquacious Fiamuamua was without words. 'Let us all sit here quietly and think of a cure,' Pesemalie suggested. 'God, I am sure, will whisper the answer to us!'

We sat and we thought. We sat and we thought. Desperately I wanted my usually faithful intuition to flash me the answer. Alas, no answer came.

'There is a man, a man who *has* cures.' Fa'afofoga, our expert fisherman, hooked us out of our drowning. We waited for it, impatiently. 'Cures for Samoan diseases, aitu diseases,' he added. Long pause as he pondered the fale's ceiling. 'I once witnessed his powers — he cured a cripple who had been crippled all his sad life . . .' Another lengthy pause.

'Get on with it!' Pesemalie voiced our impatience.

'. . . and once a leper and a madman . . .'

'Yes, but what about bad smells, and bad smells of our size?' Pesemalie hurried him.

'Not bad smells,' Fa'afofoga admitted quietly.

'You and your leader' — meaning me — 'will go and consult him anyway,' ordered Pesemalie. 'Tell him our problem and see if he can do something about it.'

'Perhaps we should consult a papalagi scientist in Apia at the Agriculture Department?' Fiamuamua suggested.

'Afterwards!' Pesemalie dismissed him.

I consider myself a modern and educated man. I therefore have little faith in traditional medicines and healers, especially healers who claim they can cure maladies caused by aitu, but I wasn't going to disobey Pesemalie.

To my surprise, Fa'afofoga's miracle healer, or taulasea, did not live in a traditional village, but in the middle of Apia, in a shabby, ramshackle neighbourhood called the Vaipe, Dead-Water — an appropriate name. Ironical for that most urbanised neighbourhood to produce what Fa'afofoga, on our bumpy way to Apia on the bus, had described reverently as 'a very wise and saintly taulasea who knows all the aitu and the illnesses they can cause.'

Vavega, the taulasea, is a decrepit wisp of an old man (more sagging skin and bone than flesh) who is almost totally blind and needs to be led everywhere by his daughter. He welcomed us, and his aiga served us a breakfast of hot tea and buttered bread.

While we ate, Fa'afofoga told him why we had come.

'This Bad Smell, how extensive is It?' he asked.

Methodically, I explained everything I knew about It. Vavega nodded periodically, the wisp of white hair on the top of his almost bald head reminding me of cigarette smoke.

'No source, no reason for Its visitation — very puzzling!' he exclaimed. Though his physical presence was like a whisper, his spiritual essence, or mana, was thickening, as it were, for me. My admiration and respect deepened. 'Its density is the same everywhere?'

'Yes,' I replied eagerly. (How did he know?)

'Very mysterious!' he muttered. 'I will come and try and defeat It!' We thanked him. 'We will come tomorrow morning — my daughter and I.'

As we stepped out of his shack, his daughter, a massive matron with small delicate hands and generous eyes, stopped us. 'My father is very frail now; we *have* to travel by taxi.'

I gave her ten dollars, which she accepted politely. 'Our village is ready to pay all your expenses,' I said.

'All we want is for your kind father to drive the Bad Smell from our humble village!' Fa'afofoga said.

'We will arrive at mid-morning,' she said. 'You will provide us with a house. No one else must live there while we are there. My father must have total privacy in order to work properly. Your village must also *act* as if we aren't there. There will be no welcome ceremonies and so on.' She paused and looked at us in turn. 'If he defeats the Bad Smell you will deposit in his bank account two hundred dollars. If he fails, no payment will be made. You must never mention money or expenses to him. He is too spiritual for that. He is an old man, and I must protect his interests. He does not believe in selling his gift, but we are a poor aiga.'

'We understand,' I replied, impressed. 'We will obey your every wish.'

That night the matai council accepted my generous offer for Vavega and his daughter to use my papalagi house, which was, according to Pesemalie, the most luxurious house in our district, and therefore most appropriate accommodation for our important guests. (My two sons and one daughter in New Zealand had sent money for the house.) While Vavega and his daughter were in our house, my aiga and I would live in our two fale.

As is the custom, each aiga was to feed our guests for a day; only the best food was to be served.

It is difficult, anywhere, for people who are bursting with curiosity to pretend that a well-known healer of supernatural diseases is *not* in their midst investigating such a freak phenomenon as the Bad Smell. But we tried, meticulously.

For instance, no one else came out to greet them when they arrived by taxi at our house on Wednesday; I took them in, showed them where everything was and then left them alone. None of the matai came; everyone kept away from the house; and all who went past behaved as if the house wasn't there. Their lunch was brought by two people of the appointed aiga and left in the sitting-room for Vavega's daughter to serve.

All day I remained in our fale, writing long letters to my children in New Zealand, describing the Bad Smell but not mentioning Vavega. Occasionally I glimpsed Vavega shuffling round the sitting-room where I had deliberately left my blackboard with its maps and diagrams of the Bad Smell. Once, he stopped and peered at the blackboard, nodding his bird-like head as though saying, Yes, yes, yes.

No one said much during our evening meal, no one dared look at our house, but as soon as the children were ready for bed some of them sneaked out and, creeping up to the house, sat at the edge of the light being cast from the sitting-room and watched Vavega, who was slumped in a chair, pondering my diagrams, trying desperately to untangle the riddle of the Bad Smell so we could be hatched. From the secure darkness of our fale, I observed him, my sleeping-sheet wrapped like a second skin around me. The whole neighbourhood, I sensed, were doing the same thing. Vavega was the fire, we were those seeking its warmth, its healing.

He sat and pondered, sat and pondered for a long, long time. The village lights went out one by one and left me alone with Vavega. He started nodding with sleep. Vavega's daughter appeared from the kitchen and helped him off to bed. A few minutes later, the house was in darkness.

Once again, the Bad Smell invaded my consciousness. We were trapped in a dead egg.

For four days, Vavega and his daughter, with our consent, moved with a quiet, undisturbed invisibility through our village and its immediate environs. I observed, surreptitiously, their every move, gathering detailed information from other people, including our children, and each night recording it in my thick, black notebook.

I have already described their first day (Wednesday); here are my notebook entries for their next three days. (By the way, V in my notes is Vavega and D is his daughter.)

Thursday. VD are up early. V is on the back verandah gargling loudly and spitting the water onto the grass. V, who is dressed in an old lavalava and ragged singlet, then parts his lavalava and makes water onto the grass. D is in the kitchen, cooking. V shuffles back into the house.

For thirty minutes I watch, but nothing happens. Then VD leaves the house through the front door; he is leaning his left hand on her strong shoulder: his right hand is with a steel walking-stick that he stabs into the ground as they walk slowly towards the centre of our village.

I wait, but they don't return until midday. She is holding him up, with her arm around his waist. (I stop myself from rushing out and helping them.) His eyes are closed; he is breathing heavily; she takes him and puts him to bed. They don't leave the house the whole of this afternoon. According to ten reliable eyewitnesses I questioned this afternoon, VD went into our church and D sat in a back pew, praying, while V went around checking every nook and cranny of the building, using his shiny steel walking-stick to tap at everything. One witness said, 'It appeared to my humble self that Mr V was *listening* to the sounds that his stick was making.'

After a thorough inspection of the innards of the church, VD then inspected the outside, especially the ground at the foot of the massive walls; this time D stabbed the steel walking-stick into the ground — at least a foot down each time — whenever V told her to, and V, after D pulled it out, examined the dirt that was on the stick. According to one witness: 'Mr V, with his fingers, would scrape some of the dirt off the stick, rub it between his fingers and then sniff at it.' One child reported that he even saw V taste some of the dirt with the tip of his tongue.

Night. After their evening meal, VD leave the house and disappear into the village. I time their absence on the gold wristwatch my eldest son sent me as a Xmas gift last year. VD are away until 11.55 p.m., when everyone else is asleep. Once again I note with concern, but I can't help him, V's state of exhaustion as D half-carries him into the house and bed.

Friday. I wake at dawn. No sign of anyone in the house, so I creep up and look in. No one.

They return, and D is looking strong and cheerful, as we are having our morning meal. Before they go into the house, he waves his walking-stick to us. Automatically just about my whole aiga, including your humble servant, wave back and then feel stupid suddenly because we are not supposed to be watching VD.

As I watch the house this morning I no longer doubt V's powers, though my education keeps telling me that I shouldn't have faith in taulasea.

VD leave at mid-morning and go to the beach, with D holding a black umbrella over V. They do not return until 1 p.m., with D once again half-carrying him.

They sleep the whole afternoon. It is raining strongly this evening and I can only reach five eyewitnesses to VD's movements that morning.

VD had spent that time exploring the whole length of beach, with D once again using V's walking-stick to stab into the sand, and under the rocks and driftwood, and provide samples of dirt for V to feel, smell and taste.

One witness said, 'On their way back, Mr V found a smooth patch of wet sand and, using a short piece of wood, drew your' (meaning your humble servant's) 'egg diagram of the Bad Smell in the sand.'

'What else happened?' I asked.

'Nothing, he just erased it with his foot, a few minutes later.'

'How did he look?'

'Very upset, almost in tears!'

As I gaze into the rain that is washing the night but is unable to clean it of the Bad Smell, I think sadly of V.

Saturday. As usual, I wake at dawn. There is no movement in the house, but I don't feel the urgent need to discover what is happening there. When my wife wakes a short while later I describe to her the strange dream I had experienced that night. Here are my words:

'I am afloat in a sea as green as young grass, looking up into an egg-yellow sky. The water feels like feathers. Suddenly above me the yellow cracks open noiselessly as if something or someone is pulling it apart, and I feel myself being sucked up into the black opening by a wind which I can't feel but which I can hear whistling and swishing and sighing. Before I reach the jagged edge of the opening, I find Vavega's steel walking-stick in my hands, it is glowing like a light bulb and feels hot, but not hot enough to burn my hands. I think of Cinderella's fairy godmother and her magic wand that changed a pumpkin into a golden coach and mice into white stallions and Cinderella into a beautiful princess with glass slippers. And I point Vavega's wand at my heart and, without an ounce of pain, stab it in, down, until all of me is glowing like a phosphorescent light bulb. I am outside myself looking at the dazzling figure that I am. There is a sudden hush, an abyss of endless silence that, within frightening seconds, is contracting around my skin like a steel shell. I am choking. "You will be our saviour!" Vavega's voice whispers in my ear. (I can't remember which ear.) And I burst out of my smothering steel shell. I wake up watching a smiling Vavega in red robes and turban (like a prophet in the Bible), shrinking steadily until he is nothing.'

'I will be our saviour!' I repeat to my wife. 'Vavega believes in my mission.'

'What mission?' she asks incredulously.

'Nothing.' She won't understand.

'He is going to fail, isn't he?' she asks.

'Vavega?'

'Yes.'

Right then the meaning of my precious dream revealed itself to me: Vavega wasn't going to defeat the Bad Smell, but, in my sleep, using his mysterious powers (mental telepathy, the papalagi call it), he had made me his heir, his knight who was to continue the war against the evil smell and conquer It. 'He may still succeed,' I lie to my wife.

I go to the house a short while later. I enter it without knocking. I search it. There is no evidence that VD were ever there. Invisible they had come and invisible they had left.

On the blackboard printed in frail yellow letters under my egg diagram is this message from V:

YOUR MAPS AND DIAGRAMS OF YOUR BAD SMELL ARE VERY ACCURATE. YOUR BAD SMELL IS AN EGG. CONGRATULATIONS ON YOUR DISCOVERY. BUT IT IS ONE THING TO ACCURATELY MAP OUT THE SHAPE AND SIZE OF EVIL AND IT IS ANOTHER TO DESTROY IT.
I HAVE FAILED.

As I hurried to Pesemalie's fale to inform him of Vavega's failure, my whole being was swimming with joy at Vavega entrusting me with the divine mission. If he had succeeded, the purpose of my existence would have been lost.

Pesemalie summoned a council meeting immediately and told them: 'The taulasea has left admitting he can't defeat the Bad Smell. He tried his best but he is very old, no longer with the necessary mana. What shall we do now?'

'Sir, perhaps, with your kind permission, we should seek the help of a scientist?' Fiamuamua offered.

When the council agreed to that, I experienced a sharp hatred for

Fiamuamua, believing that he was trying to deny me the right to save our village, but I hid my feelings well — I even offered my house for the scientist.

Fiamuamua went to Apia and, a day later, rode like a conqueror into our village in a blue Land-Rover, with a MrTrevor Mellows from the Agriculture Department.

The council gathered in Pesemalie's fale to give the papalagi a ceremonial welcome, as is the custom, but the papalagi, who is a spindly man with fire-orange hair and freckles and thin hairy legs, refused to waste time with ceremony. Cleverly, Fiamuamua interpreted politely, to the council, the papalagi's rude refusal.

The papalagi and his three aides, long-haired youths in jeans, spread out large copies of my maps and diagrams, which Fiamuamua had provided for them without my permission, on the hood of their Land-Rover and, with Fiamuamua's boastful help, identified all the landmarks and areas; then the papalagi issued orders to his aides and they all dispersed in various directions, with Fiamuamua following the papalagi like a hungry puppy.

I wanted nothing to do with their attempt; they were going to fail and I didn't want to be tainted by that aroma. Let the deserving Fiamuamua take all of it!

I spent the day repairing our kitchen fale. After the papalagi and his crew had departed for Apia at 4.30 p.m. precisely, I went round gathering information about what nearly everyone was now referring to seriously as 'Fiamuamua's papalagi and his scientific research'.

Here is a brief summary of that information, which I later recorded in my notebook

> The papalagi and his men filled small jars with soil samples dug up from various locations within the area covered by the Bad Smell and just outside Its perimeter. They also took samples of water found within the Bad Smell. The papalagi questioned a cross-section of our people, with the upstart Fiamuamua acting as his interpreter, about animals, crops, diseases and so on. Everyone reported that the papalagi refused to eat our food or drink our water.

When the papalagi and his crew did not return the next day, Fiamuamua boasted to us, 'He will bring his answers tomorrow, wait and see!'

They did return on Saturday — not with any answers, but to take samples of the air, the sea-water, our crops and other plants.

Reverend Lua's lucid Sunday-morning sermon emphasised the astounding power of modern science, describing in fervent, vivid detail such scientific miracles as heart transplants, nuclear bombs, Disneyland, space flight and the thirty-five different flavours of ice cream which he had tasted in Los Angeles when he had visited his children the previous year. (We envied him his knowledge of such wonders, and especially his visit to Disneyland.)

Nevertheless, he concluded by saying, 'However, science, without belief in God, is unholy. Science can explain much, but only our all-seeing God can explain everything!'

Fiamuamua's over-confidence deflated visibly when Monday came and passed without any sign of his papalagi and his papalagi's answers. When the same thing happened on Tuesday, Fiamuamua hid in his house, and early on Wednesday morning he sneaked into a bus and disappeared into Apia obviously to look for his papalagi, his passport back into our favour.

All day Wednesday we waited. That night I told the other matai that papalagi science was failing us, which led Pesemalie to remark, 'What do you expect from atheists?' (meaning the papalagi). 'What do you expect from half-educated boys?' (meaning Fiamuamua).

As I gazed that night at my maps and diagrams, a bubbling stream of joy washed through me. The Roc's Egg had defeated traditional healing and now modern science; it was once again up to me.

While all these events, which I have described so far, were occurring, the notoriety (fame) of the Bad Smell and our humble village spread like a flood throughout our humble country. Those of our people who were branded by Pesemalie as 'weak noses and soft stomachs' fled out of the egg, taking their exaggerated prejudices against our Bad Smell (and our village) to taint other people. 'It is good they have gone,' said Pesemalie, 'my ears were tired of their complaints and fears!'

The national response to our Odour was various. Religious fundamentalists labelled our innocent village a den of sin, a Gomorrah; the Bad Smell was our punishment. The educated were, like Fiamuamua's papalagi, interested in the natural, scientific causes of our Odour; some even visited, took samples and went home and tried to find solutions. The merely curious — and they were the most numerous, and included foreign tourists — drove slowly through our village, some holding perfumed handkerchiefs to their noses as they examined us, as though we were helpless specimens trapped in a most peculiar environment. One national leader, originally a doctor, sent a Health Department team to see if we needed some form of inoculation. The superstitious and ignorant talked of aitu, sauali'i, demons, and the Dead rising up to take their revenge.

Our responses to the varied national responses were equally various. Reverend Lua and many of us were highly elated at the attention we were attracting — the national radio station even broadcast a series of news items about our Odour. The realists, like my wife, refused to be euphoric, and got fed up with the strangers who were visiting us. As my wife put it: 'Why can't they leave us and our Smell alone?' Our fundamentalists, led by Reverend Lua, worshipped together in our church with a group of foreign fundamentalists they had invited, and then they lunched together at our expense (we are well known for our generous hospitality) in Reverend Lua's large house. Our scientifically minded, such as Fiamuamua, after the papalagi scientist's failure, refused to be hospitable to their foreign counterparts who came to experiment with us. (Fiamuamua, fearful of our wrath, absented himself from our council meetings.) Our superstitious ones welcomed their foreign counterparts, and they spent long hours echoing one another's superstitious interpretations of our Smell.

Only I stood above these biases, prejudices, false posturings, etc. I was the true guardian of our village and our Smell; only I in my objectivity could save us.

Soon after Fiamuamua's failure — and I relished his loss of standing in our community — Pesemalie, at our next council meeting, argued, quite persuasively and correctly, that as long as we couldn't get rid of our Bad Smell we had to persuade our nation that we hadn't caused It or, even more wisely, that it was a harmless, non-infectious and healthy odour, a mark of distinction and uniqueness. 'I mean, what other village in this arrogant country in this vast ocean on our sinful planet possesses such a unique smell?' he argued convincingly.

We all agreed to this truth and went home and instructed our aiga to spread it far and wide. For this campaign, I coined a very original slogan: OUR SMELL IS THE PERFUME OF THE PACIFIC; IT IS THE SCENT OF BIRTH. Our leading song-maker used it in a song which became a national hit after our village choir, the Ai-Ulu-Moto (Eaters of Immature Breadfruit), sang it at last year's national independence celebrations at Mulinu'u.

It is over a year now since our Bad Smell (or, more properly, our Odour) first visited us (or should I say, *revealed* Itself to us?). Apart from me, no one is bothering to discuss It, or find cures for It, any more. Most of us lack the stamina, the dedication, the commitment, the passion for the fight. We don't even bother with the curious visitors who come to experience It now. Occasionally, we are roused to a vengeful, fierce anger if someone insults us by flaunting in our faces our now nationally known nickname, 'Saula and the Stench'. Wouldn't you get angry?

But apart from these moments of fire, we acknowledge our Odour as an essential part of our lives, as if It has always been here since our village was founded hundreds of years ago. 'It is the air we breathe!' Pesemalie has described It, profoundly.

The other night I asked my aiga, 'Can you still smell It?' They looked blankly at me.

I refuse to give up. Secretly I have tried to devise ways to hatch ourselves out of the Egg. My satchel is full of my diagrams of these stillborn solutions. Most representative of them are these ones:

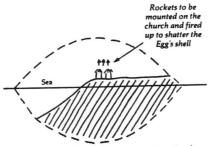

Rockets to be mounted on the church and fired up to shatter the Egg's shell

(Alas, I have not been able to procure the rockets)

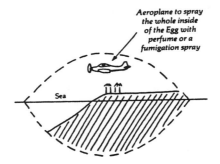

Aeroplane to spray the whole inside of the Egg with perfume or a fumigation spray

(Alas, I don't have the money to hire a plane and buy the eighteen tons of perfume needed.)

In between my scientific experimentation, I have spent my time writing, in accurate detail, all that has happened since we first became conscious of our Odour. If something happens to me before we are hatched, my written records will provide whoever is brave and committed enough to continue the valiant struggle with solid, scientific data on which to base his strategies. Not that my life is to end shortly. The Almighty in my sleep last night whispered to me that He is granting me a long life.

You may well ask: But if all your people are now living quite happily with your Odour and don't see the need to be saved from It, why are you, a weak mortal, still trying to save them from It?

My reply to that is: Sinbad the Sailor's adventures and quests were the justification for his existence. Similarly, my struggle, my mission, is the meaning of my life. I was born for it.

I will be our saviour. God has willed it so.

321

Parents & Children

Parents and their children come
to one another through many doors
that laugh, slap, clap, slash, bleed
block, cry, and let-you-through sometimes.
And by the time they meet
they've been sieved to the rags and bones
of who they were and can't remember.

Around our house mynah birds
dart and dive. I count
the holes they pierce in the sky.
My son is in the garage fixing
the brakes of his bike.
In her bedroom my daughter
Is locked into Captain America.

I've left believing in God,
my children are starting towards Him.
I carry willingly the heritage of my Dead,
my children have yet to recognise theirs.
Someday before they leave our house
forever I'll tell them: 'Our Dead
are the splendid robes our souls wear.'

The armada of mynah birds continues
to attack the trees and sky.
Their ferocity cuts wounds
in my thoughts.
Through those wounds like doors
I'll go this morning
to meet my children.

Knife

    This knife on the kitchen
table,
      black wooden handle with
two shiny eyes of rivets,
           single-

edged and curving to a metaphysical
point on which angels can't perch,
  is caught in its breathing
shadow,
  a quiet legend of itself
open to the hanging light in
  Luis Borges's dreaming.

This knife smiles a slow quiver
  of teethlight savouring
   the blood's rich message.
Whose blood? Gauchos duelling
  in grimy saloons lost in
  the myths of the pampas?

This knife hones its alertness on
  the expectation of hunting/stab
  bing/slashing/cutting,
     on crouch-
ing deadstill like its victims.

  It fits
the assassin's grip, the dueller's
mad courage, which will grant
  it shape and ferocity.
Or is it the reverse? asks Borges.

  It's more than its
shadow and smile, more than
the legend of light
in Borges's blindness, more than
the last quiver of the blood, more than
the expectation of victims and
  the dueller's triumph.

This knife is
  more than Borges's allegories.
It is
itself.
It is
a simple kitchen knife.

Shaman of Visions

Shaman of Visions, in words is the silence
before Tagaloaalagi created the dawn of solitude.
We measure ourselves against our words.

Shaman of Visions, the early dawn hours tremble
as though anticipating a lover's touch.
Words begin at the roots of our breath.

Shaman of Visions, we censor our bodies,
that is our madness.
We feel abandoned by everything.

Shaman of Visions, when a leaf falls in the heart
of the bush do you hear it? Do you feel
the pain of its lonely dying?
Shaman of Visions, through our pores our Dead see
that to love without hope
is better than not to love at all.

Shaman of Visions, we'll not live under
the dark side of Pluto afraid
of evening as much as death.

Shaman of Visions, when we die disperse
every particle of our dust into the dawn
which gave birth to the first word.

The Wall

                        Walls
            imprison/protect/cut off/shield
Walls hide/keep in secrets/keep
            out marauders
Walls frame our seeing
        Walls don't happen
        We grow them

                        The Great Wall
lives in us   Emperor Qin conquered
       the six kingdoms and dragged
the Wall across our fears   to protect
       what he'd hoarded
out of the killing
                            Centuries later
       my grandmother constructed it
across the geography of my dreaming
       and I yearned to see the truth
            of our defence against barbarians

It's raining gently   pinpricks on
       my skin as our car chases
its reflection up Juyong Pass
       The peaks are crowned
with the mist and cloud of
my grandmother's tales
       The hills display the lush flowers
of her telling
                        Suddenly
It's there   the Wall   a giant's
crooked finger directing us
       to infinity over the jagged ridges
Then we're at Badaling among
other pilgrims come
       to measure their childhood wonder

                        Michel Foucault is
dead   Umberto Eco
lives   conjurers of the vocabulary
       of decoding the illusion
   of language
and living in history
                        The Wall is
no illusion   It is more
than history   It is
black granite rising
to parapets   as wide as
six horses   that dip/rise/buck
dive/swerve   left to right
over a continent of mythology

Take the first step up   one
Then the second   (The stone
trembles beneath you)
     Push up through the stream
    of rainbow people
Now we're on the Wave
at its perfect cresting   but
it won't break and hurl us
    back into the trough
        of drowning
   Climb the steepness to
the highest watchtower   Stand
(Feel the presence of the guardians?)
Suck in the ravenous scent of
invading warriors   Listen
to their unintelligible shouting
     See the Khan in the middle?
     His eyes are beacons of terror

           A fixed defence
    constructed to the dimensions
of Qin's self-love   was no strategy
    against untamed atua who poured
arrows through the gaps   and followed
    to fit the emperor's heart
which infected them
with his civilised madness

In Foucault's language   the Wall is
    all other walls   (including
those we erect around
the heart)   and their discourses
Eco would invest the Wall
    with metaphysical puzzles

         From the watchtower
   gaze down at the plains that suck back
     the Pass and hills
   into the white soul of the north
and the labyrinths of atua
    whose 9999 names are seeded
     across oceans of applauding grass

The Wall is
greater than my grandmother's stories
    and all its possibilities
It is a wall
    that sings to the souls
    of the Dead who built it
    with their suffering
It protects nothing   the Wall
your eyes will carry
until the atua desert them

In Your Enigma

(For Reina)

You are dressed in your enigma
You shift like mist across words
that describe water
You plant signs
You invent yourself in syllables
of nightlight and winter turning
to spring on Maungawhau's shoulders

Every thing is
Every thing is earth the atua feed on
Every thing is earth moulded in Ruaumoko's belly
and thrown up to know
Tane's kiss of living air

Your ancestors left their shadows
for you to grow into
They fished islands and visions out
of tides that washed back into the Void
They dealt in imagery of bone and feather
They knew the alphabet of omens
and could cipher the silences
that once knew the speech of pain
They planted white pebbles in the mouths
of their dead and sailed them
into the eyes of the future

You are dressed in your enigma
that finds language in the gift
that is water
that is earth
that is every thing

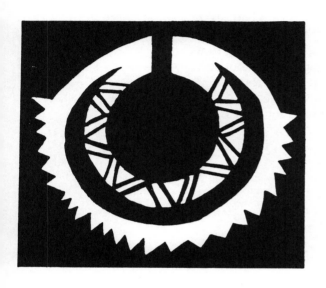

SOLOMON
ISLANDS

Sam L. Alasia

The Parrot

One fine day
I sat under a banyan tree
Listening to a parrot
Singing a piercing tune,
My heart was touched
And memories of
A loved one
Choked my throat.

LEMU DARCY

Cars You Have My Wantoks

She looks right and left
Hoping they will stop.
Wantoks whiz past,
Shining in the sun's rays.

Staggering she goes on,
Not a hope left in her —
Sun pierces her skin —
Wishing she didn't exist
On an earth full of eyeless kin.

Women and Housework

Work, work, work,
I am tired
Of marriage.
He bosses me:
Do this,
Do that.
He thinks I am
A machine.
There's always plenty to do.

He is inconsiderate;
I wish he was a woman
To taste work.

Work, work, work,
I am exhausted.
I love the family,
It is everything
To me,

But when in high spirits
He steps out and calls,
'Shut up!'
Please pass my love,
I am not what he thinks.

CELO KULAGOE

Where Leaves Had Fallen

The tree can only be seen
Where it stands.

The eye with the axe
Is also that with the chain
To cut and to haul down.

Each man with a finger
Would pick up a piece
And drag it home,
To dress, burn or ignore.

The lumber-man, he picks up
The trunk to chew,
While the squatter builds a hut
With the branches
To dream in.

The twisted twigs are only
What the old hag could bear
Down to her pot of stew,
Leaving the white chips
To the birds to cast
Over the lake as seeds.

But the gardener, he fights the wind
For the leaves —
The sight of experience
To read from their palms,
Their veins swollen with knowledge.
Their strength feeds the stump
To a new shoot.

The Toothpick

(Pacific Week)

Eat of this feast O Glutton and then
quietly belch out your hot air
(from both ends),
hide your face behind that automatic smile
and humour me by painting your face
lest your indigestion shows there.

I am your cook and dish,
at your bidding I've laid me out
rare medium and well done,
and being well-steeped in table manners
you toyed me with a nod,
picking out my bones with a toothpick
(I must tell you which are the bones)
and numbered them for your anthropological mural.

Yesterday you tagged me a cannibal
a noble savage primitive and wild.
Now you want to know whether you were right.
Yesterday you found me docile taciturn
and easy to please.
Now you want to brace yourself with my hospitality.
Yesterday you asked me not whether
I enjoyed living, and
now you have the cheek to ask me whether
I am enjoying my death.

Culture Shock

one day i long to have been
    my grandfather.
another day i long to be
    my own grandson.
today i wish i didn't have
    two hands.

My Gods

under the galip tree
my past hovers —
it's the burial sanctuary.
i fix a stick to the ground
and place another across it
to ward off the trespasser,
    and
the priest takes me
for a christian!

Julian Maka'a

An Unexpected Gift

I have owned a bicycle for some time now. Although it is getting old, I ride it to work every day. During weekends I use it to ride out of town to the industrial areas, to go to the timber mills, the rice fields and the oil-palm fields, away out of town. At other times I ride out to one of the rivers for a swim. Although the trips are regular, there is usually nothing exciting about them.

But one time I rode out past the timber mills towards the rice fields will stand out in my mind for as long as I live. The day was cloudy and very cool and I rode along whistling to the blowing wind. No one lived around there because a rice plantation covered the vast plains, stretching away into the distance. The plains were so wide and the mountains were many miles away inland, looking like a sow resting for her young to feed. A few trees could be seen here and there all over the field. These, I heard, served as shade for workers from the sun.

So there I was, enjoying my lone ride. I wasn't going anywhere in particular and intended to turn back when I was tired.

As I pedalled along, I was thinking about the past. The times when, as a child, I had been mocked and badly treated by the other children. A weakling, some said, and they used to laugh and tease me until I cried, much to their amusement: 'Ugly', 'pot-belly', 'eyes wide like an owl's', and other names would be added to the list.

Thinking about all that, I cursed. Especially when I remembered what an old man, angry when some other children and I unintentionally broke his fishing-rod one day, had said. He'd put a spell on me: I'd have bad luck until the day I died. I had not been the leader, but because I was the one the children always teased, I got the blame. And looking back, everything seemed to match up: in school, I had only managed to get further after someone who had been selected to go on said he couldn't because his parents couldn't afford his school fees, and when I finished school — because I didn't feel like continuing — I tried my best to get a good job, but couldn't. So after some months of going around every place of possible employment, I was fortunate to be given a job as an office boy. I was to post the mail, repair broken furniture, sweep the office, weed outside and water the flowers. But unlike people in other places who did the same kind of job and who had cars to drive, I had only managed to buy a bicycle after eight years. Just as I decided to turn around and start the ride back, I thought I heard someone shout. I slowed down and listened but couldn't hear anything, so I stopped. I got off the bike, deciding to walk along and listen carefully.

Not hearing anything more after walking a way, I got back on my bike and started to pedal slowly along. Then, as soon as I was gathering speed, I thought I heard the sound again. Yes! It came again — clear. But I couldn't see anything, and decided that it must have been my imagination.

Then I was suddenly afraid. I recalled a friend's story about vele men who used to kill people they met walking alone along there. I recalled something about a man being killed by a falling tree at the time when clearing of the rice fields began. I had heard that people passing along that very road often heard similar shouts — the shouts of the man who, after he'd been hit by the tree, had screamed helplessly, pitifully. The thought that what I had heard was his ghost terrified me. But then I thought: such things never happen during daytime. No ghost ever appears in broad daylight. That was what people had often told me. I decided to turn and ride away.

'Help!'

I heard it again — this time louder, more urgent. I turned in the direction of the shout and saw someone. I couldn't see who it was, but it was someone white. I turned the bike around and rode fast towards the person. Getting closer, I could make out that it was a man. He was motioning to me. He kept waving and jumping up and down. I rode faster, my heart pounding.

I was soon opposite the man — but I could not reach him by bike: he was out in the middle of the rice field. There was no road there.

Then I saw a car abandoned on the side of the road. The left door was ajar. Suddenly, I caught my breath. There was something familiar about that car. The car belonged to my boss!

Without wasting any more time, I leapt off my bike and began to run through the rice. It was hard to move quickly, and occasionally I plunged into the mud in which the rice grew and I had to struggle to get out of it. Clouds of insects that lived in the rice scattered as I disturbed them, getting into my eyes. I had to slow down and rub my eyes before I could see properly again.

I felt a sudden pain in my left foot. I knew it was a cut. But I couldn't worry about that. I had to get to my boss.

'Help! Help me! Please help me, someone,' the man kept calling. His calling urged me to go faster.

A few yards away in the field, a blackbird cried as though also urging me to go faster. I looked ahead. But I couldn't see the man.

'What's happened? Where's he gone?' I asked myself as I raced on. Then I saw him again. He was standing with his hands over his face. I fought my way through the final stretch of rice towards him. Even though I was drenched in mud, and the cut on my foot was very painful, I was determined to help him.

I was soon with him, out of breath, exhausted.

'What's wrong?' I gasped, my whole chest heaving. But the boss didn't say anything. He still covered his face with his hands.

'What's happened?' I asked. But instead of answering, he pointed to the right and nodded, seeming to ask me to go to the place he indicated very quickly.

'What's there?' I asked, still breathing heavily. I wondered why he hadn't spoken. He grabbed my hand and pulled me. We both ran. Immediately behind the next patch of rice I saw some men. He pointed accusingly at them. The men were bending over something. I still couldn't see what it was and stood gasping for air. My boss, seeing that I was just standing without haste, quickly pointed again at the men and choked out, 'My wife . . .' I quickly spun around as though I had been whipped severely on the back. I stared at my boss. Then I looked back at the men. Seeing my quick reaction, my boss seemed encouraged. He followed close behind as I started forward. As soon as we reached the men, my boss dashed ahead of me. He bent down, much to my surprise, and seized one of the men by the collar. But as he hauled the man up, the man spun around and gave him a blinding blow. My boss reeled backwards and fell to the ground. Shocked and angered, I dashed forward and, with all my might grabbed the man by the shirt. The man lashed out at me, but I ducked and landed a punch on his left cheek which sent him headlong into the rice. Then I kicked another of the three men who were still bending over my boss's wife, between his shoulders. He yelped like a beaten dog and collapsed unconscious beside the first man.

The other two, realising that a maniac was upon them, began to flee through the rice. One of them hauled up his trousers as he ran. The other, terrified, threw away his shirt as he ran. It fell not far from one of the two men lying unconscious in the rice. I grabbed the shirt and tied it around one man's eyes so he couldn't see. This way it would be easy to deal with him. I pulled the other man to a standing position and called the boss to give it to him. My boss said nothing, but came forward and punched the man in the belly. Then he punched him again and again, and yet again, until the man groaned and I released him, letting him sag down onto the trampled rice. I hauled up the other one, who was just recovering consciousness, and we gave him the same treatment until he fell unconscious again, with the shirt still covering his eyes. If the other two hadn't fled, we'd have given them the same treatment.

After we had dealt with the men, I ran over to my boss's wife, who had been sitting and sobbing where the men had left her. When I touched her, she covered her face with her hands.

'No, don't touch me. Leave me alone. Go away,' she cried. I tried to explain that it was all right and that I was her husband's office boy but she still sobbed and wouldn't stop.

I looked at her. She was completely naked. I was suddenly ashamed.

Had she been raped, or was she just about to have been? I wondered. The men, the same colour as me, and perhaps with similar beliefs and customs, had done that. Our custom strongly opposes rape or adultery, and very severe punishment was given to offenders — sometimes even death. At least, that had been the practice before Christianity. But I knew that these men hadn't done this on their own initiative. I found myself blaming the white man for the behaviour of these men. They'd probably seen it in movies, or read about it in papers. But I did not know what to do. I turned and walked toward my boss who still held his swollen face. He looked at me and I suddenly felt that I was not myself. My boss turned away and looked at his wife. The two men still lay not far away from her. I saw that she had stopped crying and was staring helplessly at him. She looked down when my eyes met hers. And then she clutched at pieces of clothes and held them around her waist. I could not look at her any more so I turned to look at my boss again. His wife rose, still clutching the tattered pieces around her.

She approached slowly. I was ashamed when I became conscious that she was staring at me unblinkingly. She seemed to hate me. But I stood there, just like my boss. She reached us without saying anything. I didn't know what to do. The three of us stood silently, staring blankly.

I still don't like to think about the incident. I wished that it had never happened. I sometimes sense that there is a reason why I was involved. Perhaps it was the old man's curse. But whatever that reason is, I don't want to know.

On our way back across the rice to the road, my boss explained what had happened.

They had been driving slowly along in their car because his wife had wanted to get a good view of the rice. She wanted to take some photographs. She had taken out the camera and tried to take a photograph out of the window, but she had forgotten to take off the lens cap. Then when she tried to remove it, it had fallen onto the road. So they stopped and reversed to pick it up. They reached the spot where the lens cap had fallen, and stopped. Four men who were working in the rice field came over to the car and asked what the matter was. They told the men about the lens cap, and the men spread around the car looking for it. There were two on each side of the car. Then one of the men began asking all sorts of unnecessary questions. My boss, knowing about the generally very good behaviour of the people, answered him. Suddenly, there was a tap on the top of the car and the four were on them. The two men on his wife's side quickly opened her door and dragged her out, one trying to lift her up onto his shoulders. But she yelled and struggled. Seeing this, my boss jumped out of the car. The other two men quickly grabbed him, punched him and then dragged him through the rice after the other two and his wife.

As soon as they reached the spot where I had come upon the scene, the two of them punched my boss until he was unconscious and then they joined the other two. When my boss regained consciousness he was too badly knocked around to help his wife. All he could do was shout for help.

That was when I heard him the first time.

The boss's wife said that the two men who had carried her into the rice started to tear her clothes off. She had tried to fight them off, but they had been too strong for her. But even though they had torn the dress off they hadn't been able to do anything else because she had fought and kicked. But they'd have succeeded if I hadn't turned up.

'Thanks. Thank you very much,' said my boss. I wasn't looking at my boss when he told the whole story. I was lost in deep thought.

'Thank you very much,' my boss said again. We were standing beside the car on the road. He was silent. I was watching him. Then he turned and looked at me.

'You can have the car,' he said. 'Because without you we'd have been killed.' Then he looked down.

The car, a brand new one. I recalled the old man's curse, that I'd have bad luck until the day I died. I was not glad. I was sorry and ashamed.

JULLY MAKINI

Civilised Girl

Cheap perfume
Six-inch heels
Skin-tight pants
Civilised girl

Steel-wool hair
Fuzzy and stiff
Now soft as coconut husk
Held by a dozen clips

Charcoal-black skin
Painted red
Bushy eyebrows
Plucked and pencilled

Who am I?
Melanesian, Caucasian or
Half-caste?
Make up your mind

Where am I going —
Forward, backward, still?
What do I call myself —
Mrs, Miss or Ms?

Why do I do this?
Imitation
What's wrong with it?
Civilisation.

A Man's World

My brother can sit on the table
I mustn't
He can say what he likes whenever he likes
I must keep quiet
He can order me around like a slave
I must not back-chat

He gives me his dirty clothes to wash
I wish he could wash mine!
If he sits on the front steps
I must go round to the back door
If the house is full
I must crawl on my hands and knees
I must walk behind him not in front
Watch my speech when he is in the house
Don't say 'face' but say 'front'
Not 'teeth' but 'stone'
Carry out my love affairs behind his back
Custom allows him to thrash both of us if caught
But he can carry on in front of me
That's his privilege
I must pay compensation
If I'm to get married
Or pregnant without a hubby
A brother can make a living out of his sisters!

Roviana Girl

Fine features,
High cheek-bones
Black as midnight
Blue-eyed and blonde
Tio — we are the same
Roviana all over.

Black and poor as I am,
Don't look down on me
My roots are bedded deep
On Roviana soil.

Brown-skinned or mulatto,
Imported blood
Slaves from headhunting days
Beachcomber and convicts
Flotsam and jetsam.

Sweet-talking our ancestors
buying land with tobacco
    and cheap trinkets
Now you buy me
    with coffee and rice.

342

Rexford T. Orotaloa

Raraifilu

One day my mother said, 'You must know something about Raraifilu, the safe side to be on. He is a fakamina, a talkative man who does no good.'

'But Mother', I said, 'Isn't Raraifilu my uncle?'

'He's your uncle all right, but he is lazy and a troublemaker. Gossiping about others — that's what he does in the village,' she said. 'Yesterday he told your father that Maoa, his wife, did not feed him properly. Your father later found out that it was untrue.'

As I strolled through the village one day I met him and he said, 'I am Raraifilu' (though I knew his name well). 'I would like to tell you something. I was a good fisherman before in this village of Suremada. I could out-fish any man. I also weaved a net all by myself. I knew how to do it.' He was talking with a frothing mouth.

Having listened carefully to his stories, I asked, 'But does everybody in the village know that you once had a net and that you were a good fisherman? I'll ask the people of the village.' He looked at me with a smile and said, 'Don't trust people of this village. They tell stories about me. Everything they tell you will be all false.' I knew he was telling lies. 'Once upon a time,' he continued, 'this village of Suremada was a village in the sun. The people did not see any fire in the village for a long time. Who would be stupid enough to make fire from the sun? In the village there was a swimming pool owned by my great-great-grandfather Kofabulu. He was a mean man. He did not allow the people to swim there. Because of Kofabulu's meanness, the gods of Suremada were angry, so they willed the village to float from the sun to this earth. Now you can see this village. It is here with us now.'

'But why didn't my mother tell me those stories?' I asked.

'This kind of story is tambu to tell a man who is not able to pay the storyteller.' 'I have nothing.' 'But your father does have some tobacco in the house.' 'Oh, so all the story needs is a piece of tobacco?' 'Yes, but when you go in the house, if your mother is around, do not tell her that I asked your father for a piece of tobacco.' I said, 'No tobacco for a storyteller.'

'What about a piece of betelnut?'

'No nothing. Like dung floating on the sea. If these things are in the house I could go and get them straight away for you, because you're a willing man to tell stupid stories.'

He was furious like an angry shark. I felt sorry for him so I went to our house and rummaged in my father's basket. Raraifilu was lucky — I found a piece of tobacco and brought it to him. He quickly changed the tone of his voice. He was happy and told me the story of Abusauru.

Raraifilu began, 'There was once a man named Abusauru. He went fishing one day in the river of Manatafa'a. As he threw his spear into the water it went through the head of a big fish. Abusauru wanted very much to get the big fish so he jumped into the river, straight into the mouth of the big fish. The fish swallowed him and took him to another island. When the fish vomited Abusauru, Abusauru found himself on a different island. On this island, man did not seek food to eat. Instead the fishes and other types of food came to the house of the man. Everything was a servant to man. What a beautiful island, something like a paradise. Would you like to go there? Mind you, don't tell anyone that I am the one who told you this story.'

'I like to live there in Suremada,' he continued. 'That is where my grandmother once lived. The people of Suremada once had only one leg, but now they have two legs, two hands, two eyes, two everything. Everything in Suremada is two. Soon these people will have three legs — their two legs and their third leg — their snake.'

'But you mustn't say that against our people,' I said.

'You're right,' he said. 'When the white men came they brought many things to this village. The natives of this village would like to live like the white men. They used spoons and plates which they bought from the stores. The white men came and changed the lives of the people. The missionaries said, "Your mode of worship isn't civilised. What is the use of too much incantation when you say prayers? And don't be stupid and thank the gods after going to the toilet." The people of this village said to the missionaries, "Kwaifasalo, our ancestor spirit, always tries to come into our house and manhandle our children. Can you come and scare it away by the power of the Christian god?"'

'Yes; so the priests, the fathers as you call them, bent on saying prayers to counteract the dynamic powers of the ancestors. Most of the things the white men tell us are found to be too absurd these days. The fact is that we haven't seen the truth in ourselves as yet. Even with Christianity. We must find the truth of our ancestor gods. I think there is no difference at all between the Christian god — the Almighty Trinity — and our ancestor gods. The truth is that our ancestors called upon the Almighty using different names. You see, in my tribe there is this god they called Tofunana Mamana, the Almighty, the centre of truth. The only question to be answered is, 'Who is this almighty god? Is it the one seen through the things in nature? The rivers, the mountains, the death of man, the successful expedition of the tribe from the sun to this earth? I don't really know myself. Maybe this is a question for the almighty god to answer himself. This question is beyond my ken.'

I said, 'Uncle, let us not go too deep into this area of thinking about the gods. Let's not dwell on this subject. It's too holy.'

But Raraifilu said, 'Let me tell you a different thing, now. You must try to make a coconut plantation, and a cocoa plantation. These are good things in life. Try to live a good life. Don't be like Adata'a, Kwilita's son. He is lazy. The other day his mother told him to go to school but he played a truant. The teacher did not see him in class. This kind of boy is dangerous and will lead you into mischievous things. Your father doesn't want you to go to prison. No, you mustn't talk or play with Roma's son either. He had already brought shame upon his family. He went and tickled another girl's nipple. This is bad for a young man like you. Let the parents arrange your marriage. How many years have you been on this earth? Ten? Twelve? Fourteen? That's infancy. You must be mature before you marry. Babies will dung your body and you will grow thin like the midrib of the coconut tree. Remember these things I tell you. Don't let them go out the other ear.'

I listened to Raraifilu's story, but I said to myself, True, you tell me some things, but why don't you have a coconut plantation of your own? That day he was talking to me, I went away after I noticed that my uncle has a big swollen testicle the size of the mountain of Kwaiasa. A funny man, this Raraifilu.

When I got to the house that day my mother said, 'Where have you been? I think you must have been listening to Raraifilu's stories. You don't understand him well. After the death of the great man Anaibolafafawa, Raraifilu stirred some people of this village to go against your father. They decided to divide the properties of Suremada amongst themselves. "Let us divide the land of Kwaitafaroa," they said. "Let us divide this village of Suremada. Who will own the creeks of Fakatari where the swamp taro grows? Why do we leave the nets undivided? The canoes of Suremada, who will look after them? The cats of this village, who will feed them? What about the spears and arrows, who will take care of them? What about the songs of Suremada? What about the sacred places? Who will look after the skulls of the ancestors? How will we go about dividing the earthworms of this soil? What about the sickness of Aniaro —Who will own them?" Raraifilu and others said they owned these things at Suremada. They said the properties belonged to them.

"'I will let the lands of Suremada to a mining company to dig for minerals. Nobody else will get the royalties," said Raraifilu. "But the people, where will they make their gardens?" asked your father. "You covet the money of the white men and forget to do right things. You're not the right man for Suremada. Be considerate. I will take you to court over this issue." Imitada went on the side of your father. Your father said "let us go to court". The president of the court said, "OK Raraifilu, OK so and so. Relate your genealogies and tell us why you say that the properties are yours."

"'My first ancestor was a man by the name of Frog, who begat two sons.

Iatekwa the first born begat Suamara — the tiller of the soil. The second son begat the people of Kwaitafaroa. Sugenasi built a sacrificial place at Fulomai. My grandfather always went there to sacrifice to the devils there. He stopped only at the arrival of Christianity." The court allowed Imitada to question Raraifilu. "Is it true that your ancestor was a frog?" Imitada asked. "Yes, but he was actually a man, not a frog. A frog is an animal." "Did Frog possess any sacrificial place at Suremada?" "Yes, at Nofufuli." "Nofufuli is a toilet for the women of Suremada", said the president of the court. "According to customs of Suremada no one on earth would sacrifice to his gods in a women's toilet." "Who was Frog's wife?' the court asked Raraifilu. "Big Hole was her name." "This earth has no such name for a woman. Sure, women have many sores on their body, but they belong to the men. The men can heal the sores of the women." Raraifilu asked Simira to be his witness in this court. "Simira will tell you that I owned this village of Suremada," Raraifilu said. "Now tell us what you know in this case, Simira," the court asked.

"'Raraifilu owned the properties at Suremada. My ancestors came to Suremada and found Raraifilu's tribe occupying the eastern part of the village. This village has a stone wall in the centre. The two tribes I am talking about made the stone wall." "What was the purpose of the wall?" the court asked. "To separate the two tribes." The court told Imitada to cross-examine Raraifilu. "What was your great-grandfather's daughter?" asked Imitada. "I don't know her name, but I remember her husband's name. His name was Abumano, meaning the one who enjoys sex very much." "What was the name of your mother's grandfather?" "Daikolu, the one who always attacks dogs from behind. He feels sweet doing it." "What was the name of the ancestor god you sacrificed pigs to?" "Kwadarfi, the god who is circumcised." The president heard that and laughed. His last tooth nearly fell off. "You must be mentally disturbed," said the president. "All the names that you mentioned weren't found in this genealogy that Abuwasia gave to the missionary Athens to write down. The names you gave in this court are fictitious names and I don't take them as genuine names of people of Suremada."

'When they held this court case at Foloasu the women who went to hear the court case giggled quietly in their hearts,' my mother said. "Ui," they said. "What kind of names of men all connected with something between a man and a woman? Perhaps Raraifilu's ancestors were not born of a woman. If they were born of any woman they would respect the names connected with the private parts of human beings." When the court heard all the witnesses from the plaintiff's side and the defence side, the court adjourned for few minutes and then gave this decision:

"'Imitada is the true owner of Suremada. He owns the reefs and the properties of Suremada. Raraifilu can only use the properties after asking permission from Imitada and his relatives. The court finds that Raraifilu covets the properties and would like to use them for himself. He isn't thinking of the rightful owners of Suremada. If Raraifilu uses the properties without asking permission from Imitada and his relatives, the rightful owners of Suremada, the court will send him to spend eternity with Satan. Who would want to spend even a minute in hell with Satan?" Raraifilu's anus emitted sparks when he heard this decision of the court. He was ashamed of himself.

After this abortive attempt at taking my father and Imitada on in court over the properties of Kwaitafaroa, Suremada and Aniaro, Raraifilu did not try to go to court again. Latona e kwaidikifi anakai halo agoago.

My mother continued, 'So that's why I tell you not to listen too much to the stories of Raraifilu the traitor. His mind is just like the spider's web hanging in the wind. It depends only on which direction the wind blows. You give him a cup of tea and he'll frequent your house until you yourself will find it hard to eat a plate of food by yourself. Raraifilu is a fanabusu. Don't ask him to accompany you to a feast. He'll eat every bit of food and you'll not be able to take any piece to the people back home.'

'But Mother,' I said. 'You tell me the truth. Does Raraifilu belong to my father's lineage?'

'Yes, exactly. He wants to override your father, but your father and Imitada are on the right side. The properties belong to the people of Suremada and an individual who tries to use them for his selfish benefits is considered as having committed the worst sin a man can perform against the gods. If you look at Raraifilu's head you'll see the scar on the right of his head. Look at his stupid head and you'll see the scar. The gods of Suremada were angry. They took Raraifilu from his house at night and hit him near the ears. Mind you son, he was unconscious. But by and by your father spent some money for someone to come and heal this stupid bastard. Relations you know. It's tambu to hate them all the time. That is against the customs of Suremada. Hating one another isn't good.

'But there is one bad thing about my uncle, Raraifilu. You see, he lost his wife. He was not wise in the handling of his four children. Raraifilu was working in his garden one day while his big daughter was weeding the paths to the taro garden. But that day his daughter was not concentrating. She did not know that she was sitting with her woman all coming out with the sharp nose. Raraifilu saw the thing and was straight away bewitched. After losing a wife for a long time and not fiddling with the nicest thing on earth, you see a thing like that open at full volume, the man underneath the trousers can spit out milk straight away. Every time he considered it a good thing to go see his daughter. I caught him one day in his house. I walked stealthily to his house and peeped in through a small hole in the wall of the house. Sure enough, I saw two turtles on top of each other. I saw Raraifilu's eyes bulging with sweat. He was very busy breaking his own egg, making love to his own daughter. I saw the daughter heighten her father's satisfaction by contracting her woman's muscle — up and down and I could hear the clacking sound the beautiful organ created — a sigh of orgasm known as mouria. After the happiest moment for Raraifilu he came out from his house. I pretended to throw stones at the little flies. He came to me wearing a big smile. I said within my mind, If I'm mature enough to kill a man, Raraifilu my uncle is the right victim. I did not tell my father about the incident. But I hinted something to my mother. My mother said, "You think your uncle is a right man? He is half man and half animal. He once did who knows what with his own sister. His brothers attempted several times abortively to murder him. Now after what you tell me, his brothers will throw him to the sea for the sharks."

But my question is, 'Why did the daughter love such a toothless old apparition?'

'Threats, you know, my son. Perhaps he threatened his daughter with a knife to make her let him use the daughter's woman. For various reasons men like Raraifilu won't live any longer on earth. You take my word, son. In many instances such a man is found dead of anything at all for the sake of the community. He might fall down from a small stump and die, a fish may bite his leg and kill him straight away.'

One day, after working in the garden, my father came home. I decided to ask him one thing. I planned to ask him without fear. He entered the house and sat down on the platform of split bamboo. 'Father,' I asked. 'Didn't my grandfather hand something to you?' 'What sort of thing are you asking about? Everything on earth has a name.' 'I am asking you about something without a name.' 'So you are asking me about something they call something without a name.' 'Magic is what I am asking you about, Father.' 'There are two main kinds. One for healing and warding off of evil spirits and the other is for menacing an enemy. Which one would you like?' 'The one for menacing an enemy.' 'But Son, you must know our customs. Magicians must not be young like you. For many reasons they must be old, this being due in part to the cumbersome character of the tambu imposed on specialists and in part to the jealous guarding of esoteric knowledge by the old men. For me to allow you to take any magic incantations would be a stupid thing on my part as a father. What exactly do you want the magic for?' 'To ask the gods to forsake Raraifilu,' I answered.

My father said, 'It's the work of the gods to take vengeance on those who break the customs of Suremada; you don't need magic for this kind of case.'

Yes, I tell you, not long after we talked about Raraifilu and all these bad things, we heard that my uncle Raraifilu drowned himself in the river. Nobody knew exactly what gave birth to his death. The children of the village found him with both his eyes missing. The villagers took him and buried him in the village cemetery. And on the tombstone they wrote:

He killed himself with shame for what he had done in the village of Suremada. He is now asking for forgiveness. May his soul rest in peace.

But others broke the custom of Kwaitafaroa and Suremada. 'Change the word "peace" to the word "agony",' they said, 'and let the sentence read "May his soul rest in agony for the many sins he did when he was alive.' But I must tell every one of you the truth. When I came to my normal way of thinking, I remembered the funny stories he once told me. I felt sorry for Raraifilu. I shed tears. I said in sorrow, 'I have lost my funny stories.' The people of Suremada mourned for him. I cried and cried.

JOHN SAUNANA

from *The Alternative*

Maduru watched the long brown mass of thick scum which separated the bluer portions of the sea from the shallows along the shoreline. Lazily his eyes followed it from one end to the other of the bay. Beyond, far out to sea, he could make out another line. This was the farthest reach of his vision. The line marked the meeting of the gentle sea swells and the blue sky above him. In the inner zone, the rounded swells broke and spilled their loads of white foam.

Then a sudden gust of breeze swept past from the land. He looked heavenwards, thinking it an early warning. A storm? But there were no rain clouds to be seen. The sky was as clear as ever. Once more he scanned the view. He was hoping to catch a white speck on the horizon which would become a ship that would take him away.

Discontented, he flung himself lengthways on the black sand, and tried to forget the misery of life in the village.

'This is the wrong place for anyone like me who has been to school. The village is full of old men and women. It's no place for a young energetic fellow like me . . . I wonder if they can ever guess what an important man I'll be when I get a job. I hope they will get a chance to see me in my air-conditioned office! I'll bet they faint with admiration when they see me in white, with black shoes. The poor bush kanakas! If they don't give a damn about me and my education, why should I respect them? No! Maduru Buru will not respect anyone who has no schooling. No! And I'll show them who's going to be the leader in the future! Yes . . . just you wait and see. I will soon be on my way to Honiara to get a job. Just you wait. Maduru Buru will swim in pound notes and silver . . . !'

Among the village people, Maduru had become shunned by all.

'Ae! Men — look at that boy Maduru. How he's become so frail and skinny . . .' said one man.

'Say what you want,' said another, 'but I think that boy hasn't been sleeping enough at night!'

'Ha! . . . what else could he be doing at night other than creeping after unprotected women and girls!' they roared. Not that they were wrong altogether. But it was the girls who were doing the chasing, for the talisman for certain success with women and girls was merely to have been away from the village to school, or to Honiara and then to come back with lies to tell.

Storytelling was important in the evenings. The gatherings sometimes attracted everyone. Maduru, of course, had much to tell of his experiences, and already he considered that he was becoming one of the most eligible bachelors on the island. But he found to his dismay that the people in his own village were never very enthusiastic about his stories. His audience was always people from other villages. In the latter, it was part of welcoming a friend to ask him to tell stories after the evening meal.

The little audience was sitting open-mouthed as Maduru told them about his first flight in an aircraft. On his part he was trying to contain himself.

'Tell us, Maduru, did you feel frightened when you were inside the aeroplane and looking down . . . above the clouds . . . and down on the islands and the sea . . .?' asked one boy incredulously.

'Not at all, Uwa. You don't feel anything once the aeroplane has taken off and starts to fly a straight course.'

'But how did you feel when the aeroplane was running to take off from the runway?' asked an old man.

'How did I feel? Well, to tell the truth, Saemaua, I felt very excited. Since it was my first time, of course, I was scared to hell because I didn't know what to do on my own.'

'Did anyone tell you what to do?' interrupted a young man who had seen aircraft flying overhead many times. He was intrigued by the thought of actually flying in one — no doubt because Maduru made it all sound so easy. And, of course, the young fellow had youth and adventure in his veins.

'Oh, sure! You see, in the small aircraft I was in, the pilot — the man who drives it — told us what we were supposed to do. But in bigger aircraft, where there is more than one person working, this is the work of young girls who are called "air hostesses" . . . '

'Ae! Is that true?' enquired a young girl shyly.

'Speak up, Niuia! We can't hear you!' broke in one of the men in the group, chuckling to himself.

'What was that?' asked Maduru, interested. 'What's your name?'

'Niuia,' replied one of the men after an awkward pause. The girl's question had just slipped out, and she hid her face in her hands and giggled with her girlfriends. Maduru was consumed with curiosity, and asked her again. This time the girl was forced to answer because the men were impatient for Maduru to get on with the story.

'Oh . . . I mean, do girls really work in aeroplanes? Really?' she asked, tailing off into giggles again. Maduru stole a glance at her and her friends, then waited for the giggling to die down.

'Yes! *really*,' he replied, emphasising the 'really'.

'They must be very pretty . . . especially if they are Europeans,' cut in an old man jokingly.

'Yes. If you go to Honiara you can see the hostesses in their bright green dresses and white hats,' answered Maduru. 'True! Man, it's true!' he added with a knowing wink to the man.

'The white women never get old. Ever!' said an old bachelor.

'Yes, that's right,' added old Onu.

'Where have you seen white women before, Onu? Are you sure you've been to Queensland? I know for certain the two of us have never left the village,' replied the first old man. 'Or is it that you've seen white women in your garden, in the big town behind our village.'

There were howls of laughter all round. Even the women, who had been quiet up till then, were aroused by the ribald exchange between the two old men.

'Ha ha ha! This is typical of the talk of the men in this village!' said one woman. 'See how easily any old man could have tricked Maduru into thinking he'd been to Honiara when in fact he'd never gone beyond the next village in his life!'

'And Maduru — you know more about the white people than we do. But if you could hear the kind of stories those old men tell us, my word, I wonder if you would stand them! But we are used to their lies now — their talk about the white women never getting sagging breasts or getting as old as we do — but it still puzzles me. Do you know if this is true? How do they do it?' asked Niuia.

But before Maduru could answer, a heavy shower began to fall, and everyone except him scampered back to their own houses. He didn't want to disappoint the last questioner. Spying a small boy, he told him to tell Niuia that he would answer her question any time she wished, and rushed to the nearest house.

The boy came back a little later with word that Niuia would like her answer that very night.

'She said for me to tell you to meet her on the beach at midnight. And so I've come to tell you without letting anyone else hear about it.' The boy waited for Maduru to thank him for his trouble. When Maduru said nothing, he slipped away into the darkness.

On the small hill above the village the school bells and gongs were ringing out as the children beat them to welcome the New Year and farewell the old. The noise woke Maduru. For a moment he thought it was some nightmare. But soon he heard other boys calling and urging him to join the fun. He leapt out of bed and in a short time was walking along with his friend, the little boy. Together they walked up the hill in the dull moonlight to the school.

Just past the first group of boys and girls who were beating the bells and shouting at the top of their voices the little boy tugged at Maduru's hand.

'Hey,' he whispered, 'there she is among those girls over there. I bet she's waiting for you. You wait over here,' and he scurried away through the knee-high grass to the group of girls. Realising the boy's purpose, Maduru began to shake with trepidation mixed with shame.

'What if she's changed her mind?' he thought. 'It's really thrusting myself on her for that little brat to fetch her for me . . . What if she tells everyone about it in the morning? Damn me! Why didn't I stop him . . .'

Then, 'Whsst!' — the signal from the small boy.

Maduru stood still; then made a dash for cover by one of the school buildings. He pressed himself to one of the verandah posts till he and the post were almost one. He could hear the voices of the boy and Niuia as they sought him out in the dark . . .

'E Kakae, you go round the other way. I'll go this way and then I'll meet you at the classroom door,' said the anxious girl, getting closer.

Stealthily, Maduru began to climb the wall to the rafters of the building where he thought he'd be hidden from his pursuers. Up, up he climbed, slowly and carefully. He was about to heave himself up on top of the cross-beam when 'crack!' — and he plummeted down like a falling coconut into the arms of Niuia.

'Eeeee! What are you doing?' she asked, surprised. 'Climbing for coconuts in the dark were you?' she laughed, mocking him.

'I . . . I . . . ' he stammered, 'I was . . .'

'Maduru,' she cut in. 'You waste my time! Did you think you could escape from me? Ha! I laugh at you!'

'I . . . er . . .'

'Ha! Look at you! You won't even come close to me,' taunted the girl. Maduru, still shaken by his fall, made no move to approach the girl. The fall had jolted the memory of his mother's warning about fooling around with girls at night.

'There will never be a shortage of girls in this world, Maduru. Your father and I will tell you when we want you to find a girl,' she'd said. 'For the present we want you to do well at school. We don't want you to marry an uneducated village girl — do you hear that? And remember! Keep away from these village bitches! We don't want to support a bastard child and some dependent, useless mother!'

But here was a girl, ripe for the picking. An arm's length away. And this same girl had mocked him for failing to make an advance. He was plunged into confusion, until the man in him came to his senses.

'What have you been doing all these years, little boy?' she asked, enticing him. 'You must have learnt something, surely?'

In a flash the serpent stirred and began to uncoil . . .

'I'm surprised you haven't learnt the one thing that's so easy. Everyone knows it,' she went on. 'But then, I can't blame you if you still know nothing about it. You're only a child . . .'

He struggled with all his will to keep the beast in check. But his will was rapidly melting away.

'If you wouldn't mind, Maduru, I might be willing to teach you that one little thing,' she whispered, 'and then you'd be the cleverest man in the world!'

And slowly Maduru was falling again for the second time that night.

He reached out to the waiting girl. His hands rested on her shoulders, then they slipped down toward her armpits, across to her warm rounded breasts. He let his fingers bathe in their pulses. His trousers could barely hold back the angry man below.

'Come on then, child! Do something! Do something quickly . . . now!' he hissed.

'Well . . .'

'I'm ready now! Come on . . .'

And under the twinkling New Year stars, with the breakers beating on the reef nearby and the music of their friends' merrymaking above them, two souls rode away to ecstasy.

Such escapades were difficult, if not impossible, for Maduru to come by when he was in his own village. There he was always under the watchful eyes of his mother. And she saw to it that her son had nothing whatsoever to do with the village belles. Maduru had constantly to be on his guard.

Wracked with indecision as to what to do when the young girls came to his house, Maduru would usually withdraw to a quiet corner of the room away from the visitors.

'Eeeee, Nanae! Is this Maduru your son?' they would ask.

'Oh, Nanae! Is this the same Maduru who used to play with me before he went away to school?'

'Hah!' his mother would snort, 'Who else? Look at him. Isn't he every inch the Maduru you used to play with?'

'Oh, really. I find it hard to recognise him after all those years . . .' the girls would often say.

On this particular occasion Maduru had had enough.

'Isn't he the exact image of his father?' said Sina. She was looking Maduru up and down, feeling pleased with herself for what she had said. And then, thinking to flatter his mother, another woman exclaimed heartily, 'Yes . . . and look at his face and eyes — aren't they his mother's?'

This shot an arrow of anger into Maduru. The talk was getting on his nerves. He looked away and then stared angrily at the woman. But none of them saw his displeasure.

'Mother! You'll have to put a stop to this nonsense. Isn't there something else you could talk about rather than this foolishness?' he protested. Then rising from where he had been sitting he stalked out, leaving the women dumbfounded.

'Nanae!' they exclaimed, 'What's upset your son?'

'Ah! Don't call him my son,' she snapped. 'I'm damned, really I'm damned. He acts like a stranger . . . he's so strange I can't understand him at all!'

'Ah. Only a fool would let his daughter marry that boy Maduru,' the women consoled themselves.

'The boy's just like his mother. Always domineering and rude!' said one. 'I wouldn't want my girl to be nagged and beaten every day by a brute like that!'

'No! No!' they all chorused. 'Nobody would, that's for sure.'

Although Maduru's grasp of English and the mannerisms of the European was crude, he was eager to impress the village people with what he had learnt at school.

'I must,' he thought, 'make these people know that the years I've spent at school have not been spent idling. I'll make them see how intelligent I am. Just like the white people . . . Oh! I wish I were white. Perhaps there's some way to bleach brown skin?'

Maduru's teachers always spoke highly of the white-man's ways. But as they themselves were not very well educated they never saw the other side of the picture. So the roots of the idea that everything belonging to the European was good took hold in the mind of the boy. And conversely, everything belonging to the village or the old ways became bad. And in this confusion he was taught to do away with anything which was not European.

At school Maduru was just another boy, expected to obey the rules like the rest. But the Maduru of the village was an entirely different character. He was no longer a boy. He was a man.

'It's my duty,' he said to himself, 'to bring the light of the white man into this dark, forsaken place. I will teach these people about cleanliness. I will teach them to sing Christmas carols and how to play soccer.'

'Who does this kid think he is to tell us that we have to wash before the morning service?' asked a disgruntled elder. 'Does he think that God will hear us better if we wash before church?'

Said another, 'Look men! Don't be childish. We've been saying our prayers unwashed for a long time.'

'No! No one will interrupt my sleep in the early morning,' vowed another. 'Not even Maduru.'

And one after the other, the men heaped scorn upon Maduru's attempts to clean up the place.

Over in Sakia's house, the men were complaining about Maduru's soccer coaching. They found it too boring and monotonous.

'Just you watch that Maduru,' complained one man. 'He's hardly finished his prayers and he's rushing out of the chapel to play soccer!'

'Yes!" agreed another. 'Last time he was jogging with the whistle in his mouth before we'd even got out of the chapel.'

'I wonder why God hasn't punished him yet?' mused another man.

'Ha! You wait. He'll be punished.'

'And I can tell you,' said Sakia, 'that when he is punished I'll be very pleased.'

'Ah, men,' said one. 'Must we wait for God to punish him? Why not do it ourselves? It'd be much more fun.'

This was greeted by a chorus of enthusiasm. One by one they denounced Maduru's carols, his refereeing and soccer coaching. Their talk wore on into the night and when they crept away to their own houses they had laid careful plans to deflate not only Maduru, but Suma, his uncle, as well.

Suma had been promised a bride, Aroaro, by his age-mate Waru in exchange for his sister. The proposal was made and the bargain sealed when they were still attending the mission school together. Both were now grown men.

Waru had married — not Suma's sister as planned, because she had died, but another girl. Suma was still a bachelor, waiting hopefully for fulfilment of his friend's pledge.

Aroaro had also grown up. Suma waited for Waru to approach him a second time, as was the custom, with a marriage proposal. But Waru had obviously forgotten his boyhood pledge and nothing was ever said. Suma, in the meantime, joined the Melanesian Brotherhood and had been away from the village for some years. When he returned he found that his betrothed had become engaged to another young man, Adua. And as was expected in such circumstances, Suma had to claim compensation for the breach of promise. When the matter was raised, Waru accused his father of breaking the family's obligation to Suma and a row had broken out between father and son over the question of compensation. Things came to a head when Adua and his father decreed that it was an affront to their dignity to sit back and watch while their rights to Aroaro were in question.

Therefore, a day was set on which Adua was to challenge Suma's rights to the girl; which meant, in effect, an invitation to fight. But all this was kept secret, so that Suma's four brothers and Maduru had all left the village when the commotion began. The huge bell used for summoning people to meetings was beaten. It brought the remaining villagers out of their houses to the mahera. Many could not understand why the meeting had been called so late in the morning when people had gone off to their gardens.

Suddenly, angry shouting was heard coming from Waru's compound — Waru's father was abusing Suma, in his absence, for trying to claim compensation. He was dancing up and down brandishing a long tomahawk. Soon he was joined by his prospective in-laws Adua and Kokai, steaming with hatred for Suma and calling on him to meet them face to face on the field of battle.

With three men dancing and pounding up and down the central mahera, hurling threats and challenges, all was confusion. Suma, hearing the noise and shouting, decided at last to investigate.

'What's the matter?' he bellowed, hoping to get the attention of his mother who was in her kitchen. 'Are those dogs at it again?'

There was no answer.

'Rauwa!' he called. 'Are you there?'

The old woman scurried around the side of the hut.

'Suma! Suma, my son! They are after you to kill you!'

'Who's trying to kill me?' he roared, amazed.

'Kokai, Adua and Tai . . . It's about the compensation,' she said, clutching his arm, trying to prevent him from going onto the mahera.

'Ha!' retorted Suma, his eyes blazing, 'If they want to kill me, I'll willingly give myself up. Ha!'

Rauwa didn't know what to say or do in her confusion. But it was clear that any advice from her now would only fall on deaf ears because Suma was already striding boldly toward the three angry men.

'Kill me if you like!' he challenged them. 'See? I'm not armed.'

The three men milled about him, ready to kill. But seeing his childhood friend in danger, Waru decided to intervene. Seizing a spear from the wall of his house he leapt to Suma's side.

'I'm with you, comrade! If they want to kill you they'll have to get me first!' he roared, brandishing the spear above his head.

A murmur ran through the crowd. Many had never seen this sort of fighting before and fewer had ever been directly involved in actual combat. It therefore fell to Suma's mother to quell the fracas. Bravely she screeched at the men, 'Shame! Shame! Shame on all of us who have reared you to fight each other like this. Adua! If you had any sense you should know that you and Suma, the man you want to kill, were suckled at the same breast! And see these hands — the same which carried and fondled the two of you when you were still infants! Selfish, young man! Have you forgotten that had it not been for Suma, who risked his life for you, you would be dead today? Where was your father when the people from the coast wanted to kill you? Now you want to kill the man who stepped in to save your life. Shame! Shame on this childish business!'

But the angry men were not to be deterred by taunts from a woman. Their rage swelled. Then suddenly, as if at a signal, the three men rushed wildly to a nearby stand of banana trees and each dealt a savage blow to a trunk. The trees fell, sprawling on top of each other, their leaves covering the bare weeded earth of the mahera. Then the men turned, and shouldering their weapons, walked away to their houses. The banana trees had represented the offending parties and, as far as the men were concerned, their felling symbolised the fall of Suma and his supporters.

Sunday. No other day filled Maduru with such satisfaction. He would be boss on the soccer field.

The soccer matches usually went on until evening, stopping only when it became too dark to see the ball. The village people loved soccer — best of all when it was raining, when the field was wet and slippery. The cold was an extra incentive for vigorous activity, for the players needed to warm their shivering bodies. The only other way to keep warm on wet days was to huddle beside a fire indoors with the old folks. Few of the men and boys wanted to do that.

The match started well, with neither side appearing to have an advantage. But it was only a matter of time before the bachelors' team began to assert its superior strength and endurance and to turn the game in their favour. As time wore on the older married men, having to chase the younger, swifter bachelors, began to show signs of exhaustion. And as the tide turned in favour of the young men, Dewiti, the referee, began to change his tactics as well, and to favour the married men. He watched the outstanding players in the bachelor's team keenly. Consequently, Maduru spent as much time arguing with the referee as playing the ball. On top of his unfairness, Maduru knew that Dewiti was following out-of-date rules from an old textbook.

Maduru was clearly the fastest and best on the field. He could outrun them all, and skilfully dribble the ball. Once there was a rush for the ball which had strayed from the field beyond the goal. Maduru sprinted past the defenders, got to the ball first, and was dribbling it back to score when Dewiti, for no apparent reason, blasted his whistle and gave a penalty against the bachelors. A little later, Maduru found himself trapped between two oncoming players in front of the goal mouth. On the spur of the moment he saw their intention to chop him for the ball. So he cunningly drew the two together, veered and swerved himself through and out of danger. The two men collided, and both had swollen legs after the match.

Tempers began to fray as the married men's team sought in vain to contain the bachelors. Maduru's goal after the first encounter was disallowed, and he was hungrier than ever to score an undisputed goal. And he knew he could.

At long last the ball came to rest at his feet and, with the quick, sure reflexes of the seasoned player, he jerked it with his foot, trapped it and began to dribble down the field into the opposition's territory. Deep into their end he paused, as though about to pass the ball, stretched out his foot to kick, then swerved and shot the ball neatly into goal. A roar of excitement rose from the spectators. They shouted encouragement: 'Beautiful! Beautiful! Shower them with goals, young man!'

But as the excitement grew, so did the married men's rage. The standard of play deteriorated rapidly. Several men began to kick and punch.

The young men's team had another chance — this time from a long overhead pass from one of their backs to the striker, who sent it spinning across to the right winger, then back to the centre man who shot. But the goalie cleared it, and the ball bounced out to the boundary.

The bachelors were to throw in. Players from both sides took their places. Each man marked his opposite number. Maduru was closely marked by Adua, and the two were nearest the thrower. Both tensed for the throw-in.

'Wheeeep!' went the whistle.

The ball rose high into the air and sailed slowly towards Maduru who intercepted and headed it away. But he was not quite fast enough, and Adua's kick caught him on the heel, sending him sprawling helplessly to the ground. Writhing in the mud clutching his heel, there seemed nothing left in him. Nothing was said, and he picked himself up and limped from the field. Coming to his mother for comfort he received only hard words.

'Hah! So you can be put down like anyone else,' she mocked. 'I thought people who boast that they know everything about soccer never get kicked. I was wrong. Adua has shown that you're just a weakling. I hope it teaches you that people like him who have never been away to school have muscle and bone as well. They can still bring you down to earth if they want!'

Maduru began to weep silently to himself. The bitter tears rolled down his cheeks and his mouth quivered in self-pity.

'Cry as much as you like. But you'll get no sympathy from me whatsoever!' said Nanae. 'Who asked you to play anyway? You never listen when I ask you to do something for me! Ask Adua to rub your foot!'

'Take it easy, ama,' said his father, comforting him, 'I warned them not to touch you again, and they'll take notice of what I say.'

Maduru was happy that his father had come to help him off the field. By now his foot had become a swollen lump and he could not walk unaided. Yes, he was thankful for his father's love and concern.

'How can I repay my father for this?' Maduru asked himself while lying waiting for sleep to come to him . ' . . . Twelve years from now, Father, I will build you a big iron house with all the European things you have ever wanted. In twelve years, Father, you will never be in need of anything . . . I will send you all my earnings in one lump sum. If only I could leave this village now . . . I can't stand being here. I'm a nuisance. Ama, I'm going to shake the dust of this place from my feet the minute I get my letter from the Education Department in Honiara . . .'

It was now the end of January. No letter had come from Honiara and there was no way of getting to Honiara except by boat. Ships had called in the past weeks, but now the bay was empty again. Maduru had taken to sitting down on the beach, watching for anything on the horizon which might turn out to be a ship. But all he'd seen had been birds or spray from the rollers out on the blue sea.

Then the letters arrived. Three in all, and he anxiously tore open the folded envelopes.

'How did I do in my exams? What are my marks?' he muttered opening the first letter with shaking hands.

'Pass with credit . . .' it said in bold letters. Then his fingers were reaching for the next — his school report: 'Frigate Bird School Report . . . This is to certify that Maduru Buru attended the school from . . . One of the best pupils for a long time . . . Shouldn't have difficulty passing the Senior Leaving Certificate . . . Above average intelligence . . . high academic ability . . . strongly recommended for secondary education . . . Headmaster, Frigate Bird School . . .'

He was now in no hurry to open the last envelope. It had a strange crest on the back, and he was sure it was from someone who he'd never met before.

'Dear Maduru Buru,' it read, 'you have been awarded a place at Prince Edward Secondary School. The school year starts on 30 January. Please make your own travel arrangements as soon as possible.'

There was a travel warrant with the letter which would get him to Auki.

TONGA

PESI FONUA

Point of No Return

'Fono, you'd better get up and go to town to see if there's a letter for us,' called Lute, my mother, from her bed at the other end of our small wooden house. The awakening message was repeated several times, but perhaps because of the mixture of heavy fumes from the mosquito coil that my younger brother, Mu'a, had lit in our living-room and the kava that I drank the night before, I felt as if I had woken to find myself at the bottom of a deep well and my mother's voice was like the rattling of a bailing bucket as it descended.

'Tamasi'i! Wake up! This is why I tell you not to over-indulge in kava. You are only a lad of seventeen, you are trying to be like Uasi — that old man with his moulting eyebrows. Mi'a, you wake up and get that boy to go and see if there's a letter for us!' called Lute to my brother, with her voice growing louder. It was something she was known for, and whenever she admonished us or we had a family discussion, the neighbourhood knew all about it.

I could hear a squeak and the forceful opening of the partition door as Lute emerged from the room where she slept with my little sister, Feketa. The partition or 'window display' as I named it, was fully pasted-up with newspaper clippings of handsome foreigners — mainly Japanese. Above it, the two-foot space between the hardboard and the ceiling was covered with red crêpe paper, its lower edge boldly serrated, and this was where our family photos hung. Most of them were Lute's, unmistakably, for she was the only figure sporting red biro lipstick on the black and white prints.

I moved my hand over my hafuni and looked up to see if Mu'a was still on his mat on the floor, but he had gone, presumably to school, for he was only eleven years old.

'You boys get up; you are so lazy, just like your father!' yelled Lute as the brown curtain to our sleeping quarters peeled open and a kick landed on my left shoulder.

'Come on, get up and go and see if there's some money for us, for the neighbours are tired of us begging for food.' My mother sounded as though she would cry, and repeatedly rubbed her eyes, then patted down her hair which looked as though she had treated it to an uku 'umea and forgotten to wash the clay off. At Lute's side, Feketa was clinging to her blue tupenu.

'Yes, I'll go when the Post Office opens at nine,' I said, and rolled over to adjust under my neck the beer bottle that I used as a pillow.

'Nine o'clock! It is now eleven!' Lute exclaimed as she dropped the curtain, and I could hear the squeaking of floorboards and the splash of rubbish that fell through the holes in the floor into the pool of water beneath the house. Our home was like a fisherman's hut out on the reef, and whenever there was heavy rain in Nuku'alofa we had to wade out to the main road, and we could not make an 'umu until the earth oven surfaced after a few sunny days.

I lay on my mat and my mind wandered back to our kava party with Uasi the previous night. Uasi, a relative of my father, did not seem to do anything else besides drinking kava. 'Our kind are few, but it's we who uphold the land of Tupou and the Chiefs,' Uasi often boasted, and many people agreed with him. Uasi was very proud of his position in the community, and maintained that it would be catastrophic if kava drinking was ever abolished. As if to prove his point, he was to be found wherever kava was being drunk in large quantities and in concentration; and if he did not attend, searchers would be sent out to take him there.

I rolled onto my back and looked up at the Seal of Tonga, screen-printed on the tapa cloth which lined the ceiling, and what Uasi had told me that night came to my mind: 'Drink a lot of kava, for you may soon go overseas and you will lose the flavour of this precious liquid.'

'Very delicious,' I whispered to myself and closed my eyes. No wonder Uasi liked drinking, for it made sleeping more enjoyable.

'Tamasi'i, lazybones, get up right now or I will hit your face with this taufale!' screamed Lute, and I felt the sting of the coconut-rib broom on the calf of my leg. I jumped to my feet and tucked the top of my tupenu tightly around my waist. The tupenu, too, was printed with a tapa pattern. I staggered to the living-room where my right foot found a hole in the floor, and I went down, instead of forward.

'Get up, you idiot!' screamed Lute, but she lowered her broom and glanced at Feketa, who was peeping around the partition door. They both looked concerned, but neither asked if I was hurt.

'It has been such a long time since we received a letter from Letio, your father, and I don't know what he thinks about us living like this; and if he has been caught and put in jail what will happen to us?' Lute lamented.

'I didn't approve at all of his staying on in Hawaii after his holiday, and even though he had been in the police force for fifteen years and had not got one stripe, at least we had food from the allotment garden. But now the estate owner has taken the tax allotment because we neglected to pay the lease for three years. Yes, it's three years since you left college, and the others left primary school, and now I don't know what the stupid old man is doing in Hawaii,' complained Lute, then she tucked in the tupenu wrapped around her.

'Come on, help me up,' I said, and raised my right arm, which Lute grasped with both hands and pulled.

There was no letter that day from my father. It was over five years since he had left, intending that we should follow at the first opportunity. But, as time dragged on, our daily living depended on the money he sent us monthly, and when, as now, no letter arrived, all we could do was beg food from the neighbours.

As I walked away from the Post Office I dreaded arriving home and being sent out to try to get some food from one of the little shops in our neighbourhood. It was one thing I never liked to do. The words of Vika, the woman who owned the shop near our home, echoed in my ears: 'Go and tell your mother she's not the only one that likes to eat tinned fish, but you must pay your fifty pa'anga debt before I will give you anything else on credit.'

'Ei, is there a loose coin?'

I looked up with surprise; it was Kalipa, a school mate of mine who had been to New Zealand recently with his father, a schoolteacher. When they overstayed their holiday, his father divorced his mother and married a palangi, enabling him to stay on in New Zealand, but Kalipa was deported, with a promise from his father that he would try to get him over soon.

Kalipa was leaning against a post of a shop verandah wearing a green cap, his souvenir from New Zealand, lowered over his eyes and when he looked at me it was as though he was trying to peep through a nail hole in somebody's wall.

'Come on, I'll get some money sent over next week and we will be rich,' said Kalipa before I had a chance to reply.

'I have nothing.'

'Ei, wealthy, have you a few cents there to make up this to buy . . .?' Kalipa begged a passer-by, but the middle-aged man shook his head and returned his wallet to his back pocket before lowering himself into his car and closing the door.

'What are you going to do today?' I asked.

'As usual, I am looking for some beer money,' said Kalipa as he stared past me to the street behind.

'Ei, girlfriend, you look rich, spare a few cents to make up this.'

'Don't trouble me, I have just scored this old man,' pleaded the fakaleiti, who supported himself on the arm of a palangi as he strolled past, wearing high heels that seemed to be on the wrong feet.

'Come on, just because you are in the money you stick your nose up,' insisted Kalipa, and dashed towards the couple, who stopped. The elderly man trembled as he handed over a five pa'anga note.

'Here, shake his hand. I told him you are my brother,' giggled the fakaleiti

Ofa, as he kissed the old man on the cheek, then they continued walking.

'It's almost enough,' said Kalipa as he put his hand in the pocket of his faded jeans and counted to himself. 'Two more pa'anga and we will be drunk.'

'Is there a stray coin to make up this for . . . ?' I asked a young man who had 'Bank of Tonga' embroidered on his shirt pocket. It was the first time I had tried to beg, and, although I did not have the looks and the style, Kalipa had been so successful I felt confident.

'Tamasi'i, why don't you go and work for your money instead of standing here begging like a fool?' said the young man. I turned to avoid his eyes, and looked the other way.

'What do you think this is? It's work all the same,' butted in Kalipa, and he flexed his muscles to bulge out of his white shirt which had both sleeves cut off at the shoulders. On his right arm was tattooed 'N.Z. 1980' and on his left were the words 'Copra Board'. The bank employee shook his head and walked away.

'Here, here,' whispered Kalipa, then he dashed to a store about three hundred metres along the road, where I could see him shaking hands with a man who had obviously just returned from overseas and was still carrying a shiny new Air Pacific travel bag. They talked for a short while and the man handed Kalipa something. Kalipa looked over his shoulder and I thought he would run away, but when he saw me looking he turned and beckoned.

'What do you think; shall we go?'

I nodded, and limped along trying to keep up, for the thong of my papa had slipped out of its socket and I had it in my hands trying to push it back into place.

'Come, we will go and visit Vai. He is a friend of mine who drives one of those black cars over there,' said Kalipa, nodding his head in the direction of a garage. Underneath a tree nearby, the drivers in their khaki uniforms stood talking.

'Have you ever ridden in one of those cars?'

Again I nodded, and with a thud my repaired papa hit the tarseal road and I slipped my right foot into it.

'You will ride for the first time, lying on the floor, of course, but you will be riding!'

Kalipa spoke with his friend for a while and then the driver removed his cap and tucked Kalipa's money inside before he replaced it firmly on his head. When we walked to the garage we found the rear door of the car open so we crawled inside and sat hunched up on the floor.

We travelled for a short while before pulling up and I heard a voice call out: 'Is there anything that the chief wants?"

'Only a few drinks to have before the midday meal,' replied the driver, then gave his order: 'Two cartons of beer, two bottles of whisky and three cartons of cigarettes.'

'The beer and the whisky are a present from me to the chief, and you remember to tell him it's from me,' insisted the barman, whose voice I recognised.

'Haven't you registered your tax allotment yet?'

'No, but I am sure it will be registered before I get sacked from this job!' said the barman, laughing.

'That is how things go,' whispered Kalipa, 'I have paid the driver, and of course it's cheaper here than anywhere else.' We abruptly kept quiet for we could hear footsteps as the two men loaded the liquor into the boot.

'Same place?' queried the driver when we pulled out to the main road.

'Yes,' called Kalipa.

We reached the destination about three miles from the centre of Nuku'alofa, and when we crawled out from the car it felt as if we had just landed after a space voyage. The feeling overwhelmed me as I emerged from the clean and shining car to the swampy ground where we were welcomed by the wild barking of skeletal dogs. We unloaded the liquor and the driver smiled farewell, tipping his cap before roaring off and raising the dust on the gravel road.

The dogs had run out of energy and were curled up in the dirt outside a fale. There was no one about except two women who were beating mulberry bark in a shelter under a feta'u tree. Leaning against the house near the dogs were several hoes, and as we approached we could hear voices coming from inside the fale: 'Come on, come on, I will give you a hiding and you'll know how bad it is to disrespect an elder,' There was a roar of laughter and I guessed that a game of draughts was in progress. When the laughter died down a cassette recorder became audible. 'Pai ta liva 'ofu Papilone,' the crowd began singing, both men and women, and it was obvious they were all drunk. I hesitated, as I was certain that if I went inside I would not get home for another three or four days. Riding in the car was good enough for me, and I realised that I should go home, for they would be waiting for me.

'You go in, I will return to town,' I told Kalipa, then we smiled at each other as the recording was drowned out by the yelling voices: 'Pai ta live 'ofu Papilone.'

'It's a farewell party for the couple who live here. They are leaving for Australia tomorrow. If you had told me, you could have gone back in the car,' said Kalipa, then he handed me two pa'anga.

'You have been so long I thought you had walked all the way to Hawaii,' commented Lute, leaning on the doorway to our house.

'There was no letter. Maybe tomorrow,' I said, and pushed my way inside.

'Siosi, Siosi! Can you give us some raw food for a haka?' called Lute to a white-haired lady in the neighbourhood who was wielding a cane-knife to trim the hibiscus fence around her property.

'Send a child over,' came the reply from Siosi, sill busy with her work.

Mu'a was sent and then I could hear the rattling of a saucepan and basin as our meal of the day was being prepared.

'This is what it's like living in poverty; no husband or tax allotment, but thank goodness we are still in Tonga.' Lute's loud comment, I was sure, was intended for Siosi's ears.

The following day I went again to check the mail, and took the opportunity to try my hand around town. I surprised Kalipa with my catch over the next few days.

'Shall we go?' Kalipa invited me one day as he got into a tricycle with some friends and a large carton of beer. 'We are having another farewell party; these two guys are leaving for New Zealand tomorrow.' I shook my head and they roared off.

'Let's go and check the mail,' I called to Mu'a, who was standing on the other side of the street. Again there was nothing, and we were not very successful in town that day either, but we went home with the hope that Lute and Feketa would be more successful when they went out looking for work that night.

Epeli Hau'ofa

From *Kisses in the Nederends*

After Bulbul had left him, Seru sat immobile for a long time thinking about what had happened and what he must do. He did not once take another swig from the bottle. He was deeply concerned with what might happen to his practice, for his family's livelihood depended largely on it. If word spread widely that because of his drunkenness he had almost brought disaster upon a national hero, they too would suffer. He knew all too well that when stories spread they grew in all dimensions and became utterly distorted.

He must see Oilei as soon as possible and get his arse fixed up. He alone must do it if his reputation were to be saved. The idea of continuing with steaming was out. Oilei would reject it outright and no one would blame him. He must be persuaded, if necessary compelled, to take from him treatment of another kind.

Seru rose, went to the edge of the jetty and smashed the bottle. He threw its neck as far out into the water as he could. Crossing the passage back home, he vowed never again to touch another drop of liquor.

In bed that night he dreamt a dream that clarified in his mind the basic causes of human illness in general, and the true nature of Oilei's problem in particular. More than that, he was convinced that he had had a vision and had been appointed by the Unseen to carry out a mission that would revolutionise the whole practice of medicine. Oilei had been appointed by the same agency to be the first beneficiary of the new approach.

Seru was woken by his dream and stayed up for the rest of the night, transported by the revelation. What he would do from then on would no longer bear much relationship to his personal life or the welfare of his family. Henceforth, he had to work for the benefit of all human beings, wherever they might be. He was a new man, a prophet.

Just before dawn, and with his drowsy wife's help, he selected five of the finest mats they had stacked on the rafters. He ordered his son to catch the biggest pig in the pen, and to prepare a large bundle of kava. Then he had his entire family accompany him to Korodamu. They left the island early to catch the seven o'clock bus to Kuruti. At the landing, Seru sent Varani on an errand into the mangroves while he and his son went into the bush behind. They returned shortly with two plastic shopping bags, each containing a different kind of leaf. Varani had already come back with seven bottles of gin, all that there was in the cache. Hardly a word passed between them, for Seru appeared to be different, possessing something the others had never before detected in him. He had an aura of authority, of a man who had seen a mystery and had solved it.

Oilei was relaxing on the divan talking with Makarita and Mere when the visitors from Rovoni appeared. They had disembarked some distance away, disrobed and wrapped tapa cloth around themselves, donned tiaras of Tahitian chestnut leaves and then proceeded slowly to Oilei's house, chanting an ancient tune about being washed up on a strange shore. The men carried their burden on their shoulders, the women bore the mats on their heads.

Mere and Makarita shifted all the furniture to the spare bedroom and brought in a large bowl, a bucket of water and a packet of pounded kava, which they placed at the far end of the lounge. There they sat down slightly behind Oilei, facing the entrance. Seru and his family entered bearing the gifts and placed them in the middle of the lounge. His son took the kava they had brought and placed it in front of Oilei, then returned to the other end of the room where his family sat. Oilei put a hand on the kava and left it there until everyone had registered his action.

Seru spoke first, with the formality, self-abasement and praise of others that went with ceremonial presentations. He thanked Oilei for honouring him and his poor, humble family by receiving them in the beautiful house only a man of wealth and renown could have built.

'Rovoni, as everyone in the Pacific knows, is rocky and infertile,' Seru continued. 'Its destitute people are unable to grow or make anything in the quality and quantity that you, who live on more favourable soils, can produce without any difficulty. But whatever little that we can produce we do with loving care, as you can see in the happy, contented face of this tiny piglet that I have dared to present to you, Oilei Bomboki, who are accustomed to receiving only great tusked boars and bulls as a matter of course. I beg you most humbly to accept this half-a-cent worth of lowly things that we have brought.

'I come to you with a heavy heart. The wrong that I have done to you came solely from the carelessness and stupidity of old men in their declining years. I beg you, therefore, to forgive me and spare the few days I have left before I heed the trumpet call that will summon me to Jehovah or to the other one, as the case may be.

'Should you forgive and spare my miserable life, I will do all there is in my power to remove from your body the pain Jehovah in his mysterious ways has visited upon you. I offer you, sir, the best that my profession can render. I, more than anyone, know that, after your near tragic experience, you would consider my suggestion an effrontery. And I would more than deserve it if you threw me out or beat me up. But, like the prophet Daniel who went, as instructed by Jehovah, into the lion's den to remove the thorn from the beast's paw, I'm risking my limbs and life, and indeed those of my family, by entering your domain, as instructed by the Holy Saviour, to remove the thorn from your, er, organ. This is my humble submission and I beg you to give it the gravest and most favourable consideration.

Oilei was very angry and would have exploded had custom not demanded that he must, in the ritual situation, behave with decorum and due ceremony. He had accepted the kava that was in front of him, and had instructed his wife to prepare kava for the visitors. In the presence of the two kava and of the much larger than normal atonement presentation in the middle of his lounge, he could not and must not show any sign of anger. What made Oilei even more inwardly furious was the way the old man had put him in a corner from which he could not escape without considerable loss of face. He could not barefacedly reject an offer nor refuse a request, especially when they were for his own benefit. To do so would bring him dishonour. Without the kava and the presentation Oilei would have had no compunction in throwing Seru and his family out of his house. He thus sat silently and absolutely still for several minutes before responding. He must deal with the old man's speech point by point and phrase his words in such a manner as to extricate himself from Seru's clutches without offending the guests.

When he spoke, it was with the utmost humility and courtesy. He thanked Seru and his family for honouring his humble abode with their very presence. They had brought with them the fresh and aromatic winds that, since creation, had swept the shores of their beautiful and justly famous island. 'I am but a poor ignorant farmer who dares not compare himself with the eminent dottores of Rovoni, the greatest healing centre in the whole South Pacific. The health and happiness of all the people of our beloved Tipota depend almost entirely on your vast knowledge of medicine and on the skills that line the palms of your hands.

'What you have given me may be worth only half a cent to people like those of your island, because you earn so much with your brains and delicately skilled hands that whatever piece of gold you choose to throw into pigsties, as is mentioned in the Holy Book, means nothing to you. But I, the poor ignorant farmer, will forever cherish the great treasure you have so generously given. This huge animal may be only a piglet to you because pigs in Rovoni are born huge. We have always marvelled at how enormous your pigs grow, larger than elephants. In all my life I've never received anything like what you have just honoured me with. I refer not to the great animal and mats and kava but to something else. No one, not even my wealthiest friend, has ever given me more than two bottles of spirits. Being so poor, I have never been able to buy more than one bottle for myself let alone for anyone else. Seven bottles of gin from one person is a fabulous gift, which only a Rovoni could give.

'Seru Draunikau, you could have chosen eight or more or six or less bottles of gin but being a great Rovoni intellectual, you have chosen to give me seven. Seven, the most magical of numbers, is impregnated with great significance and history as old as the universe. In seven days Jehovah created the solar system and the galaxy. Seven apostles finally made it into Heaven without dying first. King Solomon of the Israelites had no less than seven wives and many more than seven hundred. It's in the Book. Seven also stands for the greatest movies ever made in Hollywood: *The Magnificent Seven, Seven Brides for the Seven Brothers, The Seven Merry Wives of Windsor, The Seven Dwarfs and the Sleeping Beauty* and *The Seven Deadly Sins.* I have been most honoured and blessed today with the Seven Gins from Seru, the most unique and splendid gift ever presented in the entire history of Tipota.

'You asked me to forgive you. Who am I to forgive anyone? The Holy Book says that forgiveness is the Lord's prerogative. I have nothing in my mind but the fondest and sweetest of memories of my too-brief friendship with you. Two days ago you gave me the most enjoyable evening I'd had for a long, long time. And the gift you have just presented is worth ten times the experience that I had yesterday, although I would not voluntarily go through it again. If you have already made your peace with the Lord then that is more than I have longed for. In fact, I prayed almost all last night to the Heavenly Father to take good care of you, my friend and brother in Christ.

'Finally, I would like to say something about any further treatment of my problem. This is a matter to be decided upon between you, me and the Lord. I'm indeed honoured to have been likened to a magnificent lion with a thorn in his paw. And I can understand why the Good Lord would send his prophet Daniel into a lion's den. Lions and lionesses are the most awe-inspiring beasts in the Lord's creation, and the great English poet William Bligh, whose work I read in my school days, wrote the greatest animal poem every composed, praising the magnificent lion burning bright in the middle of the night. Yes, the Lord would indeed send a prophet to save a lion; but I doubt very much that the same Lord would despatch a prophet into a rathole to save a useless mouse, especially when the Lord himself had inflicted boils on the said rodent's er, body. I am, in other words, and in short, not worthy of any further medical attention by you or the Holy Saviour. The last thing I want is to make any further impositions on your divinely endowed skills and talents. You must, at your advanced age, be very tired by your remarkable exertions today. May I suggest, therefore, that you forget everything and have a good rest, after which you must have some refreshments before returning to your famed and fair island.'

To this unmistakable rejection of his offer, Seru very gently announced, 'As I have put it to you, the Lord Jehovah has sent me into the lion's den to remove the thorn from the magnificent beast's magnificent paw. As a devout

Christian I must obey the Almighty, even though the lion may very well tear me up for his dinner. I have entered the lion's den, and if it be the Lord's will, then whatever remains of me may be taken home by my family to be buried next to my revered father and beloved mother.'

Oilei sat there staring at Seru incredulously, realising that he had been outmanoeuvred by a foxy old man. There was nothing else he could do but submit himself once more to his ministration.

'In that case then, let the Lord's will be done. But, my good friend, I implore you most earnestly to execute the divine order with utmost care and precision, for, if anything goes amiss this time, I have only the vaguest notion of what the Heavenly Father will do to you through his humble servant, namely me. Makarita, please serve the kava,' Oilei said very calmly, bowing courteously to Seru in the way he always did to his boxing opponents just before he rose to demolish them.

When the first round of kava had been served and the formality of the occasion had thereby ended, the visitors changed into their normal clothes and sat relaxed or, more correctly, trying to be at ease with their hosts around the kava bowl. But the atmosphere was too palpably tense to allow for complete relaxation. In a little while the women left for the kitchen to prepare lunch, leaving the men to talk among themselves. Their conversation drifted inevitably to what was uppermost in their minds, the treatment. It was then that Seru revealed as a preface to what was to come his amazing dream of the human body and the creatures that lived in it.

In his vision, Seru saw the human body as a world in itself, a world inhabited by human-like creatures, the tuktuks, who organised themselves into tribes occupying territories located only in those parts of the body that contained organs and members, the most populous being lands in the lower erogenous regions. The arms and the legs were completely uninhabited, and were visited only occasionally by a few intrepid hunters.

Tuktuk territories were grouped into upper and lower zones. Uppertuk tribes were those that occupied territories above the solar plexus, the Lowertuk tribes being those that lived from the abdomen down. Within each zone, tribes were ranked according to their relative locations, above or below each other, the highest being those in the brain territories, the lowest those tuktuks who lived in the arse and the genitals.

It was the brain tribes who invented the ranking system, claiming that since they were the only ones who could see, hear and smell things outside their body-world, because of their commanding proximity to its major apertures, and that since they lived in the loftiest territories, far above the muck in the abdomen and the filth in the anal region, they were the best and cleanest tuktuks of all. They also believed that they were the cleverest since they had the good sense to live in the best part of the body-world. Uppertuks said that the worst, nastiest, dirtiest, smelliest, vilest and generally the most beastly tuktuks were those who occupied the largely swampy territories of the arse. The most degenerate, horny, porno-brained, disgustingly obscene, perverted and generally the most licentiously abandoned and loathsome were tuktuks who lived in the genital region.

Tuktuks subsisted on hunting ninongs, moose-like creatures that fed upon germs. They hunted with bows and arrows, spears and boomerangs. Because ninongs lived in different environments and fed upon different types of germs, they varied greatly in kind, size, taste and nutritional composition. The largest, tastiest, most nutritious and therefore the most desired and prized were called nambawan ninongs, found only in the genital and anal territories. These heavenly creatures fed upon a special type of germ carried around by crab lice that inhabited the nethermost regions and nowhere else. It was natural therefore that anal and genital tuktuks called their parts of the body-world the Happy Hunting Grounds.

From the milk of the nambawan ninong was made a unique kind of cheese known as liebfraufromage, which had the aroma of the Red Rose of Sodom and the combined taste of twenty species of the Forbidden Fruit. Since this cheese was matured only by being buried for ten years in anal swamps, it was the exclusive product of the arse dwellers. Tuktuks were known to have sold their entire families down the drain for a single bite of the liebfraufromage.

Since tuktuks lived entirely on ninongs and ninong dairy products, it was absolutely necessary that they trade with each other in order to vary their diet and broaden their nutritional bases. The ninong trade was conducted and controlled by tribes in the brain region who had convinced all others of their superior organisational ability and business honesty. The main trade route to and from the brain region was the spinal cord, while the nerves served as roads that branched out to the rest of the body-world. Groups of ninong traders and their long lines of carriers were always tracking from one territory to another, buying and selling. There was fierce competition among these traders for the body-world distribution of liebfraufromage and nambawan ninongs.

Between the Uppertuks of the brain region and the Lowertuks of the anal and genital territories, there was little love lost. Much of their mutual animosity arose from the Uppertuk resentment of the fact that the things they wanted most were available only in the lowest regions. To obtain these products they had to go to those areas that to them were extremely unhealthy, filthy and disgusting, and deal with tribes they considered far beneath them in intelligence and in physical and moral cleanliness. Through their familiarity with these lowest regions the brain Uppertuks had amassed a corpus of epithets that they freely hurled at Lowertuks, words directly related to the perceived characteristics of their environments. Uppertuks called Lowertuks arseholes, arselickers, buggers, bums, bullshitters, cocksuckers, cunts, fart faces, fuckwits, fucking this, fucking that, greedy guts, shitheads, turds, wankers and other luridly offensive expressions. They characterised the mental and moral capacities of Lowertuks as piss-weak and shit-awful and their achievements as cock-ups. Lowertuk tattooists, cave painters, bone carvers, nose-flute players, chanters and raindancers were referred to as arty farty bullshit artists and poofters. In the department of invective, Lowertuk were at a distinct disadvantage. They could not use the words Uppertuks had invented for them because that would only demean their surroundings, of which they were extremely fond and proud. And since not one of them had ever been to the brain lands they knew next to nothing about life in the lofty region. All they could say of the Uppertuks was that they were dunderheads, thickheads, dummkopfs, dumdums, bird-brained, nitwits, numbskulls, scatter-brained, stupid, boofy, gormless and other similarly inoffensive expressions.

Peace, stability and prosperity prevailed in the body-world as long as ninongs abounded in every territory; each tribe limited its hunting to its own domain, no one tried to monopolise or in any way interfere with the ninong trade, and tuktuks confined their conflicts to exchanges of invective.

'Human beings are healthy only as long as the tuktuks inside them live in relative peace,' Seru said. 'But since there is no such thing as a perfect body-world, tuktuks are always in strife. Sometimes they confine their conflicts within a single territory, at times two or more regions are involved and every now and then the whole body-world is at war. All diseases and illnesses in the human body and mind are caused by the messy tribal and intertribal relationships among the tuktuks.

'Oilei, your bottom's in a mess and your head's in turmoil because of long-drawn-out struggles between the arse and the brain tuktuks and among the brain dwellers themselves.'

Many years before Oilei was stricken, Seru said, a ninong trading expedition headed by Bongotuk, chieftain of the smallest brain tribe, went to the anal region to get as many of the nambawan ninongs and as much liebfraufromage as he could for the initiation feast of his eldest daughter. While *en route*, Bongotuk left the track on the only hill inside the region to attend to a call of nature. As he stepped a little distance into the bush he found a cave, the small mouth of which hid a huge natural chamber in which were stacked mounds of tuktuk skeletons. Bongotuk knew instantly that he had stumbled into the secret burial place of the anal tuktuks, the most sacred of their sacred grounds, which until then no outside tuktuk had ever seen. Being an Uppertuk who held the utmost contempt for Lowertuks, Bongotuk defecated in the cave without qualm. While squatting he picked up a shining round object and started bouncing it. He noticed that the cave was also piled high with similar objects, and said to himself, 'I must take some for my little children.' He stuffed many balls into his shoulder bag and left.

When the expedition returned home, Bongotuk bounced one ball in front of his children. As it bounced around it fell into the fireplace and exploded loudly, shattering a potful of ninongs. Bongotuk was amazed. He threw in another ball, which exploded with a terrific bang. Then he placed a trussed-up ninong near the fire and banged another ball, which killed the creature instantly. He thought for a while and, being a brainy tuktuk, searched for a strip of highly inflammable material, which he attached to another ball, lit it and tossed the lot into the air. It went off and blew to pieces a large germ flying by.

Being a cruel and unscrupulous leader, Bongotuk saw in the balls the means to attain his long-held ambition to become the paramount chief of all the brain tribes and therefore control the entire ninong and liebfraufromage trade. Accordingly, he sent his three sons and trusted minions secretly to the cave to fetch a large supply of balls, which he used to impose his dominance over all the hitherto-independent brain tribes, and united them under a single rule for the first time ever. He had also despatched a strong force of warriors to take possession of the cave and prevent anyone else from gaining access.

The anal tuktuks protested vehemently against the desecration of their sacred ground. When these protests fell on deaf ears they mounted a series of attacks on the intruders, who easily repelled them with their explosives, killing a great number. Those who survived were hounded and slaughtered mercilessly, and their families massacred. In time Bongotuk subjugated the anal and genital tuktuks, forced them into breeding nambawan ninongs and manufacturing more liebfraufromage, levying a seventy per cent tax in kind on all that they produced. Bongotuk also subjugated all the other tribes of the Lowertuk territories, and was set on conquering the rest of the body-world. At the home front, Bongotuk's tribe had formed the ruling class of the new paramountcy and had reduced all the other tribes to the rank of carriers in the ninong trade. Bongotuk was hated both at home and abroad.

'Almost a year ago, just before you started feeling the pain in your arse,' Seru addressed Oilei, 'the anal tuktuks, instigated by their intolerable oppression and the continued desecration of their most sacred ground, rose in open rebellion against their oppressors. From the beginning they have used guerrilla tactics because their weapons cannot match those of Bongotuk's forces. They normally ambush Bongotuk's troops and retreat quickly into the deepest and densest swamps, where enemy warriors will not go on account of the filth and the stench. Using bows to fire explosive missiles, Uppertuks are bombarding these swamps, thus giving you the nasty pain in the arse.

'Even more recently, the brain tuktuks from the oppressed tribes have taken advantage of the diversion caused by the Lowertuk rebellion to rise and fight for their own liberation. They are set on overthrowing the ruling class.

Bongotuk's warriors are bombarding the rebels, causing the nasty migraine that has doubled your suffering.

'The point is that there are two full-scale rebellions in your body-world. There's civil war in your brain and a Lowertuk guerrilla campaign against foreign domination. Your pains will persist as long as these conflicts remain unresolved. You will have even more pain if the other Lowertuk tribal territories rise against Bongotuk.'

'That's the most fantastic thing I've ever heard, Seru,' Oilei marvelled. 'The rebellions sound exactly like what you hear from the BBC news service every day.'

'You are at liberty to make any comparisons or draw any parallels you like, but I'm only interested in your complaints. You see, we must help the anal tuktuks drive away their invaders, and must also assist the other tuktuk tribes in the brain to overthrow the same oppressors.

In short, my recommendation is that we help the freedom fighters of the two connected revolutions, and liberate all oppressed tuktuks. Once we get rid of Bongotuk's hordes from your arse and brain, his henchmen and lackeys in the other territories will be easily swept away. Only when this is done will your pains disappear.'

Everyone in the group was profoundly impressed by Seru's revelation. They had never heard anything like it before. For long minutes they sat absolutely still, staring in awed wonderment at the old *dottore*, who appeared to each of them the very image of the Holy Physician's father. At long last it was Oilei who broke the spell.

'Pardon me, Seru, why didn't the other tuktuks look for their own explosives in other caves?'

'All the explosives in your body-world are found only in the one anal cave,' Seru explained. 'The anal tuktuks always take their dying relatives to the cave and leave them there to die among the remains of their ancestors. Just before they expire, they fart out all the methane gas in their bodies. The atmosphere in the cave is saturated with a certain type of gas found nowhere else. When each fart comes out and meets the unique atmosphere of the cave, it curls up and solidifies into a shiny, bouncing ball, which explodes when it touches anything hot. I hope that this explanation satisfies you. Now let's get back to your problem.

'You will have a series of smoking treatments of your bottom and head. It's new and untried and was only revealed to me last night. There are two types of leaves you will use as your revolutionary weapons. One is for gassing those Uppertuk invaders in your arse. The other is for the overthrow of the Bongotuk ruling tribe in your brain,' Seru paused to give Oilei a bag. 'That contains leaves that you put in a slow, smouldering fire over which you expose your bottom. I'll show you later how it's done. You will do it six times, which should be sufficient to get rid of every Uppertuk intruder down there.'

Seru gave Oilei the other bag.

'Roll some leaves from that bag in a sheet of dry banana leaf to make a cigar. Light and sniff the cigar while you're smoking your behind. That should destroy Bongotuk and all his gang living luxuriously in your brain.

'I'll keep you company for the first treatment, although my bottom isn't in any way whatsoever diseased, unlike some people I know. We'll begin when you're ready. We will need two strong wooden boxes, some dry coconut husks and banana leaves, and a place where we will have complete privacy.

'Before we start, let me tell you that this new treatment has the potential to benefit human beings everywhere. I'm certain that it will revolutionise medical science as Isaac Newton's work revolutionised physics. The discovery of tuktuks will most probably rank above Louis Pasteur's discovery of germs. Think about it.'

Oilei led Seru to an old and rather dilapidated but dry backyard shed with a concrete floor that he used as a packing and storage facility for his kava and other farm produce. Near the entrance stood a carpenter's bench on top of which was a box of tools. The shed was otherwise empty except for a few old sacks, wooden packing boxes strewn on the floor, and Oilei's farming implements leaning against a wall in the corner. He tidied up the floor and selected the two largest and sturdiest boxes. In the bottom boards of each he opened a square hole large enough to accommodate not too uncomfortably one human bottom. He placed the boxes on the ground and sat on each of them in turn; they held firm. He went out and returned with an armful of dry coconut husks and banana leaf. They had all they needed for the job.

Seru instructed Oilei on exactly what to do, and excused himself to attend to an urgent call of nature. Everything was ready on his return. Two small fires were smouldering slowly in the middle of the floor, about two metres apart. Oilei had already tossed in some green leaves, and there was a fair amount of rising smoke but not enough to befog the shed. Oilei had also rolled two six-inch cigars, one of which he offered Seru, who closed his eyes and said a brief prayer before signalling Oilei to begin. They stripped themselves naked, took a box each, stood them over the fires and sat down facing each other. Then they lit the cigars and held them as close to their noses as they comfortably could, and sniffed.

After about ten minutes, Seru realised that he could not get any more smoke up through his nostrils, although the cigar was still well alive. He tried again before he felt something odd, very odd indeed, something he had never before experienced. He had ceased to breathe, no air moved in or out of his nose or mouth. He tried again but nothing happened. He did not panic, for he was not running out of breath. His lungs and heart seemed to function as they always did, and his pulse rate was normal. Then he realised with horror what had happened. He looked sharply at Oilei, who was staring at him almost completely stunned.

'Are you having the same experience I'm having?' Seru asked in a peculiar voice.

'You mean you're also breathing through your arse?' Oilei croaked back.

Before Seru could respond, Oilei farted — through his nose. And Seru, to his own amazement, farted right back, also through his nose.

'Bloody hell!'

'Oh, shit!'

Seru was clumsily unrolling his cigar when he hard Oilei croaking like a dying Mafia godfather saying his last words.

'It's a miracle!' Oilei began giggling like a moron, but without making a sound.

'Miracle my arse!' Seru croaked angrily and almost inaudibly back. 'You've made the cigars with the wrong leaves, you stupid arsehole!'

He reached to the ground and picked up the plastic bag from which Oilei had taken the leaves for the fire. They were also wrong.

Seru rose, switched the bags, lit two new fires and tossed in the right leaves. He rolled two new cigars and lit one, his hands shaking all the while, then placed his box over one of the fires and sat with the live cigar held close to his nose.

Soon he felt the smoke being drawn into his bottom and then expelled in a loud explosion. Immediately his arse stopped breathing and air began moving through his nostrils. He drew in a long, long breath, savouring it with great relief before looking across at Oilei, who was still giggling soundlessly and obviously in a state of shock. 'Oh God, he's off his rocker,' Seru muttered as he moved over and led him with his box to the second new fire.

Seru lit the other cigar and held it under Oilei's nose. In a little while, when Oilei had begun regaining his senses and breathing normally, Seru returned to his own box.

Now that they had done the right thing, its effect began to overwhelm them. They sat zombie-like, completely lost in their respective worlds of heightened sensuality. Oilei closed his eyes, and, as the smoke circulated down below, wafting through nooks and crannies and curling up rolling hills and into other things unmentionable, he felt and all but saw Makarita's honeyed hands moving oh so lightly through dales and vales and up the weeping willow tree on their nuptial evening. The smoke that he sniffed caressed his nostrils and floated languorously through the chambers of his sinuses, then glided up the sides of his brain, giving him the sensation of Makarita's thighs rubbing delicately against his ears and the sides of his head while he was doing something unmentionable on the night of their honeymoon. There were many other things that Oilei and Seru felt, tasted, saw and smelled, and they all added up to the most extraordinary experience either man had ever had. Throughout all this, Oilei was oblivious of the revolutionary struggles that raged inside him.

When they returned to normality, the fires and the cigars were stone cold, the outside world was pitch dark and silent except for the chirping of crickets, and a lamp was glowing in the shed. Someone had obviously sneaked in and left it there. Oilei checked his watch, which said four o'clock. They had been away for over sixteen hours. They looked at each other and smiled weakly as they put on their clothes.

'This has been the most beautiful thing I've ever experienced. If all revolutions were like this, I'd fight the bloody tuktuks anytime, anywhere,' Oilei said contentedly.

'You can only do it five more times and that's it. We must suppress our desires and do what's necessary for the peoples of the world,' Seru laid a hand on Oilei's shoulder. 'Not a word to anyone about the accident, promise?'

'You can bet your arse on it,' Oilei replied.

They left the shed for the house, Oilei to his bedroom where he dozed off almost immediately, Seru to the spare bedroom where his people were sleeping on the floor. Then the old man went to the lounge and sat there thinking about the marvel of the discovery. He was still at it when the birds broke out into songs as they ushered in the new dawn. A new dawn in the history of humankind, Seru told himself as he rose, stretched his arms and went into the toilet.

While he was washing his hands, Seru looked into the mirror and froze. His nose was brilliantly pink, setting itself off against the dark background of the rest of his face. He peered carefully again but there was no mistaking it. It was pink. He unhinged the mirror, laid it on the floor, switched on the light for greater illumination and squatted. His entire end region was shimmering grey, no doubt whatever about it either. Oh Christ, he muttered, his nose and presumably his brain had turned arse-coloured and his nether end had been brainwashed. The accident had done it; that stupid Oilei!

He was just about to bellow at his host when he remembered Oilei's final words during the ceremony. 'If anything goes amiss this time . . .' Seru knew that it was Oilei's fault, but he also realised that the ultimate responsibility was his. It was his medicine, and he had ruthlessly used a ceremonial situation to manoeuvre a most reluctant Oilei into his trap. Oilei knew it too; hence the veiled but unmistakable threat. He must put as much distance as possible between himself and the former boxing champion. He tied a handkerchief around his face, below eye level. Then he went into the spare bedroom and extracted from his wife's basket a pair of dark sunglasses, which he put on. Noiselessly he woke up every member of his family, signalling them to keep quiet. When they were ready they stole out of the house and hastened away.

They were about ten kilometres from the village when the first bus to Kuruti drove by.

At the capital Seru sent his family on to Rovoni, telling them that he would follow later. He went to the Jubilee Park and slept under a low bush that hid him from any casual glance. When it was dark he hurried to the waterfront and found a fishing boat with a fifty-horsepower Yamaha engine. Anglers or divers must have just provisioned it for a fishing expedition; there was sufficient food and water to last a whole week or more. Perhaps the owners had gone to fetch more provisions? Too bad. He took the boat.

Thirty hours later he saw an island and headed straight to the beach, where to his utter amazement he found Losana Tonoka, Marama Kakase, Domoni Thimailomalangi, many other *dottores* from Tipota, and hundreds of people he had not seen before, all stark naked, practising yoga and doing other things that boggled his mind.

Marama appeared to have shed at least thirty kilograms. She was trim and looking extremely fit for her age. Seru was so warmly welcomed that he decided to stay on.

He had landed on Nanggaralevu.

Oilei woke up after noon. He lay in bed basking in the afterglow of his remarkable treatment. Then all of a sudden his senses sharpened and he wanted Makarita urgently. He could feel her thighs moving against his ears and her hands active in his groin. He raised himself to call her and in the process saw his reflection in the mirror on the dresser a few feet from the foot of the bed. He could not believe what he saw. He shook his head and blinked his eyes, but there it was, a brilliant pink nose attached to his light brown face. He scampered on all fours to the foot of the bed for a close-up view, which only confirmed what he had seen. He pinched his nose and pulled it, hoping that it was false, but it would not come off. Then he remembered the accident and the breathing through the wrong orifice. He stood up, dropped his pyjamas and bared his buttocks at the mirror, only to find that his whole bottom was glistening grey.

Oilei was shocked and outraged. Seru had done it twice to him. He jumped out of bed and shouted, 'I'll kill you, you fucking tuktuk!' as he ran into the spare bedroom.

'Where's that son of a bitch! Rita! Rita!'

Makarita bolted out of her bedroom, where she had been mending a blouse, and streaked for the front door. Before she was halfway across Oilei grabbed her and spun her around. The look of utter terror in her face struck him and overcame his rage. He drew her gently to his chest, where she broke down and sobbed and laughed at the same time. She tried to pull herself away to look at him, but he held her tight, averting his face.

'You brute! You beast! I thought you were going to kill me!'

She reached up and tore at his hair and scratched raw the back of his neck, and before they knew it they were in bed coupling away like a pair of teenagers.

Afterwards, Oilei remembered. 'Where are they?' he asked, more from curiosity than anger.

'Who?'

'The Rovoni pigs.'

'Oh. They left before anyone else woke up. Must've been in a hurry to get away.'

'Just as well. I'd have done him in otherwise. Lucky bastard.' In a little while he added quietly, 'It was really my fault though,' and told Makarita everything that had happened. By then his wife was no longer shocked by the discoloration of his nose.

'So. The brain's seeped down and the arse's risen. You should be in a nut-house,' she said, giggling wantonly.

'It was quite a revolution, though. The top dogs are in exile among giant crab lice and the underdogs have taken over. Seriously, what can we do? I can't go around with this nose.'

'Bulbul,' Makarita suggested. 'We can always ask. I'll go to the Health Centre and ring him up. But you'll have to earn it first.'

To the Last Viking of the Sunrise*

Since you left, captain,
We've missed the man
Who sliced the blue-black sea
To get to Lifuka
Before the water boiled.

You've gone, Tevita,
And the wet-winged tern from Minerva
Has flown to the rock
Where Sina sits waiting for the word
You will never send.

Moana's calling you
Who slipped the midway reef,
Set bow for the foamy straits,
Beating the wind, the wooden gods
Giving way to no one, north or west.

Oh tell us again
Of the day you raked the coral head
Then crashed the coast of Kandavu
Whence the mountains heard that he who dared the gods
Had tamed the sea.

You've gone, red-eyed sailor,
So have our fathers forever.
I mourn not you, not them,
But us you've left adrift,
Derelicts becalmed.

*The last of them has just left: Te Rangi Hiroa

KONAI HELU THAMAN

No More Guava

when you went out
to buy the paper
I wondered
if you'd come back —
so many things running
down the highway

yesterday
there were no cars no trucks
only bicycles braking
and the neighbour's kids grating
coconuts feeding the birds

i would go for water
to the community tank
firewood from uncle's
matches from the master
down the road
coming home
I'd stop for guavas
hoping my mother
would send my brother
on the next mission

i shared the guavas
with the neighbour's pigs
cursing the bats
avoiding the hornets
careful always not to break
the branches

it must have been the rain
that caused the fall
the tree
slippery and waiting
never refused me

or was it my punishment
for disobeying my mother

the hurricane came
and my family moved
to another town
where there were no guava trees
were free
all belonged to the government.

Langakali

Langakali!
Have you heard the latest?
The jellyfish at Fanga'uta swim freely in the wastes
Of Vaiola, refuge of our ailing brothers
From the north.

Hangale flowers, we'll pick no more —
Government houses have killed them all.
Yesterday I saw a child 'swimming' in an 'umu
I said, Why don't you go to the sea?
He just stared at me in silence
Then said, 'It's Sunday, can't you see?'

Must we wear this band of progress,
Stand in line for the sweat
Of our brothers' brow?
Must we now wear trousers and neckties
To be respectable?
Must you throw this medicinal branch
Out the door?
It will put out roots
And one day the tree will destroy
Your brick house,
You, and your sick son.

Today I'll polish my son's shoes
For the parade — parliament's closing.
He'll stand on the broken pavement,
Drink the sun's heat,
But would not hear the proclamation —
National airlines, royal tours, the Arabs
(We need their money but not their religion).
'Stay, help your father carve
Heads from the tamanu,
For your fees and the church.'
Must I wear this black garb for another day?
Grandma is probably laughing in her grave,
Her educated son wears leather boots
Even in the house.

Why do you weep, Langakali?
Is it because they lied to you?
Or is it because they did not tell you
The whole story?
You see, the Four Winds did send me away
To bathe in the storm clouds;
A commoner with no soul, I journeyed
In the grey hair of the sky,

But I heard the song of the sea,
Made my heart strong
That I could still find a place.

Langakali!
Did you begin to wonder
Whether I would ever return?
Would you see me again
Amidst the darkness and the soot
Of our burnt-out fale?
They said that burning is good for the soil,
But the trees suffer —
They take so long to mature;
Black coconut trunks, a dreadful sight
Headless they scorn the corrupted air.

The old man in the boathouse
Is growing weary.
He told me that he knew
The sea's origin, the moon's, the sky's
And even the sun's;
But he did not know
Why men deceive and women keep on loving them.
It was at Hala Liku that I met him
Alone, he only had the rain and the surf,
The land he gave away —
They are building runways, hotels and warehouses
On it.
It was a stormy day
When he paddled away
In a borrowed canoe.

His son, he said, had gone abroad to work
For money.
He paid the Company for airfares,
Accommodation and food, and
Came home a poor man.
Now his house belongs to the Development Bank,
His boat belongs to the chief and
He's working on a deal with the taxman
In respect of a sizeable 'gift';
Too many people are working

For money.
The sound of the conch shell
Haunts me still,
Like the cry
Of my unborn child!
I remember his face
Turning away
Trying to hide his grief.
The masters of our land
Have sold our souls
To the new religion, moneylenders,
Experts and the watchdogs of Vegas.

Langakali!
No longer do I see your face
Adorn our roads and roaming grooms
Or perfuming the evening sea-breeze.
Broken beer bottles
Greet the incoming tides
And grave-talk is no more,
For the unblinking eyes of plastic flowers
Stare away visitors from Pulotu,
Home of our warriors and conversationalists.
Pray, give me now a fast canoe
That I may join
The fish of the ocean
And together we will weep
For the works of the night.

Sunday Sadness

Smell the odour
Of the Sunday 'umu
Empty, the coals smoking
From killer waters.
The day's haunting eerie idleness
Envelopes Papa's heap
Of breadfruit crusts,
Scarred remains of futile attempts
Of toothless gums;

Pieces of Kiwi mutton-flaps
Flavour market-grown taro leaves,
Welcoming change to
Tinned 'Ocean' fish,
Saviour of now dormant fishermen
And statistical farmers.
Cold manioc, once famine-famed,
Now daily bread,
Stare from Mama's shrunken dish
At tearless people with velvet shoes
Who have ceased to walk
The good rich island earth
Of yam harvests
And plentiful Sundays . . .

Come, look through the smoke
Of the drying fire
At Grandpa's ghost weeping,
Quietly cursing
The forbidding sultry silence!

VANUATU

Grace Molisa

Custom

Custom
is an English word
English
a confluence
of streams of words
is a reservoir
of every shade
nuance and hue
sharply
contrasting
Melanesia's
limited vocabulary
supplementing
non-verbal
communication.

Inadvertently
misappropriating
'Custom'
misapplied
bastardised
murdered
a Frankenstein
corpse
conveniently
recalled
to intimidate
women
the timid
the ignorant
the weak.
'Custom'
oft-neglected
by non-conforming
advocates

the loudest
proponents
empty vessels . . .
Theoretical
'Custom'
more honoured
in omission
than commission.

A word
sandwiched
between
multifariously varied
traditional vernacular
and accidentally
occidental
Franco-Britannic
life and lingo
perplexed
by pandemonic
condominium
complex.
Custom is
as custom does!

Neo-Colonialism

Neo-Colonialism
a parasite
accommodated
by hosts
open
and susceptible to
external
influences
usually
certain
well-trained
colonial
civil servants
and weak politicians;
our bunch

of dissidents
a classic case.

Neo-Colonialism
witlessly
playing
into the hands
of foreign sharks
ready
to swallow up
unsuspecting prey.

The real game
discreetly
played
in the seclusion
of closed doors
and secrecy.

The cat and mouse
comedy
choreographed
by journalists
skilled psychologists
dishing out
diatribes
for the consumption
of the undiscerning
who legitimise
political
manoeuvres
by their
simple vote.

Status Costs

The offspring
of the well-to-do
bear the costs
over and over.
Youngsters
cannot develop
as themselves

deprived
of their own lives

Children walk
in the shadow
of parents' image
and prestige
being forced
by expectation
to wear father's shoes
and walk
in his footsteps.

The father
devotes
much of himself
to the cause
of public image
and social standing
neglecting
home
and family life

Home life
and family
suffer
while he lives
and more so
when he dies!

On the death
of a Big Man
anybody
who thinks he
is anybody
flocks
to the funeral
formalities
laying claim
to the universe
stripping
wife and children
naked.

Ni-Vanuatu Women in Development

Achievement	1980		1981		1982		1983		1984		1985		1986	
	M	F	M	F	M	F	M	F	M	F	M	F	M	F
Parliament	39	0	39	0	39	0	39	0	39	0	39	0	39	0
National Development Council	9	0	9	0	9	0	9	0	9	0	9	0	9	0
First Secretary	10	0	10	0	10	0	10	0	11	0	11	0	11	0
Second Secretary	12	1	12	1	12	1	12	1	12	2	12	2	12	4
Third Secretary	–		–		–		–		11	0	11	0	11	0
Head of Department	–		–		–		–		46	0	46	0	46	0
Deputy Head of Department	12	0	12	0	12	0	12	0	12	0	12	0	12	0
Public Service Commission	–		5	1	5	1	5	1	5	1	5	1	5	1
Teaching Service Commission	–		–		–		5	0	5	0	5	0	5	0
Judicial Service Commission	–		4	0	4	0	4	0	4	0	4	0	4	0
Doctors	–		–		–		–		–		–		10	0
Lawyers	–		–		–		–		–		–		2	0
Computer Programmers/ Systems Analysts	–		–		–		–		–		–		2	0
Forestry Workers	–		–		–		–		–		–		16	0
Transport Equipment Operators	–		–		–		–		–		–		470	0
Machinery Fitters, Mechanics, etc.	–		–		–		–		–		–		221	0
Electrical Fitters	–		–		–		–		–		–		73	0
Plumbers, Welders, etc	–		–		–		–		–		–		70	0
Total Occupation	128	1	137	2	146	2	151	2	163	3	163	3	1027	5

SAMPSON NGWELE

Peripheral Politicians

the banyan has become their House
they would convene & talk
for hours

agendaless

they would speculate, make
premature conclusions
or misinterpret

ideas & concepts

bureaucratic policies may
dominate the day's session
despite ill-information

at sundown
they all adjourn
to drink kava

& return to their
thatch houses

Island Chant

(After a poster, Beaux-Arts, May 1968)

The men in power had their way
So did Martin Luther King
The men in power had their say
So did Steven Biko
The men in power had their guns
So did Che Guevara

So let's go now:
Let's go for their universities
Let's go for their offices
Let's go for their guns

Irian Jaya! New Caledonia!

Let's go for their towers
Let's go for their palaces
Let's go for their thrones

Hawaii! Tahiti! American Samoa!

Let's go for their strongholds
Let's go for their fortresses
Let's go for their gates

Polynesia! Micronesia! Melanesia!

Let's go with their guns
Let's go to their offices
And ask why they are here.

CONTRIBUTORS

Apelu Aiavao (b. Western Samoa). Educated at Samoa College and at Ardmore Teachers' College, NZ. Teacher, broadcaster and journalist; editor of *Savali*, the government newspaper. Writes mainly in Samoan. Has also published stories for children.

Litia Alaelua (b. Auckland, 1956). Graduated from University of Auckland. Trained at Auckland College of Education. *Ghosting* is one of her first published short stories. Now teaching English at Aorere College, Auckland.

Sam L. Alasia (b. Dala, Malaita, Solomons, 1957). Educated in the Solomons and at USP, Fiji; graduated in public administration and history. Worked as civil servant; now represents Kwara'ae constituency in Parliament. Has published poetry and stories in *Mana* and a collection of poems, *Hostage* (1986).

Prem Banfal (b. Suva, Fiji, 1943). Educated in Fiji and New Zealand. Graduate of USP; taught high school. Published stories and autobiograpical pieces in *Mana* and elsewhere. Now lives in San Francisco, US.

Nora Vagi Brash (b. Kilakila, Central Province, PNG, 1944). Educated at UPNG. Journalist, actor, producer and one of the Pacific's leading playwrights; has published many plays which have been performed in PNG, Australia, and at the South Pacific Arts Festival. Has also published poems and stories in *Kovave*, *Ondobondo* and other magazines.

Alistair Te Ariki Campbell (b. Rarotonga, 1925 of Tongarevan descent). To NZ in 1933. A pioneer of Pacific literature. Editor, fiction writer, playwright and poet. First collection of poems, *Mine Eyes Dazzle*, pub. 1950; most recent collection, *Stone Rain*, 1992; has also written plays for stage, radio and TV, and a trilogy of novels: *The Frigate Bird* (1989), *Sidewinder* (1991), and *Tia* (1993).

Lemu Darcy (b. Munda, New Georgia, Western Province, Solomons, 1959). Educated in the Solomons. Has worked as a civil servant since 1978 in various ministries. Has published poems in various anthologies and magazines.

Tom Davis (b. Cook Islands, 1918). Doctor, scientist, writer and politician. Was Prime Minister of the Cook Islands; knighted for services to his country. He and his first wife Lydia wrote *Makutu* (1960), probably the first novel published by Pacific Islands writers. Published another novel, *Vaka*, in 1992. Also an expert on Polynesian navigation.

Apisai Enos (b. Central Province, PNG). Graduate of UPNG. A leading writer in the development of literature in the 1970s. Has published collections of poetry such as *HighWater* (1971), *Tabapot* (1975), and *Warbat* (1971).

Pasitale Faleilemilo (b. Western Samoa). Has published stories in *Mana*. This is one of his first published stories.

Pesi Fonua (b. Tonga, 1947). Educated in Tonga and trained in NZ and England as a journalist. Has won media and journalist awards, and published articles, essays and stories. In 1983, published *Sun and Rain and Other Stories in English and Tongan*. Publisher, editor and owner of Vavau Press, Tonga.

Epi Enari (b. Nofoalii, Western Samoa). Educated at Samoa College. Worked in American Samoa for 18 years. A trained librarian, she is now lives in Hawaii. 'The Olomatua' is one of her first published stories.

Epeli Hau'ofa (b. PNG, 1939). Educated in PNG, Fiji and at ANU; PhD in anthropology. Deputy Private Secretary to the King of Tonga 1978–81. Professor of sociology at USP since 1983. Has published books, stories and poems, a collection of short stories, *Tales of the Tikongs* (1983) and a novel, *Kisses in the Nederends* (1987).

Johnny Frisbie Hebenstreit (b. Cook Islands, 1932). Educated in Cook Islands and Hawaii and has lived in NZ since 1962. Published her first book, *Miss Ulysses of Puka Puka*, in 1948 when she was sixteen. Also published stories for adults and children, and autobiographical work. Has been active in teaching and promoting the performing arts and in women's affairs in the Pacific.

Vilsoni Hereniko (b. Rotuma, Fiji, 1954). Educated at USP, Fiji and in England; PhD in literature. Taught literature and theatre at USP. Has written and directed plays in Fiji and Hawaii; his most recent play is *Last Virgin in Paradise* (1993). Also published short stories and non-fiction. Assistant professor in Pacific literature at the Centre for Pacific Studies, University of Hawaii. Editor of the *Talanoa* series, UHP.

Jon Jonassen (b. Rarotonga, Cook Islands, 1949). Educated in Cook Islands, NZ and Hawaii; MA in Pacific studies. Active in developing the oral literature and performing arts of his country; composer and producer of many records and songs. Was Secretary of Foreign Affairs, Cook Islands. Has published non-fiction and poetry in various magazines. Now completing a PhD in political science at the University of Hawaii.

John Kasaipwalova (b. Trobriand Islands). Educated in PNG and Australia. Was influential as a writer and activist in the independence movement and the development of the Trobriand Islands. Published collections of poetry: *Reluctant Flame* (1971) and *Hanuabada* (1972), and stories and articles in *Kovave* and *Ondobondo*. Also writes verse and dance drama, including *Sail the Midnight Sun* (1980). His plays have been performed in PNG, Australia, and at the South Pacific Arts Festival.

Kauraka Kauraka (b. Rarotonga, 1951). Educated in the Cooks, NZ, Fiji, PNG and Hawaii; anthropologist, musician, photographer and writer. Published six collections of poetry in English and Cook Islands Maori, including *Return to Havaiki* (1985) and *Dreams of a Rainbow* (1987). Most recent collection of poems: *Manakonako, Reflections* (1992). Anthropologist, Ministry of Cultural Development, Cook Islands.

Ignatius Kilage (b. Simbu District, PNG). Worked as a Catholic priest for many years among the Simbu people before leaving the priesthood to work for his country's independence. Was Chief Ombudsman for several years. Published one book, *My Mother Calls Me Yaltep* (OUP, Melbourne, 1980).

Loujaya Kouza (b. Morobe Province, PNG, 1963). Published first book of poems at fifteen. Studied journalism at the UPNG and the National Music School. Published poems in *Ondobondo*. Now working in the National Research Institute, PNG.

Celo Kulagoe (b. Reko, Solomon Islands) Educated in the Solomons, PNG and at USP, Fiji; graduated as high school teacher. Has published stories and poems in *Mana* etc. Published his first collection of poems, *Where Leaves Had Fallen,* in 1980, and his first collection of short stories, *Uvipira,* in 1991. A skilled guitarist and composer.

Joyce Kumbeli (b. Milne Bay Province, PNG). Published poems in *Ondobondo* and elsewhere. Works as Secretary to the Arts Faculty, UPNG.

Jack Lahui (b. Central Province, PNG). Published his first collection of poems,

Gamblers Niugini Style, in 1975. Influential in the development of PNG literature as editor of *Papua New Guinea Writing*, and in researching PNG culture at the Cultural Studies Division of the National Research Institute. Has published poems and stories in *Ondobondo* and elsewhere.

Steven Thomas Lyadale (b. PNG). Now lectures in the Department of Language and Literature, UPNG.

Julian Maka'a (b. Tawani, Makira Province, Solomons, 1957). Educated in the Solomons and through the USP Centre there. Trained in radio communications. Published *The Confession and Other Stories* (1985). Now a producer for the Solomons Broadcasting Corporation, a dancer and choreographer.

Jully Makini (b. Gizo, Western Province, Solomons, 1953). Educated in the Solomons and at USP, Fiji. First published poetry in the 1980s under her married name, Sipolo, in anthologies and in *Mana* and elsewhere. Published two collections of poems: *Civilised Girl* (1981) and *Praying Parents* (1986).

Sano Malifa (b. Afega, Western Samoa). Educated at Samoa College and in NZ. Samoa's leading journalist and newspaper editor; owns and edits the *Observer*. Has published two collections of poems: *Looking Down At Waves* (1975) and *Song and Return* (1992), and a novel, *Alms for Oblivion* (1993).

Tasi Malifa (b. Afega, Western Samoa). Educated at Samoa College and in NZ; graduated in law. Worked in Attorney General's Office, Western Samoa. Now in private practice. Has published poems in *Mana* and other magazines.

Pio Manoa (b. Nasinu, Fiji, 1940). Educated in Fiji, worked in civil service, trained as a lay brother and priest in Australia. Taught high school in Fiji; then senior lecturer in literature and language at USP, specialising in the study of Fijian oral traditions. Has published poems in *Mana* and elsewhere.

Nemani Mati (b. Vatukoula, Fiji, 1954). Studied in Fiji at USP. Worked as a statistician in Fiji. Published poetry in *Mana* and elsewhere. Now studying at ANU.

Sudesh Mishra (b. Suva, 1962). Educated in Fiji and Flinders University; PhD in literature. Taught literature and language at USP. Published three collections of poetry: *Rahu* (1987), *Tandava* (1992), and *Memoirs of a Reluctant Traveller* (1993).

Grace Molisa (b. Vanuatu). Educated in Vanuatu and at USP. Founding member of the Vanuaku Party which took her country into independence. Worked as advisor to the prime minister. Published three collections of poems: *Blackstone I* (1983), *Colonised People* (1987) and *Blackstone II* (1989).

Satendra Nandan (b. Votualevu, Nadi, Fiji). Educated in Fiji, India, England and Australia; PhD in literature. Taught at USP 1969–87. Elected to Parliament of Fiji in 1982; appointed Minister for Health, Social Welfare and Women's Affairs in 1987. Published non-fiction, stories, two collections of poems: *Faces in a Village* (1976) and a novel, *The Wounded Sea* (1991). He now teaches at the University of Canberra.

Sampson Ngwele (b. Ambae, Vanuatu). Educated in Vanuatu and at UPNG; graduated in law and economics. First published poems while in PNG. Worked as senior civil servant in Vanuatu. In 1990, published his first collection of poems, *Bamboo Leaves*. Now Governor of the Reserve Bank of Vanuatu.

Rexford T. Orotaloa (b. Malaita, Solomons, 1956). Educated in the Solomons. Worked as a civil servant, then trained as a teacher at USP. Now teaches in the Solomons. Published a novel, *Two Times Resurrection* (1985) and short stories, *Suremada* (1989).

Ruperake Petaia (b. Western Samoa, 1951). Educated at Samoa College and USP, Fiji; BA in administration. Director of Post & Telecommunications, Western Samoa, since 1989. Has published two collections of poems: *Blue Rain* (1980) and *Patches of the Rainbow* (1992). Writes in English and Samoan and many of his poems have been translated into other languages.

Som Prakash (b. Fiji). Educated in Fiji, NZ and Australia. Taught high school and at USP in Department of Literature and Language. Has published articles, short stories and poems. Now working at Flinders University.

John Pule (b. Liku, Niue, 1962). Moved to NZ in 1964. Has published collections of poetry and a novel, *The Shark That Ate the Sun* (1992). An accomplished artist, he has had many exhibitions in NZ.

Vaine Rasmussen (b. Rarotonga, 1961). Educated in the Cook Islands; BA in administration from USP, Fiji. Edited *Ta'unga*, the first anthology of Cook Islands writing. Also published a collection of poems, *Maiata*, and several stories. Now an economist in the South Pacific Commission, New Caledonia.

Clara Reid (b. 1949, San Francisco, California, US). Moved to American Samoa in 1969. Works as a journalist. Has published poems in anthologies, *Mana* and other magazines.

Eti Sa'aga (b. Malua, Western Samoa). Educated at Samoa College. Worked as a bulldozer driver while he wrote poetry. Moved to American Samoa where he worked in bilingual education. Has published poems in *Mana* and other magazines.

John Saunana (b. Arosi Makira, Eastern Solomons, 1945). Educated in Solomons, then at UPNG; BA. First published poems and stories in PNG. Broadcaster and teacher, elected MP and appointed as Minister of Education. Later worked as Registrar at USP. Has published three collections of poetry: *Dragon Tree* (1972), *Cruising Through the Reverie* (1972), and *She* (1973), and a novel, *The Alternative* (1980).

Seri (b. Fiji). E.ducated at USP, Fiji; studied law at VUW, NZ. Has published poems in *Mana* and other magazines and anthologies and a collection of poems, *Frustrated Actors*.

Noumea Simi (b. Tuasivi, Savaii, Western Samoa). Educated at Samoa College and Massey University, NZ. Was Director of Women's Affairs, Western Samoa. Writes in both Samoan and English. Her first collection of poems, *Sails of Dawn*, was published in 1992.

Tate Simi (b. Fagalii, Western Samoa, 1952). Educated at Samoa College and in NZ. Architectural draughtsman and labour administrator; now Commissioner of Labour and Head of the Department of Labour, Western Samoa. A poet and cartoonist: *A Deeper Song* (1992) is his first collection of poetry.

Caroline Sinavaiana (b. Tutuila, American Samoa). Educated in American Samoa and America; PhD in Samoan culture. Has published essays, articles and poems in various journals and anthologies. Now Dean of Students and Lecturers in Literature at Amerika Samoa College, Pago Pago.

Russell Soaba (b. Tototo, Milne Bay, PNG, 1950). Leading figure in the cultural renaissance from 1960s. Educated at UPNG, Australia and Brown University, Providence, US; MA in literature. Has published collections of poetry including *Naked Thoughts* (1978), plays, essays, stories and two novels: *Wanpis* (1977) and *Maiba* (1985). Lecturer at UPNG.

Subramani (b. Labasa, Fiji, 1943). Educated in Fiji, at the University of Canterbury, NZ, at University of New Brunswick, Canada; PhD (1970) from USP. Taught high school; now professor of Pacific Literature at USP. His book *South Pacific Literature* (1992) was the first major study of Pacific literature. Published non-fiction, and a collection of short stories, *Fantasy Eaters*, in 1988.

Florence Syme-Buchanan (b. Rarotonga, 1963). Educated in the Cook Islands and trained in NZ as a journalist. Has published poems and short stories in *Mana* etc. Assistant Director of Media and Information Services, Office of the Prime Minister, Cook Islands.

Kumalau Tawali (b. Tawi, Manus, PNG). Educated in PNG and Canada. The first Papua New Guinean to publish a collection of poems, *Signs in the Sky* (1970). Influential poet and writer from the 1970s. Has also published plays, including *Manki Masta* (1971). Continues to publish poems in *Ondobondo* and other magazines. Since 1985, he has been teaching in the Highlands at the Christian Leaders' Training College.

Vianney Kianteata Teabo (b. Kiribati, 1962). Educated in Kiribati, at UPNG, USP, and at Massey University, NZ; MA in business studies. Journalist, broadcaster and economist. Has published stories in *Mana* and elsewhere. Now senior administrator, Ministry of Finance and Economic Planning, Kiribati.

Francis Tekonnang (b. Kiribati). Educated in Kiribati and at USP; graduated in education. Taught high school in his country for many years. Published poems and stories in *Mana* and other magazines. Died 1994.

Konai Helu Thaman (b. Nukualofa, Tonga, 1946). Educated in Tonga and NZ; BA in geography, MA from the University of California at Santa Barbara, PhD from USP, Fiji. Director of Institute of Education, Reader in Education, and ProVice-Chancellor of USP. Has published poems in many magazines and anthologies and four collections of poems: *You, the Choice of My Parents* (1974), *Langakali* (1974), *Hingano* (1987) and *Kakala* (1993).

TalosagaTolovae (b. Letiu, Savaii, Western Samoa, 1955). Educated at Samoa College and as a teacher at Hamilton Teachers' College and the University of Waikato. Taught English at Tokoroa College, NZ. Published his first collection of poems, *The Shadows Within*, in 1984. Died in August 1994.

Makiuti Tongia (b. Rarotonga, 1957). Educated in Cook Islands and USP, Fiji; MA in anthropology. Taught at teachers' college. Edited anthologies of Cook Islands writers. Published poems, including a collection, *Korero* (1979), and non-fiction. Now lecturer in Cook Islands Maori at VUW, NZ.

Thomas Tuman (b. PNG). Educated in PNG. Has published in *Ondobondo* and elsewhere. 'Kum Koimb' is one of his first published stories.

Emma Kruse Va'ai (b. Apia, Western Samoa, 1956). Educated in Samoa and NZ. Trained as a teacher. Has published stories for adults and children in various magazines and anthologies. Now lecturer at Univesite O Samoa.

Makerita Va'ai (b. Sataua, Savaii, Western Samoa). Educated at Samoa College, New Plymouth Girls' High School, teachers' training college, NZ and at USP, Fiji. Taught for many years in Samoa and then worked as Director of the USP Centre, Apia, then Director of the USP Centre, Nauru. Now Director of the USP Centre, Apia, Western Samoa. Her first collection of poems, *Pinnacles*, was published in 1993.

Joseph C. Veramo (b. Fiji). Educated in Fiji; BA from USP. Taught high school;

published collections of Fiji legends for schools. Also published short stories and poems in *Mana*, *Sinnet* and elsewhere, and a collection of stories, *Onisimo*. Now a lecturer at the USP Fiji Centre, Suva.

Momoe Malietoa Von Reiche (b. Western Samoa). Educated in Samoa and NZ, trained at Wellington Teachers' College and the Polytechnic School of Design, specialising in art. Has taught art at Teachers' Training College, Western Samoa. Has published four collections of poetry: *Solaua, a Secret Embryo* (1979), *Pao Alimago on Wet Days* (1979), *Alaoa, above the gully of your childhood* (1986), *Tai, heart of a tree* (1989). Also one of the Pacific's leading artists: her work has been exhibited in Samoa, NZ, Australia, and the US.

Vincent Warakai (b. 1956, PNG) Educated UPNG, Anglia University, England; MA in sociology from Sussex University. Now lecturer in anthropology and sociology, UPNG.

Peter Watlakas (b. New Ireland, PNG, 1953). Educated in PNG; DipEd, BA from UPNG. Now senior tutor in arts education in the Expressive Arts Department, Goroka Campus, UPNG.

Mona Matepi Webb (b. Mangaia, Cook Islands, 1960). Educated in the Cook Islands; now working as a journalist. Has published poems and children's stories.

Albert Wendt (b. Tauese, Apia, Western Samoa). Educated in Samoa and NZ. Has taught at all levels of the education system. Has published five novels, two collections of short stories, three collections of poetry, and various anthologies. Now professor of English at the University of Auckland.

Steven Edmund Winduo (b. Ulighembi, East Sepik, PNG, 1964). Graduated from UPNG and University of Canterbury, NZ. Has published a collection of poems *Lomo'ha I Am, In Spirit's Voice I Call* (1991). Now teaches literature at UPNG.

GLOSSARY

COOK ISLANDS (COOK IS MAORI & PIDGIN)

a'ae	tuna
arikiriki	pandanus mat
Aue, teia ma	Oh, here he comes
avatea	noon
ei katu	head wreaths
fau	hibiscus flower
[k]iato	cross-beams of canoe
kaikai	food
karakia	chant, prayers
karem leg	penis
korero	culture
lei	necklace, wreath
maire	scented herb used in lei
mamaiata	dawn
mamio	taro (from Mangaia)
mango	shark
mapu	youth
marae	gathering place
matakeinanga	the human component of a community
moko	lizard
mokopuna	grandchild
motu	island
pa'ata	platform
pa'e	'lee-ho'
pandanus	nut
papa'a	person of European stock
pe'e	chant
popongi	morning
popongi-avatea	morning tea time
puaka matu	fat pig
tamanu	tree, strong in hurricanes
tamure	traditional dance
tapore	village
tapu	sacred
taramea	loose woman, flirt
taunga	priest
Te Manu Ka Rere	the bird that flies

Te Moana Nui

a Kiva	the Pacific Ocean
tere	group of people moving from one place to another
toa	casuarina tree
tumukorero	experts in a certain field
tumurangi	clouds

FIJI (FIJIAN & HINDI)

a'cchar	pickle made from dried green fruit
baigani	eggplant
bau	tree
bure	Fijian house
dalo	bulbous root of which is cooked and eaten
dhoti	piece of cloth worn by Indian men
ghasita	sled
isa lei	how sad
laahgaa	long full skirt worn by old Indian women
maatha	skimmed milk
mulkaam	tree
narak	hell
orhini	piece of plain coloured cloth, shorter than a sari, worn by Indian women
pujari	witchdoctor
pyaalaa	enamel bowls
rakshasas	demons
swarg	heaven
vuniwai	drink made from roots of kava plant

KIRIBATI

babai	taro
bero [bwiroo]	small berries, like figs

403

I-Matang	European; foreigner
kabubu	preserved food made from pandanus
kamaimai	toddy molasses from coconut
kaura	tree; flowers used for garlands
kiaou	creeper used to wind on garlands
maneaba	a special meeting-house, social and political gathering place
Nei	Miss
te buka	*Wedelia biflora* tree
uri	sweet-smelling flower

NIUE

palagi	person of European stock

PAPUA NEW GUINEA

batre	father or priest
bilum	loosely woven bag
binga	ceremony
bomblam	outcast
dahaka	what
gigl yomba	?ghost
kaikai	food
kalabus	jail
kaukau	sweet potato
kiap	government officer
kimbri nem	policeman
Kipe Kangi	the devil
laplap	loincloth
lahara	wind
laurabada	wind
longlong	crazy
metar	medal
mirigini	wind
momokani	true
mundi	salt
Peng-nim kale gen nal	I'll shave your head with an axe

sarap	shut up
shule yagl	teacher
tambu	forbidden, sacred
tinfis	tinned fish
toea	ceremonial shell, necklace, currency
win moni	lottery
wantok	friend, usually from the same language group, fellow countryman

SAMOA

aiga	family group
aitu	family, extended family
alii	matai with an alii title
fa	goodbye
fa'alavelave	a family event such as a death or marriage
fafine	woman
faife'au	pastor
fale	Samoan house
fale fono	legislative house
fono	council
ie toga	a fine mat
lauga	a speech
lau paogo	leaves used to weave mats and baskets
lavalava	wrap-around garment
lotu	church service, prayers
malae	central open space of a village
matai	chief, titled head of an aiga
olomatua	old lady
papalagi	person of European stock
pepelo	to lie, liar
selau tala	100 Samoan dollars
sene	cent
tae	shit
tatao	to have a look around
tatau	tattoo
umu	stone oven

SOLOMON ISLANDS
kanaka — native
mahera — meeting ground

TONGA
hafuni — afro hairstyle
ei! — hey!
fakaleiti — transvestite
fale — house
feta'u — piece of material presented at a funeral

haka — boiled vegetables
Hala Liku — name of a road
langakali — fragrant flower
pa'anga — money; dollar
Pai ta live 'ofu Papilone — By the river of Babylon
tamanu — plant
tupenu — lavalava; item of clothing worn by men
umu — oven; hangi

405